TELEVISION
AND THE
AMERICAN
CHILD

TELEVISION AND THE AMERICAN CHILD

GEORGE COMSTOCK

S. I. Newhouse School of Public Communications
Syracuse University
Syracuse, New York

With

HAEJUNG PAIK

Department of Communication
University of Oklahoma
Norman, Oklahoma

Academic Press, Inc.
Harcourt Brace Jovanovich, Publishers
San Diego   New York   Boston
London   Sydney   Tokyo   Toronto

Copyright © 1991 by ACADEMIC PRESS, INC.
All Rights Reserved.
No part of this publication may be reproduced or transmitted in
any form or by any means, electronic or mechanical, including
photocopy, recording, or any information storage and retrieval
system, without permission in writing from the publisher.

Academic Press, Inc.
San Diego, California 92101

United Kingdom Edition published by
Academic Press Limited
24–28 Oval Road, London NW1 7DX

Library of Congress Cataloging-in-Publication Data

Comstock, George A.
    Television and the American child / George Comstock with Hae
Jung
  Paik.
      p.   cm.
    Includes bibliographical references and index.
    ISBN 0-12-183575-8
    1. Television and children--United States.   I. Paik, Hae-Jung.
  II. Title.
  HQ784.T4C69   1991
  302.23'45'083--dc20   90-27707
                                                    CIP

PRINTED IN THE UNITED STATES OF AMERICA
91 92 93 94   9 8 7 6 5 4 3 2 1

For Nora Irene Misiolek

◼ CONTENTS

IV. Knowledge, Beliefs, and Perceptions

V. Advertising

VI. Behavior

VII. Knowledge For What?

◼ PREFACE

Television was introduced into U.S. households in the late 1940s and early 1950s. It achieved instant popularity. Only the reappearance of the automobile in American showrooms after the end of World War II rivaled television in public approval and attention. Because of a freeze placed on the licensing of television broadcast stations by the Federal Communications Commission, ostensibly to review various technical issues regarding allocation of the limited amount of spectrum space (but arguably to give the advantage in the new marketplace to vested economic interests, such as the radio networks and established electronics firms), there were two distinct waves of adoption. In the first wave, beginning in 1949 in areas where stations had been licensed before the freeze, television set ownership increased from near zero to over three-fourths of all households in four years. In the second wave, beginning in 1953 in areas where the freeze delayed licensing, set acquisition was even more lightning-like, with ownership increasing in two years to almost three-fourths of all households. Overall, television sets in use increased from 10,000 in 1946 to 10.5 million in 1950. By 1960, the estimated number of sets in use had increased fivefold to 54 million. By the end of the 1980s, television sets were in more than 98% of all households, for a total of more than 90 million households. More than 90% had color sets, and about two-thirds had two or more sets.

Beyond the rapid diffusion of television sets and their near ubiquity in American households, which established a system of dissemination unmatched by any other medium and gave the medium extraordinary capacity to reach all household members, there was a steady flow of innovations that increased the attractiveness of television. Screens became larger, color was introduced, picture quality became better, and prices for a set of any given specifications declined. Broadcasting in the United States—except for the so-called public systems that attract comparatively small audiences of viewers or listeners—is supported by the revenues obtained from selling time to advertisers. The amount that can be charged is a function of audience size (the larger the better), qualified somewhat by audience quality (characteristics particularly appealing to advertisers, such as higher incomes or age groups high in consumer expenditures). Consequently, audience measurement became central to the business of broadcasting and the (in)famous ratings became the means by which less than adequately popular programs were continually being discarded, and programming progressively became honed in favor of maximal economic utility.

Meanwhile, the system of dissemination was slowly but forcefully evolving into one of increased diversity of alternatives among program sources. When broadcast television reached its maturity in the 1960s and early 1970s, television was dominated by the three networks—ABC, CBS, and NBC—and their affiliates. Between the mid-1970s and the end of the 1980s, television became a medium much more varied in programming sources. The new sources included a substantial number of independent stations in markets where they competed with network affiliates, cable, pay services, satellites, and videocassette recorders that permit in home recording and playback. As a result, between the 1960s and the beginning of the 1990s, the percentage of prime-time network audience share fell from the 90s to the high 60s. Network preeminence thus has been diminished but not ended. The revolution once promised by seers—in which technologically feasible alternatives to broadcasting would convert the medium from the seeking of mass popularity to the serving of specific interests and small audience segments, with programming often high in intellectual and cultural caliber—has not occurred.

The foremost influence of the popularity of television in modern societies almost certainly has been the increase in time spent with the mass media. Television increased the amount of time devoted to mass media consumption by the average American adult by about an hour a day; about three-fourths of this mass media consumption time is television time. The size of this effect almost certainly has increased over the years with the progressive increase in the amount of time spent viewing the television. What applies to adults also applies to children and teenagers. One of the principal effects of television has been to enlarge dramatically the place of the mass media in their lives, and to heighten enormously the place of entertainment.

From the perspective of those in the television business, the child audience is composed of persons between the ages of two and eleven years. This is the demographic category at which Saturday morning programming is aimed. This volume extends the age range of interest through the teenage years, and covers much more than children's programming. The Saturday morning audience at its peak includes more than half of all children aged two to eleven years. However, children also watch vast amounts of television produced for general audiences, and typically about 95% of the average child's viewing is of programs not specifically produced for children.

It is surely plain why the topic of television and children has been of enduring interest, not only to social and behavioral scientists and communications scholars, but also to parents, teachers, government officials, legislators, and policymakers, in addition to those in the television business. Children watch a great amount of television, and many questions can be raised about its negative or positive influence. Historically, almost all media at one time or another have been a subject of widespread concern in regard to children because the media bring messages, themes, and subject matter into the home that are beyond the control of, and sometimes in conflict with, the preferences and values of parents. Television probably is permanently established at the peak of this pyramid because of its attractiveness, ubiquitous availability, and status as a regulated medium required by the Federal Communications Act of 1934 to serve "the public interest, convenience, and necessity." Questions have frequently been raised about the kinds of legislation, rule making by the Federal Communications Commission, or industry self-regulation that would best serve the interests of children. These questions concern program content, where violence, sex, and stereotyping have drawn attention; advertising, where deception, fairness, and product quality have been prominent issues; and program quality, where the amount of cultural, educational, and age-specific programming have been at issue. To the television business, children have been important as a means of profit-making. When television was introduced, programming for children provided an additional incentive for the family purchase of a television set. In the mid-1960s, children became the direct source of profits with the development of Saturday morning programming, which was greatly facilitated by the shift away from full program sponsorship to the sale of spot announcements (which made the medium far less expensive, and thus attractive to many more advertisers) and somewhat helped by the progressive increase in multiset households (which made it possible for children to view in seclusion).

Television and children as a topic has come to interest us because of the enormous growth of the pertinent social and behavioral literature. Much of it is quite recent, with a sizable proportion appearing in the last decade and a half. The near-exhaustive bibliography, *Television and*

Youth (Murray, 1980), contains 2886 citations, with 60% appearing in the five years preceding publication. By comparison, a bibliography produced 10 years earlier (Atkin, Murray, & Nayman, 1971) contained only about 550 citations, and another appearing in mid-decade (Comstock & Fisher, 1975) contained about 1,100. Productivity has continued at a comparable rate. This growth in social and behavioral science research on television and children has had three significant consequences:

• There is a substantial body of evidence on which to draw.
• Questions once addressed by single study or by a few studies now often are addressed by a much larger set of inquiries.
• Many topics previously unaddressed now have received attention, thereby expanding the scope of inquiry.

These three circumstances arguably define real progress in scientific investigation. They increase markedly the likelihood that meaningful interpretations can be drawn from the data collected. They strengthen the confidence with which interpretations can be advanced. They make possible at least tentative interpretations of an increasingly larger number of topics. These qualities derive from the enhanced replication, the increase thereby in the possibility of discerning patterns, and the examination of new questions. The overall result is a continuing need for the collation and synthesis of the evidence, which brings us to the present volume.

We chose our title carefully. *Television and the American Child* is intended to emphasize that, in many respects, the evidence from the social and behavioral sciences on television and children is particularly pertinent to American children. Most of the research has been done in this country. For example, fewer than 5% of the 230 empirical studies of the effects of exposure to antisocial or prosocial television portrayals encompassed in a meta-analysis (Hearold, 1986) were done outside the United States. The television that enters into the paradigm, then, has been American television, just as the persons under scrutiny have been American. There is thus a control for cultural differentiation, imposed by the sites of inquiry, that makes the available data particularly pertinent and interpretable. We of course draw on research from abroad when it appears to apply to or, by contrast, casts light upon the American circumstance, but our subject is the American child of our era and not some cultureless, stateless, and timeless child.

George Comstock

◼ ACKNOWLEDGMENTS

This volume grows out of a succinct summary by the same authors, *Television and Children: A Review of Recent Research,* published by the ERIC Clearinghouse on Information Resources at Syracuse University in 1987. The authors are indebted to Dr. Donald Ely, Professor of Education and Associate Director of the Clearinghouse, for commissioning that endeavor. *Television and the American Child* is many times larger, ranges much more widely, and contains far more thoroughly arrayed support and argumentation for its conclusions. It is a mightier effort and, we hope, a more useful one, but it would not exist had it not been for his initiative.

We are grateful for recent and concise reviews of certain topics in regard to television viewing by young persons: cognitive activity (Anderson & Collins, 1988); beliefs and perceptions about sex roles (Gunter, 1986); fearfulness (Gunter, 1987); and one neither so recent nor concise concerning children and advertising (Adler, Lesser, Meringoff, Robertson, Rossiter, & Ward, 1980). They have served as useful mappings, but when we examined their original sources in a number of instances what we found and what they had found were not the same. As a result, our emphases and sometimes our conclusions are different.

The S. I. Newhouse Chair of Public Communications, which the primary author holds, provided the necessary support, and the S. I. Newhouse School provided that essential element, a congenial atmosphere. That all would have been for nothing if Joe Ingram—friend, editor, and epicurean companion—had not decided the venture was worthwhile and maintained his faith and enthusiasm through delays and the torment of time passing. The manuscript itself would not have come into being without the ability to work on several tasks at once, cleverness, and obsessive pursuit of bibliographic, graphic, and tabular quality of the primary author's editorial and research assistant, Nora Misiolek.

George Comstock

I THE EXPERIENCE

The stereotype of the child fixated by the continuous imagery of television is false, although there is no question that children find being in the vicinity of an operating television set preferable to any alternative for many hours of the day. Plain enough in the idiom of conversation, *viewing* in fact deconstructs into a number of separable elements. They include content indifference, program preferences, involvement, monitoring and cognitive activity, social circumstances, and indiscriminant viewing.

A. CONTENT INDIFFERENCE

The competition among broadcasters for higher ratings (the proportion of television households viewing a program) and shares (the proportion of viewing households tuned to a specific program), and thus enhanced profits, gives the impression that content dictates viewing. Nothing could be further from the actual circumstance.

There is abundant evidence that viewers generally are indifferent to content, with one major and one minor qualification and one important exception. Part of the evidence comes from a 12-nation investigation of time use in the mid-1960s (Comstock, Chaffee, Katzman, McCombs, & Roberts, 1978; Robinson, 1972a; Szalai, 1972) when households with television in these countries varied from close to 100% to about one out of four. Sizable urban samples in each country were asked to complete 24-hour diaries on time use. The data on television (Table 1.1) document, as would be expected, that per capita consumption was strongly related to the proportion of television households. This is obvious in

1

Table 1.1
Television Viewing Across Cultures[a]

Sample site	Percentage set ownership (1)	Percentage watched any TV[c] (2)	Minutes of TV viewing[b]			Per home viewer (5)	Percentage deviation from per home all site average (6)
			Total (3)	As primary activity (4)			
USA (44 cities)	97	80	129	92	131	7.4
Western Europe	69.33	63.33	90.17	70.17	123.83	1.5
Belgium	72	65	94	84	139	13.9
France	65	65	96	58	107	−12.3
West Germany	71	60	80.5	68.5	125.5	2.7
Eastern Europe	54.83	45.83	60.75	52.5	121.7	−.7
Bulgaria	26	17	17	16	95	22.1
Czechoslovakia	72	52	73	66	135	10.7
East Germany	85	72	100	81	124	1.6
Hungary	45	36	45	43	124	1.6
Poland	59	60	82	70	130	6.6
Yugoslavia	42	38	47.5	39	119	−2.5
USSR	52	40	45	42	109	10.7
Latin America	54	47	63	54	125	2.5
Peru	54	47	63	54	125	2.5
All sites average	65.43	55.23	77.58	62.13	122	0

[a] Single city for each nation; all industrial, with population from 50,000 to 150,000. Exceptions: France (6 cities); West Germany (one site plus 100-district national sample); USA (44-city national sample).

[b] Total represents the per capita average for the sample, including nonset owners. Viewing both as a primary and secondary activity is included. Viewing as the *primary activity* also represents the per capita average for the sample and permits the calculation of viewing as a secondary activity (Secondary viewing = Total − Primary Viewing). *Per home viewer* is the average for owners of television sets.

[c] Persons aged 18–65 in homes with someone employed.

Adapted from Robinson, J.P., & Converse, P.E. (1972). The impact of television on mass media usage. In A. Szalai (Ed.), *The use of time: Daily activities of urban and suburban populations in twelve countries* (pp. 197–212). The Hague: Mouton and Co.

the figures for those watching any television during the 24 hours, total minutes of viewing, and minutes of viewing as the "primary" (rather than a secondary) activity (columns 2, 3, and 4). The data for home viewers, those in households with one or more television sets, show that the amount of time devoted to television viewing was very much the same (columns 5 and 6). Given the great differences in national wealth, culture, hours of broadcasting, number of channels, and character and quality of programming represented by such sites as the United States, the U.S.S.R, France, Poland, Peru, Belgium, and East and West Germany, this is astounding. Part of the evidence also comes from data on repeat viewing by thousands of persons in California, New York, and Great Britain (Barwise, Ehrenberg, & Goodhardt, 1982; Barwise & Ehrenberg, 1988). The average probability is .50 that a viewer of a weekday or weekly (Table 1.2) series will be in the audience for the next episode the following day or week. In the consecutive viewing of weekly episodes (Table 1.3), the proportion remaining in the audience declines continually and reaches zero after about 10–12 episodes, so it can be fairly said that nobody views every episode. Some weekday soap operas and a network news program had higher-than-average repeat viewing, but other light entertainment programs and other news programs fall below the average. This counterintuitive pattern holds, with slight variation, for daytime, prime time, entertainment, news, and, surprisingly, even such an ostensibly fan-enamored offering as "Mon-

Table 1.2
Repeat Viewing: Weekday Series[a]

Program	[Time]	Percentage repeat viewing
"Sanford and Son"	[10:00 AM]	47
"Wheel of Fortune"	[11:00 AM]	54
"The Gong Show"	[12:30 PM]	50
"Days of Our Lives"	[1:30 PM]	55
"The Doctors"	[2:30 PM]	53
"Another World"	[3:00 PM]	65
"Marcus Welby"	[4:00 PM]	41
"Newscenter 4 at 5"	[5:00 PM]	45
"Newscenter 4 at 6"	[6:00 PM]	52
"NBC Nightly News"	[7:00 PM]	66
Average		53

[a] Day-by-day repeat viewing by viewers over age 18 of WNBC, New York City, October 1976 (Averages over all pairs of weekdays).
From Barwise, T.P., Ehrenberg, A.S.C., & Goodhardt, G.J. (1982). Glued to the box?: Patterns of TV–repeat viewing. *Journal of Communication*, 32(4), 22–29.

Table 1.3
Repeat Viewing: Weekly Series[a]

Program	[Day, time]		Percentage repeat viewing
"Rhoda"	[Monday,	8:00 PM]	64
"Muppets"	[Saturday,	7:00 PM]	40
"Price Is Right"	[Thursday,	7:30 PM]	21
"NFL Football"	[Monday,	7:00 PM]	49
"Baretta"	[Wednesday,	9:00 PM]	54
"Donny & Marie"	[Friday,	8:00 PM]	57
Average			48

[a] Week-by-week repeat viewing by viewers over age 18 of six representative prime-time weekly network programs, Los Angeles, 1976.
From Barwise, T.P., Ehrenberg, A.S.C., & Goodhardt, G.J. (1982). Glued to the box?: Patterns of TV–repeat viewing. *Journal of Communication, 32*(4), 22–29.

day Night Football." However, when television is viewed at a particular time, viewers will almost always choose the same program.

In a more modest later analysis, adults and younger viewers were compared in their repeat viewing of weekly prime-time series (Barwise, 1986). The adult average for 15 series was about 40%, compared to fewer than 30% among those aged 2–11 and 12–17, with a maximum of 50% repeat viewing for a program enormously popular among young viewers ("The A-Team"). Thus, this phenomenon is even more prominent among children and teenagers.

The explanation is that television typically is viewed when no other activity is preferable, obligatory, or necessary. Program content is not the principal factor in assembling an audience for television. The principal factor is time available, or opportunity to view. The decision to view is thus a two-stage process (Barwise *et al.*, 1982; Comstock *et al.*, 1978), with the decision whether or not to view television typically taking precedence over the decision of what to view.

The major qualification, of course, is that once television has been selected as the activity of choice, program alternatives will be carefully reviewed for the most satisfying (in the famous phrase of one television executive, "least objectionable"). Content indifference is preeminent only in attraction to the screen; thus, the importance attached by those in the television business to program popularity is justified. A minor—in terms of amount of viewing affected—qualification is that there are some spectacles or television events, such as the Olympics, Super Bowl, and the World Series, that many viewers try never to miss and some regular programs that a few viewers assiduously attend to. Such programming represents content that is distinct from the rest of television for which nothing else quite serves as a substitute; the weekly "Thoroughbred Digest" on ESPN, for example, which covers major racing events across the country that are usually ignored by local newspapers and other general circulation media. However, it is only in later childhood and during the teenage years that the social norms and personal interests that dictate such devoted attention come to play a role; thus, this qualification figures more prominently among adults than young viewers.

Children and teenagers on the whole are no different from adults in their indifference to content. About 60% of all children aged 2–11 are in the Saturday morning audience at its peak between 9 and 10:30 AM, because nothing takes them away from the vicinity of a set, and the programming is designed for them. Some in the audience on one Saturday morning at a particular time will not be there the following Saturday. The 40% who are not in the audience on any given Saturday morning, the 20% in the audience at any given time on Saturday afternoons, and the almost 50% of those aged 2–5 in the audience between 7 and 8 PM exemplify the principle of content indifference.

An important exception in regard to children and, to a lesser extent, teenagers, is their well-known inclination to develop strong if transient fondness for particular programs and television characters. This almost certainly modifies to a slight degree the preeminence of time available, by providing these viewers with increased motives to fit their activities to the television schedule, and by giving parents of younger children an increased incentive to provide an opportunity to view when a particular program is presented.

Webster and Wakshlag (1983) correctly argue that programs are not analogous to products among which resources are allocated. Instead, programs are dependent on scheduling for their popularity. This is because time use does not have the fungibility of income in its expenditure.

B. PREFERENCES

The generic program preferences of children and teenagers can be succinctly described as a function of age, sex, socioeconomic status, and ethnicity. The popularity of specific programs is transitory, of course, although there certainly have been long-running favorites (including the aptly named "Road Runner") and some characters with a claim to permanent appeal (some of the Disney cast, for example). The preeminence of content indifference means that much viewing is not expressive of preferences except when choosing among alternative programs, and then only when the choice is that of the specific viewer and not someone else in the viewing area.

The three-stage model proposed by Wolfe and Fiske (1954) in their pretelevision examination of comic book reading is applicable to the newer medium. Their notion of a "fuzzy animal" stage followed by a "superhero" phase approximates the shift from "Sesame Street" and animal cartoons, which appear earlier on Saturday mornings when younger children make up a greater proportion of the audience, to animated action–adventure later in the morning when the proportion of older children has increased. Their final stage of *realistic* content parallels the desertion of the Saturday morning audience by teenagers as they become principally consumers of general audience programming. They assert that children who became blocked at the superhero phase because of their need to follow a "perfect father figure" and for whom comics became a "religion" or opiate were "maladjusted." This parallels the conclusion by E.E. Maccoby (1954, 1964) that consumption of atypically large amounts of television or any other easy-to-attend-to pictorial mass medium may be the symptom of conflicts with parents and peers. This is apparently a robust conclusion across time, ages, culture, and technology. Tangney much more recently (1988) found, among more than 100 Los Angeles children in the fourth through sixth grades, that heavy viewing of fantasy programs and of children's programs was more frequent when parents were low in empathy, sensitivity, and flexibility in role expectation. Ekblad (1986) found in Beijing that greater television viewing appeared to reflect some estrangement from the family. Morgan, Alexander, Shanahan, and Harris (1990) attributed greater VCR use among several hundred teenagers to general conflict with parents.

Although the literature is minute on the emotionally disturbed, learning disabled, and mentally retarded child and television, what there is suggests that any pattern existing for children not so labeled is exaggerated for them (Sprafkin, Gadow, & Grayson, 1984; Sprafkin & Gadow, 1986). They are likely to watch more television, and more cartoons and violent programs; they are less adroit at processing what is viewed effectively; and their beliefs and perceptions are more likely to be affected, while any benefits television provides in the way of world knowledge may be attenuated if it is contingent on cognitive prowess; and they are likely to be more susceptible to behavioral influence. The principal caveat to an exaggerated role for television is that the inverse would occur when the outcome is contingent on the depth, quality, and extensiveness of analytic and verbal cognitive processing.

When about 160 three-, four-, and five-year-old children were interviewed by Lyle and Hoffman (1972b), almost 90% named a favorite program, with only about 7% not understanding the question. Although one program was named by one out of four children ("The Flintstones," an animated Hanna-Barbera sitcom set in the Pleistocene era), a wide range falling into eight other categories was named; thus, even this early, individual tastes are beginning to develop. The early age at which preferences can be enunciated, and the breadth of choices are striking.

The sensitivity of age-specific programming to the ages of available viewers is exemplified by the sharp decline of those naming "Sesame Street" as a favorite (from 30% to 13%) between the ages of three and five. The rise over the same age range in popularity of "The Flintstones," with only 11% naming it at age three and 36% doing so at age five, displays discrimination that marks children's preferences as a function of age; the decline from 19 to 3% in those not understanding the question indicates that as early as age three, most children understand the concept and have favorites. By age five, this is almost universal.

The shift in preferences with increasing age is documented in the questionnaire data obtained from about 1600 first-, sixth-, and tenth-grade pupils by Lyle and Hoffman (1972a). First graders mostly named situation comedies and cartoons. Sixth graders largely replaced the cartoons with action–adventure programs. Tenth graders continued to name many action–adventure programs, but added music and variety. Thus, the three-stage model requires elaboration by a format not prominent among comic books (the sitcom), and by a category of content foreign to print (music). First, sixth, and tenth graders all were especially attracted to programs with characters their own age. A.M. Rubin (1986) found, among about 160 individually interviewed children between the ages of 5 and 12, that preferences for cartoons and children's programs declined, while those for adventure–drama and comedy increased with age.

The longitudinal analyses of about 325 children over two years beginning at ages three and five by Huston, Wright, Rice, Kerkman, Seigle, and Bremer, (1990) and Pinon, Huston, and Wright (1989) enlarge upon the early phases of this process (Fig. 1.1). Viewing of "Sesame Street" and other educational programs for very young viewers declined with age, and was enhanced when encouraged by parents or, among the older children, when younger siblings were viewers. Perceived age appropriateness and the time made available to view were more important than cognitive changes in the declining exposure. Exposure to cartoons and adult comedy, with some decline at the oldest ages, increased.

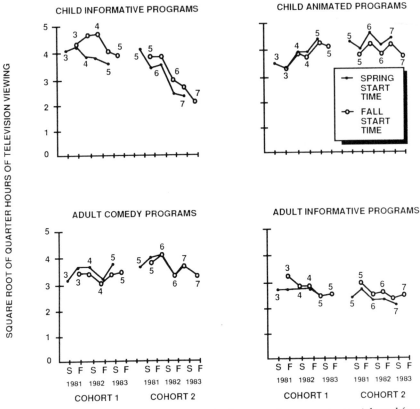

Fig. 1.1 Viewing of selected programming by age and program types. Adapted from Huston, A.C., Wright, J.C., Rice, M.L., & St. Peters, M. (1990). Development of television viewing patterns in early childhood: A longitudinal investigation. *Developmental Psychology, 26*(3), 409–420.

Exposure to adult informational programming decreased, presumably because children became old enough to leave the room when bored. This same-sex preference, exaggerated by the stereotypic, is apparently a phenomenon attributable to the development of convictions about gender identity, stability or constancy, and consistency across modes of behavior and thought. Slaby and Frey (1975) found such convictions predictive of attention to males and females in televised portrayals by boys and girls between the ages of three and about five, and that these convictions develop during this stage in that order; by five or six, the triumvirate are in place. The progression derives from the degree of simple ego involvement ("I'm a girl"; "I'll always be a girl"; "I always behave as a girl"), the complexity of the concepts, (me; always me; me in all things), and social utility (the expectations of others about behavior that is gender-specific increases with age, and behavior perceived as gender-appropriate increasingly will be rewarded and prove efficacious). The result is that young children who are male prefer activities perceived as male and those who are female prefer those perceived as female, shunning those perceived as appropriate to the opposite sex; thus, Ruble, Balaban, and Cooper (1981) found among four-to-six year olds that exposure to a television commercial linking play with gender-neutral toys to one or another of the sexes led to a decided preference for among those of the same sex and avoidance by those of the opposite sex. Recall similarly is greater for behavior of those of the same sex (Koblinski, Cruse, & Sugawara, 1978). Such gender-based predilections and antipathies are lifelong, although they will become mitigated by experience and advancement to higher stages of cognitive development. As would be expected with the typically higher status of males, these predilections and antipathies are somewhat less pronounced or constant among females. Gender thus has implications for beliefs and perceptions in response to portrayals for stereotyping in regard to the sexes (Chapter IV).

Gender plays an important role. While one might anticipate a certain unisex quality to preferences early in the fuzzy animal stage, in fact gender-related differences appear extremely early. In their interviews with three, four, and five year olds, Lyle and Hoffman (1972b) found that overall twice as many girls as boys named "The Flintstones" as their favorite (39 versus 19%), while boys were three times as likely to name a violent cartoon (17 versus 5%).

The concepts of similarity and wishful identification have been proposed by Feilitzen and Linne (1975) to help explain these processes. The former refers to a preference for characters like oneself, and is particularly pronounced among younger children. The latter refers to a preference for characters the viewer would like to resemble, and increases with age. They suggest that identification with animals is a form of similarity identification because the animal in portrayal has a dependent relationship with humans analogous to that of the child with adults. They also suggest that when older children engage in similarity identification, they prefer characters somewhat older than themselves and that age eight is the point of transition from a preference for children's programming and characters like themselves to a preference for adult programming, wishful identification, and similarity identification with those older. We concur with the sweeping portrait, but not with certain specifics. The evidence just reviewed makes it clear that similarity identification persists beyond age eight, and a turning toward adult programs—in particular, comedy—occurs much earlier. We also believe that identification with others who are different in age or other characteristics will occur as soon as the child is able to recognize or infer higher status, which presumably would be the basis for the claimed preference of those older for similar characters who themselves are somewhat older than the viewer. Thus, we argue that the dual process of similarity and wishful identification is pervasive throughout childhood except perhaps for its earliest years when the former would predominate. Crouch (1989), in a Northern Ireland sample between ages 7 and 11 years, found gender-related differences in programs named as favorites at the youngest age, with progressive shifts with increasing age, among the boys toward action–adventure and sports, and among the girls toward family, soap opera, and other stereotypically female programming. McLeod, Atkin, and Chaffee (1972a, 1972b), in a survey of more than 600 seventh and tenth graders, found that boys watched considerably more violent programming than girls; Huston and colleagues (1990) reported the same among their sample of young children.

E.E. Maccoby and Wilson (1957), among seventh graders, and E.E. Maccoby, Wilson, and Burton (1958), among college students, found more involvement with movie characters of the same sex, which implies a preference for same-sex portrayals. Sprafkin and Liebert, two decades later (1978), found that boys and girls chose to view same-sex portrayals in which sex roles were clearly conventional, and more than 80% named same-sex characters as their favorites.

Race and socioeconomic status also make a difference (Comstock & Cobbey, 1979). Lyle and Hoffman (1972a) found black children among their first, sixth, and tenth graders particularly attracted to programs with black characters. Liss (1981) found that third-grade children chose to view programs featuring characters of the same race, and Dates (1980) found that while black and white teenagers did not differ in viewing selected situation comedies with all-white casts, the blacks were much more likely to view those with black characters and to identify, to a greater degree than whites, with such characters. Surlin and Dominick (1970), in a survey of about 200 high school students, found that programs featuring families were preferred more by teenagers who were black or who were from lower income households, and that black teenagers had a much lower preference for variety programs. E.E. Maccoby and Wilson (1957) found that identification was more likely with a character who had status to which the viewer aspired than one that approximated the viewer's own. Several investigations have reported, among older children and teenagers, socioeconomic status directly associated with exposure to more serious forms of entertainment, arts programming, and informational programming (Bogart, 1972a; California Assessment Program, 1982; Frank & Greenberg, 1980; Lyle & Hoffman, 1972a).

The degree to which expressed preferences are represented in actual viewing is minimal. The average amount of viewing, content indifference, and the preeminence of time available make program favorites poor predictors of behavior. When people view substantial amounts of television, favorites and even favorite genres can only occupy a small to moderate place. Because amount of television viewing is inversely associated with socioeconomic strata (Comstock *et al.,* 1978), this becomes increasingly so as one descends the socioeconomic scale. This holds for children and teenagers as well as adults. McLeod, Atkin, and Chaffee (1972a, 1972b), for example, report only a small correlation among their teenage sample between naming violent programs as favorites and overall exposure to violent programming. However, the best example comes from the audience-segmentation analysis by Frank and Greenberg (1980).

These investigators obtained, from a national probability sample of about 2500 persons aged 13 years and older, data on 18 categories of interests (such as "comprehensive news and information", "professional sports", and "investments"), nine categories of fundamental needs (such as "status enhancement", "unique–creative accomplishment", and "understanding others"), and media use. They then performed a factor analysis that progressively divided the sample into smaller and smaller groups that were increasingly homogeneous in interests until there were 14 such segments, each ranging from an estimated 4 to 10% of the population. Gender and age were the two principal variables by which the segments could be described, with 11 made up primarily by adults, three mostly by males, four mostly by females, and four comparatively balanced. The three remaining segments were labeled youth concentration; they are pertinent because their mean ages of 22, 19, and 22 indicate that they include substantial numbers of teenagers. Their interests, needs, and media use (Frank & Greenberg, 1980):

COMPETITIVE SPORTS AND SCIENCE—ENGINEERING (average age, 22; percentage female, 5; estimated percentage of population, 7)

Teenage male students with interests in male-associated mechanical activities and competitive athletics. Avoidance of female-oriented subjects and interests. High on needs for unique– creative accomplishment, intellectual stimulation and growth, status enhancement, and escape from boredom. Low needs for understanding others and for greater self-acceptance (p. 112). *Television.* Average level of viewing. Heavy viewers of programs and program types with male personalities, especially young men who are admired because of their physical and/or social prowess. Watch programs that mock authority figures. Low on programming that is intellectually upscaled or abstract, that copes with problems that do not yield to immediate solutions, or that features female personalities in assertive roles. Generally avoid traditional authority relationships that appear to threaten their need to establish personal independence. *Magazines.* Intermediate overall readership. First on sports, automotive, and mechanics. Also high on men's and miscellaneous (*National Lampoon*). *Other Media.* Heavy users of movies. Books and movie content are escape-oriented, such as science fiction books and horror movies. Highest use rate for sports in newspapers and on radio. Radio used for broad range of content, with special emphasis on different types of music (p. 227).

ATHLETIC AND SOCIAL ACTIVITIES (average age, 19; percentage female, 83; estimated percentage of population, 4) Teenage females from high-income families. The youngest of all the segments. Interests in active, away-from-home, face-to-face activities. High need to escape from problems and to be socially stimulating. Low need for family ties (p.115). *Television.* Well below average television viewers. Lowest level of in-home availability. Heavy viewers of escape programming and programming involving male–female relationships in nonfamily, light-hearted contexts. Need to get away from problems of home life. *Magazines.* Intermediate use. Along with Indoor Games and Social Activities segment, heavy on women's services, romance, and fashion. Somewhat more use than that of other female youth segment on outdoor, automotive, and mechanics. *Other Media.* Heavy use of movies and radio, while relatively light for all types of newspapers. Escapist content for books and movies similar to previous segment, but more oriented to love, romance, and children's movies. Radio listening mainly music (p. 228).

INDOOR GAMES AND SOCIAL ACTIVITIES (average age, 22; percentage female, 91; estimated percentage of population, 4) Young, low-income females. Interests in activities, especially indoor games. Low interest in most subject matter areas. Nonintellectual. High needs for status enhancement and the need to be socially stimulating (p. 117). *Television.* Well-above-average viewers of television. Low on information or cultural program types. Above average on virtually all others. Overall profile reflects combination of youth- and young homemaker-oriented programming. Both roles coexist in segment. Television a major source of entertainment for this segment. *Magazines.* Above-average readership. Along with Athletic and Social Activities segment, heavy on women's services, romance, and fashion. Somewhat more use than the other segment of men's, service–home, general, and black publications. *Other Media.* Heavy on books and movies. Somewhat more intellectual, less escapist than other Youth Concentration segments. Somewhat high readership of biographies, religious books, world news, and business newspaper content, as well as viewing horror, science fiction types of movies (p. 228).

These profiles on the surface imply extraordinarily distinct patterns of viewing. They certainly document that the mass audience is composed of a coalition; to achieve popularity, a program must appeal to a strong degree to several segments, because approximately equal appeal to all would be a rare occurrence. They do represent segments that differ considerably in the composition of their media consumption. However, when frequency of watching programs clustered within any of 19 categories of programming (adventure, children's, crime drama, documentary, etc.) was employed as a dependent variable in a regression analysis in which the predictors were first the gender and age, then the 14 interest segments, and finally the two combined, the predictability of viewing was extremely modest. On the average for the 19, the demographics and the interest segments each accounted for 5.4% of the variance, and the two combined accounted for 8.5%. This latter figure is half again as much (55% greater) as either of the independent outcomes. This means that demographics and interests add to one another's predictive power, but more than 90% of the variance remains unaccounted for.

Preferences, viewing, and program choices are influenced by broad, underlying motives. A.M. Rubin (1979) identified six positively correlated with higher levels of viewing: learning, passing time, companionship, escape arousal, and relaxation. These motives were associated with program preferences in his examination of about 450 fourth-, eighth-, eleventh-, and twelfth-grade children. For example, those seeking arousal preferred dramatic programs, while those seeking escapism or companionship favored comedy. In a complementary vein, Babrow

(1989) found, among 360 college students, that exposure to soap operas was motivated more by opportunities for social interaction while viewing and anticipated enjoyment than by learning about life or vicarious romance. A.M. Rubin (1977) found, among about 400 nine-, 13-, and 17-year-olds, that specific motives played a decreasing role as age increased, so that viewing became more a ritualistic use of the medium for its own sake, although at all ages the predominant motives involved the seeking of divertissement and the escape from everyday cares. However, the ability of underlying dispositions to predict exposure to a category of programming is very modest because of the role of time available, the restrictions imposed by television schedules on what is available at a given time, and the attractiveness of the medium, whatever is on.

The modest role of preference in exposure is neatly exemplified by the finding of Tangney (1988) in her examination of unsympathetic parental attitudes and children's television consumption. There were more than twice as many significant correlations (25 versus 12 out of a possible 66) between such views and exposure to program types than with preferences for such types. The situation—in this case, an unhappy milieu—was far more powerful than preferences in shaping viewing; television was an escape with what was available taking pre-eminence over what was said to be preferred. Preferences, then, change and develop with age, are somewhat enduring in the short run, become much more so as adulthood is approached, and increasingly have only a modest relationship with what is viewed.

C. INVOLVEMENT

It is crucial to explicate the concept of television viewing in order to understand what a viewer experiences. Viewing has been defined as "a discontinuous, often interrupted, and frequently nonexclusive activity for which a measure in hours and minutes serves only as the outer boundary of possible attention" (Comstock *et al.*, 1978, pp. 146–147). Such a description derives from the observation of individuals while they watch television and from the mechanics of television audience measurement.

In pioneering studies, C. Allen (1965) recorded viewers in about 100 Oklahoma and Kansas homes by time-lapse movie cameras at the rate of four frames per minute, and Bechtel, Achelpohl, and Akers (1972) continuously videotaped viewers in 20 Kansas homes (Table 1.4). In both instances, viewing was recorded over an extended period of time; what was on the screen was recorded, as well as viewer behavior. In the

Table 1.4
Repeat Viewing by Number of Episodes[a]

Program	Total number of episodes	Number seen (percentage of viewers)													
		1	2	3	4	5	6	7	8	9	10	11	12	13	14
"Dynasty"	10	33	15	15	8	7	5	5	5	5	2	—	—	—	—
"Brideshead Revisited"	11	28	18	13	7	5	5	7	3	7	4	3	—	—	—
"Jewel in the Crown"	14	30	15	9	6	5	6	4	3	4	6	4	4	2	—

[a] UK viewers.
From Barwise, T.P., & Ehrenberg, A.S.C. (1988). *Television and its audience.* Newbury Park, CA: Sage.

Allen study, coders had to individually examine over 1 million stills to determine viewer behavior. In Bechtel, Achelpohl, and Akers' study, the simultaneous videotaping of programming and viewers permitted the assembly of a taped collage with viewer behavior in center screen and programming as an insert.

Allen found that for about six hours a week, the set was in use when nobody was in the room, and that for about seven hours each week, nobody in the room was viewing the screen while the set was in use. This degree of inattention amounted to 40% of all hours when the set was on, and as one might expect, was greater during the daytime (about 50%), when tasks more often accompany viewing, than in the evening (35%).

Bechtel, Achelpohl, and Akers found a similar degree of inattention. It varied from about 25% for movies to about 45% for commercials and news. Children's programming was close to movies in achieving high attention. Although as many as one-fourth of those in the audience for children's programs are adults (Comstock et al., 1978), and certain segments of the audience that place great emphasis on family activities contain adults who like to view jointly with children (Frank & Greenberg, 1980), most of the audience is made up of children (more than half) and teenagers (about one-fourth). Thus, the comparatively high attention score for children's programming means, as the data indicate (Table 1.4), that young people by the standards of television give close attention to this entertainment.

The findings of these two landmark studies, while compelling, gain support from more recent research. Hopkins and Mullis (1985), in an examination of the viewing behavior of 24 families over a two-week period, found that fathers reported watching 136 programs and said they gave "complete attention" in 75 instances, or only 55% of the time. Mothers reported watching 143 programs and said they gave complete attention in 52 instances, or 36% of the time, with their lower degree of attention largely attributable to domestic chores and child care. D.R. Anderson and colleagues (D.R. Anderson, Lorch, Field, Collins, & Nathan, 1986) found, in 4672 hours of time-lapse video recording of television viewing among 99 families with 460 members (an ample number to make it seem highly plausible that someone could be said to be watching television while a set was on), that there was no one in the room about 15% of the time.

The predominance of time available begins to occur early in life. Eron and colleagues (Eron, Huesmann, Brice, Fischer, & Mermelstein, 1983) reported the astounding datum, counter to decades of research by every imaginable means of measuring television consumption, that the viewing of both boys and girls declined decidedly between grades three and five, after rising between grades one and three (Fig. 1.2). The explanation is that the investigators employed the watching of programs named as favorites as their measure of total television viewing. Thus, what happened is not that the viewing of these children declined, but that the opportunity to view (or time available) became more important as a predictor of viewing than the presentation of a program particularly liked.

One reflection of this typically low level of involvement is the degree of miscomprehension that occurs. Jacoby and Hoyer (1982) gave six-item tests to 2700 persons on their understanding of 30-second video

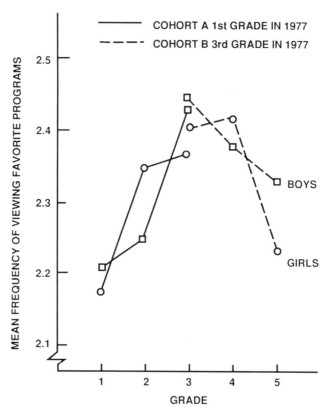

Fig. 1.2 Change in frequency of television viewing from grades 1 to 5—favorite programs. From Eron, L.D., Huesmann, L.R., Brice, P., Fischer, P., & Mermelstein, R. (1983). Age trends in the development of aggression, sex typing, and related television habits. *Developmental Psychology, 19*(1), 71–77.

segments they had just seen, taken from a wide range of formats—commercials, news, and entertainment. More than 95% misunderstood some portion of what they had viewed. On the average, about 30% of the information was miscomprehended, and the rate was about the same for all formats. The youngest group in the sample, from 13 to 17 years old, performed about as well (or more accurately, badly) as those older, so we may conclude with confidence that those younger certainly would not have done better.

This typically low involvement implies that much of what is experienced in television viewing will be processed as affective, holistic, imagistic, and nonverbal, as contrasted with verbal and analytic processing. That is, much of television is consumed as emanates from the set without much attaching of verbal labels or giving concrete thought to what is transpiring. In much popular as well as scientific—if often speculative in the latter case—writing, such processing is often identified as involving primarily the right hemisphere and alpha waves as measured by the electroencephalogram (EEG), which records rhythmic brain activity by electrodes clipped to the scalp. We agree with Rothschild and colleagues (M.I. Rothschild, Thorson, Reeves, Hirsch, & Goldstein, 1986) that lateralization is uncertain in degree, although probably significant, and that the often proposed inverse association of alpha and beta activity is speculative at best, with beta possibly an artifact of alpha activity. We thus use right- and left-brain and alpha and beta processing heuristically to distinguish between and emphasize that there is a dimension in cognitive processing with the verbal and analytic at one end and the affective, holistic, imagistic, and nonverbal at the other, and that these are conveniently thought of as two different types of processing with television more often calling forth the latter than the former.

Central to any understanding of the concept of viewing is knowledge of the mechanics of audience measurement. The concept that has evolved is a product of the techniques developed to measure audience size and characteristics. The motivations that govern our understanding thus derive from the needs of business (advertising, marketing, and television). Such an understanding may not serve other motives so effectively.

Commercial broadcast television is a profit-supported system in which the attention of the audience is vended to advertisers and whose product has been said to be not programming but the audience (L. Brown, 1971). The price that will be paid per time unit of exposure is a function of audience size and composition; large audiences, those high in disposable income, or those that predominantly represent a particular segment of the public, are preferred. Audience measurement is the means by which the price for commercials is determined. Beginning with radio in the 1930s (Beville, 1988), through trial and error evaluated by empirical investigation, a predominant paradigm has emerged to serve this end.

A person literally is counted (by A.C. Nielsen and other measurement firms) as being in the television audience at any given moment if he or she is so recorded by self or by someone assigned the responsibility of recording family viewing behavior. For many years, the most widely employed technique was to obtain data electronically on set use and the channels to which sets are tuned from a probability sample of households, thus ignoring behavior in the vicinity of the television set, and to obtain data on audience makeup from another sample by diaries reporting who was viewing what during a given time period. The two sets of data then would be justified so that set use could be reported in terms of audience size and composition. In recent years, people meters that resemble remote-control devices have replaced diaries, and the demographics are electronically recorded in accord with the coded buttons pressed by viewers. This procedure was preceded by, has been, and is complemented by a wide range of alternatives for obtaining similar information, such as diaries only, house-to-house interviews, and telephone surveys.

Such practices obviously accommodate substantial amounts of inattention, and the alternatives lead to different estimates. Nielsen figures are considerably higher than those produced by more comprehensive diary-keeping of all kinds of time use (Robinson, 1977). Videotape records give lower estimates than viewing diaries, which in turn are more conservative than reports of the previous day's viewing (Bechtel *et al.*, 1972). The procedure worked because a metric reliably comparing programs was satisfactory, and none of the alternatives was believed to offer superior estimates. It has now become subject to controversy within the television and advertising businesses because the use of people meters has been associated with declines in audience size, which means declines in profits (Zoglin, 1990). Our interest, in contrast, is in the meaning to be attached to viewing estimates. A different concept of viewing, such as one measuring eye attention to the set, the absence of any other activity other than conversation or eating, or some minimal threshold of attention, would lead to very different estimates and a different picture of television viewing.

The currently accepted concept implicitly defines viewing as typically low in personal, intellectual, or emotional involvement. Much evidence supports such a view. One out of four persons in one sample could not recall having any thoughts while watching (W.R. Neuman, 1982) when initially queried, and even after an extensive, probing interview, the average number of thoughts per viewer was fewer than eight, with decidedly more being about the medium ("analytic") than about the relationship of the content to the real world ("interpretive"). More than a third of the persons in a national sample at any given time did not specifically choose the program being viewed because they accepted someone else's choice or simply viewed what followed their or someone else's earlier choice; about one-fourth of the time programs were not watched from beginning to end; and about a third of viewers could not provide accurate accounts of the programs said to have been watched (LoSciuto, 1972; Robinson, 1972b). Among a sample of about 100 adults queried at various times during the day and evening about their activities, television viewing was consistently said to be lower in concentration required, use of skills, and challenge, and higher in feelings of passivity than any other activity except for resting and doing nothing (Kubey & Czikszentmihalyi, 1990). By the time children reach the end of their teenage years, they undoubtedly have become much like adults in their responses to television. Before that, however, their attention is probably even more discontinuous than that of adults when watching general audience programming they do not fully comprehend (D.R. Anderson & Lorch, 1983; Bryant & Anderson, 1983), and as we have seen, close to maximum when watching children's programming: entertainment designed for them, thus largely comprehensible, and also at that age somewhat novel in content (Bechtel *et al.*, 1972).

At early ages, comprehension predicts attention to the screen; comprehension increases with age; and so attention at first rises with age and then declines somewhat, as less attention is required for comprehension.

The degree to which the currently accepted concept of viewing leads to large estimates of the role of television in children's lives is made clear by comparing parent-kept diaries and time-lapse video recordings as measures of the television viewing of five year olds (D.R. Anderson, Field, Collins, Lorch & Nathan, 1985). Importantly, the data document that at this age the widely used parental diaries provide accurate estimates when viewing is defined as time spent with a television set. Visual attention averaged two-thirds of the time spent in the vicinity of the set, a figure in accord with the data of Allen (1965) and of Bechtel and colleagues (1972). The conclusion that the techniques currently employed to measure the audience for business purposes impose a limited definition on and in some ways distort children's viewing was supported by the finding that time spent with television and attention to the screen are uncorrelated. One five-year-old boy, who by conventional measurement would be classified as the heaviest viewer at about 40 hours per week spent with television, was recorded as spending only about $3\frac{1}{2}$ hours looking at the screen, which by the second criterion would place him among the lightest of viewers. If such correlations generally are null or low, it means that the two cannot be used as surrogates for one another in ranking persons as to greater or lesser viewing, and that each represents distinctive, different, and independent concepts of television exposure. The more extreme alternatives, then, lead to enormously different estimates, and impressions of the role of television in daily life that differ enormously.

Amount of television viewing is thus a function of the definition of viewing and its operationalization, and even similar modes of measurement may produce different estimates when employed in different contexts. Robinson (1977) reports obtaining an estimate using diaries comparable to those employed at the time by Nielsen of only about two-thirds of that offered by the audience measurement firm. He suggests that one reason may be that those who volunteer to have their viewing measured may not only be heavier viewers but, motivated by a desire to behave as the sponsor of the study would think appropriate, may also over-record their viewing. Timmer, Eccles, and O'Brien (1985) used a diary that measured all activities and produced estimates somewhat lower than those of Nielsen. Wartella, Heintz, Aidman, and Mazzarella (1990) invoke their own data and those of others in asserting that Nielsen and other such services overestimate the viewing of young persons. Stipp (1975), to the contrary, argues that the competitive milieu of commercial audience measurement renders the data more reliable and valid than those of academic researchers. Citing the well-known comparison by Bechtel and colleagues (1972) of global estimates of watching on a typical day, the previous day, entries in a Nielsen-type diary, and judgments based on viewing tapes of the same family members watching television filmed by a video camera mounted on top of the set, Robinson observes that the video camera often recorded no one in the room, and that the diary estimates were considerably greater than those derived from coding the videotapes. For every four hours recorded in the diaries, only three hours were estimated on the basis of the tapes.

This presents us with a conundrum. If we define television viewing to include entering and leaving the room while intermittently monitoring what is unfolding on the screen, the Nielsen estimates can be taken as accurate, with the caveat that the sample may contain some unusually heavy viewers and some over-recorders. If we define television viewing as monitoring while in the room, we must take the Nielsen figures as overestimates, with actual viewing, by this definition, about 25% less.

More stringent attentional criteria, of course, would lead to strikingly lower estimates.

We think the value placed on viewing is one key. There has been enough satisfaction for the amount of time devoted to the experience as measured by Nielsen to increase historically. We also know from data on adults collected in different places, at different times, and in different ways that use of the medium is valued even if viewing typically occurs with low attention and involvement (Barwise & Ehrenberg, 1988; Comstock *et al.*, 1978; Wober, 1988). Thus, what Nielsen measures is an activity valued by audience members.

We also have some evidence on the young when they are deprived of television. Windahl, Hojerback, and Hedinsson (1986) took advantage of the shutdown by a technician's strike of Swedish television in 1980 to examine the reactions of more than 200 teenagers. Almost two-thirds felt deprived to some degree. Those who felt especially deprived were ritualistic viewers, and especially those motivated by habit. Feelings of deprivation led primarily to other media consumption. This implies that television viewing for many serves important functions for which roughly equivalent substitutes must be found when it is not available.

We think the reliance on description inherent in all self-recording methods is another key. People record themselves or others as viewing television when they behave in accord with the recorder's unarticulated definition of television viewing. Thus, the Nielsen method elicits the amount of viewing as defined by the audience itself. In more formal terms, the time logged represents the normative concept of viewing.

These factors lead us to accept the Nielsen paradigm as effectively capturing the experience of television itself. It is demonstrably sensitive to changes over time as well as differences among strata. The behavior as measured represents a valued activity for which many seek out comparable stimuli as a replacement when involuntarily deprived, and it is in accord with the social definition of the behavior in question. Our major qualification then is that the resulting estimates when using diaries, which provide larger but, as we shall argue (Chapter II), more consistent estimates for between-group and over-time comparisons than people meters, represent the outer possible realistic limits to the amount of viewing that may occur.

D. MONITORING AND COGNITIVE ACTIVITY

Viewing does not describe what transpires in children's and teenagers' experience of television as accurately as does the term monitoring. Viewing implies visual attention to what is taking place on the screen.

Monitoring implies attention to audio, visual, and social cues as to the desirability of paying attention to the screen. That the first is descriptively inferior to the second is made clear by recent research on mental activities that occur during the television experience (D.R. Anderson & Lorch, 1983; Bryant, Zillmann, & Brown, 1983; Collins, 1981; Huston & Wright, 1989; Krull, 1983; Lorch, Anderson, & Levin, 1979).

Despite the low level of involvement that typically characterizes the experiencing of television, a great deal of mental activity accompanies monitoring (Krendl & Watkins, 1983; Meadowcroft & Reeves, 1989; Thorson, Reeves, & Schleuder, 1985). Thus, the television experience cannot be described as either active or passive without reference to what each term is intended to denote. There is justification for both labels; no good rationale can be offered for giving either term precedence; and the appropriate term depends on what aspect of the experience is being described or emphasized. It is typically passive in regard to involvement, but inherently active in regard to monitoring. The mental activity involved can be described in terms of stimulus features, viewer attributes, and situational circumstances.

Stimulus features divide into those representing format, content, and form (Calvert, Huston, Watkins, & Wright, 1982; Calvert, Huston, & Wright, 1987; Campbell, Wright, & Huston, 1987; Huston, Greer, Wright, Welch, & Ross, 1984; Huston & Wright, 1989; Rice, 1984; Rice, Huston, & Wright, 1983; Rice, Huston, & Wright, 1986; Wright et al., 1984; Wright & Huston, 1983). Content refers to topic or subject matter; format, to character, genre, and length; form, to the auditory, visual, and structural elements by which content is conveyed within a format: the zoom, close-up, accompanying music, and changes or maintenance of pace.

In the abstract, the three are independent. In practice, within a cultural context or a specific medium, the three are often related. Format (such as action–adventure, situation comedy, soap opera, game shows, made-for-TV movies, and news and sports; half-hour, hour-long, or longer programs; and series, specials, and miniseries) figures fundamentally in preferences, especially in their genre-related aspects, as the segmentation of the audience based on psychological needs by Frank and Greenberg (1980) makes clear. Content (a police detective is the killer he is assigned to apprehend; family life becomes hectic when June is a finalist in a cook-off and cannot find the recipe) plays a modest role in viewing, as the typically minute differences in audience size for different episodes of series suggest (Barwise & Ehrenberg, 1988; Wober, 1988). Although it is clear that attention varies among formats (Bechtel et al., 1972), and by implication between different contents, the elements of form would be preeminent in governing attention to the screen. Form guides attention, and because format, contents, and form are intercorrelated, such features are almost certainly responsible for much of the attentional variation associated with differences in format and contents.

Form to an important degree thus governs monitoring, because by its varied elements, a current viewer receives cues from television that continued viewing is desirable, and a potential viewer cues that attending now would be desirable. For example, music may indicate whether a portrayal is more likely to please boys or girls, whether something important is about to happen, and how an event should be interpreted (for example, as menacing or triumph), thereby enhancing comprehension and readiness to attend further. Language is associated with gender (Mulac, Bradac, & Mann, 1985), resulting in additional cues for children about the gender roles of characters. Forms typically associated with feminine or masculine characters can lead children, in the specific instance, between grades one and six (Huston *et al.*, 1984), to identify sexually neutral products in television commercials as intended either for girls or boys.

There have been several efforts to identify the form elements that are most likely to attract children's attention (Alwitt, Anderson, Lorch, & Levin, 1980; Alvarez, Huston, Wright, & Kerkman, 1988; Baggaley, 1985; Bryant, Zillmann, & Brown, 1983; Husson & Krull, 1983; Potts, Huston, & Wright, 1986). Factors that apparently facilitate attention among young children include puppets; women and children; changes in character or level of audio; peculiar voices; movement; camera cuts; sound effects; laughter; applause; a single narrator; animals if they are colorful, active, and have comical features; rapid action; and high violence. Males on the whole are higher in attentiveness, especially to violence and animation. Factors that apparently facilitate inattention include adult male voices, extended zooms and pans, eye contact with the viewer, still shots, and characters that lack color or are inactive. Increased complexity of visual or auditory stimuli will increase attention if it can be integrated into the unfolding events or somehow comprehended; continuing fast-paced music that is appealing will lead to a decrease in attention as the young viewers become absorbed in the music. Generalizations from documented linkages between attention and form are always problematic because of the possibility that somewhat different treatment or context—the crescendo or diminuendo of sound being a preeminent example (Calvert & Scott, 1989)—might lead to a different response.

A viewer attribute of primary interest is age, with chronological status understood as an imperfect proxy for the level of cognitive development. Cognitive level signifies the ability of the young viewer to understand the content, evaluate accurately the format, and interpret correctly the form features of television. Along with gender, it is a principal factor in preferences (Acker & Tiemens, 1981; Collins, Sobol, & Westby, 1981; Collins, Wellman, Keniston, & Westby, 1978; Greer, Potts, Wright, & Huston, 1982; Hayes & Kelly, 1985; Hoffner & Cantor, 1985; Hoffner, Cantor, & Thorson, 1988; Meadowcroft & Reeves, 1989; Meltzoff, 1988; Newcomb & Collins, 1979; Wright *et al.*, 1984). The principal findings are:

1. Children as young as 14 and 24 months can translate the two-dimensional events of television into an internalized representation for behaving in the three-dimensional space of the real world, and can retain this representation for 24 hours or longer. That is, at these ages they will imitate what they see, even after a lengthy delay, which would depend on such a cognitive skill.

2. The implicit recognition and response to form features precede the ability to define or describe them.

3. The ability to comprehend content, format, and form features increases with cognitive level, but even among young children, salient form features, such as action and rapid changes in scene, character, and camera treatment, attract and hold visual attention; the younger the child, the larger do such form features—and especially those visual—figure in comprehension.

4. Congruencies between content, format, and form features, that is, regularly employed conventions of television and film production, help young people learn from television, or at least better understand what they have been experiencing, as do interpretive comments and explanations from older children or adults.

5. Younger children, such as those in the second grade or below, comprehend portrayals better that resemble in various ways their own circumstances; older children are less dependent on such congruence, so that the role of congruence decreases with age.

6. Younger children are more dependent on appearances than behavior in forming beliefs about a portrayed character or the likely outcome of a story; older children make more use of behavior in making such judgments, so that the role of appearance decreases and that of behavior increases with age.

7. Skills at assembling stories, or knowledge of schema, ease the task of cognitive processing and enhance the likelihood of comprehension; these increase with age, but even children as young as preschool are similar to adults in better recalling settings and principal outcomes

than beginnings, endings, and reactions within stories, so that young and old appear to employ the same schema.

8. Regardless of cognitive level, temporally related scenes are better recalled than independent successive scenes.

9. Because of the many other factors on which comprehension depends, visual attention is an imperfect predictor even among young children who would be least equipped to draw on audio content or knowledge of schema; in fact, looking away might signal reflective, analytic processing that would enhance comprehension.

This pattern leads to a principle: Attention rises with the ability and need to assemble a narrative successfully, and falls when elements can be comprehended individually or missed elements can be readily supplied by the viewer. Thus, attention is maximal generally for movies and, among children, for children's programming. It is minimal, generally, for content that is redundant or episodic, as is the case for news, commercials, and sports, or stereotypic, so that the viewer can provide connections between episodes, as is the case for much melodrama. The finding by Bechtal, Achelpohl, and Akers (1972) that attention by teenagers for most types of programs is greater than among those younger, and for some types than among those older (Table 1.4), reinforces the contention that comprehension, in terms both of achievability and necessity, is a factor influencing attention. However, as our conclusions about the role of time would lead us to expect, the longer a presentation, the less likely it is to be viewed in entirety, so that movies generally are less often watched in entirety than are series episodes (Robinson, 1972b).

Thus, D.R. Anderson and colleagues (D.R. Anderson *et al.*, 1986) find a curvilinear relationship between attention to the screen and age (Fig. 1.3), with attention declining as the maturing child has less need to follow visual components in order to comprehend what is being portrayed. This is in accord with the finding by Pingree (1986) that comprehensibility declines as a factor as children grow older, simply because it ceases to vary much across different types of programming.

Examples of how some of these factors operate are found in the work of Collins and of Lorch and their colleagues (Collins *et al.*, 1978; Lorch *et al.*, 1979). The former showed second, fifth, and eighth graders edited versions of a commercial action–adventure program. The versions varied in the number of scenes and whether the scenes were chronologically or randomly ordered. Recall improved with age for plot-essential, nonessential, and implicit or inferred content. The logical temporal ordering led to greater recall of implicit content. Those in the two

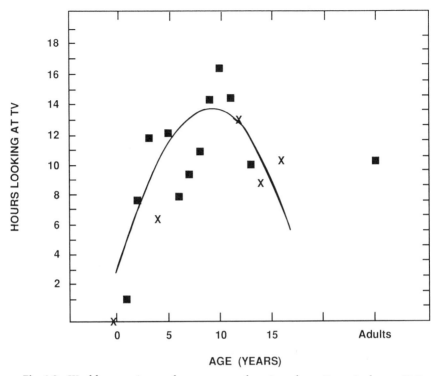

Fig. 1.3   Weekly attention to the screen as a function of age. From Anderson, D.R., Lorch, E.P., Field, D.E., & Sanders, J. (1981). Television viewing at home: Age trends in visual attention and time with TV. *Child Development, 57,* 1024–1033.

higher grades recalled implicit content better when they were also superior in recalling plot-essential content. The latter showed a 40-minute version of "Sesame Street" to preschool children, half of whom were surrounded by attractive toys, and half of whom were not. Attention to the screen was twice as great among those without the toys, but comprehension was essentially the same. Comprehension within the groups was positively associated with attention. This favors the interpretation that comprehension led to attention, over the reverse.

Young children distinguish between more and less important content, but the ability to do so increases with age. Lorch and colleagues (Lorch, Bellak, & Augsbach, 1987) found that among four to six year olds, recall of "Sesame Street" elements increased linearly with their importance, and did so much more sharply among the six year olds.

Collins and Wellman (1982) again showed an action–adventure program to second, fifth, and eighth graders, and this time interrupted it to ask what would happen next. The younger children relied far more on sterotypic expectations and on the immediately preceding event; those older, with more real-life as well as video experience to draw on, were better able to integrate what had come before in their predictions. A.F. Newcomb and Collins (1979) found that the comprehension of second graders was increased when the families portrayed were of the same socioeconomic status, while such congruence made no difference among fifth and eighth graders.

Between the preschool years and the fifth grade, children become increasingly proficient at comprehending television's techniques. Flashbacks become better understood (Calvert, 1988), replays become interpretable as a repetition of the portrayed event rather than of the behavior itself (Rice, Huston, & Wright, 1986), and essential and nonessential content become better recalled. Recall can be aided by memory aids: before the content in question, a 30-second pause, an announcement on the video, and an adult giving the same information in person (Watkins, Calvert, Huston-Stein, & Wright, 1980), or by direct questions prefaced by "You. . . ." embedded in a sequence (Tamborini & Zillmann, 1985). In the case of the flashbacks, dreamy dissolves were more strongly associated with comprehension than were abrupt cuts; in the case of the replays, those of a baseball play were sooner understood than those of a phone call; and in the case of memory aids, only the adult present in person was effective. When kindergarten children were exposed to television sequences that varied in difficulty (by altering pace, redundancy, and vocabulary) and use of techniques common to children's programming (animation, lively music, etc.), attention and recall were not only greater for those less difficult but also for those using the child forms (Campbell et al., 1987). Calvert and Gersh (1987) found that the use of sound effects to signal important and conceivably puzzling story transitions enhanced the relative comprehension of essential over nonessential plot elements among the younger of 64 children, half of whom were in kindergarten and half in the fifth grade. Morison, Kelly, and Gardner (1981) found, among about 650 second, fourth, and sixth graders, that the basis of designating a television program as realistic progresses from physical resemblance to real life to judging whether the fabricated representation presented by television is like real life, that is, from whether it is real to whether it is realistic. These findings emphasize the importance of television form, experience with television, and adult guidance.

Nevertheless, some television techniques are inherently confusing. Quarforth (1979) found that below the age of eight most children did not fully make distinctions among puppets, animated, and live characters, which is hardly surprising since the three means of depiction serve the same storytelling ends. Acker (1983) found that even among those of college age, estimates of the distance traveled and velocity of a video-taped train varied with the focal length of the lens employed, with velocity increasing with width of lens angle. The effect was inversely associated with age; it was most frequent among those in the third grade, followed by those in the seventh grade, and least among those of college age. Friedlander, Wetstone, and Scott (1974) blamed the low comprehension scores of preschool children in response to a three-minute education insert designed for that age group and broadcast nationally with "Captain Kangaroo" on the lack of redundancy, use of action to decorate rather than embody the theme, and quantity of irrelevancies, all common to television production.

Hayes and Kelly (1985) examined the recall of nodes—entangling complications or events on which a story turns—among preschool children and adults from stories told by radio and by television. Regardless of medium, the types of nodes recalled were the same regardless of age, with setting and principal outcomes better recalled than beginnings, endings, or reactions to events. The implication is that despite the lesser ability of children to focus on central rather than peripheral elements, synthesize components, and with television make use of the aural as well as the visual, children and adults use similar schema or in the language of Mandler (1983) "grammar" for cataloging story elements.

The years between seven and nine are a key period. It is during these years that young persons move from the preoperational to the concrete operational in the vocabulary of Piaget (1969; Piaget & Inhelder, 1967). In the preoperational stage of cognitive development, the ability to comprehend television programming is more limited. This is because reasoning is often binary. or black and white, so that subtleties, ironies, and inconsistencies between appearance and behavior, deed and consequence, are resolved in the direction of the most visually obvious interpretation; there is a higher degree of egocenteredness, which leads to taking in everything as part of the self so that television is taken as real and characters as beings with whom one could interact; there is lesser ability to take another's viewpoint perceptually or conceptually, so that those with a different perspective than one's own are less readily understood; and there is high reliance on the most obvious cues for understanding, which in the case of television are the visual elements and loud sound effects. Once the concrete operational stage is obtained, young people are able to comprehend general audience programming about as well as most adults, and especially so since children and adults employ the same basic schema to encode programs; it is also at this age that young people come fully to understand the persuasive intent of commercials (Chapter V).

Obviously, very complex material dependent for comprehension on experiences they have not had will continue to elude young viewers. However, the same probably applies to adults too given the fact that large proportions do not recall principal elements of programs they believe they have watched in their entirety. Thus, after this age cognitive stage probably has little to do with comprehending television programming although it may have much to do with whether a particular program is of interest. Thus, a young person in the final, third formal operational stage may be more interested in a program that deals with an abstract issue but he or she will be able to follow and comprehend the portrayed concrete events and relationships. One reason why cognitive stage no longer plays a larger role after this earlier juncture is that television programming adheres to conventions that operate against complexity and subtlety; they are designed to be popular, and thus readily understood with a minimum of cognitive skills and mental effort.

It is not true, however, except possibly during the earliest year or two that children entertain the idea that something is happening within the television set. Flavell, Flavell, Green, and Korfmacher (1990) found that three year olds had a tendency to think of television images as physically present while by the age of four the conception of them as pictorial representations was essentially universal. However, they conclude that the source of the error at the earlier age is a failure to differentiate between images and what they represent and not the belief that small people and objects populate the innards of television sets. Our own evidence for this conclusion is that we have never heard an anecdote about a child trying to open up the rear of a set to free those inside or gain access to exciting toys; in contrast, the anecdotes about children imitating what they seen on television in their play abound, and for good reason (Chapter VI).

The emphasis on age should not be mistaken for an unqualified endorsement of a Piagetian theory of stages which rigidly dictates children's responses to television. Wolf (1987), in a 10-month inquiry into the concepts about television held by children between the ages of 4 and 12, makes a convincing case that however useful stages are in making a process readily comprehensible, they also may obfuscate to some degree the process itself. The research site was a four-acre recreational facility in Austin, Texas, that included a building where they could view television. The number of children present each day varied from about 40 to about 85, and data were collected by conversing with them, by listening to conversations, and by having them produce brief television programs planned and filmed by them.

The children were quite articulate, and often displayed conscious, sometimes ingenious, efforts to interpret what they had seen (Table 1.5). The findings give a wealth of detail. Memory of (some would say, learning from) television is enhanced by favorite programs or highly novel events; initial evaluations of programs are typically brief, but children can and will elaborate; narrative conventions were understood; devices such as those used to shift scenes were recognized; use was made of nonverbal cues such as gestures and clothing; "good" and "bad" guys were identified; and on the whole the children, in the words of the author, "expressed their awareness of the use of multiple cameras and angles, editing, lighting, slow and fast motion, superimposition, process shots, and numerous other production devices" (p. 93). Among the latter was the use of music to cue events, with one boy responding to what he called "danger music" with, "Oh no! It won't be good. That song means bad things are gonna happen. If you want, we can close our eyes. You do it and I'll watch and tell." One important factor was the

Table 1.5
Child and Teenage Viewing Preferences by Type of Program

Program type	Percentage named as favorites		
	7-year-olds	12-year-olds	16-year-olds
Youth-oriented adventure	10	14	20
Situation comedy	22	17	9
Family situation comedy	25	23	9
Police–detective	3	5	6
Cartoon	24	5	1
Music–variety–talk	3	5	13
Serial dramas	—	3	9
Dramatic	2	6	13
News	—	1	1
Education–culture	4	3	2
Western	3	8	7
Game	2	4	2
Sports	—	2	2
Movies	2	4	6

Adapted from Lyle, J., & Hoffman, H.R. (1972a). Children's use of television and other media. In E.A. Rubinstein, G.A. Comstock, & J.P. Murray (Eds)., *Television and social behavior: Vol. 4. Television in day-to-day life: Patterns of use* (pp. 257–273). Washington, DC: U.S. Government Printing Office.

capability of a child to assume the perspective of a television character, particularly in regard to why things appeared as they did or were somehow obscured. These outcomes suggest a range and depth of comprehension somewhat greater than that implied by the experiments, and comprehension at younger ages somewhat beyond that predicted by a Piegetian stage theory.

Support comes from the recent experiment by Abelman (1989). He examined the comprehension of projective size—defined as "changes in object size as a way of relaying our getting 'closer' and 'farther away from' an object" (p.465), by exposing about 180 three and four year olds to either zoom-ins and zoom-outs or multiple edits with objects getting either closer to or farther away with each edit. The model proposed by Piaget (Piaget & Inhelder, 1956; Piaget, 1969) holds that children under the age of seven would not comprehend the use of projective vision techniques. Drawing on the concepts introduced by J.H. Flavell and colleagues (Flavell, Everett, Croft & Flavell, 1981; Pillow & Flavell, 1986), Abelman demonstrates that this capacity may appear considerably earlier in the preschool years, with those who possess lower level skills able to comprehend zooms, and those who possess higher level skills able to comprehend both zooms and multiple edits. The basis for the former appears to be the capacity to infer what can be seen from another's viewpoint, and for the latter, the understanding that objects may look different in different places or from different distances. In Abelman's vocabulary, children with lower level skills "infer . . . the content" (p. 476) while those with higher level skills "infer the nature, as well as the content, of another person's visual experience."

The principal implication of these two investigations is that the stage of cognitive development, along with chronological age, may mask important variation among children in their capacity to understand television, and that children ostensibly within the same cognitive stage may differ in this capacity because of their possession or lack of important perceptual skills. Age is not thereby dethroned, but merely demoted to a more modest position.

Numerous other variables affect responses to television, of course. For example, Weigel and Jessor (1973) found that teenagers who scored higher on a scale of conventionality also watched greater amounts of television. This outcome is quite plausible, given the calculated design of most television to achieve mass popularity, and the reliance on content, formats, and form features that present little to challenge viewers intellectually and emotionally (Barwise & Ehrenberg, 1988; Comstock, 1989; Gitlin, 1983). Kubey (1986), Kubey and Czikszentmihalyi (1990), and Schallow and McIlwraith (1986–87) interpret positive correlations among adults and older teenagers between negative mood states and television consumption as attributable to the use of the medium to escape from unpleasant emotions. This outcome is not only in rough accord with the evidence (Zillmann, 1988; Zillmann & Bryant, 1984) that the media are used for mood management and to maintain comfortable affective equilibrium, but also one that would seem applicable to younger persons, with one qualification: Although greater-than-ordinary use of pictorial media such as television arguably has become recognized as a possible symptom of personal maladjustment (E.E. Maccoby, 1964; Schramm, Lyle, & Parker, 1961; Tangney, 1988), young people on the whole are far more likely to turn to music than to television entertainment (Lyle & Hoffman, 1972a) when in transient states of personal distress. This tendency increases with age, as does the amount of time spent listening to music and allocation of media time to music, which comes to rival television in time use in the later teenage years (Christenson & Roberts, 1990).

Television, because of the way it has developed as a medium whose programs must achieve maximal popularity, has become a shared experience and a means of acknowledging commonalities (Comstock, 1988, 1989; W.R. Neuman, 1982). Music has developed as a medium serving small market segments with highly defined tastes, while at the same time seeking to obtain vast popularity for genres and specific offerings whenever possible, thus leading to most young persons' having very similar preferences once age, gender, and ethnicity are taken into account (Christenson & Roberts, 1990). Music can become a means of asserting self-identity, separation from or discord with parents and school, and allegiance with peers, and especially for those performing less well in school (Kubey & Csikszentmihalyi, 1990; Larson & Kubey, 1983; Larson, Kubey, & Colletti, 1990; Lull, 1985; Roe, 1983). Thus, television and music are distinct in function, not only psychologically, but also sociologically.

Situational circumstances include the availability of other stimuli, such as toys, reading matter, or incompatible media (such as recorded music), their intrusiveness in terms of size or novelty, their inherent appeal, and the presence and behavior of other potential viewers. The opportunity to engage in an alterative activity typically suppresses attention to the screen. The more attractive the alternative, the greater the degree of suppression. The importance of alternative stimuli in affecting attention to television was exemplified by the highly effective distraction research employed in the original development of "Sesame Street" (Cook, Appleton, Conner, Shaffer, Tamkin, & Weber, 1975; Cook & Curtin, 1986; Lesser, 1972, 1974). Children of nursery school age, the principal target audience, were given the opportunity to watch sequences of "Sesame Street" while in the vicinity of attractive toys. When the children turned from the screen to a plaything, the sequence became eligible for discard as less than adequately appealing. By this means, "Sesame Street" maximized the likelihood that one of the conditions supposedly necessary for learning, attention, would be present.

Young viewers also take cues from others in the vicinity of the set. In this respect, others may be employed as informants or sources of validation regarding the audiovisual signals. When other viewers turn away from the screen or turn to an alternative stimulus, the likelihood of continued attention is decreased. For example, Anderson and colleagues (D.R. Anderson, Lorch, Smith, Bradford, & Levin, 1981) found when three- and five-year-old children viewed television in groups of two or three, there was a tendency for the action of any one child (attending or not attending to the screen, looking at an adjacent distracting audiovisual slide display, or becoming highly actively involved in viewing) to be followed by the other child or children doing the same thing. Haefner and Wartella (1987) found that, among first- and second-grade children who viewed television with siblings who were either about the same age or somewhat older, evaluations of characters were influenced by the older siblings; in this instance, the cognitive and affective responses were altered by the cues from those higher in status and more knowledgeable. The most modest conceivable model of young persons viewing television is not a child seated in front of an operating set giving his or her attention to the screen, but a triad: (a) young person, (b) operating set, and (c) the situational circumstance.

We do not wish to give the impression that children never give close, continuing attention to the screen or that such attention is unrelated to type of program. We reported that the data of Bechtel, Achelpohl, and Akers (1972) indicate that children are especially attentive to programming made for them. Argenta, Stoneman, and Brody (1986) showed pairs of preschool age children of the same sex animated cartoons, "Sesame Street," and situation comedies. Visual attention was greatest for cartoons and least for situation comedies. Social interaction was markedly decreased by the cartoons; the other two types of programs led to the children dividing their time between social interaction, toys, and viewing. As the authors comment, "The image of children 'mesmerized' in front of the television set, forsaking social interaction and active involvement with their object environment, held true for only one type of programming, namely, cartoons" (p. 370). Thus, at least when there is a close match between program characteristics and viewer preferences, child viewing indeed may be intense.

The findings on the whole disabuse us of the stereotype of the fixated young viewer, although they make it abundantly clear that the audiovisual cues of television are important in regard to whether or not the screen will be attended to, and some types of content in certain circumstances may indeed mesmerize young viewers.

Nevertheless, some degree of visual dependence is created. D.R. Anderson and Lorch (1983) report that the probability of making eye contact with the screen is in part a function of whether there was eye contact during the preceding few seconds, and that this holds for three year olds, five year olds, and college students (Fig. 1.4). D.R. Anderson,

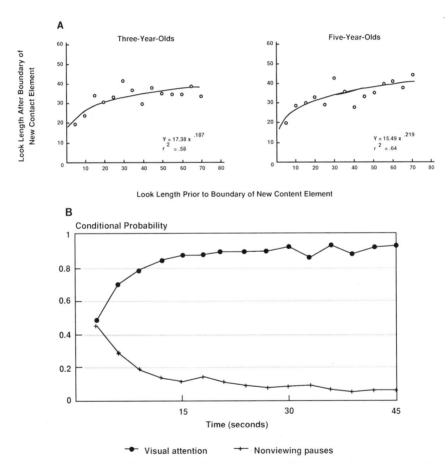

Fig. 1.4   Perceptual dependence at three ages. Adapted from Anderson, D.R., & Lorch, E.P. (1983). Looking at television: Action or reaction. In J. Bryant & D.R. Anderson (Eds.), *Children's understanding of television: Research on attention and comprehension* (pp. 1–34). New York: Academic Press.

Choi, and Lorch (1987) report that among three and five year olds, the probability of a look at the screen being maintained is a function of the length of prior attention, increasing with the length of that prior attention, and that the capability of a distracting slide to turn heads was diminished the longer prior attention to the screen had been. This process, which the authors label "visual inertia," carries viewers across sequences and from one content segment into another, thus becoming part of the process by which television holds an audience. There is also some cognitive inertia, or there would not be the persistently found lead-in effect, by which a popular program delivers some of its audience to the subsequent program (Barwise & Ehrenberg, 1988): thus, the exercise of selectivity is slightly attenuated by prior satisfaction.

A number of elements about television viewing make it intrinsically somewhat passive. People not only often view what someone else has selected, but there is also some perceptual dependence and cognitive inertia. The empirical literature we are discussing on children's cognitive processing of television attests that within this frame, a great deal of more or less autonomic activity takes place in monitoring the medium. Those who have interviewed children extensively about their viewing testify to their interest in, thoughtfulness about, and insight into what they have seen (Wolf, 1987; P. Palmer, 1986), and conclude that children are actively involved in their viewing. This conclusion, however, pertains principally to programs in which they are interested, that they choose or like to view, and are largely able to understand. A substantial amount of children's viewing is passive because, as Huston and colleagues (1990) record, it has been chosen by adults and at best is partially comprehended. Examples are adult drama, prime-time non-comedy series, and news. Huston and colleagues conclude that such viewing may occur frequently up to the age of seven, after which increased cognitive abilities widen the range of what can be understood, and the likelihood increases that children will be allowed to view on their own. We would only add that the same passivity, although to a lesser degree, occurs among those older when they want to spend time with still older siblings or parents when the latter are viewing television. This does not mean this viewing is entirely unrewarding, because, while not maximally involving or always well understood, the attention of children to television in their very early years means that often people find what they do not comprehend on television passively entertaining. Thus, the active aspects of viewing occur within a frame that varies greatly in degree of passivity.

This is far from domination by the visual elements. On the whole, children and teenagers, and certainly adults too, consume television selectively, as a function of numerous content, format, and form features, viewer characteristics, and situational circumstances. As cognitive level increases, children become more effective in monitoring television, because they become more competent in recognizing and correctly interpreting the features on which comprehension, enjoyment, and interest depend. Viewing techniques are thus acquired.

The similarity in amount of viewing across societies and cultures despite the vast differences among them, nevertheless, invites the interpretation that there is something intrinsically pleasurable about the experience regardless of content. The new evidence by Plomin and colleagues (Plomin, Corley, DeFries, & Fulker, 1990) based on 220 three-, four-, and five-year-old children in the Colorado Adoption Project (Plomin & DeFries, 1985), their siblings, and natural and adoptive parents strongly supports such an interpretation. Using the recognized methodology for making inferences about genetic and environmental influence, they conclude that in addition to a substantial environmental contribution through parents, peers, siblings, and television availability in the home there is also a sizable and significant hereditary factor. The explanation lies neither in the genetic influence on intelligence nor in temperment as such traits are conventionally measured. This confirms a hint of such a factor a decade-and-a-half ago when Loeghlin and Nichols (1976) reported a significantly higher correlation of amount of viewing between identical than between fraternal twins. The implication is that there is some variability in the pleasure derived from viewing, perhaps through susceptibility to alpha waves, or right brain processing, which many believe as representative of emotional, less critical, nonverbal, and nonanalytic thinking, are more typical of cognitive processing during viewing than the obverse, beta waves or left hemisphere processing. This in turn strongly suggests that there is a genetically based reward for viewing; thus, television everywhere is used for about the same amount of time by comparable populations.

A controversy over whether the visual component interferes with the recall and comprehensibility of the audio portion has been resolved by empirical inquiry (Calvert et al., 1987; Gibbons, Anderson, Smith, Field, & Fischer, 1986; Hayes & Birnbaum, 1980; Hoffner et al., 1988; Pezdek & Hartman, 1983; Pezdek & Stevens, 1984; Soldow, 1983). As Rolandelli (1989) argues in his review, this presumably would rest on the greater concreteness and similarity to everyday experience of the visual component compared to the greater abstractness of the audio portion, and thus the effect would be greatest among younger children and would decrease with age. The evidence clearly supports the view that young children typically pay more attention to the visual than to the audio element. The audio element can be as readily recalled and comprehended, when paid attention to, if it is linguistically within the child's range, and the visual component does not interfere with recalling or understanding the audio portion. The two keys are attention and comprehensibility. If attention is paid, and the two are equal in comprehensibility, both will be equally recalled and understood. Thus, as Rolandelli concludes, the so-called visual superiority effect is a myth.

While monitoring implies mental processing, so too does the comprehension of content, recognition of formats, and the interpretation of form features in behalf of these ends. Schramm, Lyle, and Parker (1961) argued that what the child brings to television is as important in any influence the medium has on the child as what television brings to the child. This perspective certainly applies to the concept of "amount of invested mental effort in nonautomatic elaboration of material" proposed by Salomon (1983b, 1981a, 1981b, 1979) as a factor upon which certain possible effects of television are contingent. It has a number of empirically supported implications for the influence of television and other media, and particularly in regard to learning.

Expectations about the amount of invested mental effort appropriate for exposure to a given experience—such as reading a book, attending a lecture, or watching television—to some degree govern the amount of effort that is actually expended. Salomon (1981a, 1981b, 1983a, 1983b, 1984) and Salomon and Leigh (1984) provide the evidence. In one instance, it was found that 12 year olds believed it was easier for them to learn from television than from print. Success in learning from television was more likely to be attributed to the characteristics of the medium, and success in learning from print was more likely to be attributed to the intelligence of the child. Conversely, failure with television was ascribed to lack of intelligence, and failure with print, to the characteristics of the medium (Table 1.6). In another, 12 year olds either viewed a television program or read the text, and half of each of these groups were told the experience was "for fun" and half were told it was "to learn". In effect, low- and high-demand conditions for amount of invested mental effort were created. As would be expected, children in the high-demand conditions reported expending greater mental effort. Somewhat surprisingly, there was no marked difference between those in the high- and low- demand conditions in learning from print, but children in the high-demand learned a great deal more than those in the low-demand condition from television. The implication is that print ordinarily elicits a higher amount of invested mental effort, and thus demand is not easily manipulated; the obverse apparently holds

Table 1.6
Attention to the Set by Time of Day[a]

Set in use	Total	Morning	Afternoon	Evening
Hours per week	31.8	3.5	9.7	18.6
Average number of viewers per minute[b]	1.42	1.14	1.22	1.58
Degree of inattention (hours)				
No one in room	6.0	1.0	2.4	2.6
No one viewing screen	6.8	0.8	2.1	3.9
Total inattention				
Hours	12.8	1.8	4.5	6.5
(Percentage)	(40)	(52)	(57)	(35)

[a] Figures are based on average set-in-use hours, per home, per week, over four sample sites in Oklahoma and Kansas. $N = 95$ homes (358 persons).

[b] Average audience includes all people present in the room, even if they were not looking at, or in the direction of, the set.

From Allen, C. (1965). Photographing the audience. *Journal of Advertising Research, 5*, 2–8.

for television. In a third, 12 year olds were divided into those who would read a difficult text, an easy text, or view a television sequence, with all based on the same source. Greater effort was reported for the difficult than the easy text, and least for television. Among the children with greater intellectual ability, effort was judged to be most merited by the difficult text, followed by the easy text, and least by television. The implication is that even more intellectually capable children are likely to perceive television as requiring little investment of mental effort and therefore will not learn from it in accord with their basic ability.

Compared to print, television elicits low expectations about the appropriateness of invested mental effort. In turn, amount of invested mental effort is typically low. The consequence is that not much is learned by children and teenagers from television entertainment of a cognitive or informational character, although, as we shall see, much may be learned about modes of behavior. Tests of recall or memory, and of knowledge of what has been experienced, suggest superiority for print in regard to learning. The expectation that not much mental effort is required for television viewing may carry over from entertainment to other types of programming, such as news, debates between political candidates, and other informational, cultural, and educational programming.

Self-perceived efficacy has been found to be associated positively with actual effort for print and negatively for television. The result is that the most capable children, or at least, the most self-confident, probably often employ the least effective strategies and mental operations for learning when viewing television. Thus, the "easy" medium in many ways becomes the hardest.

Gunter (1987a) gives serious consideration to the possibility that such factors may be responsible for the apparent worldwide fact that people recall very little from television news even minutes after they have finished viewing. If news and other informational programming is to be educationally useful to children and teenagers, they must be encouraged to view with the expectation that some mental effort will be required, to change motives with format and content, and to become adept at shifting from one attentional mode to another.

The data on monitoring and cognitive processing have helped elucidate and explicate the concepts *passive* and *active*. They challenge the notion of near-hypnotic control of the young viewer (D.R. Anderson & Lorch, 1983; Bryant & Anderson, 1983). They are especially significant for identifying means by which television can be made more enjoyable, better understood, and more useful to young viewers (Huston & Wright, 1989). Finally, they have increased our understanding of an everyday, seemingly trivial category of experience that in fact has some claim to complexity.

Amount and degree of recall and comprehension clearly are affected by mode of measurement.Wolf (1987) elicited much more searching, reflective, and knowledgeable responses from children about the television they were viewing than many would have expected, because he used probing, extended, unthreatening interviews and conversations. Pingree (1984) produced comparable data when she asked 18 three- to five-year-old children to reenact an eight-minute sequence from "Diff'rent Strokes" with props and dolls. Atwood and colleagues (Atwood, Allen, Bardgett, Proudlove, & Rich, 1982) found that children addressed many questions about what transpires on the screen to themselves, and concluded that much mental processing might be overlooked. Memory aides demonstrably help; the younger the child, the greater the superiority of recognition over unaided or otherwise aided recall (Evra, 1990). Nevertheless, the evidence in behalf of the relationships among stimulus features, viewer attributes, and situational circumstances is convincing; in our judgment it is level, and perhaps threshold, and not the overall pattern that is sensitive to measurement.

The concept of *indiscriminant viewing* has at least three meanings: (a) the viewing of a great deal of television; (b) viewing with minimal concern for what is viewed; and (c) a lack of motive in viewing. The phrase is frequently employed to imply that viewing is a poor use of time.

The preeminence of time available as a predictor unambiguously identifies a great deal of viewing as not driven by the desire to see particular programs. Viewers nevertheless remain highly selective in almost always watching the same program when viewing at a particular time. Young people who view a great deal are likely to watch almost all categories of programs more frequently. In a sample of more than 15,000 sixth graders (California Assessment Program, 1982), very heavy viewers rated most programs as watched more often than very light viewers, and they had a decidedly greater preference for light, comparatively undemanding entertainment. Very light viewers were below average for all types of programs, but showed a decided preference for more serious entertainment and public affairs programming. The lighter viewers, by the amount and makeup of their viewing, practiced greater selectivity, but it is hard to argue either that a preference for light entertainment constitutes indiscriminant consumption, or that the latter varies with whether the grounds for program selection are aesthetic, hedonistic, moral, or utilitarian. The preeminence of viewing over programs in the decision to view gives credence to the concept of a *motive to view*, but the subsequent selectivity hardly makes its satisfaction an undiscriminating process.

The concepts introduced by A.M. Rubin (1983, 1984) on the basis of the responses of about 750 adults to questions about their motives for viewing are more useful. He distinguishes between *ritualistic* and *instrumental* viewing. Those for whom the former is paramount seek to consume time, are high consumers of entertainment, and have a high regard for television. By comparison, more instrumental viewers seek information, are nonescapist in their motives, and are more selective in choosing programs. Both imply utility for viewing, but selectivity is lesser for ritualistic than for instrumental viewing. The predominance of one or the other would vary not only among individuals but also for the same individual with circumstances and type of programming.

Nevertheless, there may be styles of viewing that, because of the source of motivation, involve a helter-skelter use of the medium. Schallow and McIlwraith (1986–1987) found, among several hundred undergraduates, not only that television was often watched during negative moods, presumably as a source of relief, but also that such behavior was associated with fearful and guilt-arousing daydreaming and channel switching. Poor attentional control (defined as mind-wandering boredom) was associated with using television to fill time, channel switching, and fearful and guilt-arousing daydreaming, as well as with watching television when in a negative mood. Poor attentional control also was correlated positively with viewing comedy and drama, and negatively with news viewing; the former presumably would provide greater escape than the latter. Indiscriminant viewing hardly describes such behavior accurately, although the gratifications sought clearly are not easily satisfied.

Indiscriminant viewing is thus not a useful concept. It is descriptively inaccurate, connotatively misleading, and far too simplistic.

E. SOCIAL CIRCUMSTANCES

Television consumption occurs in a social as well as a personal context. In the case of children and teenagers, we think principally of siblings, peers, and parents. Television belongs to that category of technological innovations, along with the automobile and time-saving household appliances, that are often said to have changed family life. Pertinent topics include television set availability and the social setting of viewing, control of the set, and parental restriction, proscription, and prescription of viewing.

In 1960, 1970, and 1980, the Columbia Broadcasting Company (CBS) sponsored nationwide surveys about television using probability samples of about 2000 Americans 18 years of age or older (Bower, 1973, 1985; Steiner, 1963). They answer many questions, and provide data on trends.

Television sets are nearly ubiquitous in American households. The principal set or a set is in a central, accessible location in almost all households, the living room or family room. Additional sets are usually placed in bedrooms. In one-set families, more than 90% said that joint viewing by family members is typical. The figure decreases as the number of sets owned increases (Table 1.7). For example, the figures for two-set families are about three-fourths; and for three-set families, about two-thirds. In multiset households, children viewed by themselves about one-fourth of the time; the figure was similar for husbands and wives viewing together, so that for about half the time, either adults or children viewed by themselves, compared to the about one-third of the time that the entire family viewed together.

More recent data further emphasize the pattern of generational separation. Lawrence and Wozniak (1989) found, among about 150 young persons aged between 6 and 17 years, that viewing by the entire family was infrequent, and that while a majority of viewing was with another family member, most of it was with siblings. McDonald (1986) found, in a sample of 252 households with 316 persons, that most coviewing

Table 1.7
Social Setting of Viewing

Joint viewing in one-set and multiset families

| | Joint viewing likely | | | |
| | 1970 | | 1980 | |
	%	(N)	%	(N)
One-set families	94	(472)	93	(220)
Two-set families	80	(543)	75	(532)
Three-set families	66	(160)	69	(246)
Four-set families	65	(35)	63	(174)
Total for all sets	83	(1210)	75	(1172)

Viewing combinations in single-set and multiset families

| | In one-set families | | In multiset families[a] | |
	1970	1980	1970	1980
Husband–wife	17	25	26	26
Entire family	55	41	34	36
Children	13	16	26	22
Mother–child	9	9	5	6
Father–child	4	8	7	5
Other	3	1	3	5
Base: 100% =	(443)	(185)	(613)	(597)

Decisions when viewing jointly

| | Viewers | | | | | |
| Percent who report decisions made by | Mother and children | | Husband and wife | | Entire family[a] | |
	1970	1980	1970	1980	1970	1980
Group or mutual decision	27	37	53	52	42	53
Husband/father	—	—	28	28	27	32
Wife/mother	37	40	18	19	10	12
Child/children	33	19	—	—	17	10
Other/NA	3	3	1	2	4	3
Base: 100% =	(100)	(108)	(508)	(501)	(347)	(451)

[a] Viewing around all sets, combined.
From Bower, R.T. (1985). *The changing television audience in America.* New York: Columbia University Press.

occurs among persons within the same general age range, whether children, teenagers, or adults; thus, the presence of more than one set increases a tendency for younger and older persons not to view together. L.J. Baron (1985) found among a Canadian sample of 330 5 to 12 year olds, that regardless of the number of sets, coviewing was inversely related to socioeconomic status.

In short, multiple sets decrease family viewing and increase independent viewing by age cohorts; the effect is probably greatest in households of lower socioeconomic status. The likelihood that multiple-set ownership contributes to, rather than merely reflects, lower levels of family viewing is high, because the inverse association remains unchanged despite the sizable increase across decades in the frequency of multiset households. This is a significant trend, because the estimate from A.C. Nielsen Company data is that more than two-thirds of all households own two or more sets; the comparable figure for 1970 would have been one-fifth as great.[1]

The lack of and decline in coviewing by young persons and adults have implications for the effects of television (Austin, Roberts, & Nass, 1990; Buerkel-Rothfuss, Greenberg, Atkin, & Neuendorf, 1982; Desmond, Hirsch, Singer, & Singer, 1987; Desmond, Singer, Singer, Calam, & Colimore, 1985; Messaris, 1983; Messaris & Sarett, 1981; Stoneman & Brody, 1983a). What parents or other older persons say and do about what has been viewed can affect how a young person responds cognitively and affectively. Conversations during and about viewing are frequent, with one-half of a national sample of adults reporting that half of the exchanges during viewing were about television, and one-fifth saying that they talked about television after viewing (LoSciuto, 1972). If the content of conversations parallels that of thoughts occurring during viewing, the majority concern television as a medium in some way (W.R. Neuman, 1982)—the quality of the programs, the plots, and the actors. Conversations are not trivial for the young viewer, because they constitute informal education in regard to taste and judgement in the arts, entertainment, news, and sports.

However, conversations of two kinds have a special claim to importance: those that deal with the reality of what is portrayed, and those that deal with the rightness or wrongness of the portrayed behavior. In these cases, the older viewers may set limits on, mitigate, eliminate, or

[1] The painstaking reader will notice that this estimate is considerably below the more than 80% in the 1980 data of Bower. We have used the Nielsen data because they have been collected annually for decades, and a comparison of the 1970 figures from Bower and Nielsen (Bower, 1985) discloses an even greater proportional discrepancy. The repetitive measurement for at least decades of multiset households, the logical stepwise increase as the years pass, and the use of an always somewhat changing national probability sample by Nielsen leads us to prefer its estimates, and to believe that for some reason the two samples of Bower, although ostensibly probability, overrepresent multiset households, which probably means they overrepresent the middle and upper-middle classes.

give direction to any influence that television may have. This mediation arguably extends beyond the cognitive and affective to the behavioral (Chapter VI). It also seems to vary somewhat by type of program, with children interacting with each other and with parents least during cartoons; parents concerned about particular specimens thus will have to exert themselves.

The evidence suggests that parental mediation—when it employs critical discussions and interpretations of what is depicted and sets some guidelines on television use—can increase the understanding of television, improve judgments about reality and fantasy, and reduce total viewing. Desmond, Singer, and Singer (1990), based on a two-year study of 91 children who at the beginning were in kindergarten or the first grade, and a third-grade follow-up of the 29 who were the heaviest viewers, reach precisely these conclusions. As Buerkel-Rothfuss and colleagues (1982) said about their inquiry into the influence of television and parental mediation on the beliefs about families of about 650 fourth-, sixth-, and eighth-grade children:

> In particular, it appears that parents' positive intervention, such as their guiding their children toward family shows, viewing with them, commenting on show content, and maintaining control over the amount of viewing, can enhance what children learn about affiliative behavior from viewing family television shows. . . . Given the influential nature of parental comments, parents who discuss the reality and utility of such programs with their children could additionally influence the amount and kind of their children's learning from television. (p. 200)

Coviewing with one or more parents is not by itself the answer, because Dorr, Kovaric, and Doubleday (1989) found, among almost 400 second, sixth, and tenth graders, that such practices mostly reflected common habits and preferences and only modestly predicted any kind of parental mediation or conversational involvement. Parental mediation also is not invariably beneficial. As Desmond, Singer, and Singer (1990) point out, parents can also draw attention to, give implicit or explicit approval to, and in general endorse antisocial and violent portrayals, unwise or dangerous behavior, or commercials questionable in merit.

Kubey and Csikszentmihalyi (1990) conclude from the reports of adults and teenagers that amount of television viewing is associated with having positive experiences with family members and with an increase in the time they spend together. Conversely, they report that time spent with family members is rated lower in quality of experience when combined with television than when it is not. We doubt that positive correlations among teenagers between viewing and time spent with other family members reflects anything other than greater viewing by those spending more time at home, and for whom opportunity to view is thus greater. We would be taken aback if voluntary media consumption with others were not enjoyed. Of course television serves as a positive, pleasant focus when people view together. It is simply inferior in the quality of the experience to other things that family members do together. Our point is that the likelihood of family members viewing together, and especially those of different generations, has been suppressed by technology and affluence, with a reduction in at least the potential for adults to mediate the influence of television on younger viewers.

There is no resolution to the question of whether television divides or unites families because, in different ways, it does both. Brody, Stoneman, and Sanders (1980) found among three to five year olds that when watching television with their parents they talked less, were less active, and paid less attention to parents than when playing with them, but affectionate touching between parents and the child was greater when watching television. This makes intuitive sense, because television is a shared communication, and play is communicating by the rules between the participants. Television provides an opportunity to be together while placing few demands on that togetherness; no wonder nontelevision time together is assigned a higher value by teenagers. The evidence as a whole, as reviewed by D. Brown and Bryant (1990) and Kubey (1990), suggests that a considerable amount of television time involves parallel attention rather than interaction, but it is equally clear that that parallel attention is woven among a wide range of other activities and a sizable amount of inattention, so that a picture of insular viewers indifferent to others in the vicinity is hardly typical. There is no justification, then, for thinking that television has debased family life.

The decision of what to watch when family members view together, or control of the set, is more often said to be a group or mutual judgment than that of an individual (Table 1.7). Children appear to have become somewhat less influential, and that a real change took place is likely, because no shift was recorded among mutual husband–wife decisions. Adults less frequently are viewing what has been chosen by young persons. However, the increase in parental authority is somewhat illusory because, with the increase in multiset households, young dissenters can more frequently view by themselves.

These data nevertheless document one of the positive roles, an enjoyable shared experience, that television may play within families with children and teenagers. In fact, it has been estimated that as much as one-fourth of the time that young persons of elementary school age spend with their parents is spent viewing television (Timmer *et al.*, 1985), with the proportion of viewing time spent with parents recorded as high as almost half (Field, 1987) and as decreasing markedly between the fifth and ninth grades (Kubey, 1990, in press). However, as Lull (1990) argues, television may have many other roles in regard to interaction with family members. In addition to what he calls "structural" uses, which include the providing of background noise and ongoing entertainment and the punctuation by program schedules of time and activities, there are what he terms "relational" uses: the facilitation of communication by providing topics, common experience, and examples; affiliation and avoidance, in which viewing may be a shared experience that is enjoyable (as on the average it was in the data of Kubey and colleagues) or a means of avoiding conflict or threatening interaction with others; the demonstration of competence and domination, when portrayals validate behavior or permit the exercise of expertise and when television serves as a means of exercising authority, such as deciding what to view; as well as social learning, the drawing on as a guide for beliefs, perceptions, and behavior. From this perspective, television figures importantly in the means by which the members of a household relate to one another.

There has been a trend toward an increase in the restrictions, proscriptions, and prescriptions imposed by parents on the viewing of children. Since 1960, the percentage of parents who assert they have some rules or regulations in regard to when and what a child may view has increased from 40 to 50% (Table 1.8), with the decline among those with elementary school education or less insignificant because of the large decrease in their proportion in the population. Between the last

Table 1.8
Rules about Children's Viewing

| | Proportions of parents with "definite rules," by parent's education | | | | | |
| | 1960 | | 1970 | | 1980 | |
	%	(N)	%	(N)	%	(N)
Grade school	34	(230)	25	(84)	24	(26)
High school	40	(703)	43	(481)	46	(373)
College	47	(275)	46	(243)	58	(269)
Total	40	(1208)	43	(808)	50	(668)

From Bower, R.T. (1985). *The changing television audience in America.* New York: Columbia University Press.

two surveys, there has been an increase in rules about amount of viewing and hours when viewing can occur for children aged four to six and seven to nine years (Table 1.9). For those same two groups of younger children, there has been an increase in program-content rules, with more parents saying they decide about the programs that can be

Table 1.9
Restriction, proscription, and prescription of viewing

| | Age of child | | | | | |
| | 4–6 yrs | | 7–9 yrs | | 10–12 yrs | |
	1970	1980	1970	1980	1970	1980
Rules about viewing time						
Restrict amount of viewing						
Often	30	41	39	46	34	35
Occasionally	27	27	25	23	27	29
Never	43	32	36	32	34	36
Set special hours						
Often	41	49	48	58	46	50
Occasionally	26	28	18	26	22	25
Never	32	23	34	17	32	25
Rules about program content						
Decide what programs they can watch						
Often	45	50	37	46	46	40
Occasionally	28	30	25	42	38	29
Never	27	20	27	12	11	31
Change channel when program is objectionable						
Often	40	51	27	60	30	52
Occasionally	30	27	36	29	40	28
Never	31	22	29	11	31	20
Forbid watching of certain programs						
Often	39	48	39	51	52	45
Occasionally	27	25	29	30	22	36
Never	35	27	32	19	25	20
Encouragement of viewing						
Encourage child to watch to keep him occupied						
Often	18	12	13	8	7	5
Occasionally	32	38	29	38	23	16
Never	50	51	58	54	71	80
Encourage child to watch to keep him at home						
Often	9	7	10	6	5	4
Occasionally	9	11	14	21	15	14
Never	82	82	76	74	80	82
Total (N)	(197)	(138)	(217)	(215)	(189)	(187)

From Bower, R.T. (1985). *The changing television audience in America.* New York: Columbia University Press.

watched, change the channel when programming is objectionable, or forbid the watching of certain programs.

The figures for changing the channel and forbidding some programming are striking. For "often" changing the channel, the percentage increased from 40 to 51% for four to six year olds and from 27 to 60% for seven to nine year olds. That is an impressive amount of zapping. For often forbidding programming, the percentage increased from 39 to 48% for four to six year olds and from 39 to 51% for seven to nine year olds. For older children, parents report a decline in the imposition of such rules except for zapping, which increased astoundingly from 30 to 52%.

In contrast, very few parents said they often encourage viewing to keep a child either occupied or at home. The maximum figure for the former is 18% for four to six year olds: the minimum, a minute 5% for 10–12 year olds. The data of Gantz and Masland (1986), on 325 mothers of 2 to 12 year olds, confirm that few report using television as a babysitter, which they define as for parental convenience. However, these same mothers estimated that "most mothers" used the medium extensively for such a purpose (an average of 3.5 hours a day). These data suggest that ascribed motive is a crucial factor in evaluating parental behavior in regard to television, and that babysitting, while the stereotype for decades, however frequently practiced, is not a widely accepted motive; the actual role that parental convenience plays is thus moot.

Further evidence of public concern comes from a representative national sample of about 2000 persons aged 18 years and older interviewed by Roper under the sponsorship of the Television Information Office (1987). Television was named by about two-thirds as receiving "too little" attention from parents, slightly more than food and cultural activities, and more than twice the average for the three least named (career, extracurricular activities, and sports) which provides a maximal estimate of cursory or meaningless accord.

A major factor apparently is dissatisfaction with the available programming. More than half (54%) in the Roper survey endorsed the view that there were not "enough television programs suitable for children," with fewer than 10% saying there were more than enough. Bower (1985) provides supportive data. When he asked parents which programs were "the best" for their children, only eight appeared on the list, with the easy leader "Sesame Street" (39%), followed distantly by "The Electric Company" (12%). With the least named at 6% (a family comedy–drama), this means that there were few programs people would name.

Both the national survey by Bower (1985) and the study of the way children use their time, conducted among several hundred Berkeley children by Medrich, Roizen, Rubin, and Buckley (1982), record that the likelihood that parents will have rules about television viewing increases with education. Medrich and colleagues also found that while the same positive association with socioeconomic status is discernible among black households, black households at every socioeconomic level are a great deal less restrictive in regard to the television viewing of children.

To the delight of believers in a congruous universe, parents base such actions on what they believe about television. Bybee, Robinson, and Turow (1982b), in a sample of several hundred media scholars, found that when parents believed television had harmful effects, they were more likely to set rules about what, when, and how much could be watched and to interpret the meaning of and evaluate what was portrayed. When they believed it had positive effects, they were more likely to engage in interpretation and evaluation; this makes sense, because the latter would mitigate or amplify effects, while the former would delimit their opportunity for occurrence.

Abelman (1990) reports, based on his own research (Abelman, 1987; Abelman & Pettey, 1989), that the target of parental mediation varies with the type of concern over the influence of television and with the intelligence of the child. Parents concerned over behavioral effects were more likely to attempt to exert some control than those concerned over effects on beliefs and perceptions. Those concerned over behavioral effects gave the most emphasis to restricting access to television by time or program, while those concerned over cognitive effects gave the most emphasis to the critical discussion of content. Parents of intellectually gifted children were more concerned over cognitive effects, and as we would now predict, more likely to engage in critical discussion than parents of less able children, who were more concerned about behavioral effects and emphasized restricting access.

The broadcast advisory about content unsuitable for young viewers has become common. The most frequent is probably *Parental Discretion Advised*. Slater and Thompson (1984) queried 183 parents in a larger probability sample of households in a medium-sized city about these warnings. Ninety percent approved, 70% said they saw them frequently, 75% asserted they used them, and 60% favored a more detailed, graded ratings system such as that employed by the movie industry. Subsequent analyses indicated that active use of the warnings was confined to the smaller number of parents who restricted, proscribed, and prescribed in regard to their children's viewing. As Abelman (1990) concludes, this implies that advisories guide those who mediate rather than inspire those who do not to do so.

These varied data should not be mistaken for portraying the widespread, consistent, and effective regulation by parents of their children's consumption of television. For example, Desmond, Singer, and Singer (1990) conclude from their longitudinal data that active mediation by parents during viewing with children between kindergarten and third grade was "rare." Corder-Bolz (1980) found that only about half of the parents in his sample cited "often" as the frequency with which they spoke with their children about what was portrayed on television. The proportions in the nationally representative data we have presented who assert they often undertake any of the regulative measures only infrequently approximate 50%, or half of all parents. Half or more of parents "never" or only "occasionally" engage in any of these practices. Because of the widespread approval of parental involvement, we would expect any inaccuracy in reporting to overestimate the degree of regulation. However, the repeated failure of people to estimate accurately their own viewing or that of their child, the consistency with which inaccuracies are overestimates, and the finding that mothers offer estimates that are about twice as great as those of their children (Alexander, Wartella, & Brown, 1981; Anderson *et al.*, 1986; Bechtel *et al.*, 1972; Robinson, 1972b, 1977), make it irrefutably clear that in America no social stigma attaches to viewing, but only perhaps to viewing with certain motives. We do not think these are primarily normative misrepresentations, and there is absolutely no reason to think that the increase in concern is attributable to norms shifting unfavorably in regard to television use. The increasing frequency of multiset households decreases parental effectiveness by removing them from the site of the activity to be regulated, by making more difficult impositions on hours and content, and by making zapping impossible. The most can be expected from households higher in and the least from those lower in socioeconomic status, with parental education making the biggest difference (Comstock *et al.*, 1978). Thus, despite signs of increased concern, parental involvement in the television viewing of their children, on the whole, is at the most moderate and at the least nonexistent.

The likelihood of increasing parental involvement in their children's use of television by the most obvious means, providing them with more information, is low. Greenberg, Abelman, and Cohen (1990) distributed television guides reviewing programs and making recommendations, in regard to young viewers, to parent and children. The parents ignored them. The children sought out the programs designated as "warranting parental supervision or discretion."

The social circumstances that surround viewing have been somewhat altered by the VCR, although much also remains the same. This is in contrast to cable, which has increased variety and diversity somewhat (Huston *et al.*, 1990; Wartella *et al.*, 1990), without having any significant influence on the way young viewers and their families use television (Morgan *et al.*, 1990). About two-thirds of all households now have VCRs, an extraordinary fourfold increase since 1985, with the proportion somewhat higher in households with children. VCRs make a difference in what families do, what is viewed, negotiations over control of the set, and children's competencies in using television.

Lindlof and colleagues (Lindlof, Shatzer, & Wilkinson, 1988; Lindlof & Shatzer, 1990) collected data by diary, interview, and observations over several weeks on the television viewing of six families in the Lexington, Kentucky, area. Families with younger children frequently recorded favored programs, and these would be viewed repeatedly by the children. In some instances, programs were viewed as often as 10 times with no recorded declines in attention levels or enjoyment. In accord with the view that children's comprehension is an important element in attracting them to the screen, these investigators ascribe a large role to predictive recall. They quote one mother:

> It's amazing to me how many times they can watch it and never get bored . . . They really like the "Muppet Babies" . . . and they can do the dialogue back and forth, you know, one can be Kermit, the other one can be Piggy, and they can almost do the dialogue back and forth with each other. (p. 184)

The possibility of recording introduces a new area of negotiation in regard to television, that of whose interests will prevail when two sought-after programs appear in the same time slot. VCRs also encourage an accommodation to individual differences in interpretive skills and social roles. Videos can be replayed when the dialogue was misheard or the meaning was ambiguous, and the machine can be stopped or sequences repeated to allow those who must temporarily give their attention elsewhere, as in child care and meal preparation, fully to follow unfolding events.

Children's competencies at viewing also may become enhanced by VCRs. At a very early age (Lindlof, Shatzer, and Wilkinson estimate three years), they understand that content can be stored and repeated, which heightens expectations about what they can view. VCR manipulation becomes part of mastery of the television set. The viewing of favored programs repeatedly could enhance interpretive skills, because of the increased opportunities to integrate audio and visual components and match narrative to devices and techniques.

However, it would be an error to impute to the VCR, despite its increasing frequency in U.S. households, a radical transformation in how much or the way in which young people use the media. As Dorr and Kunkel (1990) argue from a number of recent studies, there remains a great deal of constancy in media use, with broadcasting (whether disseminated off the air or by cable) still easily preeminent, and VCR use comparatively modest. And within VCR use, time shifting and building a library have been insignificant compared to the renting of videos.

The time-use estimates of Sims (1989), based on a national panel of about 2650 persons aged two years and up, lead to three conclusions: (a) VCR use is much greater among children and teenagers than adults, (b) young people use VCRs primarily for prerecorded tapes, and (c) the replay of programs by young viewers is miniscule. Children and teenagers spent about half again as much time as adult males and about a third as much as adult females on VCR use. Daily use was about 30 minutes a day or three-and-a-half hours a week, with almost 90% devoted to prerecorded tapes.

Greenberg and Heeter (1987) found that young persons in households with VCRs saw many more movies per week and more movies with restrictive ratings, and Morgan and colleagues (1990) found that the predominant use of VCRs was to view rented videos. The positive correlation of VCR acquisition with higher parental socioeconomic status, and the act of acquisition itself, may signal households with a more pronounced interest in movies. Such an interest on the part of a young person could be an important motive for obtaining the device, but it seems likely that the actual consumption of movies in fact would be increased by the VCR, because of the reduced cost and increased convenience of movie watching it makes possible. Nevertheless, Wartella, Heintz, Aidman, and Mazzarella (1990) found, in a sample of urban households with children, that about one-third reported no VCR use in a week. Kubey and Larson (1990) found, among about 500 young people between the ages of 9 and 15, that ordinary television viewing accounted for three-fourths of all media time, followed by reading (9%), music listening from all sources (8%), and barely measurable amounts of video game playing (3%) and music videos and VCR use (both under 2%). In contrast, Christenson and Roberts (1990), in a California sample of teenagers, found that music consumption, including music videos, was greater than that for television. When such videos were categorized with television, music and television were close rivals in time use, with the role of music increasing with age. However, they essentially confirm that music videos have a minor role in the media use of young persons, and that among media, television remains important. Wartella and colleagues (1990) conclude that videocassettes add variety but not diversity to what children view. Dorr and Kunkel (1990) thus conclude that a reallocation of time parallel to that accompanying the introduction of television (Chapters II and III) has not occurred because "the newer media have yet to command much attention from children" (p. 12).

Teenagers apparently are highly skilled VCR users, and more skilled than their parents. A.A. Cohen and Cohen (1989) found, among 80 aged 14 and 15 years and about 160 adults whose households had a VCR, that about 90% of the adolescents knew the function of all the buttons and about 60% used the various features, while the comparable figures for adults were 40% and about 22%. Among both adolescents and adults, VCR knowledge was more a specialty of males than of females.

One might expect restriction, proscription, and prescription to be greater in households with greater media access, those with basic cable, premium services, and VCRs. This seems not to be the case (D. Atkin, Heeter, & Baldwin, 1989; Greenberg & Heeter, 1987; Kim, Baran, & Massey, 1988; Lin & Atkin, 1989), except for a slight hint that parents may be somewhat more concerned about young male than young female VCR use (conceivably because of the fear that they are more likely to seek out obscene, pornographic, or savagely violent fare), and more liberal rules about viewing R- and PG-rated movies in cable households. Greater access implies more particularized anxieties for some parents, but on the whole, those who have sought such access, as in the cable households, are less restrictive about their children's use of the media. This means that the VCR, and to a lesser degree cable, have greatly enlarged the freedom of access to content of all types by young viewers. The analysis by Morgan and colleagues (1990) of several hundred adolescents between 1985 and 1988, when the number of VCR households was increasing enormously, leads to the conclusion that for the most part, the new technology did not alter but became assimilated to established attitudinal and behavioral patterns associated with earlier television use.

The VCR nevertheless may achieve a separate identity in the minds of both young and adult viewers in regard to the satisfactions it can provide, and thereby conceivably could change the way people use television. Time available, content indifference, and low involvement could cease to be predominant. A.A. Cohen, Levy, and Golden (1988) asked 1333 young persons in the fourth, sixth, eighth, and tenth grades to rate VCRs, television, theater movies, books, newspapers, radio, and records in regard to their ability to satisfy 12 needs, such as "to succeed in life," "to learn things not taught in school," and "to have things to talk about with my friends." Books and newspapers each clearly occupied separate territories. Radio dominated, but shared a territory with television. Theater movies, records and tapes, and VCRs shared the same territory, with slight occupancy by television. Kubey and Larson (1990) report that VCR use is rated by children and teenagers as more arousing, as more emotionally involving, and as offering greater choice. These ratings seemed to be a function of the content made accessible by the technology, movies. Thus our speculation is supported by the findings that the VCR is perceived differently from television, is associated with other media where selectivity is possible and variety great, and that the content for which it is used to gain access is often especially compelling.

II TIME

The most-quoted statistic about children, teenagers, and television is that by the time of high school graduation, the average individual will have spent more hours viewing television than in the classroom, between 16,000 and 20,000 versus 14,000 (Fosarelli, 1986). This is a singularly banal statistic, however, because it tells us only that young persons view a great deal of television; we would reach much the same conclusion were we to divide or multiply by two. In order to understand the role of television in their allocation of time, it is necessary to discuss six topics: ranking among other activities; historical or secular trends; the day and life cycle; degree of centrality in the household; effects on other activities; and, qualifications to time estimates.

Prominent will be the most commonly employed measure of television exposure, the data collected by the A.C. Nielsen Company. We draw on other sources to amplify, challenge, or qualify these data. Any estimation of exposure is a function of the definition and the techniques devised to implement that definition in measurement. Exposure often involves a great deal more (or less) than steadfast attention. We introduced the term "monitoring" because it is literally more accurate than "viewing" in describing what transpires much of the time. Having settled the question of meaning, we now return to viewing and watching to refer to television consumption because they are part of the media vernacular. Monitoring will reappear only when we want to place special emphasis on the process that typifies the behavior.

One strong argument in behalf of the Nielsen paradigm is that it has evolved from decades of trial and error and empirical research to increase the accuracy of measurement (Beville, 1988). Another is that while people engage in many other activities while being counted as viewing television, it is also clear that viewing is in the forefront of activities. In his 12-nation time–use study in the mid-1960s, Szalai (1972; Comstock *et al.*, 1978) found that about three-fourths of viewing logged by Americans as either a primary or secondary activity was logged as the primary activity.

We will draw from pre- rather than post-people meter data. People meters offer many advantages over diaries, including the automatic electronic recording of demographic data, simultaneous collection of demographic and set use data to make audience information available very rapidly, and collection of set use and audience makeup data from the same sample. However, they also introduce distortions that are of particular concern to us (Beville, 1988).

People meters require that the presence of an individual be registered during the period of viewing by pressing a key on a remote control-like device. Because of lack of comprehension, fatigue, or indifference, children are unlikely to do so when viewing alone. Parents, even when in the vicinity, often will fail to enter their children. To a lesser degree, the same qualifications apply to teenagers, although nonreporting obviously is inversely related to age. Diaries make possible post hoc as well as simultaneous recording by both young persons and parents. They may somewhat overestimate exposure, but they are comparatively free of the age-related bias that would distort the patterns of exposure associated with age. As a result, they are, for our purposes, superior.

A. RANKING

During the fall and winter television seasons of the mid-1980s, the A.C. Nielsen Company (1986) estimated average household consumption of television at about 55 hours per week. The estimate for children aged 2 to 11 years was almost 28 hours. The estimate for teenagers was about $23\frac{1}{2}$ hours. These compare with estimates of about 34 hours for adult women aged 35–54 and about 29 hours for adult men aged 35–54. Older adults (in the Nielsen data, those aged 55 and over) were estimated to view considerably more (for women, eight hours more; for men, nine hours more). Younger adults were estimated to view slightly (about an hour and a half) less.

These figures represent a pattern that has persisted since the introduction of the medium. Each of the demographic age and gender categories views greater or lesser amounts of television, because on the average they are a group that spends more or less time in the vicinity of an operable television set. Children view more than teenagers because they spend more time at home, have less demanding scholastic obligations, and have more delimited social lives.

The large role of television in the lives of young persons is made more clear when we examine data on viewing during weekdays, evenings, and weekends mornings and afternoons (Fig. 2.1). Children are substantial prime-time viewers, with more than half of those aged 6 to 11 in the audience between 8 and 9 PM and almost half of those aged two to five in the audience at about the same time. Teenagers similarly reach their peak proportions during prime time but do so somewhat later, with 8 to 10 PM bracketing their major representation, and somewhat fewer are viewing at all, with a maximum of about 40% in the audience. Only slightly more children are in the audience during the peak between 8:30 and 10:30 AM on Saturday mornings, when blocks of programming are designed for them. On Sundays, when much of the programming is public affairs, religious, or public service intended for adults, the figure falls to about one-fourth during the same period. These data dispel the myth—if it is still entertained anywhere—that most of children's viewing occurs on Saturday mornings.

Timmer, Eccles, and O'Brien (1985) obtained detailed diaries representing the time use of almost 400 young persons between the ages of 3 and 17 (Table 2.1). When we examine viewing in the context of other activities, we find that:

- Television occupies more time than any other out-of-school activity;
- Television accounts for half or more of all leisure time;
- Television occupies proportionately more free or leisure time among children than adults, for whom it averages about a third (Comstock *et al.*, 1978), despite the fact that unlike adults, children engage in substantial amounts of free play; and
- The amount of television viewed by teenagers, while less than that consumed by children, ensures that the medium occupies a similar preeminence in their lives.

The prominence of television and the subordinate role of play after age nine are in accord with the time-use data on fifth graders collected

---

Fig. 2.1 Viewing by age and hour. (A) Percentage of children aged 2–5 and 6–11 years viewing television by time of day, in the fall. Monday through Friday, 7 AM to 6 PM; Monday through Sunday, 6 PM to 1 AM. (B) Percentage of male and female teenagers aged 12–17 years viewing Monday through Friday, 7 AM to 6 PM; Monday through Sunday 6 PM to 1 AM; in the fall. From Comstock, G., Chaffee, S., Katzman, N., McCombs, M., & Roberts, D. (1978). *Television and human behavior.* New York: Columbia University Press.

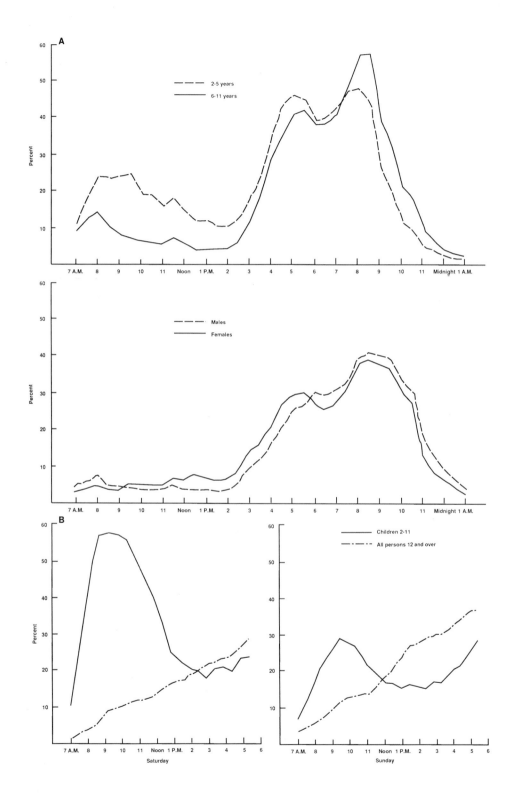

Table 2.1

Time Spent by Children and Teenagers in Primary Activities (Mean Hours:Minutes)

Activities	Weekdays*					Weekend days*					Significant effects
	3–5	6–8	9–11	12–14	15–17	3–5	6–8	9–11	12–14	15–17	
Market work**	—	0:14	0:08	0:14	0:28	—	0:04	0:10	0:29	0:48	
Personal care	0:41	0:49	0:40	0:56	1:00	0:47	0:45	0:44	1:00	0:51	A, S, AxS (F > M)
Household work	0:14	0:15	0:18	0:27	0:34	0:17	0:27	0:51	1:12	1:00	A, S, AxS (F > M)
Eating	1:22	1:21	1:13	1:09	1:07	1:21	1:20	1:18	1:08	1:05	A
Sleeping	10:30	9:55	9:08	7:53	8:19	10:34	10:41	9:56	10:04	9:22	A
School	2:17	4:52	5:15	5:44	5:14	—			—		
Studying	0:02	0:08	0:29	0:33	0:33	0:01	0:02	0:12	0:15	0:30	A
Church	0:04	0:09	0:09	0:09	0:03	0:55	0:56	0:53	0:32	0:37	A
Visiting	0:14	0:15	0:10	0:21	0:20	0:10	0:08	0:13	0:22	0:56	A (Weekend only)
Sports	0:05	0:24	0:21	0:40	0:46	0:03	0:30	0:42	0:51	0:37	A, S (M > F)
Outdoors activities	0:04	0:09	0:06	0:07	0:11	0:06	0:23	0:39	0:25	0:26	
Hobbies	0:00	0:02	0:02	0:04	0:06	0:01	0:05	0:03	0:06	0:03	
Art activities	0:05	0:04	0:03	0:03	0:12	0:04	0:04	0:04	0:07	0:10	
Other passive leisure	0:09	0:01	0:02	0:06	0:04	0:06	0:01	0:07	0:10	0:18	A
Playing	3:38	1:51	1:05	0:31	0:14	4:27	3:00	1:32	0:35	0:21	A, S (M > F)
TV	1:51	1:39	2:26	2:22	1:48	2:02	2:16	3:05	2:49	2:37	A, S, AxS (M > F)
Reading	0:05	0:05	0:09	0:10	0:12	0:04	0:09	0:10	0:10	0:18	A
Being read to	0:02	0:02	0:00	0:00	0:00	0:03	0:02	0:00	0:00	0:00	A

* Age in years.

** Market work = obligations outside the home.

A = Age effect, significant at $p < .05$, for both weekday and weekend activities unless otherwise specified.

S = Sex effect, significant at $p < .05$; F > M, M > F = Females spend more time than males, or vice versa.

AxS = Age by sex interaction, significant at $p < .05$.

From: Timmer, S.G., Eccles, J., & O'Brien, K. (1985). How children use time. In F.T. Juster & F. P. Stafford (Eds). *Time, goods, and well being* (pp. 353–369). Ann Arbor: Institute for Social Research, The University of Michigan.

years earlier by Long and Henderson (1973). This congruity across time, method, and populations attests to the validity of the overall pattern.

Among adults, television is third behind sleep and time spent at work as the major consumers of time when the 24 hours of the day are allotted among 37 primary activities, mutually exclusive categories representing the activity perceived as preeminent at any time (Szalai, 1972). Among children and teenagers, television has a similar place in competition with sleep and school.

B. HISTORICAL TRENDS

The amount of time children and teenagers in the United States spend with television has increased steadily since the medium was introduced in the late 1940s and early 1950s (Comstock *et al.*, 1978; Lyle & Hoffman, 1972a; Nielsen, 1986; Schramm *et al.*, 1961). The historical trend for children parallels a general increase in television viewing by all demographic categories (Fig. 2.2). For example, household set use increased from about six hours per day in the early 1960s to about seven hours per day in the late 1970s (Comstock *et al.*, 1978). This increase of about 15% is substantial, when the rapid acceptance, immediate popularity, and high level of viewing of television that preceded it are taken into account.

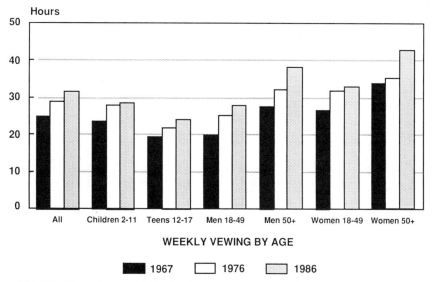

Fig. 2.2 Three decades of viewing by age. From A.C. Nielsen and Company. (1986). *1986 Nielsen report on television.* New York: Author.

Television increased overall mass media consumption by an average of about an hour a day (Robinson, 1972a), with television accounting for about three-fourths of all media consumption (Robinson & Converse, 1972). Mass media are in the business of manufacturing symbols to which people willingly give attention. Television is primarily entertainment. News and public affairs programming not only occurs in the context of entertainment, but also must meet the same criteria as entertainment in attracting large audiences attractive to advertisers (Comstock, 1989). Television covers the other entertainment media, such as movies, records, and books, as well as itself, and newspapers and magazines extensively cover the entertainment media, including television. The result is that growing up occurs in an environment in which the symbols of popular culture are present to a degree unimagined before the introduction of television.

Where does all the time come from for the mass media? This is a question asked rhetorically by Caplow and colleagues (Caplow, Bahr, Chadwick, Hill, & Williamson, 1982) when they returned in the mid-1970s to the community that had served as the site of the famous sociological studies by the Lynds in the 1920s and 1930s (Lynd & Lynd, 1929, 1937). In comparing what they found with the community of those earlier decades, they remarked not only upon the large amount of television viewing that appeared to take place but also on the extraordinary increase in the availability and consumption of media in general— newspapers, bookstores, magazine stands, movie theaters, radio and television stations. Even per capita library circulation had held its own against this competition, with fewer users taking out more books. The question gains further force from the increase in time devoted to the mass media brought about by the introduction of television (Robinson, 1972a). Caplow and colleagues decided that part of the answer lies in the adroit combining of activities. This is almost certainly true, but there is something more to be said about the historical increase in television viewing.

The progressive increase in viewing belies the once popular novelty hypothesis that the public's attention to television would decrease when it became used to the medium and, in the cliché, the novelty had worn off. The most likely explanation is that norms changed, and viewing in any given circumstance became increasingly acceptable. This is exemplified by much of the growth's coming from increased viewing during nonprime-time hours (Bower, 1973; Lyle, 1975). A related but independently important influence was the entry into the ranks of adults and parents of persons who had experienced television in their households as they were growing up. These television generations would bring firsthand knowledge and presumably greater tolerance of the medium as part of childhood to the public perception of television, making increased viewing at all ages more acceptable. A final point is that, although one knowledgeable observer (Robinson, 1969) predicted its imminent occurrence two decades ago, the ceiling on per capita consumption of television does not appear to have been reached.

A second major trend has been the increasing equalization of consumption across social strata. In the case of households in general, the trend has been observable in the progressively lessening degree to which amount of viewing is inversely related to socioeconomic status and, in particular, the educational level of the head of the household (C.C. Anderson, 1982; Comstock et al., 1978). In the case of children and teenagers, inverse relationships between television consumption and mental ability appear to have become less pronounced (Lyle & Hoffman, 1972a; Morgan & Gross, 1980). Although these long-documented inverse relationships have not disappeared, the historical trend has been toward their lessening, as the experiencing of popular culture through television has become increasingly frequent and accepted among all strata.

The third major trend has been the expansion and transformation of the means by which video content is available (Table 2.2). The developments have not been so swift, disruptive, or sweeping as had been predicted as recently as a decade ago; evolution rather than revolution is the better term (Comstock, 1989), but there have been and will be substantial changes. Our inventory includes (Comstock, 1989, 1991; Greenberg & Heeter, 1987; Heeter, 1985; Klopfenstein, 1989; Lichty, 1989):

- The enormous growth in stations not affiliated with the three major networks, which account for almost all of the increase in commercial broadcast outlets from about 500 in 1960 to about 1200 by the beginning of the 1990s;
- The steady if slow growth of cable, which has become the means by which somewhat more than half of American households receive television;
- The increase in channels available to a household, with those receiving 11 or more increasing from fewer than 10% in the mid-1960s to more than 75% by the end of the 1980s;
- The rapid adoption of the VCR, which is now in more homes than cable and almost certainly will be in about nine out of ten households by the end of the 1990s; and

Table 2.2
Video Resources in U.S. Households

Prime time audience shares (percentage)					
	1983	1985	1987		1991 (est.)
Networks	80	77	72	21 ABC	68
				23 CBS	
				27 NBC	
Independents and PBS	17	20	23	18 Independent	25
				5 PBS	
Basic cable	4	6	8		9
Pay cable	6	6	5		6

Number of channels available (percentage of U.S. households)				
Number of Channels available	1964	1972	1985	1991 (est.)
1–4	41	17	3	1
5–10	51	52	22	18
11–29	8	31	31	57
30 or more	—	—	19	24

U.S. TV households (percentage)		
	1987	1991 (est.)
TV only	28	18
TV + VCR	23	27
TV + Basic cable	12	7
TV + VCR + Basic cable	10	19
TV + Basic cable + Pay cable	9	6
TV + VCR + Basic cable + Pay cable	18	23

Overall audience shares (percentage)			
	1983	1987	1991 (est.)
Network affiliates	70	62	59
Independent stations	19	19	20
Basic cable	7	14	15
Pay cable	5	6	7
Public television	3	4	4

Adapted from Lichty, L.W. (1989). Television in America: Success story. In P.S. Cook, D. Gomery, & L.W. Lichty (Eds.), *American media: The Wilson Quarterly reader* (pp. 159–176). Washington, DC: The Wilson Center Press; and Carey, J. (1989). Public broadcasting and federal policy. In P.R. Newberg (Ed.), *New directions in telecommunications policy, Vol. 1: Regulatory policy: Telephony and mass media* (pp. 192–221). Durham, NC: Duke University Press.

Note: 1991 estimates are based on calculations by the principal author.

- The decline in audience share of the three major networks, which as the 1990s began, had slipped in prime time below 70% compared with more than 90% a decade earlier.

The proportion of households with one or more of the auxiliary sources to broadcast television (basic cable, premium cable, the VCR) is impressive (Table 2.2). The expansion in access to video stimuli has occurred amidst an electronic plethora for teenagers and, to a lesser extent, children. As Greenberg and Lin (1989) remark on the basis of data collected from about 426 seventh and tenth graders:

> Most striking . . . is the magnitude of the prevalence of all forms of electronic gadgets. . . . This suggests the continuing formation of a home video culture that now includes personal computers, video cameras, and CD players. . . . (E)ach item was possessed by more than one-half. . . . In fact, of the seven items asked about, **each** adolescent possessed an average of five of them. The media environment is . . . even more abundant . . . [for] . . . they were not asked to indicate how many radios they possessed, what software and how much, or the extent of their book, tape, record, and disk collections. (p. 87)

Nowhere, however, is there evidence that the increased options have decisively altered the amount or kind of video content consumed by the young (J.D. Brown, Childers, Bauman, & Koch, 1990; Dorr & Kunkel, 1990; Kubey & Larsen, 1990; Morgan et al., 1990; Nielsen, 1988); the increase in exposure to movies is the sole exception. The initial impact and historical increase in television consumption thereby become even more impressive.

C. DAY AND LIFE CYCLE

There is clearly a cycle of viewing by children and teenagers that reflects the role of competing activities across the 24 hours of the day. There is apparently no time segment between 7 AM and 1 AM during which there are not at least a few children or teenagers in the audience. Among younger children (aged two to five) there are about 10% in the audience at 7 AM, and an hour later there are slightly more than 20%. This peak remains until about 11 AM, when viewing declines to a midday low of about 10% between 1 and 2 PM. The proportion viewing then rises sharply to a new peak of about 45% between 5 and 6 PM. There is a third, slightly greater peak between 7:30 and 8:30 PM, after which the proportion viewing begins to decline, although even as late as

10 PM, there are about 10% of these very young children viewing television. Among older children (aged 6 to 11) there are far fewer in the audience early in the day. For example, at 9 AM the figure for these children is about 8%, while it is more than 20% for younger children. Otherwise, the day cycle follows that for younger children, except that the proportions rise about a half hour later, so that at any given moment, there is a slightly greater proportion of younger than older children viewing. They then reach a higher peak of almost 60% between 8 and 9 PM, before a decline that occurs about an hour later than for younger children. For example, at 10 PM the figure for these children is more than 20% compared to the 10% for younger children. For both groups, there is a dip in viewing between 5:30 and 7 PM that almost certainly reflects mealtimes and related chores.

The pattern for teenagers is different in two major respects: there are far fewer viewing early in the day, and noticeably fewer viewing overall. Between 7 AM and 2 PM, the figures waver between 3 and about 6%. The configuration then parallels that for children, except that fewer teenagers are viewing, so that at their peak between 8 and 9:30 PM, slightly more than 40% are in the audience. Teenagers view later, of course, so that in the later hours of the evening there are greater proportions of them in the audience than there are of children. For example, at 10 PM, the figure for teenagers is more than 30%, compared with more than 20% for older children and about 10% for younger children.

Viewing, in the sense of giving attentive interest to the screen, has been recorded as beginning as early as six months of age (Hollenbeck & Slaby, 1979). Viewing on a regular basis appears to begin between the ages of two-and-a-half and three, with daily average viewing estimated at about $1\frac{1}{2}$ hours (Huston et al., 1983). This implies a progressive increase in viewing until ages five or six, when almost all estimates of viewing, however derived, are greater (D.R. Anderson & Collins, 1988; D.R. Anderson et al., 1985; Comstock et al., 1978). The pattern through the teen years is displayed in Fig. 2.3.

Because the decline during the teenage years is attributable to competing activities, viewing remains suppressed for those who continue on to college. During the early adult years, viewing returns to levels approximating those before the teenage and college years, although slightly higher figures for those in the 35–54 age bracket suggest modest continuing suppression by child rearing, especially for those with large families (Robinson, 1977), and other aspects of young adulthood. Viewing then increases sharply among those aged 55 years or older, and television not only consumes the most time by far, but it is the sole mass medium actually to rise in consumption after this age, increasing

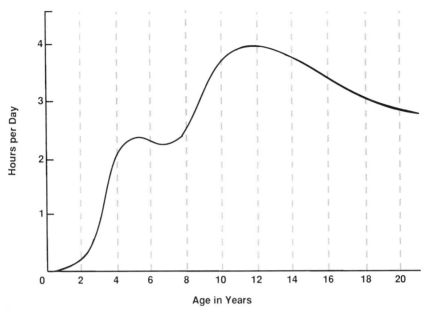

Fig. 2.3 Average hours of television viewing by age. From Comstock, G., Chaffee, S., Katzman, N., McCombs, M., & Roberts, D. (1978). *Television and human behavior.* New York: Columbia University Press.

steadily until about age 70 (Comstock *et al.*, 1978; Harris, 1974). Its role over the lifespan is nicely graphed (Fig. 2.4) by Condry (1989).

Adults and young people are alike in that television is very frequently viewed as a consequence of being in the vicinity of an operable TV set, and there being nothing else that compels one's time, attention, or presence. The increased demands of school, the freedom to be outside the home, and opportunities to engage in social and other activities that explain the less frequent viewing by teenagers than by children are simply the particular competing factors for that age.

Despite these lifestyle changes, television viewing appears to be what Tangney and Feshbach (1988) call "a reliable and consistent individual difference variable, manifested over a substantial period of time—that is, television viewing appears to be a stable behavioral trait" (p. 153). They base this conclusion on their finding that, among about 400 Los Angeles elementary school children examined over three years, there were substantial positive correlations from year to year in hours spent with television (between adjacent years, .67 and .65, and between the first and third year, .54). They observe that the programming was markedly different in the weeks examined, which simply gives further

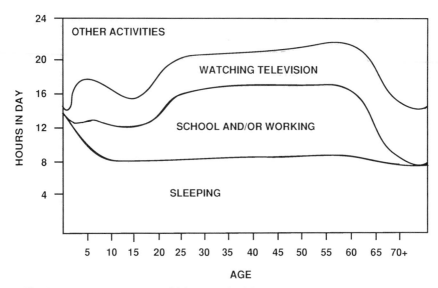

Fig. 2.4   Viewing as a part of life over the lifespan. From Condry, J. (1989). *The psychology of television*. Hillsdale, NJ: Erlbaum.

emphasis to the role of content indifference in viewing. Huston and colleagues (1990) found similar stabilities among several hundred three and five year olds over a two-year period as did Rosengren and Windahl (1989) among young persons in Scandinavia between the ages of 11 and 13, and 13 and 15. What the data attest to is not that amount of time spent with television by individuals is unchanging as they grow up, but that it changes substantially as other circumstances change, while at the same time there is some consistency across the years in media use. For some young persons proclivities toward greater or lesser consumption of television are established early. What lies behind the varied data is probably the fact that allocation of time typically does not change dramatically except at transition points—becoming a teenager, high school or college graduation, marriage, childbirth, or job loss.

Alternative uses of time also explain the decline in audience size of about 15% among both adults and young persons that occurs every summer. The most striking aspect of this statistic is not how substantial it is but how small, given the fact that much of what is on television has been presented before, and many leisure and recreational activities are not available in other seasons except in such Lotuslands as southern California, Florida, and Hawaii.

D. HOUSEHOLD CENTRALITY

In their study of time use by about 750 children in the sixth grade in Berkeley, California, Medrich and colleagues (1982) not only selected television as one of the five major domains among which children's time is allocated (the others were alone or with friends; with parents; jobs, chores, and spending patterns; and organized activities), but also proposed that families can be usefully located on a dimension reflecting behavior and norms that favor viewing (high household and parental use, and few if any rules governing viewing by young persons). We label this as household centrality of television; it proved to be strongly related to the total amount of the children's viewing (Table 2.3).

Parents determine to a large degree whether a child will be a light, moderate, or heavy viewer of television. They do so not only through rules and strictures, or the lack thereof, but in two other ways as well. They serve as examples implicitly recommending television when they themselves view a great deal; when they do view a great deal, the opportunity for a young person to view is increased by the greater number of hours he or she is in the vicinity of an operating television set. For example, J.F. Kenny (1985) found, among several hundred undergraduates, that amount of television use even in the constrained

Table 2.3
Centrality and Viewing

Ethnicity and television centrality	Child's viewing time			
	Light	Medium	Heavy	(N)
Black				
High	21	23	57	(275)
Moderate	21	36	43	(146)
Low	40	34	27	(63)
White				
High	26	35	39	(39)
Moderate	32	39	29	(43)
Low	69	21	10	(51)
All children				
High	21	25	54	(331)
Moderate	24	37	40	(232)
Low	49	31	20	(150)

Adapted from Medrich, E.A., Roizen, J., Rubin, V., & Buckley, S. (1982). *The serious business of growing up: A study of children's lives outside school.* Berkeley: The University of California Press.

circumstances of university life was predicted by amount of use of television in the home while growing up, while Rosengren and Windahl (1989) found, among young persons in Scandinavia, aged 11, 13, and 15 years, that amount of viewing was directly correlated with that of parents for those 11 and 13, and among those 15, was indirectly influenced by parents through the parent-influence on amount of earlier viewing.

The less educated the parent, the more central television is in daily life; when parents themselves view a great deal, a child is more likely to be a heavy viewer. Desmond and colleagues (1985), C. Roberts (1981), Timmer, Eccles, and O'Brien (1985), and Webster, Pearson, and Webster (1986) report similar findings, with Webster and colleagues finding, among almost 750 children from more than 400 households, that quantity of sets in the household was associated with greater viewing, thus introducing an availability component. Viewing is also much greater in one-parent than in two-parent families.

Centrality also affects what will be viewed. The 1982 CAP data documented not only that heavy viewers watch more of almost all categories of programming but that their total viewing is weighted strongly toward light entertainment. (Chapter I). Rosengren and Windahl (1989) found that the children in households where television was less central while growing up became moderate viewers of a balanced mix of programs, although as typically is the case one where entertainment was predominant, while those where television was more central became heavy viewers with a greater emphasis in the programs viewed on action–adventure, comedy, and other light entertainment. M.E. Cohen, Brown, and Clark (1981) found among about 600 households in Ontario, Canada, that centrality and its correlates, such as lower socioeconomic status and a generally more favorable disposition toward television viewing, were inversely associated with children viewing educational programming. Viewing in high centrality households is more predominantly ritualistic, and mental activity in conjunction with viewing would more often be right brain, beta wave, or affective, holistic, nonverbal, and nonanalytic. Thus, centrality figures in the relationships between television viewing and scholastic achievement (Chapter III).

It has been clear for many years that at every social stratum, blacks view more television than whites, and that the inverse relationships between socioeconomic status and (a) amount of television viewed and (b) attitudes favorable to the medium that exist among Caucasians do not hold for blacks (W.H. Anderson & Williams, 1983; Bogart, 1972a; Comstock *et al.*, 1978; Greenberg & Dervin, 1970, 1973; Poindexter & Stroman, 1981). The Berkeley data are congruent. Children in black families, regardless of socioeconomic status, were more likely to view more television and for television to score as more central in their households. For both blacks and whites, socioeconomic status was inversely related to centrality, but the frequency of centrality among blacks was dramatically greater in every stratum. Television thus occupies a particularly prominent place in the lives of young persons in black households.

The wide applicability of this pattern receives strong support from two important sources—the federally funded National Assessment of Educational Progress (NAEP) and the recent work of Tangney and Feshbach (1988). In the former (Table 2.4), data were collected from 100,000 children and teenagers in the fourth, eighth, and tenth grades in 30

Table 2.4
Socioeconomic Status, Ethnicity, and Viewing

	Viewing		
	0–2 hours	3–5 hours	6 hours or more
Socioeconomic status (parental education)			
Grade 4			
No high school diploma	26	36	38
Graduated from high school	25	42	33
Posthigh school	38	36	25
Grade 8			
No high school diploma	28	51	20
Graduated from high school	30	56	15
Posthigh school	44	46	10
Grade 11			
No high school diploma	46	43	11
Graduated from high school	50	43	7
Posthigh school	65	31	4
Race–Ethnicity			
Grade 4			
White	35	40	25
Black	21	28	51
Hispanic	31	36	33
Grade 8			
White	40	50	10
Black	21	48	31
Hispanic	34	51	16
Grade 11			
White	61	35	4
Black	36	50	13
Hispanic	55	38	7

Adapted from Anderson, B., Mead, N., & Sullivan, S. (1986). *Television: What do National Assessment results tell us?* Princeton, NJ: Educational Testing Service.

states (B. Anderson, Mead, & Sullivan, 1986) and in the latter, from about 400 Los Angeles pupils in the fourth through sixth grades over a three-year period. In both instances, the pattern of television consumption, socioeconomic status, and ethnicity paralleled the Berkeley data, and the NAEP extended the pattern to a much wider age span and to another minority, Hispanics.

E. OTHER ACTIVITIES

The relationship between television and other activities can be viewed from two perspectives: the effects of (a) its introduction, and of (b) greater or lesser contemporary consumption. The available data variously support the views that television's influence has been profound and that, for the most part, it is negligible.

The comparisons in 12 nations of the use of time by set owners and nonowners when ownership was far from ubiquitous (Robinson, 1972a, 1972b, 1990; Robinson & Converse, 1972; Szalai, 1972), data from a United States community covering the first decade of television (Coffin, 1955; Cunningham & Walsh, 1958), comparisons of children's media use in communities with and without television (Parker, 1960), data from Great Britain covering the first six years of set ownership (Belson, 1959), and various statistics from the United States (Bogart, 1972b) indicate that television substantially reduced the use of other media including movie theater attendance, radio listening, magazine reading, comic book reading, and book reading. It also decreased, if often only slightly, the degree to which people engaged in a number of activities, including housework, hobbies, social activities outside the home, time spent sleeping (but only by a very few minutes, and this might be an artifact of persons without television sets perceiving the minutes before actually sleeping as sleep time while late-night television viewers arguably would be less likely to do so), and attendance at conventional religious observances. Within the category of housework, it appeared to increase time spent shopping (a tribute perhaps to the effectiveness of its commercials and the materialistic emphases of its programming) and reduce considerably time spent gardening and tending to animals.

In the case of some of the effects on other media, children and teenagers could be said to have been directly affected, with comic book reading the most obvious example. In the case of other activities, such changes arguably would impinge on children and teenagers by changing the household environment.

Himmelweit, Oppenheim, and Vince (1958) in Great Britain and Schramm, Lyle, and Parker (1961) in the United States conducted large-scale, multifaceted, landmark examinations of the effects of the introduction of television on children and adolescents. In the case of Himmelweit and colleagues, the basic sample consisted of 1854 10–11 year olds and 13–14 year olds in four cities; in that of Schramm and colleagues, it consisted of 2688 young people from the first six grades and the eighth, tenth, and twelfth grades in San Francisco and 1708 young persons in the first, sixth, and tenth grades in five Rocky Mountain communities. In both cases, data were also obtained from hundreds of parents and teachers, and comparisons could be made between households with and without television. Both also included, in addition to the principal samples, a number of embedded studies with specialized focuses. For example, the basic sample of Schramm and colleagues comprised only three-fourths of the total number of young persons (5991) from whom they obtained data.

In both undertakings, one of the topics was leisure and other activities. Their results represent a complementary collage. In Great Britain, television reduced comic book reading. It also decreased radio listening. It reduced movie going among children but not among teenagers, for whom movie going served important social functions. It reduced participation in clubs and related activities among children but not among teenagers, presumably for the same reason. Book reading initially was decreased, and markedly so among teenagers, but with the passage of time returned to initial levels, presumably because it became clear that one does not readily substitute for the other in the satisfactions provided and needs served. Outdoor activities were somewhat decreased, but primarily those of an unorganized or unstructured nature (they give "kicking a ball around" as an example), and the authors remark that outdoor activities on the whole are too important to children and teenagers for them to be much displaced by television.

In the United States, television markedly reduced movie going, radio listening, and the reading of certain types of magazines (confessions, detective, screen, and pulp adventure) by young people. Sixth and tenth graders with television listened to radio less than half the three hours that were spent on it by those in a community yet to have television; declines for movie going and comic book reading were similar in size. Time devoted to newspapers, books, and quality and general interest magazines was unaffected, and there was some evidence that the reading by the young of general interest magazines actually (and ironically, since such exemplars as *The Saturday Evening Post, Collier's, Life,* and *Look* failed to survive the competition of television) was stimulated somewhat by television. With television, children were recorded as going to bed slightly (about 13 minutes) later, a figure about the same as that obtained for adults in the 12-nation time-use study

(Robinson, 1972b; Robinson & Converse, 1972; Szalai, 1972). Among very young children, time spent in play was slightly reduced. Total time spent on the mass media by children and teenagers was markedly increased, with the estimate of about an hour to an hour-and-a-half again similar to that for adults in the 12-nation study. The investigators conclude that, among young people, the introduction of television "reorganizes leisure time and mass media use in a spectacular manner" (p. 169).

The principle that television use does not displace personally or socially important activities is so robust that it may be considered an axiom. For example, S.B. Neuman (1988) recently reported that in a sample of 70,000 aged 9, 13, and 17 years there was no association between amount of viewing and engaging in sports or spending time with friends. She also reconfirmed an equally longstanding pattern (Brown *et al.*, 1990; Kubey & Larsen, 1990; Lyle & Hoffman, 1972a) that as young people become older, and especially as they pass from early to late adolescence, television diminishes and music increases in importance, often becoming predominant among media. Pervasiveness in western culture is attested to by Rosengren and Windahl (1989), who report essentially confirmatory findings for both social interaction and leisure and for music among Scandinavian youth.

T.M. Williams (1986) and colleagues examined the effects of the introduction of a single government-owned Canadian Broadcasting Corporation (CBC) channel in a remote British Columbia community of about 650 that could not receive a signal until late 1973. They collected varied data on both young persons and adults before the advent of television and two years later at this site, which they called Notel, and compared the outcomes with those from two similar communities, one that could receive only the CBC channel (Unitel) and one that could receive a variety of channels, including the three major American networks (Multitel), thereby creating a three-community naturalistic experiment.

They found that the introduction of television decreased participation in the total number of community activities engaged in (Fig. 2.5), and much more so among youths (persons in the seventh through the twelfth grades) than among younger adults (55 years or younger). Television reduced attendance at clubs and meetings, but clearly so only for adults, a finding concordant with the view of Himmelweit, Oppenheim, and Vince (1958) that television does not displace activities socially important to young people. There was some evidence, but it was far less clear, that community involvement in "special days" (defined as weddings, funerals, and elections) and "entertainment" (defined as special movies, parades, and bingo) declined.

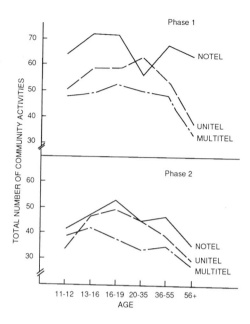

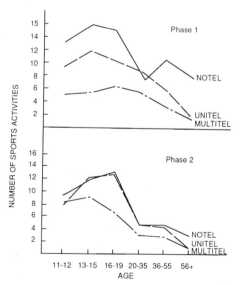

Fig. 2.5 Participation in activities before and after the introduction of television. Adapted from Williams, T.M. (Ed.) (1986). *The impact of television: A natural experiment in three communities.* New York: Academic Press.

The greatest overall decline in participation in activities occurred among older adults, those over the age of 55. The decreases in participation registered for young persons, younger adults, and older adults suggest that one effect of television is to increase age segregation and to lessen the contact that children and teenagers have with adults, and especially with senior adults.

They found the same rapid adoption of television as had been observed in the United States where, once the medium had become familiar to the public, saturation reached 75% of households within two years after signals became available (Fig. 2.6). Within two years, viewing in Notel equaled that in Unitel, and while viewing was slightly greater in Multitel with its multiple channels, the authors observe that "the differences were less striking than the similarities, especially if hours of availability are considered" (p. 245) (the broadcast day was

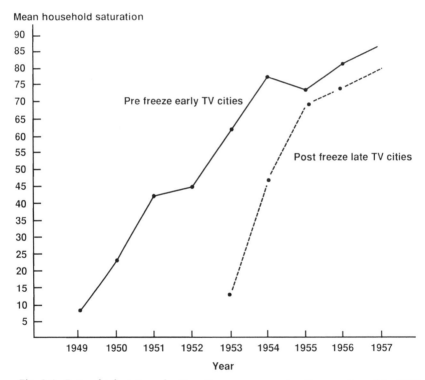

Fig. 2.6 Rate of television adoption. Freeze = no station licenses issued by FCC; prefreeze = stations were licensed in late 1940s; postfreeze = stations were licensed in early 1950s. From Cook, T.D., & Campbell, D.T. (1979). *Quasiexperimentation: Design and analysis issues for field settings.* Chicago: Houghton Mifflin.

considerably longer in Multitel than in Unitel or Notel), and conclude that it is the presence or absence of television and not the quantity, character, or variety of programming that has an effect, if any, on time. This is in accord with our conclusions from the 12-nation study (Chapter I). They also report a decline similar to that in the United States in movie attendance. Because the patterns of use of other media and use of television were very stable over the two years in Unitel and Multitel, but not in Notel, they suggest that the introduction of television may alter the way people use other media; however, they are unable to pinpoint any instances of clear-cut displacement except for movie going.

Murray and Kippax (1977, 1978) obtained data from about 100 children and their parents in each of three Australian communities with very different television availability. In the No-TV town, none received. In the Low-TV town, a single government-owned channel that devoted about a third of its schedule to educational programming for use in the schools had been received for about a year. In the High-TV town, that channel had been received for five years and an additional channel devoted almost exclusively to entertainment, sports, and news had been received for two years. They found only somewhat greater television viewing by children in the High-TV than in the Low-TV town. The frequency of engaging in a number of kinds of leisure activities declined linearly across the three communities. The declines were most prominent for spectator and participant sports and other outdoor activities and for certain media usage (movie going, radio listening and record playing). Comic book reading was decidedly lower in the towns with television, and total reading time was somewhat less, but the number of books reported as read per week was greater. Among both mothers and fathers, they found declines across the communities in radio listening, movie going, listening to recorded music, theater attendance, and hobbies, and among fathers, in spectator sports, reading, and listening to public addresses. They also found that two-thirds of the children in the High-TV town said they viewed when they were bored, compared with only about 40% who said so in the Low-TV town. They too propose "a major restructuring of one's conception of the media and patterns of daily activities" (Murray & Kippax, 1978, p. 42) as a consequence of television availability.

The distinctly different perception of the use of television by children in the Low-TV town almost certainly reflects the extraordinarily high educational emphasis of the only television available. When content is different from what we ordinarily think of as television, the medium is differently perceived, while time spent viewing is little if at all affected.

J.R. Brown, Cramond, and Wilde (1974) obtained data from very small groups of children in three Scottish villages (N = 18, 18, and 11, respectively), one where television was newly acquired, one where it had been in place, and one in which it was not available, four months before and eight months after the arrival of television in the village newly acquiring it. They found outdoor activities decreased, but contrary to Himmelweit, Oppenheim, and Vince (1958), it was the rule-governed, of which sports is a fine example, rather than laissez-faire activities. There was less radio listening, less comic book reading, and children had come to think of indoor activities, as more enjoyable. Like Murray and Kippax (1978), they see television as leading to a restructuring of children's time use.

Himmelweit, Oppenheim, and Vince (1958) introduce the concepts of functional similarity, transformed activities, and fringe or marginal activities to interpret the findings on the introduction of television. The first leads to the functional displacement hypothesis. It holds that one medium will displace another when it performs the function of the displaced medium in a superior manner, either by being more rewarding at the same cost or convenience, or equally rewarding at less cost or greater convenience. For example, television displaced comic book reading and for younger children, movie going, because it provided similar satisfactions in a superior manner. The second refers to changes within a class of activity, such as the role radio has assumed among young persons. As Schramm, Lyle, and Parker (1961) observe, with the arrival of television, radio ceased to be the primary medium around which the family would gather and became a secondary medium frequently employed by young people to listen to music while doing something else. The third refers to activities largely unaffected and therefore not relevant to the new medium, such as teenage social activities and (in their data) organized outdoor sports. T.M. Williams (1986) and colleagues contribute several additional concepts (our italics):

> Television seems especially powerful at displacing other activities. Proponents of the functional equivalence argument contend this is because television is the least specialized medium and therefore able to satisfy the most needs, or to satisfy them best. This may be true, but several other factors strike us as equally if not more important. The first is *time-sharing*. People are likely to spend more time with a medium that can be time-shared with other activities, including other media, than with one which cannot (e.g., ironing can be done while watching TV or listening to radio, but not while reading; reading can be done while watching

TV, but listening to records cannot). The second is *perceived ease* of the medium. Salomon (1983) has shown that by comparison with print media, children perceive television to be an easier medium and one at which they are more expert. . . . In addition to ease of time-sharing, *ease of access* undoubtedly is important. For example, we found that television displaced participation in community activities outside the home, but there was little evidence to indicate it displaced private leisure activities, including ones typically conducted inside the home. Participation in organized community activities requires more effort than watching television, whereas some indoor leisure activities can be time-shared with TV. (p. 242)

In certain instances, we can say with confidence that television continues to suppress an initially depressed activity because it remains below a historical peak achieved before the introduction of the medium. Examples of such activities are comic book reading and, for children if not clearly so for teenagers, movie attendance. However, often we cannot be sure about continuing effects for two reasons.

First, the data from Great Britain on the first six years of television set ownership (Belson, 1959) and from the United States community on its first decade of television (Coffin, 1955; Cunningham & Walsh, 1958) make it clear that introductory suppressions are sometimes followed by recoveries. In the British instance, both frequently and less frequently engaged-in activities were suppressed when a television set was acquired. Examples of the 20 activities examined are gardening, movie attendance, and reading. By the end of six years, the less-frequent activities had recovered to their pretelevision levels, but frequently engaged-in activities remained somewhat below pretelevision levels. The introduction of television delimited the opportunities of which children and teenagers could avail themselves, but with the passage of time, family life became much like it once was, except for a modest diminution of initially frequent activities. This hints that the price of television is a slight curtailment in pursuit of major interests, but no reduction in the variety of activities engaged in.

This is a key to the effect of television on time use. If it added an hour on the average to media consumption per day, then in its absence, something would have to be done with that hour. It is more likely that people would devote it to familiar and convenient activities on which they already spend considerable time than invent novel things to do. At the same time, they would not give up infrequent and by that fact special or unusual activities in which they occasionally engage for television viewing. Contrary to the popular view, television thus adds to the variety of experience.

Second, secular trends may vitiate initial television effects. The change in an activity over time may be so great that any initial effect becomes comparatively insignificant, and thus ambiguous as to its continuation. An example is library circulation (Cook & Campbell, 1979; Parker, 1963). The investigator (Parker, 1963) took advantage of a natural experiment on the grand scale designed unintentionally by the federal government. In the late 1940s, the Federal Communications Commission (FCC) halted the licensing of television stations and did not resume until several years later. Ostensibly, the purpose was to better analyze allocation of spectrum space to preclude conflicting signals, although Winston (1986) asserts that the real purpose (at least for the length of the freeze) was to give the big companies with major financial interests time to divide up the market and exclude newcomers. The result was a country divisible into communities with and without television. Television and nontelevision sites could be identified with ease because of the rapidity with which sets were acquired where stations were licensed (Fig. 2.6). This made possible the use of a research design labeled by Cook and Campbell (1979) as an "interrupted time series with switching replications." They write:

> Imagine two nonequivalent samples, each of which receives the treatment at different times so that when one group receives the treatment the other serves as a control, and when the control group later receives the treatment the original treatment group serves as the control. . . . External validity is enhanced because an effect can be demonstrated with two populations in at least two settings at different moments in history. Moreover, there are likely to be different irrelevancies associated with the application of each treatment and, if measures are unobtrusive, there need be no fear of the treatment's interacting with testing. (p. 223)

Library use clearly was affected by the introduction of television (Figure 2.7), with per capita circulation reduced. The decline was primarily confined to fiction titles. This, along with the decline in comic book reading, is an example of functional displacement (Comstock *et al.*, 1978; Himmelweit *et al.*, 1958; Schramm *et al.*, 1961). Television provided fictional entertainment in a manner more satisfying than fiction library titles and comic books. These data illustrate how a change attributable to a new circumstance may be dwarfed by secular trends. The best guess is that library circulation is slightly depressed today compared to what it would be in the absence of television.

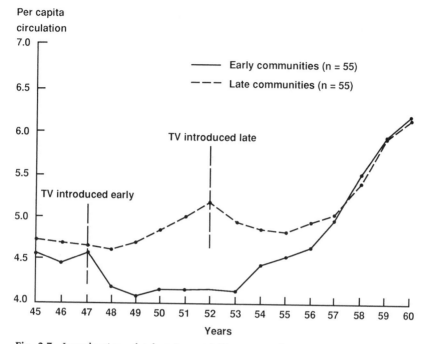

Fig. 2.7 Introduction of television and library circulation. From Cook, T.D., & Campbell, D.T. (1979). *Quasiexperimentation: Design and analysis issues for field settings.* Chicago: Houghton Mifflin.

However, we say this with less confidence than we assert that the introduction of television had an effect.

Secular trends may diminish the importance one would attach to any continuing effect, unless the medium is a major contributor to the trend itself. In the case of library circulation, entertainment as well as news and public affairs programming may have stimulated interest in some topics, but the increases certainly largely reflect an increasingly better-educated population for whom, however much they may use and enjoy it, television does not satisfy many of their interests.

A question asked persistently is whether television takes children and teenagers away from more constructive activities. If what is implied is that television displaces activities that a young person has the skills, opportunities, and motives to engage in, the answer, with one major exception, is largely no. If displacement of time were a major factor, we would expect heavier and lighter viewers to differ markedly in their participation in various activities such as taking lessons, visiting museums, playing sports, and participating in organizations such as the Boy and Girl Scouts. A number of investigations of time use do not consistently find such differences, although a few do emerge. Lyle and Hoffman (1972a) collected extensive data from about 1600 Los Angeles area young people in the first, sixth, and tenth grades. They concluded that among the sixth and tenth graders, participation in a wide range of social and recreational activities ("extramural sports and organizations, hobbies and artistic activities, after-school chores or work") was not necessarily related to amount of television viewing, although first graders who were heavy viewers engaged in less play. Sixth and tenth graders who were high print and high television users "were among the most active in all areas, while those low in use of both media were among the least active." This implies that a disposition toward involvement lies behind both media use and engaging in other activities, and this would mitigate any displacement of the latter by the former. Timmer, Eccles, and O'Brien (1985) found no associations between amount of viewing and time spent on each of more than two dozen other activities except for small negative associations with personal care and churchgoing. S. Neuman (1988), of course, found no association between time spent with friends or at sports and viewing. Rosengren and Windahl (1989), found no evidence among Scandinavian children and teenagers, of any incursion of television viewing into time that might be spent with friends or on other leisure, and some signs that the opportunity to engage in other activities reduced slightly the amount of time spent viewing television. Heyns (1976), in a study of out-of-school summer activity, concluded that playing and pursuing hobbies were unrelated to television viewing.

Medrich, Roizen, Rubin, and Buckley (1982), among those 750 Berkeley children, found only some minor and no striking inverse relationships between amount of television viewing and engaging in other activities such as lessons, sports, clubs, hobbies, and play. There was certainly no consistently negative linear relationship between viewing and engaging in other activities. However, when they turned to the centrality of television in the household (Table 2.5), they did find some clear-cut positive associations between noncentrality and activities but, except for reading, only among whites.

This pattern (of stronger relationships for centrality than for viewing, and the presence of the former largely among white households) seems plausible when it is recalled that television is viewed when other compelling activities are absent, the providing of such opportunities has much to do with parents, schools, and communities, and nothing to do with the availability of television, and the special place television has in black households. It emphasizes the importance of norms rather than viewing as a factor that suppresses other activities.

Table 2.5
Centrality and Selected Activities

Activity and Ethnicity	Television centrality (Percentages)		
	High	Moderate	Low
Takes fine arts lessons			
Black	27	27	32
White	19	34	43
All children	26	27	35
Reads every day			
Black	11	10	18
White	11	27	37
All children	12	15	22
Visits cultural places with parent			
Black	10	8	10
White	31	31	43
All children	13	11	21

Adapted from Medrich, E.A., Roizen, J., Rubin, V., & Buckley, S. (1982). *The serious business of growing up: A study of children's lives outside school.* Berkeley: University of California Press.

Some young persons who are heavy viewers are in circumstances that facilitate engaging in other activities, while others view heavily because the opportunity to engage in such activities is restricted; as a result, there is an uneven relationship between viewing and other activities in which engaging in them is either about as frequent as or only marginally less so than among light viewers. Greater centrality in white households almost certainly reflects lesser interest or capability on the part of parents to encourage or join their children in engaging in activities. Black households are not parallel because the more favorable disposition toward and greater use of television make centrality a weak correlate of parental interest or capability in regard to children's activities.

If there is an exception, it is reading. The introduction of the medium not only reduced overall print media use at the time, but a greater amount of television viewing appears to be associated with less frequent reading. Heyns (1978) concluded as follows:

> The two activities which have the largest inverse relationship in terms of time allocation are reading and watching television. Children tend to spend equivalent amounts of time playing or pursuing hobbies irrespective of how much time is spent watching television; but reading behavior is strongly inversely related to time spent watching television. (p. 301)

She speculates that children allocate their time between active and quiescent and solitary activities, and that reading and television are tradeoffs. Medrich, Roizen, Rubin, and Buckley (1982) also found television use to be strongly inversely related to regularity of reading (Table 2.6). Among white families, children reading for fun five or more days a week increased from 21% for heavy viewers to more than double, 46%, for light viewers. Among black families, the comparable figures were 19% for heavy viewers and 31% for light viewers. This congruity between the races makes this a particularly convincing finding. They did not find any association between viewing whether some reading occurred, but only with frequency of reading. This disparity holds an important lesson: It is not use but degree of use that is sensitive to changes in time allocation, and to collect data on the former rather than the latter is a waste of time. Thus, in the case of reading, not only norms but viewing appear to be suppressive. However, as we would suspect, not all data are consistent. For example, reading was among the many activities unassociated with viewing in the time-use data of Timmer, Eccles, and O'Brien (1985).

The varied data suggest that it was the introduction of television and its subsequent ubiquitous presence that has had the greatest influence on the activities in which children and teenagers engage. Time spent currently on viewing does not seem to make a great deal of difference, except probably for reading. Among white families, the environment established in regard to television, or its centrality, seems to make a greater difference. Among black families, centrality seems to make a difference only for reading. In this context, the remarks of Medrich and colleagues (1982) become an admonition not against television but in behalf of the value of time in the lives of young persons:

Table 2.6
Viewing and Reading Regularly for Fun

Child's viewing time	Children who read five or more days a week (percentages)		
	Black	White	All children
Light	31	46	36
Medium	24	36	26
Heavy	19	21	19

From Medrich, E.A., Roizen, J., Rubin, V., & Buckley, S. (1982). *The serious business of growing up: A study of children's lives outside school.* Berkeley: The University of California Press.

Even if television viewing had no measurable effects on children . . . it would still be argued that it is an inadequate agent of socialization and a poor use of time relative to other alternatives. Furthermore, while television may have few measurable negative consequences, it has few measurable benefits for children either. . . . Most children watch too much television given the time-use options. Their time might be better spent, in the sense that doing other things might teach them more about their world and foster development of talents, intellect, and physical abilities. (p. 227)

III SCHOLASTIC ACHIEVEMENT

There is no question that the amount of time spent viewing television by American children and teenagers is negatively associated with their academic performance. We begin with an examination of the degree and shape of this relationship. We then turn to the possible effects of viewing on cognitive behavior that might contribute either positively or negatively to scholastic achievement, beginning with the evaluations of "Sesame Street," turning then to interests and vocabularies, the role of mental ability, and finally to hypothesized effects on traits and abilities—spatial, perceptual, and temporal responses, impulse control, imaginativeness, and creativity. Then we return to the inverse association overall between achievement and viewing, to examine the evidence in behalf of one contributing causally to the other, and the processes or means by which any causal contribution might come about.

A. ASSOCIATION

A meta-analysis (Glass, 1978; Glass, McGaw, & Smith, 1981; Hunter, Schmidt, & Jackson, 1982; Rosenthal, 1984) encompassing about two dozen samples varying widely in sizes, ages, sites, and measures produced a small average negative effect size for the relationship between television viewing and scholastic achievement (P.A. Williams, Haertel, Haertel, & Walberg, 1982), but a conclusion need not rest on any such arithmetic aggregation, and fortunately so, because an examination of the studies leads to the conclusion that they vary so much, and particularly in quality and representativeness, that the outcome totally lacks credibility. It also need not rest on discerning a pattern in a set of findings in which some seem to be in conflict with others. Outcomes in this instance are compelling because of (a) the quality of measurement, (b) the size and comprehensiveness of the samples, and (c) the consistency of the results.

There are five major sources:

1. The 1980 California Assessment Program (CAP) data and successive follow-ups (1980, 1982, 1986);

2. The 1980 High School and Beyond (HSB) data collected by the National Center for Educational Statistics (Keith, Reimers, Fehrman, Pottebaum, & Aubey,1986);

3. The 1983–1984 NAEP data collected by the Educational Testing Service (ETS) under support of the Office of Education (B. Anderson *et al.*, 1986);

4. The synthesis of data from eight state assessments such as that of California representing more than 1 million children and teenagers (ESA) (S. Neuman, 1988); and

5. A sample of several thousand sophomores, drawn from the 1980 HSB data, from whom data were again obtained two years later when they were seniors (Gaddy, 1986).

We will begin with and give most of our attention to the California data because of (a) the extremely large sample size and (b) the representation of the greatest variety of achievement.

In the spring of the 1980 school year, the state-run CAP obtained data on mathematical, reading, and writing achievement and television exposure for everyone present in the sixth and twelfth grades on the day of testing. The number for the sixth grade was 282,000 and for the twelfth grade, 227,000; this represented 99% of the enrolled population.

It is not only size of the data set that promises quality, however. It is the sponsorship—not because they do things so well in California, but because any such nationally visible endeavor sponsored by a state department of education would represent the scientific norm of highest achievable quality, or reliability and validity.

The combination of two grades and three kinds of achievement leads to six sets of data. Because the pattern of results for each kind of achievement is about the same, we will focus on reading because it is the skill most thoroughly represented throughout all the data. At both grade levels and for each of the three kinds of achievement (Fig. 3.1 and 3.2), there was a negative association between amount of television viewed and achievement. Similarly, for each level of family socioeco-

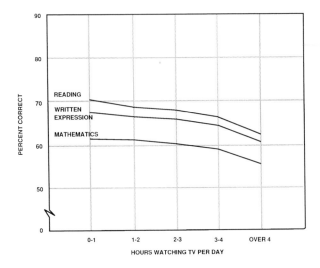

READING ACHIEVEMENT BY HOUSEHOLD SOCIOECONOMIC STATUS

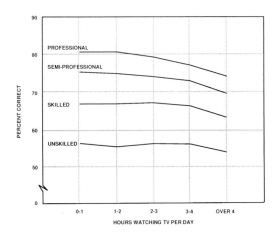

NUMBER OF STUDENTS BY SOCIOECONOMIC STATUS					N/R	TOTAL	
PROFESSIONAL	15,713	11,176	7,022	3,787	4,918	337	42,953	15%
SEMI-PROFESSIONAL	15,634	12,927	9,449	5,812	9,631	495	53,948	19%
SKILLED	23,713	21,283	16,966	11,301	21,795	1,189	96,247	34%
UNSKILLED	10,408	9,391	7,591	5,2111	11,451	769	44,821	16%
NON-RESPONDENTS	11,505	9,866	7,286	4,627	9,481	1,173	43,938	16%
TOTAL	76,973	64,643	48,314	30,738	57,276	3,963	281,907	100%
PERCENT	27%	23%	17%	11%	20%	2%		

Fig. 3.1 Television, achievement, and socioeconomic status: Sixth grade. Adapted from California Assessment Program. (1980). *Student achievement in California schools. 1979–80 annual report: Television and student achievement.* Sacramento: California State Department of Education.

ACHIEVEMENT IN THREE SUBJECTS

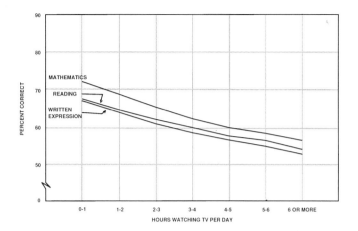

READING ACHIEVEMENT BY EDUCATIONAL LEVEL OF HEAD OF HOUSEHOLD

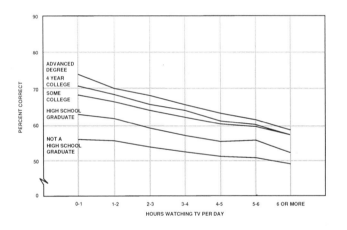

NUMBER OF STUDENTS BY EDUCATIONAL LEVEL OF HEAD OF HOUSEHOLD							TOTAL	
ADVANCED DEGREE	16,923	9,244	6,128	3,424	1,730	818	1,323	39,590	17.4%
4 YEAR COLLEGE	14,928	10,097	7,725	4,613	2,425	1,127	1,656	42,571	18.7%
SOME COLLEGE	17,679	14,017	12,305	8,149	4,491	2,233	3,366	62,240	27.3%
HIGH SCHOOL GRADUATE	13,090	11,865	11,850	8,822	5,294	2,714	4,101	57,756	25.4%
NOT A HIGH SCHOOL GRADUATE	5,097	4,968	5,074	4,127	2,462	1,403	2,261	25,392	11.2%
TOTAL	67,717	50,211	43,082	29,135	16,402	8,295	12,707	227,549	
PERCENT	29.8%	22.1%	18.9%	12.8%	7.2%	3.7%	5.5%		100%

Fig. 3.2 Television, achievement, and socioeconomic status: Twelfth grade. Adapted from California Assessment Program. (1980). *Student achievement in California schools. 1979–80 annual report: Television and student achievement.* Sacramento: California State Department of Education.

nomic status, there was a negative association with viewing for each of the types of achievement, as exemplified by the data on reading.

In contrast, among pupils whose English was limited in fluency, amount of television viewed was positively associated with achievement. Even a downturn at the level of greatest viewing did not produce average scores below those for the lightest category of viewers.

There are five important qualifications or amendments:

1. Family socioeconomic status is inversely associated with achievement, and this relationship is far stronger than the negative one between achievement and amount of television viewed.

2. The inverse association between amount of television viewed and achievement increases as family socioeconomic status rises, with the strongest relationship occurring for pupils from the highest recorded category of status, a phenomenon readily visible in the increasingly sharper declines in the slopes for achievement.

3. The inverse relationship between amount of television viewed and achievement is stronger at the twelfth-grade than at the sixth-grade level, a pattern readily discernible by comparing the differences in scores for those low and high in television exposure at the two grade levels.

4. For the lowest level of family socioeconomic status, the inverse relationship is sometimes barely observable, and occasionally there is a rise in achievement, with an increase in amount of television viewed before the decline in achievement appears, although these phenomena appear confined to the lower grade level.

5. The numbers recorded in the highest viewing categories, where declines in achievement are sharpest, are not trivial, with about 30% in both the sixth and twelfth grades reporting that they watch three or more hours a day.

Only the most mulish would challenge these data in regard to their wide applicability to American children and teenagers, although obviously they might not apply to narrowly defined subgroups. However, in this instance we have highly supportive data, extraordinary in both quantity and quality.

Keith, Reimers, Fehrman, Pottebaum, and Aubey (1986) analyzed the relationship between television viewing and achievement scores equally weighted between mathematics and reading of more than 28,000 seniors in the HSB data. B. Anderson, Mead, and Sullivan (1986) report on the relationship between viewing and reading among about 100,000 fourth, eighth, and eleventh graders in 30 states in the NAEP data. S. Neuman (1988) aggregated the outcomes for viewing and reading, vocabulary, and study skills from eight statewide evaluations (California, Connecticut, Maine, Illinois, Michigan, Pennsylvania, Rhode Island, and Texas), using samples of 18,000 from where the N's were in the several hundred thousand (California and Michigan) to make the task feasible on today's computers, with a representative, weighted total sample of about 173,600. Gaddy (1986) drew samples ranging from about 2400 to 5000 from the HSB data representing the same students as sophomores in 1982 and as seniors in 1984 and examined the outcomes for viewing and reading, vocabulary, and mathematics.

In every instance, there was confirmation of the CAP outcomes. For example, the NAEP data parallels the CAP pattern at all three grades for socioeconomic status, viewing, and reading (Table 3.1), while the HSB sophomore–senior panel does so at both grade levels, and provides direct evidence that the degree of inverse association increases with household education resources, such as number of books, having an encyclopedia, or subscribing to a newspaper (Table 3.2). If the black samples are taken as surrogates for groups, on the average, of lower socioeconomic status compared to their white counterparts, both the NAEP and HSB data further confirm that the prominence of a negative association increases with socioeconomic status, for it is less pronounced among the blacks than among the whites.

A CAP follow-up (1986) provides evidence that the phenomenon is not confined to basic skills (Table 3.3). With data representing every student available for testing (more than a quarter of a million) in the eighth grade in the state, amount of television viewing was inversely associated with achievement not only in reading, writing, and mathematics, but also in science, history, and social science.

There is a question of curvilinearity, with achievement rising with a few hours per day or week of television viewing and then falling continuously as viewing increases. The raw 1980 CAP data, the largest and most comprehensive by subject matter and grade, give only the slightest hint of such a shape among the comparatively flat sixth grade curves for those from households of the lowest socioeconomic status although it is visible for those with limited fluency in English. The eighth grade curves for all five subjects similarly are essentially flat among those reporting viewing two or fewer hours a day. Fetler (1984), in his analysis of a sample of 10,000 sixth graders (Fig. 3.3) in one of the follow-ups to the 1980 California assessment again covering achievement in reading, writing, and mathematics, concluded there was some evidence of curvilinearity. Inspection of the data (Fig. 2, p. 112) shows that they are almost entirely attributable to the lowest socioeconomic strata, and

Table 3.1

Reading Proficiency (0–500) and TV Viewing by Ethnicity
and Parental Education

	Hours of TV viewing per day		
	0–2	3–5	6 or more
Ethnicity			
Grade 4			
White	232	228	213
Black	200	201	190
Hispanic	208	204	193
Grade 5			
White	274	268	253
Black	246	248	236
Hispanic	249	249	238
Grade 11			
White	301	291	275
Black	272	267	262
Hispanic	277	268	254
Parental education			
Grade 4			
No high school diploma	201	207	195
High school graduate	220	220	206
Posthigh school	237	231	210
Grade 8			
No high school diploma	247	252	236
High school graduate	262	259	246
Posthigh school	279	271	255
Grade 11			
No high school diploma	274	272	260
High school graduate	287	279	268
Posthigh school	305	295	279

From Anderson, B., Mead, N., & Sullivan, S. (1986). *Television: What do National Assessment results tell us?* Princeton, NJ: Educational Testing Service.

that otherwise, the shapes are either partially or wholly downward. Potter (1987), in examining about 550 pupils between the eighth and twelfth grades in a small midwestern community, found a threshold effect of about ten hours of viewing per week, or fewer than 1.5 hours per day, before amount of viewing became negatively associated with a composite measure of varied scholastic achievement, and concluded there might be some curvilinearity. S. Neuman (1988) concluded, from her ESA aggregation, that there was a comparable threshold, and in the eight-state pooled data, found a curvilinearity that was most visible

Table 3.2
Correlations between Media Use and Achievement Variables[a]

Achievement measure	All students Sophomore $n = 5074$	Senior	Blacks Sophomore $n = 2365$	Senior	Females Sophomore $n = 4997$	Senior
Vocabulary	−.158	−.176	−.031	−.023	−.177	−.186
Reading	−.160	−.155	−.042	−.011	−.168	−.160
Math level 1	−.173	−.188	.008	−.011	−.202	−.196
Math level 2	−.157	−.169	−.021	−.030	−.159	−.176
Grades	−.128	−.127	−.032	.021	−.146	−.136

	High resource Sophomore $n = 2974$	Senior	Medium resource Sophomore $n = 3960$	Senior	Low resource Sophomore $n = 3112$	Senior
Vocabulary	−.241	−.220	−.076	−.121	−.037	−.094
Reading	−.226	−.174	−.064	−.089	−.064	−.086
Math level 1	−.211	−.204	−.105	−.122	−.084	−.109
Math level 2	−.171	−.175	−.097	−.110	−.073	−.113
Grades	−.189	−.148	−.080	−.089	−.051	−.074

[a] Smallest significant correlation (one-tailed alpha = .05, corrected for design effect) for all students is .032; for blacks, .047; for females, .032; for high-resource group; .042; medium-resource group, .036; and for low-resource group, .041. Calculated using Fisher's r to Z transformation.

Adapted from Gaddy, G.D. (1986). Television's impact on high school achievement. *Public Opinion Quarterly, 50*, 340–359.

Table 3.3
Television Viewing and Achievement in Five Areas (Eighth Grade)

Amount of TV viewing (hours)	Percentage of students	Percentage correct scores Reading	Written expression	Mathematics	History– Social science	Science
0	2	68.1	63.6	59.0	58.2	61.8
0–½	4	67.7	64.0	59.1	57.9	61.6
½–1	9	67.4	63.5	58.7	57.4	61.0
1–2	19	67.6	63.7	58.7	57.4	60.9
2–3	22	66.4	62.5	57.0	56.1	59.7
3–4	17	65.0	61.0	55.2	54.7	58.7
4–5	11	63.6	59.5	53.4	53.3	57.2
5+	17	58.3	54.6	48.8	49.3	53.7
$N = 285,743$						

From California Assessment Program. (1986). *Annual report 1985–1986.* Sacramento: California State Department of Education.

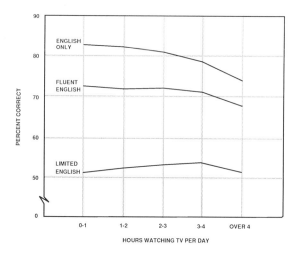

NUMBER OF STUDENTS BY ENGLISH FLUENCY LEVEL

						N/R	TOTAL	
ENGLISH ONLY	59,285	47,665	35,538	22,343	42,655	2,570	210,056	75%
FLUENT ENGLISH	11,109	11,015	8,562	5,705	10,117	657	47,165	17%
LIMITED ENGLISH	2,713	2,995	2,095	1,403	2,233	350	11,789	4%
NON-RESPONDENTS	3,866	2,968	2,119	1,287	2,271	386	12,897	4%
TOTAL	76,973	64,643	48,314	30,738	57,276	3,963	281,907	
PERCENT	27%	23%	17%	11%	20%	2%		100%

Fig. 3.3 Language proficiency, television, and reading achievement: Sixth grade. Adapted from California Assessment Program. (1980). *Student achievement in California Schools. 1979–80 annual report: Television and student achievement.* Sacramento: California State Department of Education.

at the intermediate, less so at the elementary, and not at all at the high school level, which essentially parallels the CAP data, where any sign of curvilinearity is confined to the earlier, sixth grade (Fig. 3.4). Keith and colleagues (1986), however, with the very large HSB sample, found no evidence of curvilinearity with mathematics and reading achievement.

There is no case for universal curvilinearity, but a good one at intermediate, and a fair one at earlier grades, among those from households lower in socioeconomic status. This suggests a developmental pattern, with a little television viewing having a different—and for some more beneficial—role in the middle and earlier grades than later. The shape of all the curves nevertheless is downward for most or all of their slopes, reflecting a negative association between all categories of achievement and amount of television viewing.

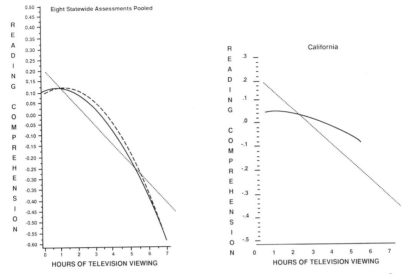

Fig. 3.4   Television, reading, and shape of slope (best-fit regression equation lines). Elementary —; intermediate – – –; high school -----. Adapted from Neuman, S.B. (1988). The displacement effect: Assessing the relation between television viewing and reading performance. *Reading Research Quarterly, 23*(4), 414–440.

B. COGNITIVE BEHAVIOR

1. "Sesame Street"

The status of "Sesame Street" as an institution in American childrearing is well described by a social psychologist whose own analyses have raised serious questions about the degree and range of its educational effects, Thomas Cook (Cook & Curtin, 1986):

> By almost any criterion, "Sesame Street" has been a success. It has won numerous awards from professional groups in television and education and has received rave reviews from media critics; the series has been adopted and adapted in many countries and languages; countless parents attest to its wholesomeness, particularly when compared to the alternatives available on commercial television; and product spin-offs have been numerous and commercially lucrative. The series has also passed perhaps the most difficult test of all. It has survived for more than 15 years in an era in which most other educational television programs aimed at

national audiences have not been renewed after a few seasons of production. "Sesame Street" is a national institution, and arguably a global one. (p. 3)

That 15 years has now become two decades. The goal of the series was "to promote the intellectual and cultural growth of preschoolers, particularly disadvantaged preschoolers" (Cooney, 1968, as quoted in Cook et al., 1975, p. 7); that is, children two-to-five in age. Widely publicized initial empirical evaluations played a large part in this success (Cook & Curtin, 1986) because they appeared to document pedagogic effectiveness.

These evaluations were conducted by the Educational Testing Service (ETS) of Princeton, New Jersey, the organization responsible for the Scholastic Achievement Test (SAT) and Graduate Record Examination (GRE). Ball and Bogatz (1970; Bogatz & Ball, 1971) attempted a series of field experiments that would permit comparing the intellectual growth of nonviewers with that of viewers. Measures primarily covered symbolic recognition (letters, numbers, etc.) and basic cognitive processes (classification, relations).

When "Sesame Street" was first broadcast, public television was available in only about 60% of American homes. Because of this limited potential reach and the unprecedented nature of an unreservedly educational children's series, however entertaining, there were fears that not enough preschoolers would watch to make such field experiments possible.

As a result, a sizable proportion of homes within the designs were to be contacted regularly by Educational Testing Service–Children's Television Workshop (ETS–CTW) representatives. During the first and second years of "Sesame Street" (1970, 1971), the representatives visited the homes before the season began, to talk to parents and children about the importance of viewing, and to leave promotional materials such as balloons, buttons, and magazines. During the first year, they continued to visit the homes weekly to encourage the children directly. During the second year, visits were scheduled monthly. About two-thirds of homes in the evaluation design in the first year, and about half in the second year, were so treated.

However, "Sesame Street" immediately became so popular that the scarcity factor was not viewers, but nonviewers. As a consequence, the field experiments collapsed, for lack of control groups, into the comparing of children who viewed greater or lesser amounts, a mishap somewhat rectified during the second year by the use of cable systems.

Several years later, Cook and colleagues (1975) re-evaluated the original evaluations in the context of later research in *Sesame Street Revisited*. Ball and Bogatz had concluded that the regular viewing of "Sesame Street" increased the learning of numbers, letters, and cognitive reasoning skills, and that such learning occurred for children varying widely in characteristics. Cook and colleagues concur that among regular viewers there was learning from "Sesame Street," and that it occurred among "black and white children; urban, suburban, and rural children; and children of both sexes." This was a considerable accomplishment, for teaching with television that is also supposed to be entertaining is much harder than it looks. Friedlander, Wetstone, and Scott (1974) found an average comprehension score of less than 50% among preschoolers in response to a three-minute educational sequence ostensibly designed for children of that age—an outcome they attribute partly to the conventions of television production that are contrary to effective pedagogy; that is, inadequate redundancy, irrelevant action, and unnecessary details.

Where Cook and colleagues and Ball and Bogatz disagreed was on the breadth of effectiveness, the degree to which any effectiveness was attributable to exposure to the program instead of the combination of viewing with encouragement, and the introduction of effects on equality of scholastic achievement as a criterion for evaluating success. Cook and colleagues conclude that the pedagogic value of "Sesame Street" was limited and modest. They found learning attributable to viewing confined largely to recognition of letters and numbers (associational tasks), with scant if any contribution to the acquisition of reasoning skills (inferential tasks), with much of any success attributable to the added influence of the ETS–CTW visitor.

These conclusions alone would have been horrifying to CTW, dependent as it was and is on the contributions of government, foundations, and private industry, while deriving supplementary income from the franchising of products. However, Cook and colleagues took a step beyond, denying much of the scientific basis of CTW's public acceptance. They also argued that "Sesame Street" was increasing the disparity between the disadvantaged and the advantaged.

The result was controversy. As the president of the sponsoring Russell Sage Foundation describes events (Freeman, 1975), the manuscript was initially submitted in 1972, but only published three years later. In the interim, the document was meticulously examined by ETS and CTW, and the foundation convened an expert panel. As part of this process, opinions were solicited from three prominent authorities on research of the type examined by Cook and colleagues, the sociologists James Coleman and Peter Rossi and the social psychologist Donald

Campbell. A number of suggestions about alternative analyses were made; Cook and colleagues took some of them. Peer review is common but usually quick (generally at the insistence of publishers—in this case, the Sage Foundation). Three years of intensive scrutiny is rare, and testifies not only to the prodigious energies of CTW and ETS but also to the sacred status of "Sesame Street." When published, the concluding commentary by Ball and Bogatz (1975) stated uncompromisingly, "We have examined this work in great detail, and we reject its major conclusions" (p. 388).

Much of the debate centered on the criterion of narrowing the achievement gap. CTW repeatedly has asserted that its goal never was to decrease the gap but to provide a valuable experience for all preschool children (Ball & Bogatz, 1975; Lesser, 1974). Yet, what is one to make of the frequent justification of the series by CTW supporters on the grounds that it would serve the needs of the disadvantaged, or the evidence that the initial federal funding was based on especially serving such children (Cook et al., 1975)? It is naive to think that CTW would not take credit were the data to indicate that it had closed the gap. Perhaps even more sensitive is the question raised by Cook and colleagues that we would also raise: could CTW have designed the series to have greater impact on the disadvantaged?

We believe that a different paradigm (one that made the disadvantaged the focus for program development, with those elements most attractive to them emphasized at the expense of those appealing to the more advantaged) might have produced a series with greater benefits for the disadvantaged, but we think this is a case where the norms of television and the realities of funding have to be taken into account. Television has an unequaled capacity among the media to reach huge audiences, and it is hard to justify not doing so when the opportunity exists. Politically, purposefully ignoring the great majority of the potential audience might have made support for the series most difficult to obtain and probably impossible to sustain; the political key is the success of "Sesame Street" has been its essentially universal appeal.

As for the introduction of the achievement gap criterion, the issue is whether or not an organization should be allowed to impose its preferred goals in the assessment of performance. Experience with the automobile, nuclear power, oil, and pharmaceutical industries says "No." We do not think CTW is an exception. The issue merited attention because such concerns have been paramount in federal educational policy, and much of CTW's funding has come from the government.

Nevertheless, the failure to have closed the gap is probably the price of an enterprise such as "Sesame Street." As Cook and colleagues argue, children from middle class families may have watched such educational programming more frequently and consistently, and even if their viewing was matched by that of the disadvantaged, they more often might have been in environments culturally and educationally richer and therefore more facilitative of learning; thus, the gap may even have been widened.

However, these circumstances may no longer hold. When "Sesame Street" was inaugurated, public television reached far more households higher in socioeconomic status because of the predominance of UHF channels hard to receive except on the best equipment, and the geographical location of stations (Comstock et al., 1978). The presence of cable in over half of households, and a vast increase in number of stations, have largely eliminated this disparity (Comstock, 1989). Rice and colleagues (1990) provide data. In a two-year examination of more than 300 children beginning at ages three and five, they found no socioeconomic or ethnic differences in viewing of "Sesame Street." They also found a contribution to improved vocabulary attributable to viewing rather than viewing with parental involvement. What Cook and colleagues examined in regard to a wide range of educational effects was the introduction of "Sesame Street" with and without a program designed to involve parents and children in viewing; in sharp contrast, Rice and colleagues two decades later examine the role of parental coviewing, and find that vocabulary learning is not dependent on it. These are compatible outcomes that lead to optimism rather than pessimism in regard to the current effectiveness of viewing "Sesame Street" on at least one kind of achievement.

Another caveat is that the greater centrality of television in black households and those of lower socioeconomic status suggests that children in such settings may more often view "Sesame Street" with their parents in the vicinity, and this may lead to a greater amount of verbal exchange, prompting, and practice, which might compensate for the advantages of middle class children. The two findings that parents use television as a means to teach language (Lemish & Rice, 1986) and that the best predictor of coviewing is total amount of television viewed by children and parents (Dorr et al., 1989) support such a view.

We would emphasize that:

1. "Sesame Street" provides an educational as well as entertaining experience that children can consume profitably on their own, or even more profitably with participation by adults.
2. "Sesame Street" is viewed regularly (defined as four or more times weekly) by an estimated 50 to 60% of all children between the ages of

two and three (we extrapolate from the meticulous calculations of Cook and colleagues to take into account the increase in the reach of public television to more than 90% of households. We cannot use Nielsen or comparable estimates because they are averages for a point in time, while with an educational series like "Sesame Street," there will be few if any benefits if viewing is not regular).

3. "Sesame Street" attracts very large numbers of viewers from ethnic minority households and those of lower socioeconomic status that proportionately are not appreciably smaller than those from white, middle class and more affluent strata; in fact, over the years, much of the claim of public broadcasting that it appeals to all strata has rested on the viewing of its educational programming by children from such households.

4. "Sesame Street" and similar educational programming is expensive to produce (the 1988 budget of CTW, which also produces "The Electric Company," was $13 million) but because television is such a successful mass medium, the cost per year per child viewer is extremely modest, with the most recent estimate $1.25 ("Inouye plans bill . . .", April 17, 1989).

"Sesame Street" is an example of a general rule. Use of the media for social ends may exacerbate differences, at least initially, because those least in need or most able to benefit may predominate among early users, may make more effective use of what is offered, or may have superior access.

The analysis of Cook and colleagues survived the criticisms of those with vested interests, a special review panel, and several distinguished experts. The same cannot be said of many, if any, reassessments of the analyses of others. We concur with their conclusions that the cognitive effects of "Sesame Street" are limited, reasoning is not much benefited, and the size and number of effects to an important degree are contingent on intervention by an adult. We did not find in the bibliography of research on "Sesame Street" by CTW (1989) any study that purports to document long-term, wide-ranging influence either as proximate as the midelementary school years or as distant as high school graduation. In the absence of such evidence, it is difficult to evaluate the contribution of "Sesame Street" to cognitive development. Even if we accepted fully the interpretation that Ball and Bogatz place on their findings, we would not be better able to make such an evaluation, because small or large, wide or narrow, the gains measured have been short-term. This does not reflect negatively on "Sesame Street;" it holds for all attempts to advance young children's mental skills. What Gerald Lesser, the Harvard professor of education and psychology who had a leading role in designing the series to adhere to the scientific evidence on children's reasoning, wrote more than a decade-and-a-half ago (1974) remains true:

> Sadly, we have not been able to show in any conclusive way that any program of early education has definite or lasting effects on children . . . (O)n balance, no one can claim to know how and why we educate young children. (p. 15)

2. Interests and Vocabularies

Himmelweit, Oppenheim, and Vince (1958) found only scant evidence in behalf of an influence of television on the interests of young people. Some teenagers did seek out books that had been dramatized, thereby widening reading tastes and experience. However, there were some surprises in regard to television's ostensible ability to stimulate participatory involvement by drawing attention to a topic or activity.

They assessed the effects of coverage of a museum collection on an ongoing British Broadcasting Corporation (BBC) series by interviewing young persons at the museum before and after the broadcast. The number visiting was about the same in both time periods, only 10% of those in the second period had seen the program, and not all of them were there to see the part of the collection given coverage. There was no evidence, when young persons from households with and without television were examined, that frequency of visiting museums and art galleries in general differed. Expressions of interest in visiting an exhibition, museum, or art gallery similarly did not differ. Interest in an additional array of cultural activities also did not differ—going to a concert, opera, play, or ballet; discussing politics; reading books; and writing a play, poem, or story. They also found television availability unrelated to the liking or disliking of 20 different school subjects. They perhaps betray some disappointment when they observe:

> Television stimulates interests, but only fleetingly. It is up to the adults around the child to maintain these interests and turn them into action: by rendering accessible the books that have been dramatized, by helping the child to find materials needed to make things suggested on television, by encouraging him to visit places (such as art galleries or exhibitions) that have been featured (p. 47)

Schramm, Lyle, and Parker (1961) found temporary and specialized effects on vocabularies. When they compared children in communities with and without television on their performance on a nationally used test of general vocabulary, they found evidence that children with television entered the first grade about a year ahead. When they examine specialized vocabulary, which they describe as consisting of "timely and topical" terms such as satellite, war, and cancer (enduring would be more descriptive), the results were similar. Such outcomes were clearer for those high or low than for those average in mental ability. Among sixth and tenth graders, they found no evidence of a contribution by television to miscellaneous knowledge except for information about entertainment figures. By the sixth grade, any general vocabulary advantage had disappeared. Yet there is ample evidence that children and teenagers learn brand names from television (Adler *et al.*, 1980). These results suggested that television increases general vocabulary early, that such effects disappear with time, and that any continuing effect is limited to the content in which television specializes.

T.M. Williams (1986) and colleagues thoroughly examined vocabulary differences in their three-community natural experiment. They employed three nationally recognized widely used measures of vocabulary—the Stanford–Binet (S–B) vocabulary subtest, the vocabulary subscale of the Wechsler Intelligence Scale for Children (WISC), and the Peabody Picture Vocabulary Test (PPVT). At no grade level and on none of the tests did the data support an initially hypothesized contribution by television to vocabulary. These results hint that the early effect found by Schramm and colleagues may have been an introductory phenomenon that no longer occurs because of the near-universal diffusion of any once-novel language employed on television. In retrospect, the outcome is not surprising.

Selnow and Bettinghaus (1982) report a small negative correlation among preschool children between amount of television viewing and language competency, and a positive association between quality of language in programs viewed and language ability. This suggests that children of greater mental ability, who would have superior command of language, are somewhat more likely to view programs more in accord with their abilities, and that typically the television that children view is unlikely to improve or broaden their use of language.

Nevertheless, television does seem to figure in the acquisition of vocabulary. Lemish and Rice (1986) found that a great deal of verbal interchange emphasizing vocabulary occurs between children and parents drawing on television, and particularly ongoing viewing. Rice and Woodsmall (1988) demonstrate that children of nursery school age can acquire object and attribute words by exposure to their use in a television sequence. Initially, Rice (1983, 1984) and colleagues challenged the view held by most developmental psychologists that television is relatively unimportant in language acquisition. They argued that television is important because of (a) the quantity of children's viewing, and the high motivation to see a program that sometimes accompanies that viewing; (b) the near-universal use in children's programs of dialogue that is child-pertinent (presumably, the only exceptions would represent failures by writers and producers), with many programs featuring repetitive phrases and stressed words that would facilitate imitation; (c) the opportunity for children to learn the meanings of words through their use in program dialogue; and (d) the frequency with which children borrow from television things to say (and do) in play. However, the research by Rice and colleagues (1990) leads to a more conservative interpretation. They collected data from several hundred children over a two-year period beginning when they were three or five years old. Among the younger children, they found that the regular viewing of "Sesame Street" was associated with increased vocabulary later, while the viewing of animated cartoons had no association with later vocabulary. The implication is that the entertainment designed for children that most children view makes no contribution, while educational programming does.

The data indicate that television by itself does not at present significantly boost vocabulary over what it would have been in its absence. As Harrison and Williams (1986) observe:

> It is possible that television has the potential to have a positive impact . . . Whether this occurs, however, probably depends on what the child would be doing if she or he were not watching TV. If older children spend some of that time reading, or if younger children are read to (by siblings, parents, babysitters), then it becomes a question of which activity is most effective for teaching vocabulary knowledge. (p. 114)

They cite in support the finding by Meringoff and colleagues (1983) that the recall of figurative language [in this instance defined as expressions without referential meanings, such as phonetic refrains, repeated chains of words, or fanciful and symbolic descriptions of characters (e.g., leopard-of-the-terrible-teeth)] by children of preschool age was substantially less after exposure to a televised dramatization than it was when the same story was presented by having a picture book read to them.

In sum, television is now part of the process by which language is learned, and would probably have a larger, more beneficial role if more programs were designed to instruct. General vocabulary, even among young children, is probably not greater than it would be were television less prominent or absent from their lives. The language employed by children and teenagers is probably more grounded in entertainment than was the case before the arrival of television.

3. Mental Ability

Numerous investigators have concluded that mental ability is a major factor in the orientation of young persons toward television and other media (Fig. 3.5). Schramm, Lyle, and Parker (1961) refer to it as "one of the great building blocks (along with personal relationships and social norms, and, of course, age and sex) which go into the structure of a child's television viewing patterns" (p. 79). They propose a model, based on their data, in which television serves different functions that change with advancing age for children who are higher and lower in mental ability, that has not been contradicted since by either empirical inquiry or common observation. They found that brighter children typically were initially heavy viewers because it was part of a broader pattern in which brighter children make greater and more enthusiastic use of the opportunities offered them. They give an example:

> In one school system we had the opportunity to study a group of fourth- and fifth-grade children who had been brought together, because of their very high intelligence scores, for some special classes. These were most remarkable children. They were studying nuclear physics with great interest, specifying the different shells of the atom and considering the tables of periodic weights. They were handling mathematics in a way that would have done credit to most high school and some college students. They were

PRESTIGE RANKINGS BY EIGHTH-GRADE CHILDREN

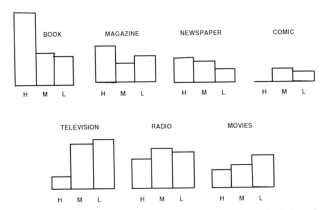

Fig. 3.5 Mental ability and orientation toward media. Mental ability, high = H; moderate = M; low = L. From Schramm, W., Lyle, J., & Parker, E.B. (1961). *Television in the lives of our children.* Stanford, CA: Stanford University Press.

voracious readers. We rather expected that their broad intellectual curiosity and their wide reading would eat into their television time. But quite the contrary! Their television time was proportionately nearly as high as their reading time. They seemed to have an almost inexhaustible fund of energy for mental activities. They did *more* of everything—more television, more movies, more reading, more discussing, more investigating on their own. (p. 79)

They observed a marked change between the ages of 10 and 13. Young persons at every level of mental ability typically reduce the amount of television viewed when they become teenagers. They also typically reduce the proportion of media time spent on television and increase that spent on print. However, the change for brighter children began to occur earlier, and the proportionate decrease in time spent with television became much greater. The brighter teenagers made more use of print (except for light fiction and journalism, characterized at the time as comics and pulp, detective, and screen) and less use of television. When the brighter teenagers did view television, they were much more likely than those lower in mental ability to view news and public affairs programming, to enjoy it more, and to be better able to identify public figures featured on such programs. Those lower in mental ability were more likely to remain heavy viewers, to consume more comics and pulp, detective, screen and similar magazines, and otherwise to be lower in use of print.

The authors employ the concepts of fantasy and reality as descriptive of media experience in interpreting these changes. They see television on the whole, along with the print media favored by teenagers lower in mental ability, as offering primarily the former while other print far more often offers the latter. Reality in this context denotes much more than the portrayal of events and the expression of opinion. It stands for content, factual or fictional, that is intellectually stimulating, increases the range of experience as well as knowledge, and calls upon various skills (such as interpretation, comprehension, and insight) in its consumption; that is, content that contributes to the maturation and the ability to cope of the young person. Thus, brighter teenagers make more productive use of the media. In a sense, they outgrow television. The investigators comment:

Both the high and low groups, in mental ability, are therefore settling into adult patterns. The high group will use television less, and more selectively, and will turn to other media for much of its serious information needs. The low group will use television

> more, and printed media less. As their teen-age behavior suggests,
> they will use television heavily for crime mysteries, situation
> comedies, Westerns, variety and popular music. (pp. 46–47)

Internalized norms and social relations had a far less significant role
in television use, and mental ability was a factor in their influence.
They found that the number of young persons high in print but low in
television use grows markedly between the sixth and tenth grades, and
that they are more likely to have accepted the norms of deferred gratification, self-betterment, and improving their skills at coping that are
associated with upward mobility. Young persons with such norms, if
mental ability is high or at least moderate, are more likely to become
serious users of print and more selective in their television viewing,
favoring reality content to a greater degree. In regard to social relationships, they found that conflicts with parents or peers increased television viewing among those high in ability and high in socioeconomic
status, but did not do so among those low in both ability and such
status. As E.E. Maccoby (1954) concluded, this probably reflects the
typically much lower levels of viewing that occur among those high in
ability and socioeconomic status, so that there was plenty of time
available for escaping unpleasant reality by watching more television.
The data collected by Himmelweit and Swift (1976) on several hundred
British male teenagers over 20 years confirms the persistence of this
pattern. Television and print use and the emphasis on reality and fantasy in later life varied with mental ability and socioeconomic status as
they had earlier. Those who were high in consumption of the dominant
media of entertainment and undemanding content of the time, movies,
later were higher in television viewing. The teenage years thus are the
locus of the establishment of lifelong consistencies in media use.

T.M. Williams (1986) and colleagues in their three-community experiment found that when they pooled all the young persons in grades
three and up and divided them into four groups on the basis of mental
ability, there was an inverse, linear relationship between amount of
television viewing and mental ability. However, this relationship was
primarily attributable to Notel, where television was a novelty; in
Unitel and Multitel there was no such relationship. In Unitel and
Multitel, young persons high in mental ability used certain print media
more, such as newspapers, magazines, and books, and read comics less.
Thus, the model proposed by Schramm and colleagues requires the
modification that an accommodation to television takes place as people
become accustomed to it. As we have documented, differences in viewing associated with socioeconomic status and mental ability with the

passage of time have become somewhat reduced. Thus, mental ability becomes less forceful in predicting television use but remains forceful in predicting consumption of a much greater proportion of what they called reality content.

Morgan and Gross (1982) conclude from a review of previous research that there is a negative relationship between mental ability and amount of television consumed among young persons, although they do not dispute the model of Schramm and colleagues that before the ages of 10–13, children of high ability are often heavy viewers. In the analysis of their own data, they confirm such a negative relationship, and find it is largely independent of the inverse relationship between socioeconomic status and television viewing; that is, mental ability and household socioeconomic status are each independently inversely related to a young person's television viewing.

They also present two challenges to the paradigm by which the role of television has been assessed. First, they divide a sample of over 600 sixth through ninth graders into those low, moderate, and high in mental ability, and analyze the relationships for males and for females between television exposure and seven areas of scholastic achievement, such as reading comprehension, language usage and structure, vocabulary, and math concepts. Significant correlations and even their signs differ between the sexes and mental groupings, suggesting that television may have different relationships with achievement depending on the type of achievement, and gender and mental ability of the student. Second, while they find a negative association between time spent reading and time spent viewing television at any given time, when analyzing the data over time from the same panel of respondents, they find that amount of first-year television viewing predicts amount of time spent reading in the third year with such factors as mental ability, socioeconomic status, gender, and first-year reading taken into account. This hints that earlier viewing may stimulate later reading, possibly through increasing interest in various topics.

They thereby challenge the assumptions—implicit in the way data are often analyzed and interpreted—that narrowly defined subgroups do not differ enough to matter, and that same-time associations are informative about over-time outcomes. However, the data at best are suggestive because of, in the first instance, the modest sample sizes and extremely small magnitudes of the correlation coefficients in any of the cells (which total 48 when a composite achievement score is added to the seven measures of intellectual achievement), and in the second, the very modest size of the over-time correlations and the failure to measure type of reading, which easily could consist of increased hours of comic book and other light reading while monitoring television. Their contribution, then, is not to what we know about these processes but to the way we might think about them.

4. Traits and Abilities

a. Impulse Control Television variously has been accused of contributing to hyperactivity, reduced attention span, failure to control impulses and direct efforts toward a goal, and perseverance (Halpern, 1975; Swerdlow, 1981; Winn, 1977). Hornik (1981) aggregates such hypothesized outcomes as an intolerance for the pace of schooling. We will now examine the evidence that television exposure somehow impairs children in their ability to cope constructively with their environment.

Friedrich and Stein (1973; Stein & Friedrich, 1972) provided about 100 children in a nine-week-long nursery school program with three different television experiences during the middle four weeks. One group saw 12 violent cartoons such as "Batman" and "Superman." Another saw 12 episodes of a program designed to help children to cope, "Mister Rogers' Neighborhood." The third saw 15 children's programs that contained neither violence nor the prosocial emphasis of "Mister Rogers' Neighborhood." Those who saw the violent cartoons decreased in rule obedience and tolerance of delay as measured by observation of actual behavior. Those who saw "Mister Rogers' Neighborhood" and the variety of children's programs displayed greater tolerance of delay. Among children high in mental ability, those who viewed "Mister Rogers' Neighborhood" displayed increased persistence.

D.R. Anderson, Levin, and Lorch (1977), Gadberry (1980), and Tower, Singer, Singer, and Biggs (1979) also examined the effects of specialized educational programming. Anderson and colleagues examined 72 preschool children in regard to their performance (a) on a puzzle-solving task designed to measure perseverance, (b) on a figure-matching task designed to measure impulsivity, and (c) on their activity levels in free play after they saw versions of "Sesame Street," edited either to be extraordinarily fast or extremely slow in pace, or were read a story by a parent. There were no differences in perseverance, impulsivity, or activity level among the groups. Gadberry compared the performance on the same figure-matching task of six-year-old children whose television viewing was unrestricted or had been restricted to about half the ordinary amount, with much of the abandoned programming consisting of violent entertainment and much of the restricted viewing consisting of educational programming such as "Sesame Street" and "The Electric

Company." She found boys whose viewing had been restricted to display greater impulse control. Tower and colleagues observed 58 preschool children in regard to their concentration during play, defined as continuing in an activity, ignoring distractions, and not becoming hyperactive, who for 10 days either saw "Mister Rogers' Neighborhood," "Sesame Street," or a variety of educational films. Children high in imaginativeness, whose concentration was great enough initially that it may have been at its ceiling, did not change, but those low in imaginativeness increased in concentration in all three conditions.

Salomon (1979); J.L. Singer, Singer, and Rapaczynski (1984); J.L. Singer, Singer, Desmond, Hirsch, and Nicol (1988); Desmond, Singer, and Singer (1990); and C. Anderson and McGuire (1978) provide data on school age children. Salomon examined the perseverance of 114 Israeli children in the second grade in checking numbers read out loud in tables of random numerals after they had either watched "Sesame Street" or a variety of entertainment and nature films for eight days. He found that those who had seen "Sesame Street" displayed less perseverance. Singer and colleagues first examined 63 nine-year-olds in regard to their restlessness and ability to sit still in conjunction with television-viewing diaries covering the previous two years. They found small positive correlations between the viewing of violent entertainment and both restlessness and inability to sit still. Later, they collected data from 66 children in kindergarten and the first grade over a one-year period, and decided by its end that only among very heavy viewers whose parents were comparatively low in involving themselves in the child's experiences was there any positive association between television viewing and restlessness. Desmond and colleagues (1990), on the basis of their two-year longitudinal study of about 90 children and their parents, and the third-year follow-up of about 30 of the heaviest viewers covering ages five through nine, concluded that heavy television viewing was positively associated with greater restlessness, and that parental mediation was ineffectual either because it was rare, or when employed, often drew attention to violent scenes rather than discrediting them by moral judgment. Anderson and his colleague found similar small correlations between teacher ratings of impulsivity among several hundred third-, fourth-, and fifth-grade children and the viewing of violent entertainment by the third- and fourth-grade children and the total viewing of the fifth-grade children.

Thus, we have mixed results in regard to impulse control and its concomitants. There is some evidence, because of the positive findings that are reported, that television can affect these modes of behavior, but the effect is not strong, not entirely consistent for the same stimulus

("Sesame Street"), and it is unclear whether it is television itself (as is the case in some instances) or specific content (as is the case in others), except for the consistency with which violent programming has negative effects.

b. Perceptual, Spatial, and Temporal Responses It has been variously hypothesized that television can improve, at least under some conditions, the capability of young persons to employ skills in encoding, interpreting, drawing inferences from, and comprehending visual stimuli. However, both the amount of evidence and direction of results differ by type of skill.

Salomon (1974, 1979) offers four experiments on perceptual skills. Subjects were given either full exposure to a televised example of the use of a skill, an abbreviated example, the opportunity to practice the skill, no such experience, or some combination of these, and then were tested on the skill. Principal outcomes were that television can teach visual skills, and that effectiveness of such television instruction depends on initial skills.

In the first experiment, 80 eighth graders were randomly assigned to one of four conditions. In addition to the control group, there were three treatments. In each, subjects as they observed three paintings by Breughel under different circumstances were asked to record 80 details. In one, they simply saw slides of the paintings (which the investigator labels "activation"). In another, they saw 80 pairings of each painting with a subsequent detail ("short-circuiting"). In a third, they saw a television sequence that for each painting 80 times displayed the painting and then zoomed in on and then out from the detail ("modeling"). Subsequent performance in identifying distinct items from a new, complex visual montage was superior for those of low visual aptitude in the modeling condition but superior for those of high aptitude in the activation condition (Fig. 3.6).

This paradigm was varied somewhat in three subsequent experiments. Subjects were in the second, eighth, and ninth grades. Manipulations encompassed the effects of verbal rehearsal and truncated modeling and activation; modeling and short-circuiting in regard to the new task, the ability to transform three-dimensional objects into two dimensions or floor plans; and modeling and short-circuiting effects on children for a third task, the ability to recognize a displayed object from a different perspective.

The results of all four experiments are mutually supportive. Exposure to a visual process or conversion by television may be internalized; that is, learned. However, such internalization requires extensive exposure. Processing depends on initial aptitudes. There was an interaction not

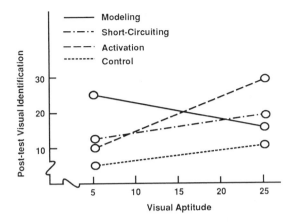

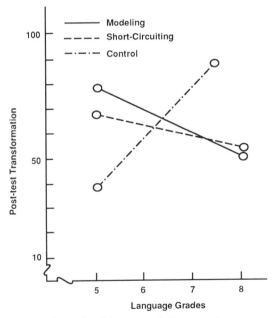

Fig. 3.6 Interaction of visual and language skills with televised instruction in visual processing. Adapted from Salomon, G. (1979). *Interaction of media, cognition, and learning.* San Francisco: Jossey-Bass.

only with visual skills but also with language skills (Fig. 3.6), with those better skilled doing well without televised instruction. Because everyday use of such skills would approximate the activation conditions, this implies that television may augment the visual skills of those low in such aptitude or lacking in compensatory language ability without adversely affecting those better prepared for such tasks. The net effect, if the demonstrated effect were to occur widely, would be to expand cognitive capacities.

Later, he presented preschool, second-grade, and third-grade Israeli children with six months of "Sesame Street," presumably a novel stimulus for them. On two tests of perceptual skills, the ability to order pictures in a logical sequence and the ability to discern a figure embedded in a pattern, the performance of schoolage children increased, while that of the preschool children did not. In addition, the schoolage children, on tests given only to them, increased their performance in recognizing elements part of a larger aggregation, understanding differences in perspective, and relating details to the whole. Over time, knowledge of the subject matter of "Sesame Street" did not predict the acquisition of perceptual skills, but the level of perceptual skills predicted acquisition of knowledge. Together, these findings suggest a "learning to learn" in which television teaches skills used in encoding its subject matter as well as teaching the subject matter. This interpretation is reinforced by the finding that correlations between amount of viewing and amount learned increased progressively over the six months.

Such effects occur with comparatively brief as well as lengthy exposure. When Salomon showed one group of second-grade Israeli children "Sesame Street" and another group entertainment and nature films for eight days, he found improved performance on the same set of perceptual tests just described by those who saw "Sesame Street."

Gadberry (1980) and Rovet (1983) provide supportive findings. The former found that six-year-old children placed on a restricted television regimen emphasizing educational programming improved in their ability to identify visual details. The latter examined the use of film versus practice with the physical objects to teach Canadian third-grade children to recognize whether an object seen from different perspectives had the same shape, the spatial rotation problem. Those who saw a film that explicitly and completely reviewed the rotation process and those who physically examined the objects did better and equally so, both immediately after the experience and two weeks later. Merely presenting the beginning and end states on film had no effect, while those who saw a portion of the process improved in performance but distinctly less so than for those viewing the complete operation.

Henderson and Rankin (1986) found, among 135 children of preschool age, that brief television segments demonstrating visually and by other means, such as verbal instruction, the principle of serial order (such as from large to small or tall to short) increased their performance at a seriation task. However, Hofmann and Flook (1980) found, among 24 four-year-old children, that a 24-minute film designed to teach shape recognition failed to have any effect, while a pretest, or actual practice, did; they interpret these outcomes as challenging the view that concrete–operational thought as construed by Piaget (Piaget & Inhelder, 1969) can be improved at this age by television programs.

It has been hypothesized (Greenfield, 1984) that television may enhance the ability to deal with spatial problems because of its implicit instruction in the rearranging of visual imagery. The sole empirical test of such a phenomenon occurs in the three-community experiment by T.M. Williams (1986) and colleagues. They had no hypothesis; they included a measure of spatial ability because it was part of a package with two other measures of cognitive performance, vocabulary and creativity. They employed the WISC block design subtest, which requires reproduction by manipulating blocks and by drawing of designs presented by the test administrator. Criteria are accuracy and speed. No interpretable findings emerged, except for a hint of the introduction of gender differences not present before the arrival of television. Scores for boys were higher than those for girls in Unitel and Multitel, while in Notel there was no gender difference before it received television.

In regard to temporal skills, B.Z. Hirsch and Kulberg (1987) asked about 100 children between the ages of 4 and 11 to judge the length of a variety of time segments whose beginning and end were signaled by an audio tone. Accuracy increased with age, but the amount of preschool television viewing was negatively associated with accuracy at later ages. On the other hand, Hayes and Kelly (1984) found among about 60 preschool children that the temporal ordering of events is much better understood when the presentation is visual than when it is aural. The former implies that greater everyday viewing interfered with the ability to estimate passage of time while the latter not only further documents the reliance of young children on the visual to interpret television but suggests that when they misunderstand the motives and consequences of actions or story narrative it may be because temporal order was conveyed aurally rather than visually.

The evidence indicates that sequences designed to do so and instructional programming can improve the perceptual skills of children and teenagers, but thorough, repetitive display of the process enhances the likelihood of such an effect. Perceptual skills in turn increase learning from educational programs. The small amount of evidence available confines such effects to those of school age. Television entertainment might have some positive effects, but they would be limited because, however varied the visual techniques, they are not designed, ordered, or repeated for instructional impact. There is no evidence that ordinary noninstructional television improves spatial abilities, and some, that it may interfere with the development of temporal judgment. There is also some evidence that the greater difficulty young children have in relating motives to behavior and subsequent consequences, and thus understanding televised narratives, is attributable to the conveying of temporal order by aural rather than visual means.

c. Imaginativeness It has been argued that by presenting visual images that are self-sufficient, occur at a predetermined pace, and are continuous, television inhibits young viewers from reflection, elaboration, supposition, and invention in regard to the narrative (J.L. Singer & Singer, 1981, 1983). Reading and radio listening, by comparison, ask more of the consumer, and thus ostensibly would be more effective in stimulating imaginative mental activity.

Lyle and Hoffman (1972a) found that half of their sample of about 275 children in the first grade told them that they sometimes or often used what they saw on television as a model for play with others, and 30% said they did so when playing by themselves. The anecdotes of parents invariably produced accounts of their children imitating something they had seen on television. The question that arises in regard to imaginative activity, which includes fantasy play, is whether such contributions are negative or positive. Do they represent the narrowing of options and the precluding of alternatives from which the child might otherwise draw, thereby stereotyping play, or do they provide a source for enjoyable, fruitful, rewarding experiences?

J.L. Singer and Singer (1976) assessed imaginative performance of 45 preschool children by observing whether elements not in the "perceptual environment" were introduced into play for two weeks before and after they had either seen a daily episode of "Mister Rogers' Neighborhood," seen those episodes with an adult who directed attention to important elements and encouraged emulation, or engaged in games with an adult. They report that all three groups increased in imaginativeness of play, with the games group increasing the most and the television-only group increasing the least.

Later, J.L. Singer and Singer (1981), in a longitudinal analysis, observed the play of 141 three and four year olds at four different times over a year, and each time obtained diaries from parents of their children's viewing, representing a two-week period before the observation.

Imaginativeness was unrelated to television viewing, although it was positively associated with states that most would judge favorably— language ability, positive affect, elation, and liveliness. It was also very stable over this period, suggesting that imaginativeness might be quite resistant to any influence of television.

Greer, Potts, Wright, and Huston (1982) observed the play of 32 same-sex pairs of children of preschool age after they had seen either high- or low-salience commercials, and found somewhat greater imaginative play after exposure to the high-salience commercials. However, this occurred only when they were clustered and not distributed over the accompanying program, suggesting that such an effect for child-pertinent television advertising requires concentrated exposure.

Tower, Singer, Singer, and Biggs (1979) similarly measured the use of imaginative fantasy by observing the play of 58 preschool children before and after two weeks during which they saw either episodes of "Mister Rogers' Neighborhood," "Sesame Street," or a variety of educational films, and hypothesized that effects on imaginativeness would be in descending order. No significant changes were recorded.

James and McCain (1982) observed the outdoor play of 36 children aged from three to seven years over seven weeks at a daycare center. They recorded 20 television-based games, which included physically imitating television characters; using television as the basis for play with objects, such as clothing a doll; repeating language from television; pretending to be television characters; and social interaction based on television. Some of the play was predominantly social by involving others; some was self-explorative by giving the child a chance to play a role, such as a strong "Super Woman." The themes of the television-based play were quite limited, but they were also themes that occur in nontelevision-based play. The authors conclude that television can "have positive consequences in terms of helping the children have fun, learn more about their feelings and abilities, introduce more variety in their play and interact with others" (p. 799).

Huston-Stein, Fox, Greer, Watkins, and Whitaker (1981) observed the play of 33 same-sex pairs of children of preschool age after viewing programs that varied in violence and activity. High-violence–high-activity programs decreased imaginative play; low-violence–low-activity programs increased it.

D.M. Zuckerman, Singer, and Singer (1980a) measured (by teacher ratings) the use of imagination in play of 232 children in the third, fourth, and fifth grades in a middle-class suburb. These ratings were positively related to intelligence and to the viewing of fewer programs featuring fantasy violence.

J.L. Singer, Singer, and Rapaczynski (1984) measured the imaginativeness of 63 children, aged from five through eight, over several years, by the Human Movement Inkblot test, an interview about favorite activities and games, and observation of play with blocks. Television viewing was measured by diaries maintained by parents. Lower preschool viewing, and especially less viewing of violent or physically arousing programs, was associated with superior inkblot performance at age eight. Two additional associations recorded include a positive one between interview scores and exposure to fantasy rather than realistic violent entertainment, and a negative one between the viewing of action–adventure programs and scores on the block play. The associations with television viewing were very small, if statistically significant, and more substantial predictors of the measures were attributes of the mother—the valuing of imagination, nonrigid child-rearing practices, orderly routines, and engaging in cultural activities.

Alexander, Ryan, and Munoz (1984) examined the interactions of six- and nine-year-old brothers while viewing television over several months, and concluded that a major amount of conversation derived from television was used to facilitate fantasy play. Reid and Frazer (1980) observed the behavior of nine families over a three-month period in regard to the responses of children, who ranged in age from 5 to 11, to commercials. They concluded that the commercials led to nontelevision activities, the making of social plans, conversations with parents, and fantasy play in front of the set.

C.C. Peterson, Peterson, and Carroll (1987) found, among about 300 West Australian males and females aged from 10 to 14 years, that heavy television viewers scored less well than light viewers on a test of imaginativeness. Similarly, Tucker (1987) found, among about 400 males with an average age of 15, that amount of television viewing was inversely correlated with a scale measuring imaginativeness.

Greenfield, Farrar, and Beagles-Roos (1986) and Greenfield and Beagles-Roos (1988) describe a series of experiments comparing children in the first through the fourth grade in their response to radio or television. When presented with identical, unfinished stories except for the animated component of the television version, imaginativeness in finishing the stories was greater for the radio version. However, comprehension, recall, and inference making were superior for the television version. Greenfield, Bruzzone, Koyamatsu, Satuloff, Nixon, Brodie, and Kingsdale (1987) describe several experiments comparing music videos with music alone among those varying from 10 years through college age. The younger the person, the greater the degree of lack of comprehension of the lyrics. Videos were analogous to television, and music to radio, in effects on imaginativeness or at least diversity in the way the meaning of a song was described. Greenfield and Beagles-Roos (1988) review a number of studies, encompassing an age range from preschool to adulthood, in which recall of principal story elements from television is superior to that from radio (Barrow & Westley, 1959; Gunter, 1979, 1980; Hayes, Kelly, & Mandel, 1986; Siegel, 1973; Vig, 1980; Waite, 1976), and speculate that historically "the growing importance of television means that children socialized by this medium may have more information but be less imaginative" (p. 88).

McIlwraith, Schallow, and Josephson have conducted a series of studies (McIlwraith & Schallow, 1982–1983, 1983; McIlwraith & Josephson, 1985; Schallow & McIlwraith, 1986–1987) on imaginative processes in regard to a variety of media among children and undergraduates. Typically, they find no association between amount of television viewing or any other quantitative measure of media consumption (book reading, movie going, or record listening) and positive constructive daydreaming or fantasy construction, defined as that which is "vivid" and "considered to be useful and pleasant." However, they do report continuities between type of fantasy and content, such as positive associations between science fiction consumption and ruminating about how things work. Among those of college age, viewing of general drama and comedies, and to a lesser degree music videos and entertainment features, were positively associated with pleasant, constructive fantasy. Fantasies of guilt and failure were positively associated with use of television to dispel negative mood states and with channel switching, and not with specific content or amount viewed, thus suggesting that these kinds of cognitions impel searchful viewing for relief rather than being attributable to what is seen on television. These data give no support to the view that television viewing interfered with imaginative processes.

We do not agree with D.R. Anderson and Collins (1988) that an alternative explanation for the apparent differential effects of radio and television is that the latter provides more information, so that "completing the story requires less elaboration" and completions are "more succinct and less repetitive" (p. 56), because we do not understand why a medium ostensibly richer in information, television, should lead to briefer, less complex accounts. Compared to radio and print, greater concrete information typically is an inherent property of television storytelling, and therefore greater informational delivery, while theoretically important, is not an alternative explanation but precisely the issue.

The evidence in behalf of some nefarious effect of television on imaginativeness is sparse. The reported inverse correlations with exposure are small and ambiguous as to causality. As a trait, it is stable and therefore not readily open to media influence. There is some evidence that it contributes constructively to play and fantasizing. Any effect is probably short-term, given the much stronger relationship imaginativeness has with factors in the family and home environment. There is some evidence that other media may be more provocative for imaginativeness, and thus use of one medium rather than another may stimulate greater or lesser imaginative activity at that time.

d. Creativity   Creativity is defined by the *Dictionary of Behavioral Science* (Wolman, 1989) as "The ability to produce something new, such as a new idea, a new scientific system, a new solution to a problem, a piece of art, sculpture, painting, architecture, or a piece of film, drama, music, or ballet" (p. 79). This is somewhat lofty to apply to children, but the emphases are the same—the ability to generate new ideas or to think about things in new or different ways.

Peirce (1983) evaluated the creativity of stories written by about 100 fifth-, seventh-, eighth-, and ninth-grade pupils on the basis of "entry into the world of fantasy, elaboration of creative ideas, use of dialogue and point of view." Creativity was negatively associated with amount of television viewed and positively associated with number of books read and with parental involvement, through rules and commentary, with television viewing.

Watkins (1988) asked about 80 young persons in the third, fifth, and eighth grades to write stories about real life and for television. Real-life stories were more complex than television stories, but this difference decreased as amount of viewing increased. By the eighth grade, the television stories were about three times more complex than real-life stories among those high in viewing. They were also longer, and higher on measures of affective tone and use of thoughts and emotions. Overall, television stories were more in accord with what is typical of the medium, and Watkins concludes that viewing shaped the way stories were told, including nontelevision stories. However, the characteristics of the eighth-grade television stories by heavy viewers hardly suggest any association between viewing and creativity.

Runco and Pedzek (1984) examined divergence of thought and ideational fluency—that is, originality and the generation of new ideas—among 64 children equally divided between those in the third and in the sixth grade after they heard a story by radio or heard and saw the same story on television. There were no differences between media, but as would be expected, the older children performed much better.

T.M. Williams (1986) and colleagues in their three-community experiment used the Alternative Uses and the Pattern Meaning tasks to assess the creativity of young persons in the fourth and seventh grades. The former asks for novel applications for such common objects as a chair, button, shoe, or car tire, while the latter seeks the identification of things that ambiguous drawings might represent. Neither places a limit on the number of answers. The first is considered a measure of divergent thinking, the second of ideational fluency.

The principal outcome was that the arrival of television in Notel was accompanied by a decided decline in scores on the Alternatives Uses task (Fig. 3.7). In the cross-sectional analysis (comparing different samples of the same grades in the three communities before and after Notel had television), young persons in Notel initially scored much

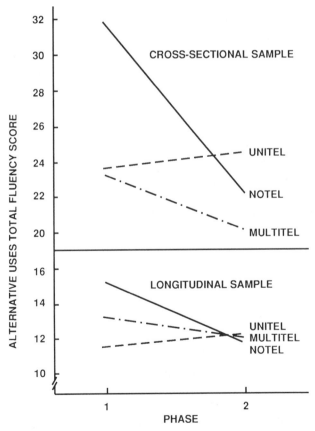

Fig. 3.7 Creativity and television. From Williams, T.M. (Ed.). (1986). *The impact of television: A natural experiment in three communities.* New York: Academic Press.

better than those in the two communities with television; after television arrived, the scores for the three communities were much alike. In the longitudinal sample (comparing scores for the same persons in the three communities at the two points in time), scores for the Notel sample decidedly decreased while those for the other two communities did not. This mutual support from two distinct modes of analysis gives the finding considerable credence.

Their conclusion that the introduction of television reduced the creativity of young persons is somewhat weakened by the failure of the Pattern Meanings task to lead to any interpretable differences. This is surely not because television enhanced the spatial abilities of young persons, since there is little if any evidence of such an effect. Thus, any effect is limited to divergent thinking, or the production of new ideas.

When they analyzed cross-sectional data on amount of television viewing and performance on the two tasks, neither in Unitel and Multitel before Notel received television, nor in the three communities after its arrival were there any relationships between viewing and either measure of creativity, except for a marginal negative one for Pattern Meanings at the second measurement, when data for all three communities were combined. When they examined such relationships for all the cognitive measures (alternative uses, pattern meaning, vocabulary, and block design), only for block design and only after Notel had received television was there a consistent negative association with viewing.

The evidence again gives no support to the view that television enhances spatial abilities. While the introduction of television may have decreased divergent thinking, the far more important finding (because television is about as disposable as the California freeway system) is that greater or lesser amounts of contemporary viewing would seem to make no difference.

C. CAUSATION

The role of television in the inverse association between viewing and achievement is far less clear than the fact that such a relationship exists. Is television the root, or the fruit?

One possibility is causation. Television would be required to contribute to the lesser levels of achievement, and the viewing would have to precede the lowered achievement in time order even if, in practice, they are observed synchronously.

Another is symptomatology. Greater television viewing would be the sign of the influence of some other factor. Nominees include lower mental ability, poorer prior grades, concurrent low achievement, social relationships that involve conflicts with parents or estrangement from peers, and family norms.

Much of the evidence concerns reading. It is the only subject on which there is direct evidence, it has been examined more often than any other, and it merits priority as the fundamental skill for achievement in many areas. It is possible (in fact, likely) that the involvement of television varies somewhat with subject matter, but on the whole, we would anticipate that what would hold for one would largely hold for others.

T.M. Williams (1986) and colleagues in their three-community experiment reach the conclusion that, despite some disparate outcomes, their data identify a negative effect of television on reading scores in the second and third grades and between the eighth and tenth grades. Their judgment is based on (a) the superiority, with intelligence controlled, of second-grade boys and girls in Notel before it received television (p. 50, Fig. 2.1); (b) the precipitous decline in third-grade cross-sectional scores adjusted for intelligence in Notel after the acquisition of television (p. 53, Fig. 2.3); (c) the failure of Notel teenagers to increase their scores between the eighth and tenth grades, while those in Unitel and Multitel did so (p. 60, Fig. 2.7); and (d) the much lower scores adjusted for intelligence in the eighth grade throughout in Multitel, while Unitel and Notel did not differ from one another (p. 55, Fig. 2.4).

We are less sure. First, in two of these instances the two other communities exhibit trends similar to those of Notel, if somewhat less pronounced (p. 50, Fig. 2.1; p. 53, Fig. 2.3). Second, the almost identical eighth-grade scores for Unitel and Notel throughout, while Multitel scored much lower, are incompatible with the interpretation that television had a negative effect (p. 55, Fig. 2.4). Instead, Notel scores should have declined, and Unitel scores should have resembled those for Multitel, not Notel. Third, the longitudinal scores between grades two and four (that is, when the same children were measured before and after Notel received television) are strikingly inconsistent with a negative effect of television (p. 57, Fig. 2.5). In the second grade, before television arrived, Notel children scored better in reading ability when intelligence was taken into account than did those in the other two communities. Between the second and fourth grades, the scores of these Notel children increased at the same rate as the scores of those in the other two communities, and Notel maintained its superiority in the fourth grade. Thus, there are elements not supportive of or inconsistent with a negative effect.

Hornik (1978) obtained data on reading progress between the seventh and the ninth grade of three samples of teenagers in El Salvador. Some of the families obtained television sets during this period; others did not. Hornik concluded that the acquisition of a television set impaired achievement by about 10%.

This leaves us with the reported correlations between television exposure and achievement. One test of the plausibility that television contributes causally is whether the negative associations survive when controls are imposed for other variables. If so, alternative explanations for the association are eliminated, and the causal hypothesis is strengthened.

However, there are three important caveats. First, post hoc analyses, in the absence of theory that is either supported or disconfirmed by the configuration of findings, cannot be convincing in regard to causal linkages. Second, no correlational analysis can fully eliminate the possibility that an unmeasured third variable is responsible for an observed association between two measured variables, although the probability decreases with the number and pertinence of the variables controlled. Third, variables controlled and ages vary across studies, and the role of the former may vary with the latter, so that crucial combinations may have been ignored.

Because of the huge number of cases on which they are based, the negative associations so far recorded in the CAP, NAEP, the two HSB sets, and ESA data are impressive. As we have seen, the negative association in the CAP data survives controls for subject matter, three grade levels, and socioeconomic status, and in the NAEP data, survives controls for three grades, socioeconomic status, and ethnicity.

However, there are several studies in which a wider range of variables is controlled. These include three very large samples, about 28,000 seniors in the HSB data (Keith *et al.*, 1986), about 10,000 eighth graders in a CAP follow-up (Fetler, 1984), and about 5000 in the sophomore–senior HSB panel (Gaddy, 1986). Among the others, sample sizes range from about 125 (Burton, Calonico, & McSeveney, 1979) through several hundred to a few thousand (Morgan & Gross, 1980; Potter, 1987; Ridley-Johnson, Cooper, & Chance, 1983; D.F. Roberts, Bachen, Hornby, & Hernandez-Ramos, 1984; Walberg & Tsai, 1984–1985). Ages have ranged from the first grade through high school seniors. Variables have included mental ability; parental involvement, either generally or in television use; availability of other media; socioeconomic status, gender, and ethnicity; beliefs and perceptions about the media; and engaging in homework. All report, before the imposition of the control variables, statistically significant negative correlations between

amount of television viewing and achievement, which in three cases
was for reading (Ridley-Johnson *et al.*, 1983; D.F. Roberts *et al.*, 1984;
Walberg & Tsai, 1984–1985); one for an average of language, mathematics, and reading (Burton *et al.*, 1979); one for a balanced combination of
reading and mathematics (Keith *et al.*, 1986); one for a scale covering a
variety of areas (Potter, 1987); one for reading, vocabulary, and mathematics (Gaddy, 1986); and two for reading, writing, and mathematics
(Fetler, 1984; Morgan & Gross, 1980).

Gaddy's analysis of the sophomore–senior HSB panel data gives the
impression that when other variables are controlled, the negative associations between viewing and achievement disappear (Table 3.4).
However, we believe that a careful examination of the data leads to a
very different interpretation. Gaddy controlled for an extraordinary
number of variables and then calculated the association between earlier

Table 3.4
Cross-Lagged Coefficients between Sophomore and Senior Years—Television as
Independent Variable Including All Control Variables[a]

Dependent variable	All students beta n = 5074	Blacks beta n = 2365	Females beta n = 4997
Vocabulary achievement	−.004	.015	−.004
Reading achievement	−.001	.006	.006
Mathematics level 1	−.012	.012	−.014
Mathematics level 2	−.009	−.017	−.017
Grades	−.008	−.008	−.003

Dependent variable	High resource beta n = 2974	Medium resource beta n = 3960	Low resource beta n = 3112
Vocabulary achievement	−.001	.023	−.012
Reading achievement	.011	.015	−.013
Mathematics level 1	.000	.000	−.004
Mathematics level 2	−.014	−.017	−.022
Grades	−.002	−.009	−.013

[a] In addition to the variables listed above, each cross-lagged regression equation includes sex, race, hispanicity, private school attendance, academic program, father's and mother's education, number of siblings and parents at home, family income, educational possessions (5 measures), homework (two measures), absenteeism and tardiness, frequency of reading for pleasure and the front page of the newspaper.
All underlined coefficients are significant at .05 (one-tailed, corrected for design effect).
Adapted from Gaddy, G.D. (1986). Television's impact on high school achievement. *Public Opinion Quarterly, 50,* 340–359.

(sophomore) amount of viewing and later (senior) achievement. This procedure (a) confines any contribution to *changes* in achievement over the period that, this late in the educational process, one would expect to be minor at best, and (b) includes as controls some factors that may in fact be the *consequence* of extensive amounts of viewing. It eliminates any synchronous contribution of television viewing. The two-year lag is additionally problematic, given the evidence (Chapter II) that earlier viewing predicts no more than about a fourth (and with a cavalier allowance for unreliability, far less than half) of viewing two years later; this means that the earlier measure is no substitute for a later measure. His controls for educational resources in the home eliminate the influence of number of books, availability of an encyclopedia, and subscribing to a newspaper, but these are artifacts whose availability may be foreclosed by the centrality of television in the household or heavy use of the medium by the young respondent; the same can be said for controlling for early amount of reading, reading achievement, and vocabulary. Thus, the design minimizes the likelihood of recording an association; the controls may in part mask the process by which television may have a negative effect.

Our interpretation is that variation in achievement is so constrained that negligible associations with viewing are inevitable and thus do not impugn the frequently reported negative correlations between viewing and achievement. The data permit a test. If we are correct, the association of other variables with achievement also should be very small, because those associations would be constrained by the same controls. As the author comments:

> One logical basis for comparison is the set of estimates for other media activities, such as reading for pleasure or reading the front page of the newspaper, and "obvious" sources of academic effects such as high school program, private school attendance, and time spent on homework.

He continues:

> The estimated effect of TV (measured by betas averaged across the four achievement tests for the total sample) . . . is not radically different in absolute value from the other estimates: reading the newspaper (.001), private school attendance (.019), homework time (.021), reading for pleasure (.034), and being in an academic program (.042). (p. 355)

The test is passed.

It is of passing interest that the association of achievement with television is the only one with a negative sign, but we would conclude nothing from this, because of the minute magnitude, other than the one that Gaddy reaches: the data clearly support the hypothesis of no benefit. The major point is that the data do not challenge the likelihood of some negative influence of viewing on achievement.

Of the remaining eight, the negative association survives in five (Burton *et al.*, 1979; Fetler, 1984; Keith *et al.*, 1986; Morgan & Gross, 1980; Potter, 1987), although in one instance (Morgan & Gross, 1980) only for reading among the three basic skills examined, fails to do so in two (Roberts *et al.*, 1984; Walberg & Tsai, 1984–1985), and is not throughly tested in one in which the authors argue that socioeconomic status as a factor is ruled out by the use of homogeneous populations (Ridley-Johnson *et al.*, 1983). In one failure (Roberts *et al.*, 1984), the degree of association drops below the threshold of statistical significance, but the signs remain negative. Those that survive include the two largest samples (Keith *et al.*, 1986; Fetler, 1984), a sizable variety of control variables (six and five, in the most populous cases), and the full range of ages. These data modestly but importantly support a causal interpretation. They are ambiguous as to time order, but they document, within the variables examined, an independent contribution to lowered achievement by television viewing.

The remaining alternative is to examine the evidence on the process by which one or another relationship might come about. In so doing, we examine the strength of the varying explanations of *how* rather than of *what*, in hope that we may find one with better support than another.

D. PROCESS

1. Cognitive Factors

D.R. Anderson and Collins (1988) draw on a number of sources to propose an elegant and subtle mechanism by which television viewing might interfere with reading ability, and thereby achievement in general. They speculate that "the comprehension skills developed through television viewing are initially irrelevant to reading or may even interfere with reading" (p. 64). They cite the finding of Pezdek, Lehrer, and Simon (1984) that when children in the third and sixth grades were presented with stories by television, radio, or text with pictures, the comprehension of radio and text was positively associated, but there was no association between comprehension of television and text. They suggest at these ages "a synergistic audiovisual integration unique to TV viewing" (p. 64). That is, the addition of the visual imagery of television changes the processing of the audio from being similar to that for print to something different. They cite as supportive the findings of Beagles-Roos and Gat (1983) and Greenfield and Beagles-Roos (1988), in which recall by children of stories conveyed by radio or television differed in quantity, creativity, and inferential bases, and an analogous finding by Meringoff (1980a) in comparing the recall by seven and nine year olds of stories conveyed by an illustrated book or by television; in each case, television was associated with greater recall of action and greater reliance on visual imagery. They suggest that "extensive experience with television may subtly retard the ability to listen without a visual frame of reference" (p. 64)—and by implication, we would emphasize, the ability to process text, or read. Finally, they conclude that if such an effect occurs, it is limited to the younger ages, because Field and Anderson (1985) report that the correlation between looking and listening to television decreases with age, and Pezdek, Simon, Stoeckert, and Kieley (1985) report that, among young adults, comprehension of text and television are positively correlated. Although the conjectured effect would occur at the ages when reading ability is being acquired, the evidence on the whole does not support the view that the visual imagery interferes with the processing of the audio, but that it takes precedence over it. If what occurs is distraction from rather than disruption of textual processing, then any effect on the acquisition of reading skills would be negligible.

Armstrong and Greenberg (1990) interpret deficits among college students in the performance of cognitive tasks completed in the presence of an operating television set as attributable to a suppression of cognitive capacity. Affected were reading comprehension, spatial problem solving, and cognitive flexibility. The 84 subjects completed these and other tasks with or without television programming as background. The data favor a diminution of capacity over alternative explanations such as heightened arousal, decreased linguistic processing, or the diversion of attention. They suggest that "those who habitually combine homework, reading, and other intellectually demanding activities with television are likely to be getting less benefit from them," and that such effects "could easily translate into substantial cumulative effects on intellectual achievement" (p. 379).

There is some evidence that television viewing, and in particular the viewing of violent entertainment, might contribute to a lowered degree of impulse control. If so, we would expect television to affect achievement negatively by reducing the ability of children to stay with a task, and this would be especially deleterious for reading in the first through third grades, when children are acquiring the basic skills (Chall, 1983).

Both the large-scale inquiries into the introduction of television in Great Britain (Himmelweit *et al.*, 1958) and in the United States (Schramm *et al.*, 1961) found that, in a limited way, television might facilitate achievement by encouraging reading. In the British study,

programs sometimes stimulated interests, and these often were translated by children and especially teenagers into subjects they pursued by
reading. In the American study, intellectually brighter young children
actually viewed greater amounts of television because of their wide-
ranging curiosity, implying that a topic made salient by television
might be pursued by reading. However, such effects are likely to occur
only among those who have no problems with reading, and therefore
any contributions by such inducements to achievement would be null
or minor.

One-half to three-fourths of the variance in achievement scores typically is accounted for by mental ability (Fetler, 1984). What remains
does not seem readily attributable to the effects of television on cognitive performance. The most likely candidate, despite the mixed evidence, is impulse control, because of the ages that would be affected.
The interference process (D.R. Anderson & Collins, 1988) is not supported by the evidence, and the decreased capacity effect (Armstrong &
Greenberg, 1990), while probably real enough for some young persons
in some circumstances, does not seem to explain much. Fetler (1984), in
his CAP sample of about 10,600 eighth graders, found only a comparatively minute association (negative) between homework-in-front-of-
the-television and achievement—about one-fourth of that for amount
of viewing (negative), one-seventh of that for amount of homework
(positive), and one-tenth of that for socioeconomic status (positive).

2. Displacement

T.M. Williams (1986) and colleagues propose that television displaces
time that could be spent learning to read. They argue that learning to
read is hard work for a child, while television offers an intellectually
undemanding alternative. Such displacement would permanently suppress scholastic achievement by leaving children and teenagers below-
par readers.

Chall (1983) specifies the key period as the first through the third
grade. Mastery of the alphabet and the matching of letters to spoken
words occurs in the first and second grades. The foundation for reading
fluency is laid in the second and third grades, when reading occurs
primarily as skills practice rather than for information or enjoyment. By
the fourth grade, basic skills have been acquired, and children begin to
read for the rewards of content.

Once basic skills are acquired they will be retained regardless of later
experience, including amount and content of television viewed. This is
why Williams and colleagues place particular emphasis on their

second- and third-grade data, which they interpret as identifying a negative effect of television during the important acquisition period.

Those most affected would be those least able to cope. As T.M. Williams and colleagues write:

> Television provides a more attractive alternative, for most children, but especially for those who have most difficulty learning to read and who need to practice most, namely, those who are less intelligent (or have a learning disability). The brighter children either need less practice and get enough practice in school or practice more. (p. 397)

The CAP, NAEP, and HSB sophomore–senior panel data and the displacement model are reminiscent of the findings of Schramm and colleagues (1961). The latter found an inverse relationship among children scoring high on tests of mental ability between amount of television viewed and scholastic achievement; among those scoring low, there was a positive relationship; and among those of moderate ability, viewing was unrelated to achievement. In all four sets of data, an inverse relationship between viewing and achievement is clearest among those from whom the most would be expected: in the CAP and NAEP cases, those from households of higher socioeconomic status; in the case of HSB, households with greater educational resources; and in the case of Schramm and colleagues, those of greater mental ability. In all four sets of data, the relationship is null, weak, or even to some extent positive among those from whom the least might be expected: in the CAP and NAEP cases, those not fluent in English or lowest in socioeconomic status; in the HSB case, those minimal in household resources; and in the case of Schramm and colleagues, those of lower mental ability.

The pattern invites an expansion of the model proposed by Williams and colleagues: Television viewing is inversely related to achievement when it displaces an intellectually and experientially richer environment, and it is positively related when it supplies such an environment. This is not only consistent with the few signs of a limited positive association, but also with the less pronounced CAP negative association in the sixth than the twelfth grade, where academic demands would be greatest.

The developmental model described by Schramm and colleagues (1961) is pertinent. Self-selection of media experience in amount, type, and character is a function of mental ability and social background. It predicts, as occurs in the CAP and NAEP data, that heavy viewers, but particularly those in the upper strata, would perform less well scholastically. Their famous dictum that what the child brings to television is as important as what television brings to the child also applies, for some or all of the positive slopes may represent those broadening their experience by moderate viewing rather than what television provides educationally, and this would be particularly likely among those not fluent in English. Thus, the extremely limited extent to which positive or even neutral slopes are found indicates that contributions to scholastic achievement by television are few or nil.

3. Social and Environmental Influences

In addition to the ESA aggregation, S. Neuman (1988) analyzed a 70,000 NAEP sample of 9, 13, and 17 year olds for factors associated with the inverse association between reading achievement and viewing. The amount of time spent reading, outside of assignments, on the average declines somewhat between 9 and 13. This does not contradict the model of Schramm and colleagues (1961), which proposed a proportionally greater emphasis on print use with increasing age, and especially so among those of greater mental ability, a group distant from the average. Reading achievement was positively associated with reading outside of assignments. On the whole, achievement was greatest for regular readers and moderate viewers. Heavy viewing (more than six hours a day) was consistently associated with lesser achievement, regardless of the regularity of reading. Reading for enjoyment and reading frequency, as one would expect, were positively associated. Thus, reading, reading achievement, and television viewing are compatible at moderate but not heavy levels of viewing.

S. Neuman (1988) surprisingly found only a minute negative association between frequency of reading and amount of viewing, although a possible explanation is the insensitivity of the reading measure (rarely, monthly, weekly, or daily), which is akin to whether print is used at all. The initial CAP data measured television use, homework, and outside reading by amount of time spent daily, and are more valid (Fig. 3.8). In the sixth grade, the associations between viewing and these two activities are inverse, while in the twelfth they are positive, and more time is spent on homework and outside reading.

Nevertheless, except for those who in the twelfth grade spent a very great deal of time on outside reading, there was, in both grades and at every level of time spent on homework or outside reading, a negative association between reading achievement and viewing. These data suggest a developmental change in which the relationship between the medium and homework and outside reading changes from displacement to compatibility, with the implication that to some degree, be-

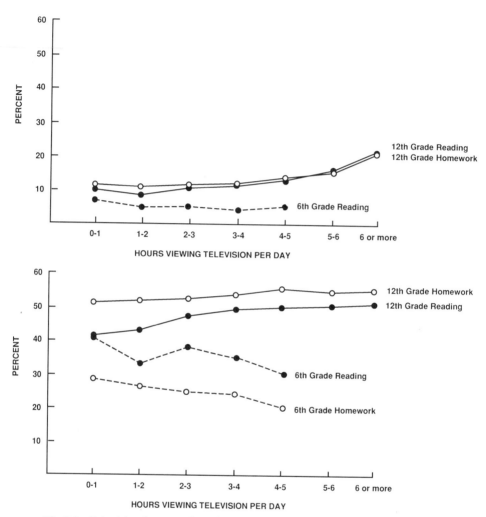

Fig. 3.8   Television, homework, and reading in the sixth and twelfth grades. Adapted from California Assessment Program. (1980). *Student achievement in California schools, 1979–80 annual report: Television and student achievement.* Sacramento: California State Department of Education.

cause of the increased likelihood that they are done in conjunction with viewing, the quality of the latter two may be adversely affected.

S.B. Neuman and Prowda (1982), using a sample of about 7800 drawn from the fourth, eighth, and eleventh grades for the 1978–1979 Connecticut statewide assessment of reading proficiency, found amount of viewing inversely associated with reading ability, with the magnitude of the negative association increasing with grade level. In contrast, reading for pleasure consistently was positively associated with reading ability.

Morgan (1980) in a sample of about 200 males and females from whom data were obtained over three years found that the reading comprehension scores of those high and low in mental ability tended to converge as amount of television viewing increased, and as one would expect the narrowing of differences is primarily attributable to the sharp decline in scores of those high and moderate in ability. In the larger sample (Morgan & Gross, 1980) from which the panel of 200 was drawn, amount of viewing and reading achievement were negatively associated and this association withstood controls for sex, grade, socioeconomic status, mental ability, time spent on homework, and time spent reading for oneself. Over the three years, the correlation between television viewing and reading for oneself shifted from negative to positive. This provides strong confirmation of the developmental trend in the CAP data in which associations between viewing and homework and outside reading shift from negative to positive between the 6th and 12th grades. Morgan also records a qualitative difference in reading for oneself in the later period:

> Heavy viewers are significantly more likely than light viewers to prefer stories about love and families, teenage stories, and true stories about stars. Light viewers . . . choose science fiction, mysteries, and general non-fiction. (p. 164)

Morgan concludes that "these favorite genres suggest that the reading content of heavy viewers reflects common television programming"; we would say that the reading of light viewers includes a greater proportion of reality content. These data indicate that not only may the homework and outside reading of heavy viewers be inferior in execution because more of it occurs in conjunction with television viewing, but that the subject matter of what is read by heavy viewers is less likely to make any contribution to achievement.

Keith and colleagues (1986) found, in their sample of more than 28,000 seniors, that homework was positively associated with achievement, and that parental involvement in these young persons' lives was associated with increased time spent on homework. At the same time, they found no evidence that television and homework competed for the same blocks of time, because the amount of homework typically demanded was modest. This implies, at least for the older teenager, that while those viewing very great amounts of television might score higher on achievement if they substituted homework for some of that viewing, for most young persons the two activities are not in serious conflict. Morgan and Gross (1982) similarly reported associations among high school students between poor reading skills and lower intelligence, greater television viewing, lower family socioeconomic status, and less reading.

In the spring of 1981, the CAP (1982) collected data from more than 15,000 sixth graders (a sample of 7%) in which the relationships between family socioeconomic status, television viewing, and achievement found in the much larger sixth- and twelfth-grade data collection the previous year were confirmed. The major contributions concern heavy and light viewers (Table 3.5), and programs viewed (Table 3.6).

Heavy viewers (defined in this instance as those above the ninetieth percentile in amount of viewing) were above average in doing homework in front of the set, and watching in the morning and late at night, below average in watching public television, and said they watched more than when younger. Light viewers (defined in parallel fashion—those in the bottom 10% of viewers, excluding those who said they viewed no television at all), exhibited the opposite in each of these respects. They were below average when heavy viewers were above average, above average when heavy viewers were below average, and said they watched less television than when younger.

Table 3.5
Heavy versus Light Viewers: Sixth Grade

Area rated	Heavy viewers	Light viewers
Amount of viewing	68.7	34.6
Overall achievement	44.2	53.4
Parent occupational status	46.2	53.6
Homework while viewing	53.0	46.5
Viewing before school	53.9	45.7
Watch TV late	54.3	44.9
Parents watch same programs	52.4	46.8
Discuss TV with parents	53.9	47.8
No rules on what you watch	51.3	47.6
Watch public TV	45.1	51.8

Note: The heavy-viewer group watched more than 6 hours, while the light viewers watched less than an hour per day. Between-group comparisons were significant at $p < .001$ for all variables in the profile.

From Fetler, M. (1984). Television viewing and school achievement. *Journal of Communication, 34,* 104–118.

Table 3.6
Popularity of Selected Programs: Sixth Grade

Overall popularity ranking	Title of show	Percentage responding "regularly"				
			Socioeconomic status by quartile*			
		Overall	1	2	3	4
1	"Dukes of Hazzard"	63.3	52.2	64.2	67.9	65.2
2	"Happy Days"	62.4	49.1	56.1	69.9	74.1
3	"Love Boat"	57.0	51.4	55.2	59.2	60.4
4	Cartoons	51.5	38.1	47.3	58.6	59.7
5	"Different Strokes"	51.5	42.6	50.6	52.5	66.5
11	"M*A*S*H"	41.1	40.1	45.8	43.0	34.2
16	"Dallas"	33.8	25.5	35.0	36.0	40.0
20	"Incredible Hulk"	27.7	14.3	24.7	30.7	42.3
25	"Charlie's Angels"	24.2	14.5	23.2	24.3	37.6
35	"National News"	17.5	17.0	19.4	15.4	19.4
39	"Lobo"	13.8	8.0	9.4	17.1	20.6

* 1 represents the highest, and 4, the lowest socioeconomic status quartile.
From California Assessment Program. (1982). *Survey of sixth grade school achievement and television viewing habits.* Sacramento: California State Department of Education.

Overall, the most popular programs at this time for this age group were "Dukes of Hazzard," "Happy Days," "The Love Boat," cartoons, and "Different Strokes." Of 81 programs on which data were obtained, all but six were watched more by children from households low in socioeconomic status. The six watched more frequently by those from households of high socioeconomic status were "M*A*S*H," "Benson," "Sneak Previews," "All Creatures Great and Small," "60 Minutes," and "Jacques Cousteau."

As reported earlier (Chapter I), there were differences in the types of programs preferred by heavy and light viewers. For most programs, heavy viewers were more likely to have watched than light viewers, but there was a much greater emphasis on light entertainment—in particular, situation comedies, prime-time soaps, and action–adventure—in their 15 most-watched programs. By contrast, the 15 most-watched programs of light viewers were largely informational in character, with some comparatively serious entertainment. These are not merely reflections of socioeconomic differences, because for the total sample the upper and lower quartiles were much alike in the relative frequency with which specific programs were viewed. Young persons who are comparatively very light viewers thus are instrumental and information-oriented in their use of television; for them, television does not distract from consumption of what Schramm and colleagues called reality content and probably enriches it.

Centrality of television in the household thus is a dimension that has implications for scholastic achievement. At the extremes, amount of viewing is a predictor of types of programs viewed. Very light and very heavy viewers are distinct groups differing from each other not only in how much, but also in what they view and in the social circumstances of their viewing.

4. Patterns

What, then, should one conclude? We believe several patterns are discernible:

1. The inverse associations between socioeconomic status and reading, and between mental ability and reading, the turning away from television toward print with the passage from childhood to the teenage years, and the special population that apparently makes up young people who are very light viewers lead us to believe that young people who are able and especially those who are highly efficient at reading will come to watch less television. Thus, some of the negative association between viewing and reading and other achievement is caused by the behavior of brighter young persons who are able or highly proficient readers.

2. Television consumption is typically greater among young persons of lower mental ability, those with conflicts with parents or peers (except probably for those from households low in socioeconomic status for whom viewing typically already is high), those in households where the centrality of television is high, and those who perceive no other activity as more necessary or rewarding than watching television. These same factors (representing individual traits, social relationships, household norms, and personal values) would be expected to be associated with lower achievement. In most cases, they would interfere with effective acquisition of basic skills, with the mastering of any subject, and with the completion of assigned tasks. In the case of households high in television centrality, we would expect the interference with achievement to go far beyond the amount of time devoted to television. Young persons in such households typically will have parents who have a low regard for reading and high esteem for television (remember, these are households in which parents themselves are typically high in television consumption); infrequently will have examples of adults reading, and especially of adults reading what Schramm and colleagues (1961) called reality content; and seldom will have reading material, and especially of that kind, available in the home. Young persons in such house-

holds would experience few constraints in the dividing of their time between television and other activities, such as homework, in a way that decidedly favors television, thus implying that along with a low regard for reading, there will be a low regard for scholastic achievement, or at least the means by which it must be attained. For blacks, of course, centrality makes less difference as a variable because of the much greater frequency of high centrality among households higher in socioeconomic status; however, one would expect the same argument to apply to those in households lower in socioeconomic status when centrality is high. Thus, a portion of the negative association between television viewing and achievement is attributable to young persons not performing well because of traits, dispositions, circumstances, or some combination of the three.

3. Greater amounts of television viewing until the late teenage years are associated with lesser amounts of reading for oneself, although the two (at least when the term monitoring is taken as accurately describing the experience of following a television program) are certainly compatible. However, this compatibility is probably limited to lighter reading, and reading that can be done episodically. On the whole, those who view more, read less, and this applies in particular to regular reading and to the consumption of more demanding content. In the later teenage years, the earlier inverse associations between viewing and reading become positive. The same pattern holds for homework. However, at all ages, there is an inverse association between achievement and viewing, and this holds regardless of the amount of time spent on homework or reading for oneself. The sole qualification is that the negative relationship is markedly less pronounced among those who read a very great deal for self-satisfaction; their level of achievement is distinctly higher. An analogous pattern for homework is only marginally observable. The amount and quality of both reading and homework appear to be negatively affected by viewing, and particularly reading, so that reading and other skills would not be maintained. The quality of the experience is a particularly important factor among teenagers. We have no doubt that a major contribution is made by the viewing behavior of those who in any case would perform less well, but the data thus hint that a small share of the negative association between achievement and viewing is attributable to the influence of viewing.

4. In the three-community experiment of T.M. Williams and colleagues (1986), we were about as impressed by the gains and maintained superiority of Notel between the second and fourth grades (p. 57, Fig. 2.5) and the ambiguous trends (p. 50, Fig. 2.1; p. 53, Fig. 2.3) and standings (p. 55, Fig. 2.4)—all evidence counter to a negative effect—as with the transient superiority of Notel boys and girls before television

arrived (p. 50, Fig. 2.1) and the precipitous decline in third-grade scores in Notel after the arrival of television (p. 53, Fig. 2.3). Thus, in the sole instance in North America of a direct, experimental test of a causal contribution by television to lowered achievement, the evidence in regard to reading is contradictory.

5. Television viewing, at certain points in life when basic skills are being acquired, nevertheless may displace or conflict with their effective acquisition. In the former, television would take time away from needed practice. In the latter, it would cultivate cognitive processing skills not entirely compatible with the processing of audio or textual content. Both processes are tenable, but between the two, we assign greater credibility to the former. Most of the attention has focused on reading, but we believe that the same paradigm in which there is a critical period for acquisition of basic skills essentially applies also to mathematics and writing. Thus, the evidence supports some contribution by television viewing to lowered achievement.

6. The negative associations between television viewing and reading achievement are greatest for heavy viewers, the socioeconomically advantaged, and those of higher mental ability, and the types of programming most likely to be involved in these associations are action–adventure, comedy, cartoons, and other light entertainment. This is the type of programming favored on the whole by the viewer who would be described as ritualistic. These outcomes emerge from our analyses, but they are in accord with the conclusions of the recent review by Beentjes and Van der Voort (1988), who specify these four factors as putting young viewers at risk in regard to reading.

7. Negative associations between viewing and achievement have been recorded across a wide spectrum of grades, basic skills, and other subjects; at the higher grades there is no sign of curvilinearity or flatness, and the negative slope is more pronounced. Persisting deficits in basic skills surely account for some of this, but the intercorrelations across the years in amount of viewing are insufficient to explain this pattern. This leads to the rejection of displacement at a critical period as the sole process, despite the likelihood of lower achievement by most and higher viewing by many of those affected earlier. The evidence thus supports a three-factor process in which large amounts of viewing not only (a) displace skill acquisition but also (b) interfere with further practice, or skill development and maintenance, and (c) lower the quality or value by decreased capacity of practice done in conjunction with television.

If there is no more than symptomatology, we argue that, in the case of scholastic achievement, the symptom is part of the problem. Part of the

solution, however achieved, is shifting some of the television viewing
time to more scholastically relevant activities.

We reach a somewhat different conclusion. We display our interpretation (acknowledging that not all data are in agreement) in a mock path
analysis (Fig. 3.9). We have based our paths and the direction and
strength of the association on the sample sizes, quality of measure, and

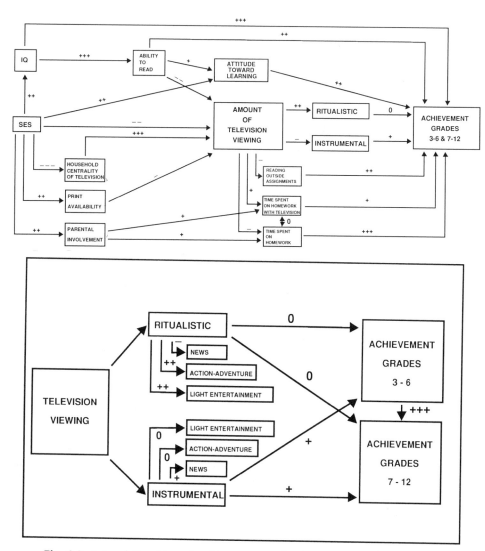

Fig. 3.9 Interrelationships of achievement and other variables. Large (>.50) =
+++/−−−; substantial (.21–.49) = ++/−−; small (.06–.20) = +/−; null (.00–.05) = 0.

frequency of outcomes in the various sources. Why do we not simply use the one path analysis available (Keith *et al.*, 1986)? Because it only includes seven of the nonachievement variables, so we incorporated its findings in constructing a more comprehensive picture.

We see mental ability and household socioeconomic status as fundamental, and the household environment (centrality of television, availability of print media, and parental involvement, in our model) as a substantial predictor of amount and kind of television viewed. For blacks, centrality by itself is less significant; however, we would expect the other factors to apply and for centrality to play a role in households lower in socioeconomic status. Reading outside of assignments and completion of homework affect achievement, and are negatively associated with amount of television viewed. We take age into account, with a few of the factors having different strengths of association with achievement early (grades 3–6) and late (grades 7–12), with early achievement a major predictor of later achievement. We take the ideologically cowardly but analytically conservative and (we think) justifiable route of partitioning the relationship among the possible explanations with somewhat more accorded to nontelevision than television factors. We think the pattern applies to scholastic achievement in general, because the principal factors are independent of any special characteristics of reading. The empirical justification, of course, is that wherever measured, the results are largely parallel, whatever the area of achievement. Thus, we think the evidence indicates a modest causal contribution by television to lesser achievement, with viewing in excess of a modest-to-moderate amount the major factor.

KNOWLEDGE, BELIEFS, AND PERCEPTIONS

IV

What it means to view, and what viewing means for time, has brought us to questions of what time spent with television means. Our initial focus was on scholastic achievement and associated abilities. We now turn to a more diffuse, less socially circumscribed range of cognitive behavior—what young persons know, believe, and perceive. We begin with general knowledge and conclude with social cognition, or the synthesizing of impressions into a world view. In between, we examine three specific topics: violence, sex roles, and ethnicity.

A. GENERAL KNOWLEDGE

Both Schramm, Lyle, and Parker (1961) in the United States and Himmelweit, Oppenheim, and Vince (1958) in Great Britain, in their large-scale inquiries, found limited effects on knowledge attributable to the introduction of television. Schramm and colleagues concluded that most effects involved knowledge about television entertainment. Himmelweit and colleagues found increases in knowledge about geography, science, sports, music, handicrafts, and household chores, but none for English literature, history, nature or rural studies, art and architecture, current affairs, or religion. One would expect such effects to have been more frequent in Great Britain because they would be contingent on broadcast content, and the BBC, chartered to serve educational and cultural needs, far more often covered such topics than the profit-driven American system.

Television nevertheless may contribute to what young persons believe in important ways, when it brings them information not available

139

from alternative sources. The examination by DeFleur and DeFleur
(1967) of occupational knowledge provides an example. They interviewed about 240 children aged from 6 to 13 years, using 4 × 5 inch
cards with figures drawn to represent three distinct sets of occupations:
personal contact occupations, or those the child ordinarily would encounter; television contact occupations, derived from a six-month analysis of entertainment programming; and general culture occupations,
defined as those with which adults would be familiar, but children
would not. The children were asked to describe the occupations, and
they were ranked in regard to prestige by both the children and their
mothers.

The children expressed greater understanding of occupations with
which they had no experience that were featured regularly on television
(Table 4.1). The pattern was the same for accurate ranking of occupational prestige. Upper- and middle-class children performed better than
those from households of low socioeconomic status. The rankings became more similar as age increased, and increasingly came to resemble
those of the mother, reflecting either socialization by the parent, ac-
culturation, or both. There was more sameness in the rankings among
the children and greater agreement in the rankings by children and their
mothers for the occupations featured on television. This suggests stereotyping and homogenization—portrayals that are similar across programs leading to impressions that resemble one another.

The contemporary validity of these findings is attested to by several
studies. Wrobleski and Huston (1987), found among 65 fifth and sixth
graders, that knowledgeability about occupations frequently portrayed
on television was equal to those often encountered in real life. In a
sample of 640 high school students, Ryan, Bales, and Hughes (1988)
found, among those from households low in socioeconomic status, that
the amount of television viewing was associated with heightened occupational expectations, rising for those anticipating high-status jobs
from 28% for light viewers, to 36 and 50% for moderate and heavy
viewers. Messaris and Kerr (1984) found among about 300 first, third,
and fifth graders that the perception of television characters as representative was associated with whether or not mothers emphasized their
reality, and knowledge about their occupations was positively associated with viewing and discussing programs with mothers. Babrow and
colleagues (1988) interviewed about 120 second, fourth, and sixth graders in regard to the bases for their impressions of peers in real life and on
television, and found that, while complexity increased with age, the
bases essentially were the same.

There is ample evidence that children and teenagers acquire and

Table 4.1
Occupational Knowledge and Television Viewing

Age of child	N	Personal contact occupations	Television contact occupations	General culture occupations
Mean role–knowledge scores				
6	29	57.86	24.21	16.48
7	37	65.89	38.95	24.71
8	44	80.93	64.77	40.75
9	42	83.76	71.24	46.52
10	35	93.57	86.40	52.94
11	34	99.23	88.47	60.50
12–13	15	108.6	98.80	71.13
All ages	236	82.44	65.56	42.78
Sameness of prestige rankings by age (coefficient of concordance)				
6		.08	.13	.14
7		.32	.28	.32
8		.40	.53	.26
9		.50	.76	.42
10		.61	.83	.52
11		.60	.79	.61
12–13		.79	.78	.53
Agreement of prestige ranking by child and mother (mean coefficient of ordinal association)				
6		.30	.27	.19
7		.31	.45	.21
8		.44	.64	.31
9		.46	.76	.36
10		.51	.82	.49
11		.63	.86	.55
12–13		.56	.67	.42

From DeFleur, M.L., & DeFleur, L.B. (1967). The relative contribution of television as a learning source for children's occupational knowledge. *American Sociological Review, 32,* 777–789.

retain information disseminated by television in a format intended to teach (D.F. Roberts & Bachen, 1981). Among very young children, "Sesame Street" is an obvious example. The Columbia Broadcasting System (1974) found that 90% of several hundred children aged 7–11 years, interviewed in three cities, described "Fat Albert and the Cosby Kids" in accord with the intended prosocial messages, and about one out of seven of these messages was said by the children to pertain to their own lives. Similar results were obtained by Christianson (1986) when he showed situation comedies with moral themes to 156 children in kindergarten or first, third or fourth, and the sixth grade. At the earliest age almost none had a high level of understanding, but about half achieved a middle level; by the sixth grade understanding at middle or high level was 100%. Among teenagers, the CBS "National Citizenship Tests," a series intended to teach facts and change beliefs about U.S. institutions, is an example (Alper & Leidy, 1970). Data were obtained from about 4500, representing viewers and nonviewers, before and after a broadcast, and six months later comparable data were obtained from a national sample of 9000. Viewing was positively associated with changes in beliefs and knowledge, of which many appeared to persist after six months.

Although neither children nor teenagers were the principal focus, the field experiment by Ball-Rokeach, Rokeach, and Grube (1984) involving "The Great American Values Test," a 30-minute program designed to change beliefs, merits attention. Certainly they would have been in the audience in sizable numbers, but our main reason is that it illuminates a psychological process by which television might affect cognitions.

The documentary featured Ed Asner and Sandy Hill, then anchor on ABC's "Good Morning America," and was broadcast on a winter evening by all three major network outlets in the Tri-cities (Richland, Pasco, and Kennewick) area of eastern Washington state. During the first half, values were defined, their measurement described, and statistics cited on what Americans believe. During the second half, there was a concerted effort to create dissatisfaction among viewers over the importance they attached to two, equality and the environment. The rationale was that self-esteem could be restored by giving these more importance, which in turn could lead to changes in behavior.

The authors obtained data from representative samples totaling about 2750 in the treatment site and a control site (Yakima). They measured outlook by mail questionnaire, and behavior by response to separately mailed solicitations seeking contributions to three real-life organizations.

The program was watched by one or more persons in one-fourth of the households, or about two-thirds of all those watching television at the time. The strongest finding came in response to the financial solicitations. The rate of 8.3% in the treatment site was not large, but it was much larger (about 60%) than the 5.2% for the control site. This is impressive because it represents truly comparable populations, the whole samples, thus ruling out any influence of self-selection in viewing. There were no significant differences in outlook between the total samples in the two sites, but effects easily could be masked by the large number of nonviewers. When they divided the treatment sample into those who identified themselves as full, partial, or nonviewers, differences in outlook were largely as hypothesized. There was further evidence of behavioral change with average contributions from full viewers much higher than those from partial or nonviewers.

The authors propose a concept applicable to children and teenagers, *media dependency*, with those who scored high relying more on the media for information and guidance. They found that those who scored high were more likely to have viewed the program. This difference was attributable to those whose motives for media use paralleled the two themes of the prebroadcast promotional campaign, self-knowledge and social knowledge.

Studies of the use of television news by children and teenagers lead to a number of conclusions (B. Anderson *et al.*, 1986; Atkin, 1978; Chaffee, McLeod, & Atkin, 1971; Chaffee, Ward, & Tipton, 1970; A.A. Cohen, Harrison, & Wigand, 1974; Comstock *et al.*, 1978; Drew & Reeves, 1980, 1984; Henke, 1985; Hollander, 1971; Huston *et al.*, 1990; Johnson, 1973; Meadowcroft, 1986; A.M. Rubin, 1976; Tan, Raudy, Huff, & Miles, 1980; Tolley, 1973). They include:

1. A large majority of children and teenagers believe they get most of their information about public events from television, ranking television far above teachers, parents, peers, or other media.

2. Exposure to television news among children and teenagers is substantial. The average ratings for the national network evening news for those aged 2–11 is about three-fourths, and for those aged 12–17 is about one-half that of adults aged 18–55. About one-third fairly frequently view national news and somewhat more, local news. In one recent national sample of about 100,000 (Table 4.2), 41% of fourth

Table 4.2
News Viewing by Children and Teenagers

Grade	Daily	Frequency of news watching*		
		Weekly	Monthly or less	Never
4	41	25	11	24
8	45	34	11	10
11	49	33	13	5

* $n = 100,000$

Adapted from Anderson, B., Mead, N., & Sullivan, S. (1986). *Television: What do National Assessment results tell us?* Princeton, NJ: Educational Testing Service.

graders, 45% of eighth graders, and 49% of eleventh graders said they viewed news daily, and those who said they never viewed decreased from about 25% in the fourth grade to 5% in the eleventh grade.

3. Exposure to news programs increases factual knowledge about public events, as does exposure to newspapers and other print media, but children and teenagers are far more likely to see news than to read news, so television is the primary provider of such knowledge. Learning from news by children and teenagers increases when the information is repeated, film is used, and when the items are emotionally affecting.

4. Exposure to news programming by children and teenagers is increased when parents have a high interest in the topics currently receiving coverage. News exposure increases as children enter the teenage years and is no longer a correlate of greater or lesser amounts of television viewing. It becomes a type of programming selected by some teenagers—mostly those of greater mental ability, from households of higher socioeconomic status, or with parents who stimulate discussions about events—for its own merits. Thus, viewing in early childhood can be thought of as predominantly the passive consequence of being in the room when the news is on. In later childhood, when they can leave the room or, in multiset households, watch other content if they wish, viewing may be taken as an expression of some interest. By the teenage years, it frequently has become motivated or instrumental. Among teenagers there is also an increase in use of print news media, and especially newspapers, between junior and senior high school. This socialization toward greater use of a wider range of news media during the teenage years now extends to the Cable News Network (CNN).

5. The opinions of children and teenagers at least on major public issues have been found to correlate positively with the perceived opinions of parents and not with the inferred opinions of favorite newspersons. This indicates that while television may supply information, it is primarily parents who influence opinions, with the caveat that to do so they must express those opinions clearly.

Their exposure to television news shapes the way young persons perceive reality. Cairns, Hunter, and Herring (1980) provide a good example. When they asked about 200 young persons in the fifth and sixth, and the seventh and eighth grades to explain what ten ambiguous pictures represented, those in a community on the west coast of Scotland, where only television from northern Ireland could be received, much more often mentioned bombs and bombings than those in a community without such access. When asked to invent newscasts, the older children in that Scottish community much more often included an item such as, "A bomb has just gone off in Belfast, and that is the end of the news."

Young persons also perceive the news as adhering to conventions. A.A. Cohen, Adoni, and Drori (1983) and Adoni, Cohen, and Mane (1984) queried several hundred ninth and twelfth graders in Israel about the degree to which various social conflicts differed in complexity, intensity, and solvability. Those younger consistently perceived television news and reality as more alike. However, in regard to the topic they were most familiar with, those in both grades perceived television as portraying the conflict as less complex than was actually the case. For a variety of areas of conflict, those older perceived television as portraying conflicts as less complex, more solvable, and less intense than they judged them to be. Reitzes and White (1982) found that when 60 sixth and eighth graders were asked to make up endings for events taken from programs popular with young viewers and from network news, negative outcomes were assigned to news twice as often as to entertainment (43 versus 19%).

Television certainly has changed the accessibility of news and public affairs information among young persons, and especially children. We emphasize children because of the change in media use of teenagers between junior and senior high school, with use of print media and especially newspapers for political information increasingly markedly (Chaffee *et al.*, 1970); television remains important, but proportionately less so for older teenagers. This informational use of the media parallels the changes in regard to media use in general discussed earlier (Chapter III) in regard to mental ability and age. The sum is a greater probability of exposure to news events than would be the case if the alternatives were print media and radio. Thus, television has increased not only the role of entertainment but also the presence of—given the values and conventions that shape news (Comstock, 1989)—bad tidings in the lives of young persons.

Does television play as important a role in their exposure to public events as children and teenagers say? The data of Robinson and Levy (1986) on adults invite skepticism. They found that interpersonal conversation was about as frequent a source as media exposure. However, young persons and especially teenagers often would not have the initial knowledge or interest to stimulate such conversations, and often would lack suitable partners. When parents and young persons share knowledge and interest, the result would be heightened news viewing by young persons. Thus, the media are the principal sources of news for the young, and television, especially so, for children. Our reasoning gains strong support from Drew and Reeves (1980), who found, in a sample of more than 400 elementary school pupils between the third and seventh grade, that only about 10% said they regularly had conversations with friends or parents or discussions in the classroom about the news.

Several surveys small to moderate in scale record modest associations between news viewing and political beliefs and perceptions (Atkin, 1977; Atkin & Gantz, 1978; Berman & Stookey, 1980; Chaffee, Jackson-Beeck, Durall, & Wilson, 1977; Conway, Stevens, & Smith, 1975; D.F. Roberts, Hawkins, & Pingree, 1975; A.M. Rubin, 1978). Among third to sixth graders, correlations were positive between the viewing of commercials for presidential candidates, but not between the viewing of news programs and liking for a candidate. Among children, but not among teenagers, expression of a party preference was associated with news viewing. Among teenagers, but not among children, acceptance of political conflict as an unavoidable part of issue resolution was associated positively with news viewing. Some of the data suggest no association between cynicism over and belief in the efficacy of the political system with news viewing at any age, while one survey found among teenagers a negative correlation between both total viewing and news viewing and favorable feelings for federal, state, and city governments. Among children between the ages of 6 and 11, positive correlations between interest in politics and news viewing occurred. These outcomes border on the disparate, and lead only to the obvious conclusion that such associations vary with age.

However, a survey of major scope, with a nationally representative sample of about 1650 high school seniors and almost 2000 of their parents, suggests profound influence of the media over time (Jennings & Niemi, 1968). There was a noteworthy correlation between parental and teenage beliefs and perceptions only in regard to party identification. This implies a substantial opportunity for media influence, and one that would have increased progressively with the secular decline in party identification (Comstock *et al.*, 1978; Nie, Verba, & Petrocik, 1976). Chaffee and Miyo (1983) found at best only modest evidence of selective exposure to a presidential campaign (the conventions, advertisements, and speeches, mostly by television) as a function of party preference among about 375 adolescents, with liking for both major party candidates increasing when initial levels of liking were held constant. The first documents that media effects other than reinforcement of initial positions are possible among young persons, and the second records that they occur. Dennis (1986) found, among several hundred young persons between the ages of 10 and 17, that two predictors of their labeling themselves as independents during a presidential campaign were whether their parents were independents and exposure to television news and newspapers. He concludes that television may weaken the role of political parties by the emphasis it gives to individual politicians, and the role of primaries in selecting candidates.

A series of studies by Chaffee and colleagues (Chaffee & McLeod, 1972; Chaffee, McLeod, & Wackman, 1973, Chaffee *et al.*, 1971, 1972a, 1972b), in which data were obtained from more than 2300 seventh and tenth graders in a number of communities and from more than 1800 of their parents, have established communicatory values within the family as predictive of media use and political involvement among teenagers. They conceived of two dimensions on which families might differ in regard to interpersonal communication:

- *Social harmony,* varying from low to high in the emphasis on maintaining amiable relations among and between individuals.
- *Expression of ideas,* varying from low to high in the emphasis on exchanging opinions and thoughts, including controversial ones, among and between individuals.

They found that these were largely independent of one another, so that a family might be high or low on either or both, leading to four family types which they labeled as consensual (high, high); pluralistic (low, high); protective (high, low); and laissez-faire (low, low). They found such families to exist in roughly equal proportions. The picture that emerges (Table 4.3):

Table 4.3
Family Communication Patterns and Teenage Media Use

Type of media use	Grade	Family communication pattern*			
		Laissez-faire	Protective	Pluralistic	Consensual
Total TV time	Junior High	+02	+35	−38	−01
	Senior High	+08	+22	−18	−07
TV entertainment	Junior High	+02	+08	−15	+03
	Senior High	−07	+16	−04	00
TV news	Junior High	−21	−15	+11	+21
	Senior High	−22	−06	+14	+17
News reading	Junior High	−16	−35	+20	+25
	Senior High	−19	−09	+15	+14
N	Junior High	161	145	138	197
	Senior High	184	131	179	156

* Standard scores with row mean = 0, σ = unity.
Adapted from Chaffee, S.H., McLeod, J.M., & Atkin, C.K. (1971). Parental influences on adolescent media use. *American Behavioral Scientist, 14,* 323–340.

- An emphasis on expression of ideas leads to greater use of print, greater consumption of news and information from the media, and less television viewing.
- An emphasis on social harmony does not inhibit political participation when the expression of ideas is also emphasized; it is inversely associated with knowledge of public affairs, presumably because of the constraint placed on exchange of views and the consequent introduction of new information and rehearsal of old. Thus, teenagers from consensual and pluralistic families differ in knowledge but not in participation. Those from protective and laissez-faire families are average or below average in both information and participation.
- Teenagers from homes where social harmony is emphasized and the expression of ideas or controversy is not (that is, protective families) are the heaviest television viewers and are quite high in the viewing of violent entertainment. Teenagers from homes where the expression of ideas or controversy is emphasized and social harmony is not (that is, pluralistic families) are comparatively low consumers of television and of violent entertainment.

Within the four family types, teenagers differ somewhat from their parents in political activity and media use, suggesting some influence by the media. An emphasis on social harmony encourages television viewing generally, perhaps because the experience—normative for behavior and conventional in substance—is unlikely to disrupt social relations and reduces the opportunity for conflicts among family members.

Meadowcroft (1986) found, among several hundred parents and children, that the correlation between socio-orientation and political knowledge was positive among those in the fourth and fifth grades and negative among those in the eleventh and twelfth grades. Because those younger are in an early stage of Piaget's (1971) hierarchy of development (concrete instead of formal operations), she suggests that they may not be able to grasp the family emphasis on harmony and conformity yet may have "a natural curiosity about the world of politics" (p. 202). We vastly prefer her alternative that some parents adapt their emphases to the child's age, with socio-orientation in some households preceding a concept-orientation. We base our choice on the data: (a) the frequency of socio-orientation decreases, while that of concept-orientation households rises with grade level, and (b) a "natural curiosity" about politics at the earlier cognitive stage strikes us as implausible. Otherwise, the data support the general pattern: (a) interest, knowledge, discussions, and use of mass media in regard to politics increases with age, and (b) there are positive associations between the political interest, knowledge, and mass media use of parents and their children.

Other research reinforces the view that this is a meaningful way to examine media use by the young. Messaris and Kerr (1983) found among 336 mothers of elementary school children that concept-orientation was positively associated with talking to the child about the moral implications of what occurred in television programs; with the offering of geographic, historical, or scientific information in connection with what was shown on television; and with emphasizing that television was make-believe. Socio-orientation, in contrast, was associated with emphasizing the reality of the way television portrays the world. Abelman (1985) compared 286 pairs of mothers and fourth- or fifth-grade children in regard to whether the mothers were "inductive" or "sensitizing" (Aronfreed, 1976) in their disciplinary practices, with the latter emphasizing the exertion of power and the former, communication, thus placing inductive practices close to a concept-orientation. He found that when the mother was decidedly inductive, children watched more programs portraying constructive behavior and expressed a greater propensity to employ such behavior. Similarly, J.L. Singer *et al.* (1988) found among about 65 children in kindergarten and the first grade that parental emphasis on discussion rather than prescription was positively associated at the end of the year with the children's comprehension of television, level of general information, and early reading readiness.

However, it would be a severe mistake to conclude that the heightened intrusion of news and public affairs into the business of growing up is leading to greater interest in, attention to, and knowledge about current events. A recent collation of survey results covering the past 50 years, *The Age of Indifference* (Times Mirror Center for the People and the Press, 1990), documents that the trends have been in the opposite direction. Adults under 30 are less interested in, pay less attention to, and are less knowledgeable about major and continuing stories of national and international significance than those older; in decades past, this was not the case. The three exceptions are sports, extremely violent events, and social issues directly affecting young adults, such as abortion. Consumption of the news from all sources, including television, but especially from newspapers, has declined compared to two decades ago for younger adults; they show a greater preference for lighter treatments of public affairs as exemplified by *People*. Parallel declines have occurred in the likelihood of voting and in being critical of American institutions and political figures. Generational differences usually have been issue-based, as exemplified by much greater support among younger voters in the early 1970s for amnesty for those who avoided the draft, open abortion, and a lessening of restrictions on marijuana use; currently, generational differences reflect a comparative indifference by the young to events unless they are entertaining, spectacular, or affect them directly.

As we have said (Chapter II), television consumption changes with the life cycle. This well-documented phenomenon (Bower, 1973; Comstock *et al.*, 1978) conceivably may be somewhat modulated by the differing experiences of generational cohorts. We would expect news and public affairs to be much more sensitive to cohort effects than media use in general because the historical events accompanying childhood, adolescence, and young adulthood (World War II, the Korean War, the Civil Rights movement, Vietnam) might have lasting effects on the importance attached by many to such content. Danowski and Ruchinskas (1983) make a convincing case for such an expectation by their documentation that use of television to follow the eight presidential campaigns between 1952 and 1980 was predicted largely by two factors—whether one was a young adult when television began to provide major coverage of presidential campaigns, a cohort effect, and by the closeness of the contest, an event effect.

Based on an analysis of more than 900 Dallas teenagers, C.J. Cobb (1986) devised a fourfold typology in which fully a third (the largest group) were categorized as apathetic readers who infrequently looked at a newspaper, spent comparatively little time with it when they did, and did not place much value on newspaper reading as an activity. As a group, they ranked themselves comparatively low in academic performance, and they had parents who provided few examples of reading. By the teenage years, media use probably is not highly correlated with that of parents (Chaffee *et al.*, 1971) because of the reduction in viewing that would attenuate the magnitude of any correlation and the increase in amount of time spent outside the home, but there remains the environment, established by parents, that has persisted since childhood, that would affect media use through norms and availability (Chapter II; D.F. Roberts *et al.*, 1984). In fact, Cobb provides much evidence that parental behavior in regard to print media is a major determinant of whether adolescents will fit into one of her three categories of more devoted readers: "scanners", who read newspapers frequently but spend little time with them; "sporadics", who read them less frequently but spend more time when they do; and "heavy readers", who read them frequently and spend considerable time when they do. In any case, mental ability and household media environment again appear as important determinants of the media consumption of young persons.

Overall television exposure frequently has been reported as negatively associated with interest in or knowledge about public affairs (Chaffee *et al.*, 1970; Jackson-Beeck, 1979; A.M. Rubin, 1976). This almost certainly reflects the fact that, among those who watch a great deal of television, public affairs and news programming is insignificant, not only in proportion but also in both the importance attached to it and the degree to which it is watched with a motive for obtaining information.

The facts depict an unhappy set of paradoxes. Despite the increasing availability of news and public affairs information—and especially so in the most convenient of media, television, where number of channels and minutes per week have increased over the past two decades, although admittedly primarily among magazine and other softer formats (Comstock, 1989; Gunter, 1987a; Bower, 1985)—the exposure of young persons to the news has declined. Although the technological capacity for the extended and in-depth treatment of the news has increased, and educational levels among the young are higher than ever, the demand for such treatment apparently has not increased among the young. Interest in, attention to, and knowledge about the news are all proxies for involvement, which typically would increase with the degree of threat or range of personal consequences ascribed to events. It is unsettling that such a minor psychological principle should translate into differences between generational cohorts that somewhat undermine the basis, public knowledge and participation, of democratic politics.

In sum, effects on general knowledge are limited by the emphasis of American television on entertainment. The impressions given by entertainment may lead to knowledge and beliefs less varied than real life would provide, and thus to deviations from reality in what is thought. Programs designed to influence can be effective. Children and teenagers almost surely vary in their dependence on the media. Television is the only news medium to which children have much likelihood of being exposed. Young persons consider television a major source of public affairs information, learn from the news when they view it, are guided in their news exposure and opinions on major issues by the interests and views of their parents, and are more likely to become motivated news consumers and to use print as they grow older. The media influence the political outlook of young persons, and this is exacerbated by the overall decline in party allegiance. The key period for such socialization is the early teenage years. Parental communicatory values affect media use. Television use is high where conflict is avoided and print use and attention to the news media is greater where the exchange of ideas is encouraged. Historically, there are some signs of a decline in interest, attention, and knowledge in regard to public affairs; this ironically occurs when the availability of such information in the most convenient of means, television, has increased.

B. VIOLENCE

A number of studies have examined relationships between television exposure and beliefs and perceptions about violence. Some focus on the distinctions that young persons make in regard to media content, others on possible media influence.

Snow (1974) interviewed 50 children between the ages of 4 and 12 as to whether certain portrayals were violent. About one-fourth so described a "Road Runner" cartoon; about one-half, a fighting clown sequence; about two-thirds, a scene from a western; and all, news footage of battle action. Younger children somewhat more frequently described the cartoon and fighting clowns as violent. The chief rationales for not using the label were that the portrayal was make-believe, funny, or both.

T.P. Meyer (1973) interviewed 180 boys and girls aged from five to seven in regard to behavioral situations with alternative ethical resolutions. In each case, the child was asked what friends would do, what parents would prefer, what was right or wrong, what favorite television characters would do, and what he or she would do. Most attributed admiration of a character to its being "funny" or "fun to watch". Favorites generally were perceived as behaving in socially desirable ways, but a sizable minority of males perceived favorites as using violence and meriting emulation. The behavior attributed to favorite characters resembled the child's own choice, value judgments, and perceived choice of best friend more than the perception of what parents would prefer.

Drabman and Thomas (1974) exposed 44 boys and girls in the third and fourth grades either to a western with many violent events or to a no-film experience. Each child was then asked to take responsibility for the welfare of two younger children playing in a distant room whose behavior they could monitor by television. What the child actually saw was a videotape in which two children play quietly, then become progressively destructive, with the sequence culminating with a physical fight in which the television camera is demolished. Those who saw the violent western on the average tolerated greater violence before seeking adult help.

Additional evidence on desensitization is provided by Cline, Croft, and Courrier (1973). First, they showed 80 boys, between the ages of 5 and 12, who over the preceding two years had either viewed very little or a great deal of television (4 or fewer versus 25 or more hours per week), a 14-minute black-and-white film with three segments: (a) two minutes of nonviolent ski action, (b) a four-minute chase, and (c) eight minutes of a brutal boxing match. Physiological arousal to the segments was measured by pulse amplitude, a type of heart response measured by a physiograph. Second, they repeated the procedure with about 40 boys similarly divided, but with the addition of another measure of physiological arousal. Arousal by the boxing sequence was much less among those with high than with low prior exposure; the two groups did not differ in physiological arousal before being shown the film segments; and the findings were consistent for both measures.

Thomas, Horton, Lippencott, and Drabman (1977) replicated the Drabman and Thomas (1974) experiment with 3–5 year olds as the subjects with several important changes. The treatment and control were made more equivalent in excitatory potential, with the former, scenes from a violent prime-time police series and the latter, a sequence from a championship volleyball game. The dependent variable became emotional responsiveness to the videotape of the children fighting as measured by galvanic skin response (GSR), and data were collected on the children's viewing at home. Both boys and girls who saw the police drama displayed lower levels of emotional response to the video, and there were substantial inverse correlations between the regular viewing of violence at home and responsiveness to the video. These findings eliminate the alternative explanation that distraction from the task was wholly responsible.

M.H. Brown, Skeen, and Osborn (1979) compared 64 six and seven year olds in the degree of reality they attributed to animated and live-actor versions of "Star Trek." These young viewers rated the live-actor version as being more realistic.

In Great Britain, Chaney (1970) found, among about 60 twelve year olds, that lower mental ability was a factor. For both boys and girls, it was associated with greater liking for and perceived realism of favorite series, and the greater the violence, the greater the perceived realism among boys low in mental ability and highly involved in their favorite series.

Greenberg and Reeves (1976) collected data from about 200 children equally divided between boys and girls in the third through the sixth grade in regard to whether they judged a specific character, an area of content, or television in general to be like real life. The perceived views of friends and family were major predictors of such an attribution. Rating television as like real life was negatively associated with mental ability and age, and positively associated with the amount viewed.

Specific characters were more often said to be like real life than was television in general.

Dominick (1974) collected data from about 370 fifth-grade children in white- and blue-collar communities. For both boys and girls, the viewing of crime and police programs was positively associated with identification with a character representing law enforcement, the belief that criminals usually get caught, and knowledge of the civil rights of those arrested. Knowledge about legal terms was positively associated with their frequent portrayal on television.

Greenberg and Gordon (1972a, 1972b) asked almost 600 boys in the fifth and eighth grades to rate four violent programs. Age, race, and socioeconomic status made a difference, but principally socioeconomic status. Enjoyment, approval, and the degree of humor, realism, and amount of violence perceived were inversely associated with such status, with the difference in amount confined to the earlier grade.

Dominick and Greenberg (1972) obtained data from almost 850 boys and girls in the fourth, fifth, and sixth grades on dispositions favorable to the use of violence. Both degree of parental approval of the use of aggression and amount of exposure to violent television drama were positively associated with such dispositions among both boys and girls; however, the association was stronger for perceived parental opinion than for exposure to television violence.

The two surveys by Lovibond (1967) in Australia support the proposition that there is a positive association among teenage males between an ideology favoring use of force, and exposure to violence in the media (Table 4.4). The first involved a sample of about 375 before the introduction of television, and the holding of such an outlook was greater among those who read more violent comic books. The second involved a sample of more than 90 after the introduction of television. Comic book reading was less frequent, and now the amount of exposure to television and a preference for violent programs were also positively associated with the holding of such an outlook.

Carlson (1983) found, among about 600 in the sixth through twelfth grades, that the viewing of crime shows was inversely although modestly associated with scores on a scale measuring support for civil liberties. With the application of statistical controls for a variety of variables, the association remained negative and statistically significant for those older and for those from households higher in socioeconomic status.

Elliott and Slater (1980) found, among a sample of about 550 male and female teenagers, that overall viewing of programs focusing on law enforcement was positively associated with perceiving selected exam-

Table 4.4
Media Use, Ideology Favoring Force, and the Introduction of Television

Comic book reading and favorability	Before TV			After TV		
Number of comic books read per week	0–1	2–5	6+	0	1–3	4+
Mean CF Scale score*	79.2	82.2	95.3	79.0	88.6	91.3

Television viewing and favorability						
Number of hours TV viewed per week	None	1–2	3–5	6–10	11–15	16–20	21+
Mean CF Scale score*	72.0	77.0	81.4	86.7	82.7	87.4	111.4

* CF Scale (Children's F Scale): Scales on ideology of using force in the domination and exploitation of the weak by the strong.
From Lovibond, S.H. (1967). The effect of media stressing crime and violence upon children's attitudes. *Social Problems, 15,* 91–100.

ples of them as realistic; this perception was lower among those who had had some formal instruction in law enforcement and higher among those who had an arrest record. Rarick, Townsend, and Boyd (1973) found, among a small sample of 49 teenagers, that there was little variation in the images held of police on television, but those of real-life police varied substantially across a positive–negative dimension, and the two were largely uncorrelated. Thus, there is stereotyping and it seems convincing to some.

Several studies have examined the perception by young viewers that something on television is frightening. Himmelweit, Oppenheim, and Vince (1958) found that children were more likely to be frightened by realistic than by ritualistic violence (at the time represented by westerns), by horror or space dramas, by a dagger or sharp instrument (as contrasted with a gun), or if it involved a threat to a favorite animal, such as Lassie. Cantor and Reilly (1982) and E.L. Palmer, Hockett, and Dean (1983), across the second, sixth, and tenth grades, found age inversely related to the frequency of fearful reactions. Among the second graders, two-thirds said they avoided programs they thought would frighten them; by the sixth grade, only about 10% said so. Frightening programs were popular, and especially among the older viewers. By the sixth grade, a majority said they enjoyed such fare. Sparks (1986) found, among children ranging in age from 4 to 11, that younger and older children differed in what they often found unpleasantly frightening. Younger children (up to the age of seven) were frightened by what he calls "impossible content"—transformations and grotesque and ugly characters. The older children were frightened by "possible content"— events that were within the realm of possibility, if low in probability. Sparks and Cantor (1986) found fearful reactions to "The Incredible Hulk" to differ by age, with children aged 3–5 years experiencing more fear *after* and those aged 9–11 more *before* than during or after the character transformation. Cantor and Hoffner (1990) found, among children in kindergarten through the second grade, that fearfulness was greater when a threat was presented as possibly occurring locally, and that the appearance of those portrayed in a 1958 Paramount horror vehicle was somewhat more frightening than their behavior. Cantor, Wilson, and Hoffner (1986) surveyed parents about the reactions of young viewers to one of the most-viewed, made-for-TV movies of all time, *The Day After*. Although levels of fear on the whole were modest, fear in this instance increased with age.

Given the frequency with which television news reports on horrendous events, one would expect an extensive body of research on the reactions of children and teenagers to such occurrences. None exists. Except for a few examinations of the reactions of young persons to the assassination of President Kennedy (Sigal, 1965; Wolfenstein, 1965), which essentially found their responses parallel to those of adults, the sole example is interviews by Wright, Kunkel, Pinon, and Huston (1989) with 122 fourth-, fifth-, and sixth-grade boys and girls six days after they viewed the Challenger space shuttle disaster. Although they almost invariably reported sadness and grief for the death of the schoolteacher, Christa McAuliffe, and sympathy for her family, the children coped well; a special protocol to be invoked if a child was upset by discussing the event was not once invoked. Boys were more likely to have followed the space program on television and were more favorable toward it after the disaster than girls; girls were more upset. However, despite statistical significance, these differences were very small, so that reactions were much alike regardless of gender and age.

There have also been efforts to explore ways by which fearful reactions can be ameliorated. B.J. Wilson and Cantor (1987) found, among children aged from five to seven and eight to nine years, that exposure to a documentary portrayal of snakes reduced fearfulness to a scene from *Raiders of the Lost Ark*, and the effect held for both ages. B.J. Wilson (1989a, 1989b) found, among children between kindergarten and the fifth grade, that prior experience could reduce fearfulness while viewing a frightening movie sequence and increase the acceptability of the featured creatures, but that a popular technique to shield themselves from fear had opposite effects at different ages. In one experiment, the demonstration of petting and handling a live lizard, but not exposure to one, reduced negative reactions to a scene from a movie called *Frogs*, in which lizards are responsible for a man's death. In another, encouraging children to cover their eyes during a suspenseful scene from *To Kill a Mockingbird* decreased fear among those younger, but increased it among those older. Cantor and Wilson (1984) and B.J. Wilson (1987) both examined children of preschool age and those aged 9–11 years. In the first instance, the authors found that fearfulness over the scene in *The Wizard of Oz* in which Dorothy is captured and threatened by the Wicked Witch of the West could be reduced among the older, but not among the younger viewers, by inducing a mental set that it was make-believe. In the second, the author found that exposure with commentary to a mock-up tarantula, as well as verbal rehearsal of phrases describing the spider as not harmful, reduced fearful reactions among both younger and older viewers to a movie episode in which a mob of tarantulas kills a human being. A majority said they hated tarantulas. This is pertinent, because Condry (1989) argues that the tarantula is an example of the distortion of beliefs by the media. Tarantulas frequently have been portrayed as villains and are arguably generally feared (and certainly so by the principal author), while on the basis of his daughter's having one as a pet, Condry testifies confidently that they are gentle and shy. Hoffner and Cantor (1990) found, among those both aged from 5 to 7 and 9 to 11, that anticipatory fear in response to a snake attack in *The Swiss Family Robinson* was increased by a forewarning and decreased by assurances of a happy ending, while neither clearly affected responses while viewing.

If a portrayal is perceived as humorous or make-believe, children are less likely to think of it as violent; violence, to children, is serious, not playful. They typically perceive admired television characters as behaving in socially desirable ways and being much like themselves in how they would act. For a sizable minority of boys, this means perceiving a person behaving violently as acting in a socially desirable manner and being worthy of emulation. They become emotionally desensitized to seeing violence by exposure to violence on television, but the effect is far clearer for responses to the media than to real-life events, because so far it is only responses to events conveyed by television that have been assessed. Greater realism is attributed to television by those of lower mental ability, those more involved in their viewing, those younger in age, those whose friends and families are perceived as judging television to be like real life, and those who view greater-than-average amounts of television. Viewing of crime and police programs is associated with identification with those who enforce the law, the belief that criminals usually are caught, and knowledge of the rights of those arrested. Violent television scenes are perceived as portraying acceptable behavior, as being more like real life, and are better liked by children and teenagers who are lower in socioeconomic status. Greater exposure to violent media is positively associated with an ideology favorable to the use of force and indifference to civil liberties. The frequency with which perceptions of the reality of television are in accord with those of friends and parents indicates that the social climate established by interpersonal exchange about the validity of what the medium portrays plays an important part in the credibility assigned to it; the cues that the medium supplies directly about the reality of its portrayals are interpreted in the context of the norms about television established socially.

Young viewers are more likely to be frightened by violence that is novel, forcefully presented, involves instruments to be found around the house, threatens someone they care for, or might occur locally. Typically, fright reactions decrease with age, but there are cognitive qualifications. Because young children do not fully comprehend the concept of character transformation, they are more frightened by the result than the process, while for older children, the prospect is more frightening than the outcome. In the case of *The Day After*, fright was greater among those who could comprehend more about international conflict and nuclear war. On the whole, children seem well able to cope with fictional and real events that would seem or in fact are upsetting. Fright reactions can be reduced by changing the way events will be perceived, but this is generally harder to do among younger than older children. Many young viewers enjoy media that instill some degree of fright, and a majority of young children will avoid such portrayals, while only a few older children do so, presumably because the latter comprehend better the make-believe character of what is presented and are more able to abandon their reactions once a scene or program is over.

C. SEX ROLES

Sex roles are those activities widely considered to be appropriate for and typical of one or the other of the genders. *The Dictionary of Behavioral Science* (Wolman, 1989) defines sex role as:

> Behavioral patterns expected from individuals by their social group believed to be typical of their sex. Some sex-determinant behavioral patterns are biologically determined, such as menstru-

ation and pregnancy in females. Certain behavioral patterns are culturally influenced, such as ascendance–submissiveness, or occupational choice. Sex role is often called psychosexual role. (p. 313)

Such differing expectations continue to be widely held, and certainly the roles of males and females are portrayed differently in television entertainment (R.C. Allen, 1985; Cassata & Skill, 1983; Greenberg, 1980; Gunter, 1986; Katzman, 1972; Kalisch & Kalisch, 1984; U.S. Commission on Civil Rights, 1977, 1979) as well as in other mass media. Signorielli (1989), based on the analysis of almost 20,000 characters in television storytelling (14,011 males and 5691 females) representing more than a decade-and-a-half of programming, offers a succinct conclusion descriptive of the evidence as a whole:

> . . . Sex role images, over the past 10–15 years, have been quite stable, traditional, conventional, and supportive of the status quo. (p. 341)

We begin with relationships between exposure and sex-role beliefs, perceptions, and preferences, turn to gender-based differences in response to portrayals, and finally to relationships between the sexes.

Birnbaum and Croll (1984) found among 43 preschool children that emotional reactions to a television program differed by sex, with boys displaying more anger and girls displaying more happiness and fear. McArthur and Resko (1975) showed preschool children brief video sequences in which the behavior of adult men and women either were stereotypic and traditional or in which the roles were reversed. Same-sex behavior was recalled and reproduced more frequently than opposite-sex behavior, whether it was stereotypic or nonstereotypic; this held for both boys and girls. Cordua, McGraw, and Drabman (1979) produced identical data on misperception of portrayals among about 130 five and six year olds, and additionally found that real-life exposure to male nurses and maternal employment enhanced correct identification. Ruble, Balaban, and Cooper (1981) found, among 100 four to six-year-old boys and girls, that display of a toy being played with exclusively by one or another of the genders in a commercial strongly suppressed desire to play with the toy among those of the opposite gender, and this effect occurred only among those who had reached a cognitive stage where gender is recognized as comprehensively invariant—which is thought to occur typically by about the age of five and certainly usually by the end of the sixth year; those who had yet to recognize this primarily imitated the kind of play engaged in regardless of the gender of the portrayed child. Conversely, DiLeo, Moely, and

Sulzer (1979) demonstrated among 120 boys and girls in nursery school, kindergarten, and the first grade that counter-normative portrayals of toy play decreased the choice of sex-typed toys, and additionally found that sex-typing was more frequent among those older and among males. Tan, Raudy, Huff, and Miles (1980) showed half of 120 children in the third, fourth, and fifth grades, evenly divided between boys and girls, a 15-minute newscast delivered either by an adult female or male. Both boys and girls recalled more of the male newscast, and a decidedly lower degree of recall occurred for the girls exposed to the female newscast. Silverman-Watkins, Levi, and Klein (1986) challenged the implication of sex bias on the grounds that the male newscaster had an advantage because the topics were masculine. They concocted a 12-item newscast balanced between masculine, feminine, and neutral topics with a male or female voice, and showed it to about 100 fifth, sixth, and seventh graders. The gender of the newscaster made no difference in recall, but boys and girls recalled stories linked to their gender best, and overall more children remembered the newscaster as male than female. Mayes and Valentine (1979) showed Saturday morning cartoons to 30 children between the ages of 8 and 13, evenly divided between boys and girls, and measured the degree to which they perceived male and female characters as possessing 14 traits readily ascribable as more or less masculine or feminine. Boys and girls perceived male and female characters very differently, and the perceptions were highly stereotypic. Miller and Reeves (1976) found, among 200 boys and girls in the third through the sixth grades, that four-fifths of the boys compared to one-half of the girls, who named television characters as people they would want to be like, named same-sex characters, although only slightly more than half named any television character.

Several studies focused on very young children. Beuf (1974) interviewed 63 boys and girls between the ages of three and six and found them overwhelmingly conventional in regard to occupational sex roles, with relationships strongest for those who viewed greater-than-average amounts of television. When Drabman, Robertson, Patterson, Jarvis, Hammer, and Cordua (1981) showed preschool children and those in the first grade a brief video sequence of a female doctor and a male nurse, they found that most of the preschool and first-grade children subsequently identified the photograph and name of the male as the doctor. Durkin (1984) in Great Britain conducted in-depth interviews with 17 children, ranging from preschool to nine years old, after showing them four varied television segments featuring sex-typed behavior, and found even the youngest knowledgeable about social conventions. Flerx, Fidler, and Rogers (1976) interviewed 76 children between the ages of three and five about their sex-role beliefs, subjected the four and five year olds (the three year olds were thought to be too young) to brief daily sessions over a week, in which they were read picture books that were either stereotypic or nonstereotypic in regard to sex roles. They repeated the manipulation with another 46 five year olds, with the addition of a nonstereotypic film condition. Conventional sex-role beliefs were much more predominant at age four than at age three; the nonstereotypic picture books were effective in reducing such beliefs; the film was even more effective than the picture books; and effects remained (although at a reduced level) after a week. Davidson, Yasuna, and Tower (1979) showed 36 five-year-old girls cartoons that either featured females engaging in stereotypic or nonstereotypic ways or were irrelevant in regard to sex roles. Subsequent stereotyping of personality characteristics was less frequent among those who saw the nonstereotypic than among those who saw the other two versions. Cobb, Stevens-Young, and Goldstein (1982) showed 36 boys and girls aged from four to six years videos that associated unisex toys with one or the other of the genders, and subsequently each sex more frequently chose a toy that had been linked to their gender. Rosenwasser, Lingenfelter, and Harrington (1989) found, among about 115 preschool and second graders, that there was a modest positive association between knowledge of nonstereotypical commercial programs, such as "Who's the Boss?" and "The Cosby Show," and holding nontraditional views on sex roles.

A larger number included or are confined to older children. Pingree (1978) showed 227 children in the third and eighth grades, about evenly divided between boys and girls, sets of real commercials featuring women in either traditional or nontraditional roles. One-third of the children were told that those they would see were real people who actually did the things portrayed, one-third that they would see actors who did not do such things in real life, and the final third were given no instructions. Subsequent stereotyping was reduced at both grade levels and for both sexes among those who saw the nontraditional versions when told the people were real, and in general among those told the characters were acting. However, stereotyping was heightened among eighth-grade boys after exposure to the nontraditional portrayals. B. Meyer (1980) examined 150 girls aged 6–8 and 10–12 from working class families in regard to sex-role beliefs, aspirations, and perceptions of behavior. He found no association between any of his several measures and television exposure, although between the two ages, sex-role outlooks became more varied and more like those of the mother. Drabman *et al.* (1981) found that fourth-grade children resembled the preschool and first-grade children in erroneously naming or identifying the female doctor and male nurse, while those in the seventh grade were almost wholly correct. Freuh and McGhee (1975) and McGhee and Freuh (1980) obtained data at two times 15 months apart from 64 boys and girls in kindergarten, and the second, fourth, and sixth grades, evenly divided between boys and girls, who could be classified as heavy (25 or more hours per week) or light (10 hours or fewer) viewers at both times. The amount of television viewing was positively associated with stereotyping of both males and females, and stereotyping tended to increase with age, but decreased among those who were light viewers. Miller and Reeves (1976) found, among their third through sixth graders, that those who expressed familiarity with female characters in nontraditional roles on currently broadcast television programs judged such roles to be more appropriate and more frequent in real life. List, Collins, and Westby (1983) found, among about 85 third graders, that recall of gender-relevant information from television programs was greater for those who had a stereotypic outlook. Wroblewski and Huston (1987) found, among their fifth and sixth graders, that females who viewed more programs with traditional sex roles had more conventional aspirations. Eisenstock (1984) found, among about 240 boys and girls between the ages of 9 and 12, that identification with a counterstereotypical female character in a television program was greatest among boys and girls scoring high in traits conventionally said to be feminine and unrelated to scores on masculine traits. As part of the formative research (Cook & Curtin, 1986; Lesser, 1972, 1974) to develop the 13-episode "Freestyle" series, F. Williams, LaRose, and Frost (1981) showed segments designed to counter stereotyping to more than 650 children in the fourth, fifth, and sixth grades. Factual recall was high; recognition of intent was moderate, averaging about 50%; liking for the characters was substantial; and desire to be like the characters was low. There was a lack of consistency among and between the males and females in the rating of personality traits, activities, and occupations in regard to the sexes, leading the authors to conclude that stereotyping among the young is not "a general and fundamental mediator" of other responses. Comprehension and liking were enhanced when the male television characters were perceived more stereotypically; comprehension was enhanced when the female characters were perceived less stereotypically; and liking among boys was enhanced with perceiving the female characters less stereotypically—a pattern suggestive of more attention to and approval of modes of behavior traditionally associated with maleness. Alexander (1985) found, among 230 sixth and seventh graders, that broken homes and problems with peers predicted soap opera viewing, but little evidence, in our view, that viewing affected the belief either in the efficacy of talking to solve problems or the fragility of personal relationships, two soap opera staples (Cassata & Skill, 1983; Katzman, 1972). Finally, Perloff (1977), among 11–12 year olds, found no association between amount of television viewing and sex-role beliefs, although he did find a modest association between conventionality of beliefs and the behavior and outlook of the mother.

There are also a few studies that focus on teenagers. In their three-community experiment, T.M. Williams (1986) and colleagues administered a 61-item scale, measuring the stereotyping of peers, to all pupils in the sixth and ninth grades before the arrival of television in Notel and two years later. Altogether, data were obtained from about 430 young persons in the three communities; scores for both boys and girls increased decidedly over the next two years (Fig. 4.1). Tan (1979) found

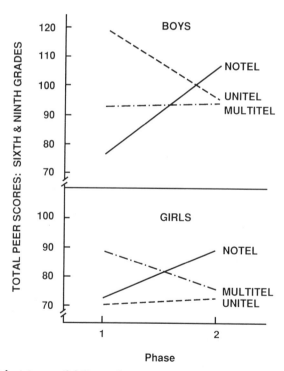

Fig. 4.1 Television availability and stereotyping. From Williams, T.M. (Ed.). (1986). *The impact of television: A natural experiment in three communities.* New York: Academic Press.

that, among 56 high school girls between 16 and 18 years, those exposed to 15 network beauty commercials subsequently attached greater importance to being popular with men and accorded beauty characteristics more importance "for you, personally" than those who saw 15 commercials with no beauty themes or products. L. Ross, Anderson, and Wisocki (1982) found, among 78 college students, that holding sexually stereotypic views of themselves was positively associated with watching programs with stereotypical sex-role portrayals, but not with overall television viewing. F.L. Geis, Jennings (Walstedt), and Brown and colleagues (Jennings (Walstedt), Geis, & Brown, 1980; F.L. Geis, Brown, Jennings, & Corrado-Taylor, 1984; F.L. Geis, Brown, Jennings (Walstedt), & Porter, 1984) conducted three different experiments in which replicas of off-the-air commercials portraying the two genders either duplicated or reversed the roles of the sexes. College-age women responded to the reversed roles by rating females as higher on dimensions where males stereotypically are ascendant, such as dominant–submissive; by writing essays about life 10 years from now that less frequently emphasized homemaking and more frequently emphasized achievement outside the home, so that males and females were equal in the emphasis on achievement among those seeing the reversed version while among those seeing the original version males were ascendant in emphasis on achievement; and displayed more independence on a standard psychological measure of such behavior.

Morgan (1982) brings life to small numbers (in this case, correlation coefficients) in an adroit analysis of data obtained from about 350 young persons in the second and third years of a panel study that began in the fall of 1974 and ended in the spring of 1977. At the time of the second-year data collection, the sample, roughly divided between males and females, were in the sixth through ninth grades. Correlations between amount of viewing and stereotyping were positive at both times and for both males and females, although they only remained so for third-year males when controls were entered for other variables (Table 4.5). When the simple correlations were examined by level of mental ability, the third-year correlations for males turned out to be primarily attributable to those with medium ability, while in both the second and third years, the correlations for females were primarily a product of those of high ability. When viewing and stereotyping were correlated across the years, the pattern was unambiguously opposite for males and females. When other variables were taken into account, earlier stereotyping by males was positively associated with later viewing, and earlier viewing was unassociated with later stereotyping. For females, earlier stereotyping was unassociated with later television viewing, while earlier television viewing was associated with later stereotyping.

Table 4.5
Television and Stereotyping: Synchronous and Longitudinal Correlations

Viewing and sexism scores

	Boys		Girls	
Variables[a]	Second year	Third year	Second year	Third year
Simple *r*	.20**	.34**	.16*	.21**
Grade	.17**	.30***	.11	.17**
SES	.18**	.34***	.14*	.19**
IQ	.07	.20**	.10	.09
Mother works	.19**	.35***	.16**	.21**
All	.04	.18*	.03	.02

Viewing and sexism scores by IQ

	Second year		Third year	
IQ group	Simple *r*	Partial *r*	Simple *r*	Partial *r*
Boys				
Low	.16	.17	.12	.22
Medium	.13	.03	.38**	.43**
High	.08	.07	.10	−.02
Girls				
Low	.04	−.02	.03	.00
Medium	−.01	−.04	.08	.07
High	.25*	.18*	.26*	.27*

Viewing and sexism scores over time

	Correlation of second-year TV with third-year sexism		Correlation of second-year sexism with third-year TV	
Variables[a]	Boys	Girls	Boys	Girls
Simple *r*	.14*	.28***	.30***	.11
Second year sexism	.04	.24***	—	—
Second year TV	—	—	.23**	.00
IQ	−.03	.20**	.18**	.04
SES	.13	.27***	.29***	.09
Grade	.11	.24***	.26***	.05
All	−.09	.14*	.15*	−.07

   * $p < .05$.
   ** $p < .01$.
   *** $p < .001$.
   [a] Simple and partial cross-sectional correlations between amount of television viewing and sexism scores.

From Morgan, M. (1982). Television and adolescents' sex role stereotypes: A longitudinal study. *Journal of Personality and Social Psychology, 43*(5), 947–955.

He argues that the pattern for females represents a convergence phenomenon, with those least likely to hold stereotypes (those of higher ability) being brought closer to the average by greater viewing. As for the boys, he speculates that those more sexist to begin with view somewhat more television because it so consistently confirms their beliefs and perceptions.

In two similar analyses of correlation coefficients by subgroups, Rothschild and Morgan (1987) and Morgan (1987) found further evidence, consistent with a very modest contribution by viewing, to the holding of traditional sex-role beliefs. Among about 900 persons between 10 and 14 years, Rothschild and Morgan found positive associations between viewing and stereotyping when family cohesion and rule-making in general were low, or when there was a great deal of cohesive interaction (viewing together and discussing programs) centered on television. In their view, household norms either suppressed or facilitated the influence of television, with the latter occurring when parents placed a great deal of emphasis on the medium. In a sample of almost 300 adolescents, Morgan found small positive associations between amount of viewing and conventionality of beliefs, but none with behavior, and some signs of an incremental contribution over six months. We are somewhat puzzled by the fact that such influence seemed greatest among boys who were low and among girls who were high in conventionality, which might be taken as undercutting his earlier deduction of convergence, but also might be attributable to some unmeasured symmetry in what these groups watched or the firmness of their beliefs.

The most substantial body of evidence on what can and cannot be achieved by the calculated use of television to shape beliefs and perceptions about sex roles comes from the evaluation of the federally funded "Freestyle." The series of thirteen 30-minute episodes broadcast on public television was designed to broaden the perspectives and motives of children aged 9 through 12 in regard to sex roles, as exemplified by the episodes "Helping Hand" and "Grease Monkey" (Table 4.6). The evaluation encompassed over 7000 children in seven different sites across the nation, which varied in whether the treatment condition consisted of viewing in classrooms followed by discussion, viewing in classrooms without discussion, or viewing in the home.

Johnston and Ettema (1982) propose a variety of useful comparisons (Figure 4.2), and they wisely attempt a criterion for evaluating the meaningfulness of an observed difference. They conclude after reviewing the suggestions of several authors (J. Cohen, 1977; Horst & Tallmadge, 1976; Tallmadge, 1976), that pre- and post-treatment differences are best evaluated as a proportion of the pretreatment standard

Table 4.6
"Freestyle" Episodes: "Helping Hands" and "Grease Monkey"

"Helping Hands"

Synopsis:
   Walter thinks tutoring math will be a cinch until he discovers that his pupil, newcomer, Dolores Cabrillo, can't read math problems which are written in English. Dolores, fearing disgrace, swears Walter to secrecy and he and his bilingual buddy, Ramon, help Dolores prepare for her math exams. With their helping hands Dolores, of course, passes.

Themes:
   (1) *Behavioral skill:* nurturing skills for boys.
      Message: Tutoring, like other nurturant activities, requires "helping skills": including empathy and patience.
   (2) *Pre-occupational activities:* nurturant activities for boys (specifically, tutoring younger children).
      Message: Nurturant activities such as tutoring can be rewarding activities and boys can be competent in them.
   (3) *Adult work–family roles:* teacher and other occupations related to tutoring.
      Message: If a child enjoys nurturant activities such as tutoring, there are a variety of occupations he or she may wish to consider.

"Grease Monkey"

Synopsis:
   Chris is very interested in automobiles. She applies for a summer job at a nearby gas station and convinces the crusty old owner to hire her on her merits. While tending the station alone she takes on a job that's too big for her and disaster follows. She summons up the courage to return to work and a mechanic teaches her the fundamentals of auto repair. The next time there's trouble she's prepared to handle it.

Themes:
   (1) *Behavioral skill:* risk-taking.
      Message: Jobs for which one is not prepared are unreasonable risks. The same jobs may, however, be reasonable risks once one has had some training for them.
   (2) *Pre-occupational activities:* mechanical–technical activities for girls (specifically, auto mechanics).
      Message: Girls can learn to be competent in mechanical–technical activities such as auto mechanics.
   (3) *Adult work–family roles:* auto mechanic.
      Message: Auto mechanics can be an interesting occupation.

From Johnston, J., & Ettema, J.S. (1982). *Positive images: Breaking stereotypes with children's television.* Newbury Park, CA: Sage.

deviation with effects categorized as small (.20), modest (.22–.29), sizable (.30–.39), and very large (in excess of .40).

By far the most effective treatment was viewing in classrooms with discussion, where there were numerous changes in the desired direc-

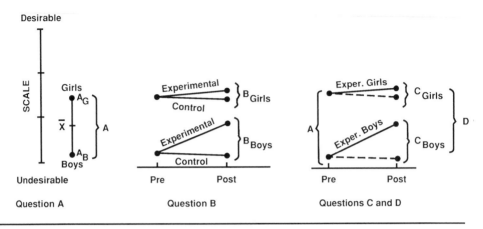

Question A: What were boys and girls like before Freestyle?

Question B: Did Freestyle change the experimental groups by a statistically significant amount relative to the control groups?

Question C: If yes to B, by how much did the experimental groups change (educational significance)?

Question D: Was the gap between boys' and girls' perspectives reduced?

Fig. 4.2   Questions asked by "Freestyle" Evaluation. From Johnston, J., & Ettema, J.S. (1982). *Positive images: Breaking stereotypes with children's television.* Newbury Park, CA: Sage.

tion of sufficient size to be meaningful (Table 4.7). When outcomes were arrayed by type, the descending order of effects in frequency and magnitude was attitudes toward, beliefs about, and interest in engaging in an activity. This parallels the usual pattern for public information campaigns in which effects are greatest for knowledge about the campaign, modest to sizable in acceptance of its messages, and null to modest in behavioral change (Comstock, 1983a). Most of these effects remained after nine months, although typically diminished in size. Viewing in the classroom without the subsequent discussion and viewing at home had very limited effects. As the authors write:

> It is clear that "Freestyle," when used to best advantage in the classroom, can produce some impressive effects. Most notable among these effects are more positive attitudes toward those who engage in a variety of nontraditional pursuits. "Freestyle" was particularly successful in promoting greater acceptance of (a) girls

Table 4.7
Summary of "Freestyle" Outcomes (Classroom Viewing with Discussion)

	Beliefs about			Attitude toward			Interest in		
	Females		Males	Females		Males	Females		Males
Childhood preoccupational activities	ooo	Boys in helping roles	x	o	Boys in helping roles	o	—	Helping	o
	x	Girls in athletics	oo	ooo	Girls in athletics	ooo	ooo	Athletics	—
	o	Girls doing mechanics	ooo	ooo	Girls doing mechanics	ooo	o	Mechanics	—
		—			—		x	Science	—
Childhood behavioral skills	a	Girls as leaders	a	oo	Girls as leaders	ooo	—	—	—
	x	Girls being independent	x	oo	Girls being independent	ooo	—	—	—
	x	Girls being assertive	x	a	Girls being assertive	a	—	—	—
	x	Girls taking risks	x	x	Girls taking risks	a	—	—	—
Adult work and family roles	oo	Sex of those in traditionally male jobs	oo	oo	More women in "male" jobs	ooo	x	"Male" jobs	—
	oo	Sex of those in traditionally female jobs	oo	ooo	More men in "female" jobs	ooo	oo	"Realistic"	—
	o	Wives doing male housework	o	ooo	Wives doing more "male" housework	o	o	"Enterprising"	—
	oo	Husbands doing female housework	o	oo	Husbands doing more "female" housework	ooo	—	"Female" jobs	x
	x	Wives support family	x	x	Wives support family	x	—	"Social" jobs	o
	x	Husbands support family	x	x	Husbands support family	x			

Key: — = concept not measured or inappropriate for audience.

Size of Effect: ooo = large, oo = medium, o = small, x = not educationally significant, a = "homogenizing" effect only.

From Johnston, J., & Ettema, J.S. (1982). *Positive images: Breaking stereotypes with children's television.* Newbury Park, CA: Sage.

who engage in athletics and mechanical activities, assume positions of leadership, and display importance; (b) boys who engage
in nurturing activities; and (c) women and men who choose nontraditional careers. "Freestyle," in short, changed some of the
children's norms about sex-appropriate behavior. (p. 204)

We reported earlier (Chapter I) that several investigators (E.E. Maccoby & Wilson, 1957; E.E. Maccoby *et al.*, 1958; Sprafkin & Liebert,
1978) have found that children and teenagers display greater interest in
and give greater attention to television and film characters of the same
sex. They also appear to express greater liking for them (Joy, Kimball, &
Zabrack, 1977, as described in T.M. Williams, 1986, p. 285; Sprafkin &
Liebert, 1978). However, greater interest, attention, and liking are by no
means necessary conditions for taking television characters as models.
Status contends with and often takes precedence in influence over such
obvious factors on which perceived similarity would depend as sex and
race (Bandura, 1973, 1986; Comstock & Cobbey, 1979). Thus, there is a
tendency for portrayals of males to be more effective in influencing
young females than are portrayals of females in influencing young
males. Enhanced receptivity to portrayals of the same sex, heightened
when the portrayed behavior is consonant with conventional expectations, nevertheless lays a foundation for influence on beliefs and perceptions about sex-pertinent behavior.

The conventionality or nonconventionality of sex-role beliefs and
perceptions certainly would have some influence on male and female
interaction, but other studies have focused on questions directly pertinent to relationships between the sexes. The outcomes fall under three
topics: desensitization, contrast, and callousness.

Linz, Donnerstein, and Penrod (1984) and Linz (1985) exposed male
college students to varying quantities of commercially released R-rated
"slasher" films such as *Texas Chainsaw Massacre, Maniac, I Spit on
Your Grave, Vice Squad,* and *Toolbox Murders,* that depict graphic
violence against women. In the first instance, viewing these five films
at a rate of one a day for five days was associated with perceiving them
as less violent and believing them to be less degrading to women, and
there were declines in reported anxiety and depression after viewing. In
the second instance, the viewing of two such films was sufficient to
produce the same effects. Krafka (1985), using a similar design, found
that female college students similarly declined in reported anxiety and
depression with repeated exposure but, unlike males, their perception
of violence did not decrease. Zillmann and Bryant (1982) found that
male college students were less likely to judge films as pornographic or

violent after extensive exposure to films in which women were victims of violence or sexual abuse. These same two authors later (1984) exposed 160 undergraduates equally divided between males and females to either a "massive" amount (almost a total of five hours in six weekly sessions) of film portrayals of nonviolent heterosexual activities including anal intercourse, coitus, cunnilingus, and fellatio, a moderate amount (half as much), or none. Increased exposure was associated with decreases three weeks later in perceiving such films as offensive, pornographic, or eligible for restrictions in regard to access by minors or broadcast use, and increases in beliefs about the frequency of sexual behavior other than conventional intercourse. Linz, Donnerstein, and Adams (1989) exposed about 60 male undergraduates to 90-minute video anthologies of slasher scenes or of other exciting scenes, including nonviolent sexual intimacy. Those who saw the slasher anthologies subsequently were less physiologically aroused by a scene of violence perpetrated by a male against a female but registered no change in mood, while those who saw the other anthology registered increases in hostility, anxiety, and depression in response to the new violent scene.

In their review of the scientific evidence on the effects of pornography, Donnerstein, Linz, and Penrod (1987) propose a "contrast effect" in which exposure to an unusually attractive person depresses evaluations of more ordinary-looking individuals. For example, Kenrick and Gutierres (1980) showed male college students either an episode of "Charlie's Angels" or a slide of Farrah Fawcett in a magazine advertisement, and then asked them to rate, on the basis of a photograph, the attractiveness as a potential date of an average-looking female. Those who first saw either of the celebrity stimuli gave lower ratings. Cash, Cash, and Butters (1983) found that female college students who were exposed to female models in magazine advertisements rated their own attractiveness lower than those not so exposed. Kenrick, Gutierres, and Goldberg (1989) found that male college students rated the attractiveness of a photographed nude as lower after prior exposure to *Playboy* and *Penthouse* nudes than after exposure to art works or nudes of average attractiveness. The implication is that exposure to highly attractive persons suppresses ratings of more ordinary mortals.

Our discussion of callousness draws on two bodies of research. One concerns the effects on aggressive behavior of exposure to violent erotica. The other focuses on changes in beliefs and perceptions—that is, attitudes toward women or toward ways of interacting with them.

There is much evidence that, within the setting of a laboratory experiment, the exposure of males of college age to violent erotica under certain conditions will increase subsequent aggression against a female of similar age. Such experiments are well described in several recent reviews (Donnerstein, 1984; Donnerstein *et al.*, 1987; Malamuth, 1984; Malamuth & Billings, 1986). The experiment of Donnerstein and Berkowitz (1981) is representative:

> (M)ale subjects were first angered by a male or female confederate. Following this instigation they were given the opportunity to view one of four films. The first was a neutral film. . . . The second . . . was a nonaggressive–pornographic film. . . . The third and fourth films were of an aggressive–pornographic nature. They depicted a young woman who comes to study with two men. Both men have been drinking, and when she sits between them she is shoved around and forced to drink. She is then tied up, stripped, slapped around, and raped. . . . In the positive–aggressive film the ending shows the woman smiling . . . (t)he narrative also indicates that she becomes a willing participant. . . . In the negative–aggressive version . . . the narrative indicates that at the end she finds the experience humiliating and disgusting. After viewing the film, all subjects were given an opportunity to administer electric shocks to the male or female confederate (Donnerstein, 1984, p. 66)

In this and similar investigations, a pretext is offered for the delivery of the noxious stimulus. Typically, subjects are told that when the confederate errs on a task in another room they will be informed by a signal, and must let the confederate know by delivering the stimulus. These stimuli can vary in frequency or intensity, which become the measure of the degree of aggression. In the present instance, the typical outcomes are (a) aggression against a male target does not differ among the conditions; (b) erotica without violence does not increase aggression; (c) aggression against a female is increased in the negative–aggression condition when the subjects have been angered by the female confederate; and (d) aggression against a female is increased by the positive–aggression condition with or without prior provocation by the female confederate. Greater arousal to the rape depictions was eliminated as an explanation by the similarity among the four films in measures of physiological arousal while viewing. Thus, film content appears to be responsible.

In the absence of prior provocation by a female, only exposure to the portrayal of positive consequences increases aggression against a female, but when subjects have been angered by a female, the portrayal of negative consequences also increases aggression against a female. In the first circumstance, the positive portrayal presumably lowers inhibitions about aggressing by changing beliefs and perceptions either about the behavior or the target; in the second circumstance, the prior provocation provides a motive for and perhaps some pleasure from aggression against a female. Cues may link the real-life target with the victim in the portrayal. In the example, both were female; aggression against males, with or without prior provocation, was unaffected. Finally, a portrayal of violence against a female in the absence of any sexual behavior has been found to increase subsequent aggressiveness against a female, although the strongest effects appear to occur when violence and erotica are paired.

Erotica without violence has been found variously to increase, decrease, or leave unaffected levels of aggression. Mild erotica typically has no effect or decreases aggression; more compelling erotica often increases aggression. Sex of subject and sex of target or their pairings (male–male, etc.) do not make any difference, so there is no evidence that the exposure of young males to erotica especially increases aggression against females. Excitation transfer, level of arousal, dominant response, attentional shift, and hedonic valence (Donnerstein, Donnerstein, & Evans, 1975; Sapolsky & Zillmann, 1981; Zillmann, 1971; Zillmann, Bryant, Comisky, & Medoff, 1981; Zillmann & Sapolsky, 1977) become pertinent.

The likely explanations for mild erotica's having no effect are either its failure to induce sufficient arousal or its capacity to shift attention. More compelling erotica, while able enough to shift attention, will induce much greater arousal. Aggression will be increased only when it is the dominant response or those higher in the repertoire of responses cannot be put into effect; otherwise, some other form of behavior would be enhanced. Hedonic valence makes a difference, because a negative mood state—which may be attributable to the portrayal as well as to some other experience—increases the likelihood that aggression will be the dominant response. The effects on aggression of exposure to erotica without violence thus vary, but one likely outcome is that a young male, highly aroused but offended or disgusted by an erotic film, will behave more aggressively.

The failure of erotica to affect aggression differentially by sex of target obviously does not absolve it of any role in aggression against females. It is fairer to say that *violent* erotica does *not* endanger males than to say that erotica does not endanger females, or that erotica is *equally* likely to facilitate aggression against males and females.

The investigations of extended exposure to erotica, violent erotica, and slasher films cited earlier in regard to desensitization also examined other effects. Zillmann and Bryant (1984) invite the adjective "marathon" by beginning with six weeks of initial exposure of male and female undergraduates to varying quantities and kinds of erotica, followed by the measurement over three weeks of various outcomes. Exposure varied from massive (36 films) to null, with two intervening levels. Principal outcomes were that the greater the exposure:

1. The greater the reported enjoyment, the lower the reported negative valence, the lower the recorded physiological arousal, and the lower the degree of aggression directed against a peer of the same sex subsequent to exposure to another erotic portrayal; the authors (correctly in our view) attribute the reduced aggression to the combination of increased enjoyment, decreased negative valence, and decreased arousal.

2. The greater the degree of callousness explicitly expressed by males in agreeing with such statements as, "A woman doesn't mean 'no' until she slaps you," and "A man should find them, feel them, fuck them, and forget them."

3. The lower the jail sentence proposed by subjects for the perpetrator of a rape described in a newspaper article.

Zillmann and Bryant (1982) earlier had reported parallel outcomes for massive exposure to video erotica among both male and female college students in regard to expressed callousness, incarceration for rape, and support for the women's liberation movement, although they were more pronounced among males than females. Linz, Donnerstein, and Penrod (1984) and Linz (1984) found comparable effects for slasher films, with the latter finding that as few as two were sufficient to alter the outlook of viewers. On the other hand, Donnerstein, Linz, and Penrod (1987) describe (p. 79) research by Linz in which extended exposure to nonviolent theater and hotel movie channel erotica (such as *Debbie Does Dallas*) had no comparable outcomes. They suggest that effects may depend on the consistency with which portrayals are demeaning to or abusive of women. Linz, Donnerstein, and Penrod (1988) provide supportive data by their finding that among about 160 college-age males, those who saw R-rated nonviolent teenage sex films (*Fast Times at Ridgmont High*, etc.), X-rated nonviolent erotica (*Debbie Does Dallas*, etc.), or no films did not differ in their response to a rape trial, while there was weak evidence that those who saw slasher films became less sympathetic to the victim and more indifferent to rape generally; in fact, they invoke precisely this rationale, heterogeneity of portrayals within films, for their failure to find differences in rape myth acceptance and other measures of callousness attributable to film exposure.

While extended exposure to erotica may reduce aggressive responses to subsequent exposure, it does so at the cost of desensitizing viewers to erotica, and increasing callousness toward women, as expressed in statements endorsed and reactions to the crime of rape. Extended exposure to violent erotica and slasher films similarly desensitizes viewers. A corollary of desensitization is greater acceptance of the public availability of such stimuli. Thus, extended exposure cannot be said to be particularly beneficial for relationships between the sexes. Malamuth (1989) argues that even if direct effects of the various classes of erotica are minor, the indirect effects may be socially important by creating an environment in which the beliefs and perceptions of male peers are relatively indifferent to and even mildly supportive of violence and especially sexual violence against women.

The likelihood of the influence of television on responses related to sexual interaction is enhanced by the large role found by Courtright and Baran (1980) for the media—in this instance, television and films—in the acquisition of sexual information. Among about 400 high school and college students, media and peers appeared to be the principal sources. This is in accord with Bronfenbrenner's (1970) conclusion that these two have become preeminent as agents of socialization. Those more sexually active ascribed less potency to media portrayals, suggesting again that those without experience on a topic are most likely to be influenced by the media.

In sum, the findings attest to very modest but positive associations between television exposure and the holding of stereotypic beliefs by children and teenagers of both sexes. Sex differences abound, and much the same can be said when subjects or respondents are differentiated on other variables. The impression gained from studies covering a brief time span, whether experimental or correlational, is often not the same as that obtained when data are collected over a lengthy period. The record is one of success for altering stereotypic beliefs by nontraditional portrayals. This has been demonstrated repeatedly in the short term, and the "Freestyle" evaluation documented that it will occur in naturalistic settings with sustained effects, when such portrayals are accompanied by discussions that reinforce their themes.

We believe that conventionality is a key interpretive concept. Television viewing for young persons is a highly conventional use of time, and we would not be surprised to find that those who view more than average are more conventional than average in outlook. Television is somewhat out of step quantitatively in its portrayals, as Signorielli (1989) points out, by underrepresenting females in general and females in the workforce and by remaining stable over the past decade and a half when norms about sex roles have been changing. However, being out of step is not standing in opposition; television has accommodated these changes by some shifts toward more prominent roles for women in soap operas (Cassata & Skill, 1983), commercials (Bretl & Cantor, 1988), and major prime-time series (Reep & Dambrot, 1987), such as "Cagney and Lacey," "Hill Street Blues," "Remington Steele," "Who's the Boss?" and more recently, "L.A. Law." With each passing decade since television has been a presence in American society, there has been a widening of what is considered appropriate or acceptable, if not necessarily normative, for both genders. Television quantitatively distorts in the direction of still widely accepted norms which accord men higher status. Thus, we would not expect much of a contribution by viewing in general, because so much of what television presents will be in accord with what has been learned from other sources. We would even entertain the possibility that the demonstrated short-term effects of nonstereotypic portrayals simply depend on the activation or heightened salience of impressions of such activities, rather than the actual changing of beliefs or perceptions. Although stereotyping by young people is readily detectable, there is also plenty of variation in the outlook of young persons so that it is far from a monolithic, but surely important factor in the way they construe the world.

We do conclude, however, that television certainly reinforces and thus contributes to the holding of conventional beliefs. Programming is typically stereotypic and generally favors male ascendancy (Comstock, 1989); males appear more frequently, more often exert authority, display bravado, or demonstrate competence or expertise, and occupations are linked to gender both in kind and by status. The male secretary is a device for humor; the female a fixture. Tough cops don't use seat belts; lady partners do. The news is an excellent example—men predominate in presenting the news and in what is considered newsworthy. Thus, the inference that it was frequency of masculine topics that gave the male newscaster the advantage in recall in fact supports the conclusion that the news as it is ordinarily televised contributes to a conventional perspective on sex roles.

Certainly television portrayals may play a pernicious role in relationships between the sexes. Portrayals in television and other media of highly attractive persons may encourage dissatisfaction or lowered evaluations of the attractiveness of those of the pertinent sex in real life. Exposure to erotica, violent erotica, or violence against women in a sexual context, and especially the latter two, may facilitate male aggression against females and may encourage callous attitudes toward females, and particularly toward their sexual abuse. Exposure to such stimuli may desensitize viewers, so that the stimuli become rated as less pornographic, violent, or offensive, thus initiating a cycle in which the acceptability of such audiovisual entertainment increases. The increased acceptability, accompanied by increased liking, for such stimuli reduces the likelihood that they will increase aggression. However, violent erotica and violence in a sexual context presumably would retain some capability to do so because their prowess rests on more than arousal and negative valence. These additional factors include the portrayal of rewarded abusiveness when victims enjoy their plight; the linking of sexual expression with aggressive behavior, thereby enhancing the likelihood that the former also will elicit the latter; and cues in the portrayal, such as the gender and gender-associated attributes of the victim, that may increase the likelihood of aggression against a female. Even if long-term exposure to erotica may not facilitate aggressiveness directly, it may do so indirectly by creating an atmosphere in which aggression against females by males is more tolerated among males.

D. ETHNICITY

In the first major inquiry into the effects of the media on young persons, the multivolume Payne Fund series on the movies in the early 1930s (Charters, 1933; R.C. Peterson & Thurstone, 1933), the investigators found that films could have a major influence on beliefs and perceptions about those differing in ethnicity. Young persons numbering more than 1000, between the ages of five and eight, saw a movie about once every two weeks, and those older, between the ages of 9 and 19, saw a movie about once a week. When the movies consistently portrayed a non-white or non-American population favorably or unfavorably, beliefs and perceptions were decidedly altered in the direction of the portrayal. The films apparently often made strong impressions, because at all age levels, factual recall as well as a change in outlook were measurable, not only the next day but three weeks and six months later. Typically, effects increased with number of films seen with similar emphases, but there was at least one instance in which a single film had a large effect.

The applicability of these findings to television must be qualified by the differences between the two media. Theater movies may be seen regularly, but in comparison to television, infrequently. Theater movies in their polish, dramatic prowess, powerful imagery, and effective acting are more comparable to television miniseries, specials, and made-for-TV movies than to weekly series. This leads us to believe that the initial viewings of an unfamiliar series might somewhat affect outlook, and that this shift probably would be maintained by continued viewing. However, we would expect only effects comparable to those recorded for movies from comparable stimuli.

Such programming would be exemplified by the eight-part series "Roots." Surlin (1978) reviews the small literature, and a survey of urban residents too late to include (Hur & Robinson, 1978) essentially corroborates the earlier findings. Unfortunately, only two (Hur, 1978; McAllister-Johnson, 1977) deal with young persons, and these were teenagers. As we would expect, inclusive exposure was not common, with the average number viewed between five and six, despite the fact that by the end of the decade *six* of the episodes ranked among the top 20 most-watched programs of all time (Steinberg, 1980). As we would expect, more blacks than whites viewed. A large majority of the teenagers of both races perceived the series as accurate and discussed it with parents or others, although such discussions were reported more frequently by blacks than by whites. Taking the teenage and adult evidence together, the series appears to have induced guilt in many whites and anger or emotionality in blacks. However, there was scant evidence of changes in beliefs or perceptions, although many apparently believed the series made whites more sympathetic toward blacks and blacks more hostile toward whites.

Lambert and Klineberg (1967) collected data from 3300 American white children, aged 6, 10, and 14 years on their sources of information about four different peoples, those of Africa, China, India, and Russia. Among the six year olds, television was predominant, followed by parents. Among the ten year olds, television remained predominant, but school had become important and parents, negligible. Among the 14 year olds, school was predominant, followed by mass media generally. Television and movies were the major source of information about the peoples of Africa at all ages. D.F. Roberts and colleagues (1974), in their evaluation of the General Electric Company series designed to make American children feel more favorable toward children in other lands with different ways of life, "Big Blue Marble," concluded that viewing of the program had measurable effects in the intended direction. Bogatz and Ball (1971) in their evaluation of "Sesame Street," which includes characters varying in ethnicity, concluded that after two years of fairly regular viewing, both black and white children of preschool age had increased in the favorability of their beliefs and perceptions about children different in ethnicity; however, this outcome was confined to those in the special treatment condition in which viewing was systematically encouraged (Chapter III), and thus cannot be said to be typical of children viewing in the absence of such treatment (Cook *et al.*, 1975). Gorn, Goldberg, and Kanungo (1976) found that "Sesame Street" inserts portraying children different in ethnicity increased the willingness of children of preschool age to play with such peers. Mays and colleagues (1975) found that viewing 16 half-hour "Vegetable Soup" episodes, featuring children different in ethnicity interacting led both blacks and whites aged from six to ten years to express greater friendliness toward those different in ethnicity, and among the blacks, enhanced acceptance of their own ethnicity. Graves (1975) found significant shifts among white children aged from six to eight years in the assigning of positive or negative adjectives to blacks after a single exposure to an animated cartoon with either favorable or unfavorable portrayals of blacks, and more citing of positive adjectives when blacks in the portrayal numerically were in the minority and not the majority. Kraus (1972) similarly reported greater positive effects on evaluations of blacks for integrated portrayals in films aimed at white high school students. On the other hand, Dorr, Graves, and Phelps (1980) found, among several dozen children between kindergarten and the third grade, no evidence of shifts in outlook in regard to blacks immediately after viewing an episode of "The Jeffersons" that ostensibly portrayed blacks negatively.

Greenberg (1972) examined the responses of 300 white fourth- and fifth-grade children to black characters on television. He found that four out of ten indicated they would like to be like one or another black character; four programs whose casts included blacks were among their favorite top ten; and television was cited by about four out of ten as their major source of information about blacks. However, exposure to blacks on television was unrelated to beliefs and perceptions about real-life blacks, and both Greenberg and Reeves (1976) and Greenberg (1972) reported that the degree to which the portrayal of blacks on television was said to be realistic by children was positively associated with their amount of real-life experience with blacks. Atkin, Greenberg, and McDermott (1983) subsequently found among more than 300 whites in the fourth, sixth, and eighth grades that perceptions of the traits of blacks on television was positively associated with beliefs about the traits of blacks in real life; there was little evidence of exposure to blacks on television by itself influencing such beliefs. The degree of identification with black characters was much less overall, which may reflect changes in the characters portrayed on television at the two different times as well as anomalies between the samples. Even so, more than one-fourth of the whites said they would like to be one of the characters then current. In the CBS (1974) examination of the effectiveness of "Fat Albert and the Cosby Kids" in communicating positive messages, liking for the program among about 700 7–11 year olds was only slightly greater among blacks than whites. Among the white children, race was more often mentioned spontaneously in describing (essentially with approval) the cast than sex or age.

Vidmar and Rokeach (1974) found among a sample of about 240 American white teenage viewers of "All in the Family" that many identified with the bigot Archie rather than the tolerant Mike (Meathead); saw Archie as winning arguments; and found nothing wrong with his racial and ethnic slurs. Such responses were positively correlated with scores on a scale measuring ethnocentrism. This finding gains credibility from the essentially identical results among adults reported by Surlin (1974). This kind of selective perception in regard to ethnic groups other than one's own has been recorded frequently, with an early memorable example the "Mr. Bigot" cartoons of World War II, in which subway posters designed to ridicule racial prejudice were interpreted by the prejudiced as presenting arguments in its behalf (Cooper & Jahoda, 1947).

Wilkes and Valencia (1989), during an analysis of ethnic portrayals in television commercials, found that a black coder ascribed more significant roles to blacks than did a white or Hispanic coder, while the Hispanic coder perceived more Hispanics and ascribed more significant roles to them than did the other two. This suggests that while only a minority of characters and personalities on television are from ethnic minorities, they may enjoy a perceptual dominance among young minority viewers. This fits nicely with the positive correlations among black children reported by Stroman (1986) between amount of viewing and self-concept and by McDermott and Greenberg (1984) between self-esteem and favorable perceptions of black characters, and between each of those two measures and parental expressions of interest in the characters. Thus, despite their scarcity, portrayals of ethnic minorities may be a factor in self-esteem of such viewers, and especially when they are esteemed, as they typically appear to be.

Children and teenagers frequently cite television as an important source of information about other ethnic groups, and exposure to film and television portrayals of ethnic groups can affect beliefs and perceptions about them. This can occur with a single exposure, especially when the portrayal is compelling and forceful. Effects apparently occur not only for ethnic groups different from that of the viewer, but for beliefs and perceptions about the viewer's own ethnic group. Whites accept black characters, in some instances naming them frequently as persons they would like to be like and citing programs that include black characters as among their favorites. Portrayals that are ambiguous in regard to their interpretation by viewers as depicting positive or negative attributes are likely to be interpreted in accord with the viewer's preconceptions, thus reinforcing rather than changing beliefs and perceptions about race. There is far less evidence to draw on in regard to ethnicity than was the case for sex roles, and the complaints by Graves (1980) and Stroman (1986) in their reviews, that the effects of television on beliefs and perceptions related to ethnicity have not received much attention, remain valid.

E. SOCIAL COGNITION AND SCENARIOS

So far, we have confined ourselves to specific elements of the more or less coherent set of expectations or world view based on experience that serves as a guide for behavior. We now turn to the organization of such social cognition into a comprehensive, interconnected, systematic whole.

The best known example of such an approach in connection with television is the cultivation research pioneered by Gerbner and colleagues. Morgan (1988) in the *International Encyclopedia of Communication* provides a description:

> Much research and debate on the impact of television has tended to focus on individual messages, programs, episodes, series, or genres, usually in terms of their ability to produce immediate changes in audience attitudes and behavior. Cultivation analysis is concerned with more general and pervasive consequences of cumulative exposure to cultural media. . . . In its simplest form cultivation analysis has been utilized to determine whether people who spend more time watching television are more likely to perceive the *real* world in ways that reflect the most common messages and "lessons" of the television world than people who watch less television but are otherwise comparable in terms of, for example, important demographic characteristics. (p. 430)

Because so much that is pertinent to children and teenagers is scattered among other topics, and some issues can be addressed only by turning to data on adults, we will attempt to convey the pattern of outcomes without first cataloguing the findings. Although much criticism, controversy, and many proposed amendments have been made regarding this formulation (Comstock, 1982b; Cook, Kendzierski, & Thomas, 1983; Doob & MacDonald, 1979; Gerbner, Gross, Morgan, & Signorielli, 1980, 1981a, 1981b; Hirsch, 1980a, 1980b, 1981a, 1981b; Wober, 1988; Wober & Gunter, 1988), a fairly coherent picture has emerged.

Numerous null associations certainly have been reported, but they

have not overwhelmed in number the many positive associations recorded between amount of television exposure and a belief or perception in accord with the demographics or emphases of television. Morgan's (1988) catalogue includes "images of violence, sex- and age-role
stereotypes, conceptions of occupations, science, education, health,
family life, minorities, political self-designations and orientations, religion, and other issues" (p. 432). However, over the years, the focus
increasingly has been on violence.

There is no doubt that there always has been a great deal of violence
on television (Head, 1954; Smythe, 1954). Morgan (1988) asserts that
"Crime in prime time is at least ten times as rampant as in the real
world, and an average of five to six acts of overt physical violence per
hour involve well over half of all major characters" (p. 431). The cultivation hypothesis is that subscription to *mean world* beliefs and perceptions (of risk, abrasiveness, and dishonesty) is increased by greater
television exposure because of the predominance of violence on television.

The evidence requires, for interpretation, the introduction of two sets
of concepts (Comstock, 1982b). The first differentiates between the
types of relationships by which television exposure and a mean world
outlook might be connected: (a) *association* (are the two positively
correlated?), and (b) *causation* (does one contribute to the other?). The
second distinguishes between the types of outlook involved: (a) *fearfulness*, or beliefs about self, and (b) *pessimism*, or belief about circumstances in general. The first can be said to be personal, or affective;
oneself is the subject. The second, societal, or cognitive; the world at
large is the subject.

Association is well documented. It has been found not only for adults
(Doob & MacDonald, 1979; Gerbner & Gross, 1976; Hughes, 1980), but
also among children and teenagers of both sexes and at all ages (Carveth
& Alexander, 1985; Gerbner, Gross, Eleey, Jackson-Beeck, Jeffries-Fox,
& Signorielli, 1977; Gerbner, Gross, Jackson-Beeck, Jeffries-Fox, & Sig-
norielli, 1978; Gerbner, Gross, Signorielli, Morgan, & Jackson-Beeck,
1979; Gerbner *et al.*, 1980; Hawkins & Pingree, 1980, 1981; Hawkins,
Pingree, & Adler, 1987; J.L. Singer *et al.*, 1984).

The case for causation is less certain. Hughes (1980) provides the
most useful analysis, although his data are from adults, because of the
large sample size of about 2000, the use of the same "anomie" scale
frequently employed by Gerbner and colleagues, and his simulta-
neously controlling for the influence of nine demographic and personal
variables, while others have controlled fewer or one at a time (Table
4.8). With no controls, all five items behave as hypothesized, with four

Table 4.8
Mean World Beliefs and Television Viewing[a]

| | Hours watched per day | | | eta–beta[b] | N |
	0–2	3	4+		
(1) World affairs					
Before	.311	.342	.466	.144*	
After	.342	.354	.413	.066*	1333
(2) Public officials					
Before	.579	.693	.723	.139*	
After	.613	.686	.667	.066*	1333
(3) Lot of the average man					
Before	.496	.625	.618	.125*	
After	.534	.619	.555	.066*	1312
(4) Child into the world					
Before	.338	.404	.466	.113*	
After	.386	.378	.400	.015	1325
(5) Afraid to walk alone					
Before	.419	.421	.475	.051	
After	.451	.419	.418	.033	1362

[a] Before and after controlling for sex, race, education, income, age, hours worked (per week), number of memberships, church attendance, and population size.
[b] measures of association
* Significance level $p < .05$
Question Wording and Codes
(1) Do you think it will be best for the future of this country if we take an active part in world affairs, or if we stay out of world affairs?
1 = stay out, 0 = active part
(2) Most public officials are not really interested in the problems of the average man.
1 = agree, 0 = disagree
(3) In spite of what some people say, the lot of the average man is getting worse, not better.
1 = agree, 0 = disagree
(4) It is hardly fair to bring a child into the world the way things look for the future.
1 = agree, 0 = disagree
(5) Is there any area around here—that is, within a mile—where you would be afraid to walk alone at night?
1 = yes, 0 = no
From Hughes, M. (1980). The fruits of cultivation analysis: A reexamination of some effects of television violence. *Public Opinion Quarterly, 44*(3), 287–302.

achieving statistical significance. However, simultaneous control for the demographic variables of sex, age, and socioeconomic status are critical, because each is strongly related to both amount of exposure and fearfulness (Doob & MacDonald, 1979), with females, the elderly, and those lower in socioeconomic status, higher in both. Such variables as church attendance, employment status, organizational membership, and population of place of residence might play a role by differentiating among frequency and type of contact with the outside world. With controls, the nonsignificant item reverses in directionality; one loses significance, and three retain it.

Some would make much of the fact that there is no uniformity in the degree of exposure at which the holding of the belief in question increases and some signs of modest curvilinearity, but we see no reason to expect that different beliefs should be equivalent in the amount of television exposure required to influence them or that influence should be linear. These findings weaken but do not demolish the case for causality.

The four items achieving statistical significance before the introduction of controls fall under the concept of pessimism; three of these retained significance after their introduction. The item initially failing to achieve significance and subsequently reversed in direction falls under the concept of fearfulness. Thus, the case is not only stronger for association than for causation, but for either relationship, distinctly stronger for pessimism than for fearfulness.

This conclusion draws strength from impressive supporting data. Tyler (1978, 1980, 1984) found, in samples of adults in various sites across the country, that exposure to crime in the media increased estimates of the crime rate, but did not affect estimates of personal risk. Tyler and Cook (1984), in a direct test of the propositions that societal- and personal-level crime judgments exist independently and that they are differentially affected by the media, found firm and consistent support in three studies varying in design, topics, and populations.

The original cultivation formulation held that it was television as a whole that affected beliefs and perceptions. Yet, the mean world became a focus because of the frequency of violent portrayals, which implies a concern for kind rather than quantity of exposure. The emerging evidence supports such a reformulation, with beliefs and perceptions varying with differences in exposure to different kinds of television programming (Bryant et al., 1981; Carveth & Alexander, 1985; Hawkins & Pingree, 1980, 1981, 1982; O'Keefe & Reid-Nash, 1987; Potter & Chang, 1990; J.L. Singer et al., 1984; Slater & Elliott, 1982; Tamborini, Zillmann, & Bryant, 1984; Weaver & Wakshlag, 1986) with mean world beliefs and perceptions more clearly associated with the viewing of crime dramas and documentaries and news than with television in general. There is additionally some evidence (Potter, 1986) that, contrary to the implied universal cultivation effect, such an outcome is at least partially dependent on ascribing a high degree of realism to what is portrayed or accepting television as a truly informative window on the world.

The original formulation also has been expanded by Gerbner and colleagues to include *mainstreaming* and *resonance.* In the former, television is said to increase similarity of outlook; in the latter, to heighten real-world influences when it reinforces them. Morgan (1982) interpreted the convergence over time in sex-role stereotyping among females as an example of the first, while the finding by Doob and MacDonald (1979) that a mean world outlook was greater among residents of an inner city higher crime area when they watched greater amounts of television has been offered as an example of the latter.

In several instances, effects have been demonstrated experimentally (Bryant *et al.,* 1981; Tamborini *et al.,* 1984; Weaver & Wakshlag, 1986). This enhances the plausibility of some causal contribution by viewing. Such effects typically have been transient, and those with some signs of durability have not followed upon exposure to violent entertainment but exposure to factual documentaries of crime and violence.

There also is some evidence of reciprocity between a mean world outlook and selection of mass media. The classic examination is that of Boyanowsky, Newston, and Walster (1974) who found the murder of a female college student followed by increased attendance by females from the same dormitory at a film about psychopathic killers. The authors interpret this as fear control, with anxiety induced by the real-life crime stimulating a motive to experience violent crime in a safe setting, in which the apprehension of the perpetrator(s) is assured. Wakshlag, Bart, Dudley, Groth, McCutcheon, and Rolla (1983) found among about 60 undergraduates that those who were initially apprehensive about crime were more physiologically aroused while watching a made-for-TV crime movie, and reacted more strongly to various aspects of the film, while there were no differences in response to a noncrime-related commercial. Wakshlag, Vail, and Tamborini (1983) found among about 100 undergraduates that those made apprehensive about crime by exposure to a documentary subsequently selected films low in the portrayal of victimization or high in the portrayal of bringing the malefactors to justice.

Overall, the impression is one of some contribution by television to mean world beliefs, but not in the way construed by the cultivation formulation. The posited cumulative impact may not occur at all. Instead, exposure to violent television stimuli may simply activate or heighten the likelihood of recall of thoughts of a more pessimistic nature. Frequency of exposure in this instance may not be a measure of the history of viewing but of the likelihood of recent exposure to violence or distressing events in entertainment, news, or other programming.

If television induces a certain degree of pessimism, it also becomes party to a circularity. The pessimism would motivate the selection of television programming able to provide temporary relief, while at the same time frequently reinforcing the initial motivating state, as would be the case with crime stories or the popular retribution tale.

The findings on knowledge, beliefs, and perceptions give credence to the perspective offered by a number of observers that a principal influence of television lies in its shaping of internalized mental phenomena given such labels as framing, mapping, prototypes, schema, schemata, scenarios, scripts, neoassociation, and, of course, social cognition (Bandura, 1986; Berkowitz, 1984; Collins, 1983; Davis & Abelman, 1983; Janis, 1980; T.M. Williams, 1986). These phenomena in one sense have lives of their own, by affecting thoughts and feelings without necessarily affecting behavior. In another sense, they are linkages between experience and subsequent behavior. In this respect, television may be thought of as an influence on behavior by providing "mental models, beliefs, and expectations which are built up and modified through experience" (T.M. Williams, 1986, p. 403).

In the general model (Abelson, 1976, 1981; Schank & Abelson, 1977), television would be only one among many sources of experience. Cultivation thus is a special case of a more general phenomenon, the construction of an interpretation of social reality. It takes television as a holistic source, whose world view would transfer intact as an addition to what is otherwise experienced. The challenge in regard to the general model is to specify when television makes a contribution, and in making such an attempt, we replace the holistic view of television influence for one in which effects are selective by type of programming.

Real life would be the primary source, because affect is personal, risks are real, and rewards and sanctions, whether material, emotional, or ideological, are truly experienced. The directly observed behavior of others would have a secondary but important place because, through such responses as admiration, empathy, and identification, it would not be devoid of these elements.

The media, and particularly television, because it is by far the medium most attended to by children and teenagers, enter by supplying nonredundant information. Television programming is filled with images and experiences not available locally to most young viewers. When programs pertain to knowledge, beliefs, and perceptions for which alternative sources have been absent, television may function as a source of information. One important factor would be the consistency with which events are portrayed, but a very large proportion of such elements would be consonant with and redundant to other experience; little if any independent influence of television at any time would be expected. This leads us to expect more in the way of influence in regard to violence, where television for most young people is in contrast with real life, than for sex roles, where on the whole, it is not. This makes of television largely a factor reinforcing the status quo in regard to sex roles. It is for these reasons that nontraditional portrayals apparently have had some success in altering stereotypes; they are not redundant to the rest of television. In addition to the two somewhat paradoxical factors of consistency and nonredundancy of portrayals, we would expect television to contribute to internalized mental phenomena when it is given credence as a reliable source (that is, realistic), involvement is high, or identification pronounced. We would expect situational cues to play a crucial role in eliciting these stored mental elements. Thus, it is when the real world partially overlaps with what has been experienced principally from the media that we would expect behavioral effects.

V ADVERTISING

The influence of television advertising on children and teenagers has been the subject of continuing controversy for two decades. By the end of the 1970s, the average child aged between 2 and 11 years saw about 20,000 commercials, with the figure ranging from about 5500 for light viewers to 33,000 for heavy viewers (Rossiter, 1980b). Contemporary estimates (Condry, 1989; Condry, Bence, & Scheibe, 1988) would be about double, or 40,000 per year for the average child. This reflects the shift from 60-second to 30-second or shorter commercials in general audience programming; by the late 1970s, 30-second commercials were already the standard in children's programming (Meringoff & Lesser, 1980). Our examination covers the evolution of the controversy, the points of contention, the empirical evidence, and the policy options.

A. EVOLUTION OF THE ISSUE

Television advertising and its effects on young persons were placed on the public agenda as an issue in the late 1960s and early 1970s. Particularly prominent were Action for Children's Television (ACT), and its founder, Peggy Charren, who remain preeminent among those pressing for change and reform. Also extremely active was the midwestern advocate, Robert Choate, who for a considerable time directed the Washington, D.C.-based organization, Children, Media, and Merchandising.

During the preceding two decades, television advertising attracted almost no public attention in connection with young viewers. Saturday and Sunday morning programming carried as many as 16 minutes an

188

hour of nonprogram material, most of which were commercials, compared with an industry code prime-time ceiling at the time of 9.5 minutes. This occurred, not because of a belief by broadcasters in the greater forebearance of young audiences, but because these hours were categorized as day segments; advertising ceilings were higher to ensure profitability when audience size was smaller. However, this circumstance invited public displeasure, once displeasure had some advocates. As L. Brown recounts in *The New York Times Encyclopedia of Television* (1977):

> During the early years of the medium, the appeal of television to children was exploited for the sale of TV sets; later, when most households had but a single TV set, programs were aimed at children on the theory that the young controlled the family viewing until bedtime. . . .
>
> Although children helped to build circulation for stations, and good will for the new television medium, they were not initially perceived as a major marketing group for products. Television was considered too high-priced for child-oriented products in the 50s and early 60s when the single or dual sponsorship of programs was the rule. Prime time programs were particularly expensive, considering that they reached a large proportion of adults who were not targets of the advertisers. But a number of factors converged around 1965 to make children's programs a major profit center of networks: first, the proliferation of multiset households, which broke up family viewing and loosened the child's control over the program his or her parents would watch; second, the drift to participation advertising as opposed to full sponsorships, which encouraged more advertisers to use the medium; and third, the discovery that a relatively "pure" audience of children could be corralled on Saturday mornings (and to a lesser extent on Sundays) where air time was cheaper, advertising quotas were wide open and children could be reached by the devices used years before by comic books.
>
> By the late 60s television programming aimed at children was confined, with few exceptions, to Saturday mornings in the form of animated cartoons. Moreover, the animation studios developed a form of limited animation for the undiscriminating youngsters, involving fewer movements per second, which was cheaper than standard animation. Recognizing that children enjoy the familiar, the networks played each episode of a series six times over two years, substantially reducing costs. And while prime time pro-

grams, under the Television Code, permitted 9.5 commercial minutes per hour, Saturday morning children's shows carried as many
as 16 commercial minutes per hour. Citizens groups did not become aroused, however, until the networks began to deal excessively—in their competitive zeal—with monsters, grotesque
superheroes and gratuitous violence to win the attention of
youngsters. Advertisers, by then, were making the most of the
gullibility of children by pitching sugar-coated cereals, candy-
coated vitamins and expensive toys. (pp. 82–83)

(C)ommercials directed specifically at children . . . became a
highly controversial aspect of television, raising questions on the
morality of subjecting children to sophisticated advertising techniques. In the 70s consumer groups began protesting the differing
commercial standards for children and adults, as well as other
allegedly abusive practices, among them promoting nutritionally
inadequate foods, using program hosts as salesmen, tempting purchases by offering premiums, and advertising expensive toys in a
deceptive manner. (pp. 81–82)

ACT emphasized the clutter, the quantity, ostensibly dubious practices and techniques, and the alleged inherent unfairness or deceptiveness of advertising directed at children. It argued that many members of the audience were too young to understand the self-interested
motives behind commercials, and therefore could not properly evaluate
them. Choate emphasized the harmful behavior that advertising might
encourage, such as dangerous use of adult products in play, and in
particular, the consumption of highly sugared and nonnutritious foods.
In fact, he can be credited with almost single-handedly pressuring the
giant cereal makers into nutritionally upgrading their products by persistently documenting, before innumerable investigatory bodies, that
the food value was less than it could be. Through appearances before
congressional committees, petitions to the Federal Communications
Commission (FCC) and the Federal Trade Commission (FTC), complaints to broadcasters and advertisers, and coverage by the press, they
jointly created an atmosphere in which some conciliatory response by
broadcasters and advertisers, fearful of governmental interference or
public hostility, was almost inevitable.

The result was a number of significant if not revolutionary reforms.
The discrepancy between the amount of nonprogram material on children's programming and during prime time was first cut in half, then
reduced to zero. Advertising of vitamins named, packaged, and hawked
to appeal to children was ended. Restraints were placed on the use of

television characters and personalities (specifically, "host selling" was banned, in which hosts would peddle products on the same programs in which they were featured), although as any close attention to present-day Saturday morning programming would verify, their use in other contexts has not ended. The various codes ostensibly governing television advertising directed at children, consisting at that time of those prescribed by the National Association of Broadcasters (NAB), National Advertising Division (NAD) of the Council of the Better Business Bureaus, and those of each of the three major networks generally were strengthened. Later conciliatory shifts include the use of so-called "bumpers" or separators—brief segments, neither program nor commercial, that appear before and after commercials and supposedly help children to identify advertisements for what they are.

ACT and its allies eventually were successful in placing their demands for federally imposed restrictions on advertising directed at children on the agenda of the FTC. More recently, they have asked the FCC to bar programs featuring characters and devices coincidentally marketed as toys as program-length commercials (PLCs). The first led to a major series of FTC hearings on the possibility of new federal rules for children's television advertising. The latter has led to a federal stance that at best can be said to be convoluted and at worst, indifferent to both children and logic.

B. POINTS OF CONTENTION

There have been five principal points of contention. They include the recognition and comprehension of television advertising, the possibility of harm if the persuasive message is accepted, the influence on effective parenting, the role of advertising in providing programming for children, and the use of program content to promote products.

1. Recognition and Comprehension

Critics argue that commercials directed at children are inherently deceptive and unfair, because before reaching some age, they may not be able to distinguish between commercials and program content, may not perceive commercials as persuasive rather than informative, and may not recognize that the statements made by brand representatives are in the self-interest of the advertiser. They argue that the audiovisual techniques employed may mislead young viewers about product attributes, and that premium offers distract them from these attributes, ostensibly the correct basis for choosing among products. The reply has been that early in their years of viewing, children perceive commercials as differing from program content, even if they cannot define what advertising is. They assert that children cannot be damaged, even if unaware of persuasive intent and self-interest, because they lack the disposable income to act on desires created by commercials, which can be converted to consumption only with the cooperation of parents. The identifying of commercials is thus a problem for only a few children, and comprehension of the nature of advertising is irrelevant because children do not make consumption decisions independent of adults. They hold that to ensure truthful appeal, the techniques employed are governed by stringent self-regulatory codes, and that a premium in fact is a product attribute that merits consideration.

2. Harmfulness

Critics argue that acceptance of some or all of a commercial message may result in psychological or physical harm to a young person. The former include the inducement of feelings of inferiority, lack of self-esteem, and relative deprivation either through the attractiveness and skills of those portrayed or the failure to have use of an advertised product and the purchase of toys that do not match the expectations created, leading to anger, frustration, or disappointment. The latter include the consumption of heavily sugared and fast foods, to the detriment of nutrition and body weight, and the imitation of behavior that might harm self or others, such as operating a microwave, using chemically dangerous cleansers, or manipulating the controls of an automobile. The rejoinder is that puffery, placing the product in the best light, and the use of attractive characters are inherent in advertising; that nutrition is unaffected because advertising influences product and brand choices, but not basic preferences where parents and habit predominate; and that the rare act of unexpected imitation should not be the basis for a general standard. However, there is general agreement that commercials should be barred if they are actually misleading or have the properties of an attractive nuisance, that is, invite harmful behavior.

3. Parenting

Critics argue that television advertising directed at children often initiates a secondary persuasive process in which they seek the compliance of parents. These products may not be the first choice of parents, may be judged to be undesirable by them, and may not be unambiguously affordable. Nevertheless, refusal may lead to conflict. The avoidance of conflict constitutes an incentive for parents to accede, although giving in may be counter to their best judgment. The reply is that the phenomenon is exaggerated and misunderstood. Conflict is said not to be substantial enough to merit remedy, and requests can be used to teach children the bases for rational consumer choice (do we need it? do we want it? is it affordable? how does it compare in attributes and price with competing products? is there a less expensive alternative different in kind with which we would be just as satisfied at this time?). However, most codes have tacitly acknowledged the legitimacy of the concern by specifically barring appeals that instruct children to ask their parents for a product.

4. Programming

Critics argue that reliance on advertising to support programming for children diminishes its quality and value. Popularity across a wide age range becomes the goal, because revenues increase with size of audience. Animation, swift scene changes, loud music, violence, and other narrative techniques to hold attention predominate, with educational, affective and cognitive benefits, and programming for particular ages, assigned a minor if any role at all. This is in addition to the time taken up by commercials, which could be used for other purposes, such as public service announcements (PSAs) aimed at children. When questioned how programming could be supported without advertising, the critics assert that the FCC could require broadcasters to present a minimal number of hours for young viewers as a condition for license renewal. The reply is that the popularity among children of the television entertainment designed for them documents that it is what they want; the authority of the FCC to mandate programming so specifically is open to question; and any such step is highly unlikely, because the agency has never mandated programming on such a scale.

5. Program Content

Critics point out that the 1980s saw the emergence of numerous series either designed to portray existing toy lines or concocted in conjunction with the development of new toys, and that the result is a program-length commercial. The distinction between program and nonprogram content ostensibly then becomes one merely between which product is being promoted. The critics see this as an enormous escalation in precisely the type of practice that earlier restrictions on the use of television characters and personalities in commercials were supposed to restrain. The counterarguments are that the practice of marketing toys in conjunction with television characters and personalities has a long history including such notables as Mickey Mouse and Donald Duck, and the programs contain no persuasive messages in behalf of purchase. The FCC essentially concurred by ruling in the late 1980s that programs featuring characters, devices, and personalities sold as toys do not, by that fact, constitute commercials in behalf of those products.

C. EMPIRICAL EVIDENCE

The most comprehensive examination of the effects of television advertising on young persons is by Adler and his five colleagues (1980). This special task force was convened by the National Science Foundation to provide some empirical basis for the FTC deliberations on the topic that began in the latter part of the 1970s, and ended in 1981, and to make public the evidence to date. They evaluated dozens of studies; their bibliography contains more than 450 items; and they found 26 studies worthy of annotating in depth as an appendix. Although the authorship is made up entirely of academics or those not affiliated with the advertising or broadcasting businesses, we take their conclusions as conservative in phrasing, because the enterprise was conducted with an advisory committee containing the full spectrum of interested parties: public interest groups, advertisers, and broadcasters. Sociologically speaking, this is not an atmosphere conducive to soaring like an eagle.

Nevertheless, although our interpretations are sometimes different, we recommend their work with two additional qualifications. The first is that some new evidence, which we try to take into account, has appeared since they completed their analysis. The second is that they confined themselves to children between the ages of 2 and 11, while we give attention also to teenagers. We acknowledge that for teenagers, issues of recognizing and comprehending the nature of advertising are irrelevant, and those of parenting, reduced if not absent, but those of deception in general and harmful effects from acceptance of an advertising message remain fully relevant. In our society, protective concerns are either topic-specific (drug use, etc.) or age-graded (the status of minors before the law, etc.); teenagers qualify on both.

We divide our discussion into three broad areas:

1. Recognizing, comprehending, and evaluating commercials;
2. Accepting the message of a commercial; and
3. Exchanges between parents and offspring.

In regard to the first, we cover four topics: distinguishing commercials from programs; understanding the persuasive intent of advertising; the effectiveness of alternative audiovisual techniques in commercial comprehension; and the role of premiums in judging product desirability. The second encompasses five: source appeals and endorsements; threats to self-esteem; use of proprietary over-the-counter and illegal substances, and the consumption of alcohol and its abuse; food consumption and nutrition; and the role of amount and frequency of exposure. The third, three: purchase requests, conflicts and parental yielding, and consumer socialization.

1. Area #1

Adler and colleagues conclude that the mental capability to distinguish commercials from programs and to understand the persuasive intent of advertising increases with age, as one would expect, but that a "substantial proportion of children, particularly those below age seven or eight, do not draw upon the concept of selling intent in defining commercials, in distinguishing them from programs, or in explaining their purpose, suggesting little comprehension and/or low salience of persuasive intent as a critical feature of advertising" (p. 214). We believe it is crucial to distinguish between:

- Identifying commercials as different from programs, versus
- Understanding their persuasive intent, or identifying them for what they are.

The data unambiguously document that children below the ages of seven or eight recognize commercials as different in some way from programs. P. Zuckerman and Gianinno (1981) showed photographs of animated characters from either commercials or programs to 64 four, seven, and ten year olds, asked questions about the photos, and asked them to define a commercial. The younger children could not define a commercial, but most could identify who the characters appearing in commercials were and could match them with the products they vended; in fact, in testimony to their inability to comprehend the concept of "commercial," more could make such matches than were correct when asked which characters were "in a commercial." Levin, Petros, and Petrella (1982) asked 72 children aged between three and five years to identify 84 ten-second videos that varied in audio, visual, or audiovisual modality as from programs or commercials. Correct identification was inversely associated with age; correct labeling was predominant, with the minimal misidentification about 20% of the time for the five year olds; and there were no interpretable modality effects. Macklin (1987) found among 120 children of preschool age that only a minority correctly selected a picture of a boy and girl with a woman making purchases at a supermarket checkout counter from an assortment of ten, as indicating what the commercials they had just seen *wanted* them to do. The rate for four year olds was about 8%; for five year olds, 20%. In a follow-up study, 45 such children, after viewing commercials, were asked to choose a play environment that satisfied the same query, one of which was a play store. About 13% made the correct choice, although the figure was 40% for five year olds and zero for three year olds. Similarly, Butter, Popovich, Stackhouse, and Garner (1981) found that while a majority of 80 preschoolers could recognize commercials as different from the "Captain Kangaroo" sequence in which they were embedded, even larger majorities could not define commercials or say why they were on television. In a complementary vein, Ward and colleagues (Blatt, Spencer, & Ward, 1972; Ward, Reale, & Levinson, 1972; Ward & Wackman, 1973) found that, among those aged 5 to 12 years, the younger children distinguished commercials from programs on affective (they were funnier) or coincidental (they were shorter) grounds, while older children often introduced the criterion of purpose (they sell).

The distinction is made quite clear by the research of Blosser and Roberts (1985) who exposed 90 children varying in age from preschool to fourth grade to a variety of television messages, such as excerpts from the news, commercials, and instructional PSAs (Table 5.1). Their findings concur with the earlier evidence that ability to identify categories of content increases with age. When the criterion of comprehension was recognition that a commercial presented something that *could* be purchased, more than half before the age of seven could recognize a commercial. However, when the criterion of perceiving the message as persuasive in intent was employed, it was not until age eight or later that a majority could be said to recognize a commercial. News was identified earliest, commercials were next, and PSAs came last; this exemplifies the problematic nature of commercials for children's comprehension, because they without doubt exceed news in prior experience and yet become fully understood only at a later age.

We would also draw on the experiment by Gentner (1975), ignored by Adler and colleagues, in which she examined the acquisition of the verbs have, give, take, sell, buy, and spend. Children ranging in age from three-and-a-half to eight-and-a-half years were asked to make two Muppet dolls from "Sesame Street," Bert and Ernie, who were seated behind tables on which there were money and objects, engage in these activities. A typical instruction was, "Make Ernie sell a truck to Bert." Even those in the youngest of the five yearly age brackets (between three-

Table 5.1
Age and Comprehension of Message Intent

| | Age (years) | | | | | |
Message type	0–5 (N = 10)	5+–6 (N = 24)	6+–7 (N = 19)	7+–8 (N = 14)	8+–10 (N = 13)	10+ (N = 10)
Percentage comprehending message content						
News	30	21	53	50	77	90
Child commercial	80	83	95	93	100	100
Adult commercial	40	67	84	86	92	100
Educational	100	83	90	93	100	90
PSA	60	92	95	100	100	100
Percentage correctly labeling each message type						
News	60	88	95	100	92	100
Child commercial	10	62	53	71	85	100
Adult commercial	10	58	63	79	92	100
Educational	0	0	0	7	23	30
PSA	0	0	0	7	23	20
Percentage articulating correct message content						
News	0	38	63	86	100	100
Child commercial	0	0	16	36	77	60
Adult commercial	0	13	11	21	61	60
Educational	0	8	11	36	62	40
PSA	0	8	5	29	39	60

Adapted from Blosser, B.J., & Roberts, D.F. (1985). Age differences in children's perceptions of message intent: Responses to TV news, commercials, educational spots, and public service advertisements. *Communication Research, 12*(4), 455–484.

and-a-half and four-and-a-half) understood give and take, with the former almost universally grasped and the latter comprehended by four out of five. There was little sign of comprehension of buy and sell. Comprehension of these concepts increased with each advancing age bracket, until for the oldest (between seven-and-a-half and eight-and-a-half), it reached 95% for buy and 65% for sell. Except for those in the second bracket (four-and-a-half to five-and-a-half), when comprehension of the two was about equally modest (25–30%), sell consistently and sizably lagged behind buy.

Buy and sell involve more complex transactions than give and take. In addition to prior or future possession, they call for the exchange of money on the condition that there is an exchange of object. Sell probably lags behind buy because it is less familiar to children and possibly (as proposed by Geis, 1982) because it is associated with an ego gratification that children have yet to experience. The argument that the inability to role-play the transaction symbolically represented by a commercial interferes with the full comprehension of advertising is supported by the finding of Faber, Perloff, and Hawkins (1982) that, among 65 first and third graders, comprehension and the ability to role-play were positively associated. In any case, we are convinced that many children below the age of eight cannot comprehend the persuasive intent of commercials, and that this absence of comprehension increases markedly with decreasing age.

In this context, the importance of children being able to distinguish commercials from program content takes on a reduced significance. If children cannot make the distinction, they cannot recognize their persuasive intent, unless one wishes to take the cynical view (and in the case of children, a rather optimistic one in regard to their inferential capacities) that all of television has a persuasive intent. If children cannot recognize their persuasive intent, their ability to distinguish commercials as different from the program is irrelevant.

If we hold for children the same standards we hold for adults, then television advertising directed at them is deceptive for many children under the age of eight, and the proportion for whom it is deceptive increases markedly with decreasing age. Adults are conventionally protected from being deceived by advertising that might be mistaken for legitimate news reports by the label *advertising* or an equivalent warning. The rationale is that if they do not recognize the persuasive intent, they may be misled; if children do not recognize the persuasive intent of commercials, deception by the standards held for adults is inevitable.

Thus, we do not interpret recognition as comprehension. We would not take choosing a picture of a child in a supermarket from one or more alternatives as evidence of comprehension of a commercial among very young children as Donohue, Henke, and Donohue (1980) or Macklin (1985) have, although we do not doubt that the correct selection was frequent, increased with age, and an increase in the options decreased the number of correct responses, as they report. Instead, we would consider these and similar outcomes as more evidence that very young children associate characters and elements of commercials with marketed products.

Rossiter and Robertson (1974), in regard to Christmas toy and game choices, found that among about 290 first-, third-, and fifth-grade children, cognitive defenses (the ability to discriminate between commercials and programs, and a comprehension of the persuasive intent of commercials) became increasingly important, while affective or attitudinal defenses (liking for, attributing believability to, or general wanting of things advertised) became less important in resisting persuasion with advancing age. Christenson found some effectiveness for knowledge about commercials as a defense against persuasion. In an early experiment (1982), he found that exposure to PSAs warning about the nature of commercials increased understanding of their persuasive intent among first- and second-grade children. Among both first- and second-grade and fifth- and sixth-grade children, exposure to the PSAs led to a lowered belief in the truthfulness of commercials and lower flavor ratings of two subsequently advertised gums, although ratings went unchanged for a third advertised game; ranking among competitors for all three products went unchanged. Later (1985), he found that, among fifth- and sixth-grade children, mistrust of advertising was inversely associated with increased favorability toward a new product, a result he attributes to the extrathorough cognitive processing that mistrust would encourage. In our view, these varied findings imply that only among older children do these cognitive factors matter and have meaning.

Commercials obviously employ as many recognized means of attracting and holding attention as possible. In the case of young persons and especially children, this means high levels of action, pace, scene shifts, and visual change; familiar or highly appealing characters or personalities; and verbalizations that are catchy and invite imitation. Here, we are concerned with the use of techniques ostensibly employed to improve the recognition of a commercial or the comprehension of product attributes. The first has been represented by the use of so-called bumpers or separators to demarcate commercials from program content. The second is exemplified in the use of disclaimers, usually verbal appendages at the bottom of the screen.

Both have been adopted by advertisers and broadcasters in response to their critics. In fact, an extraordinary one-third of commercials on Saturday mornings contain disclaimers (Stern & Harmon, 1984). Neither seems to have the support of empirical evidence. For example, Palmer and McDowell (1979) found that the then-standard separator of a voice-over to animated characters announcing " '(Program title)' will be right back after these messages" did not increase the recognizability of commercials among young children. Stutts, Vance, and Hudleson (1981) found, in a sample of 108 three, five, and seven year olds, that separators were ineffective at ages five and younger; they were helpful for the seven year olds, but these children are reaching an age at which help is not necessary. Similarly, R.D. Liebert, Sprafkin, Liebert, and Rubenstein (1977) found that the then-standard disclaimer "Assembly required" was understood by few children, while most understood the more colloquial "You have to put it together." Stutts and Hunnicutt

(1987) provide supportive data from children of preschool age for the phrases "Each sold separately" and "Batteries not included." Meanwhile, Ballard-Campbell (1983), while giving added support to E.L. Palmer and McDowell (1979) in their finding of null efficacy for regularly employed separators, found that a more intense colloquial version that presented a symbol of termination was far more effective among boys aged four, six, and eight years. The voice-over declared, "O.K., kids, get ready, here comes a commercial" while the visual accompaniment was a red stop sign. However, the use of child-oriented techniques is not common, for Stern and Harmon (1984) in their analysis of disclaimers in commercials found they typically were in audio and used adult language. Paget, Kritt, and Bergemann (1984) found, in a sample of 84 ranging in age from preschool to young adults, that the ability to place oneself in the role of others, including advertisers, was comparatively quite low at the earlier ages and increased with age; of particular pertinence, they found that the persuasive intent of a commercial was recognized at a much earlier age when a spiel is directed at the viewer, rather than the common television format of portraying interaction among persons in connection with a product. Donohue, Henke, and Meyer (1983) found that among 75 children between the ages of six and seven the understanding of television commercials could be increased by both a videotape of Saturday morning commercials, which the instructor stopped intermittently to ask questions about their purpose and the techniques employed, and by role-playing in which the children developed commercials for a cereal product. R.P. Ross and colleagues (1984) found, among more than 400 boys between the ages of 8 and 14, that the use of live auto-racing footage in a commercial for a toy race car led to overestimates of its size, speed, and complexity.

We are not at all surprised to find that separators and disclaimers are not effective. It is in the interest of whatever channel is being viewed not to disrupt ongoing monitoring and risk channel shopping; disclaimers are not information an advertiser wishes to convey, but serve as a legitimization of the message. Similarly, it is hardly surprising that various conventions of commercial design discourage the recognition of a persuasive attempt and encourage exaggeration of the positive attributes of the product; both, again, are in the interests of the communicator.

In regard to premium offers, Adler and colleagues (1980), in their concluding summary, assert that the "inclusion of a premium in a commercial does not seem to distract children from other product attributes (as measured by recall of the content of the commercial), nor does the premium appear to increase children's evaluation of the product. These negative results should be interpreted with caution, however, since they are based primarily on a single study in which only one commercial was tested" (p. 216). However, when we examined the review by Ward (1980) that this summary purportedly represents ["Adler and colleagues" refers to the work as a whole or jointly authored sections; signed chapters are referred to by the individual author(s)], we encounter several studies that bear on the question of the effects of premiums on product evaluations, and are led to a somewhat different conclusion.

For example, Ward reports that R.S. Rubin (1972) and Shimp, Dyer, and Divita (1976) found premium offers effectively competed with product attributes in responses to cereal commercials. The former found that among first-, third-, and sixth-graders, premiums at every age were better recalled than product attributes; decidedly few at every grade level perceived the cereal as what the commercial was supposed to make them want, with the maximum score for the cereal when there was a premium included, but half that when there was no premium offer; and more first graders perceived the premium than the product as what the commercial was supposed to make them want (Table 5.2). The latter found a modest association between brand choice and liking for the premium. Atkin (1975b, 1975c, 1978a) found that more than three-fourths of mothers of children from preschool to fifth grade reported that their child cited a premium in asking that a cereal be purchased, and almost 10% of children's requests unobtrusively recorded in a supermarket included mention of a premium. A national survey by a marketing research company is described in which, among about 900 children ranging in age from 6 to 14, those younger consistently cited the premium as more important in choosing a cereal than such factors as "were nutritious," "were natural," or "were enriched or fortified." We interpret the evidence as suggesting that:

1. Premiums figure importantly in the response of young persons to advertised products;
2. Among younger children, recall of product attributes is lower than among those older, while recall of premiums is superior to that of product attributes;
3. Younger children perceive premiums to be more important than product attributes in choosing among products; and
4. Premiums are cited frequently by children when they ask a parent to purchase a product (the almost-10% supermarket figure is certainly an underestimate of premium-based requests, because one would not

Table 5.2
Premium Offers, Product Recall, and Perception of the Intent of a Commercial by Age

Recall of Specific Commercial Elements (number)

	Premium			No premium		
	First grade	Third grade	Sixth grade	First grade	Third grade	Sixth grade
Brand name						
Accurate	2	4	7	2	5	9
Cereal only	8	4	4	8	7	3
Symbol						
Accurate	8	8	7	7	9	12
Other animals	3	2	0	5	2	0
Premium						
Accurate	9	11	12	—	—	—
Other objects	2	0	0	—	—	—
N	12	12	12	12	12	12

What Children Think They Are Supposed to Want After Exposure to a Commercial (number)

	Premium			No premium		
	First grade	Third grade	Sixth grade	First grade	Third grade	Sixth grade
Cereal	1	3	5	9	8	10
Cereal (emphasized) plus premium	0	5	4	—	—	—
Premium only	4	3	3	—	—	—
Other	1	0	0	2	1	1
Don't know	6	1	0	1	3	1
N	12	12	12	12	12	12

From Adler, R.P., Lesser, G.S., Meringoff, L.K., Robertson, T.S., Rossiter, J.R., & Ward, S. (1980). *The effects of television advertising on children: Review and recommendations.* Lexington, MA: Lexington Books. [Reprinted from R.S. Rubin, (1972). *An exploratory investigation of children's responses to commercial content of television advertising in relation to their stages of cognitive development.* Unpublished doctoral dissertation, University of Massachusetts.]

expect many children spontaneously to recall, in the bustle of a store, an offer seen hours or days earlier on television).

Premiums are undeniably often the basis of product choices, and especially among those younger. However, with products as fungible as those marketed to children (who would wish to assert that one or another cereal differs enormously from the rest in nutritional value, or that one or another toy or game within a genre is inherently better than some other choice?), a premium often is as rational a basis as any for a decision.

2. Area #2

In regard to endorsements, Adler and colleagues (1980) reach a firm conclusion: "A number of studies have demonstrated that the mere appearance of a character with a product can significantly alter children's evaluation of the product, with the evaluation shifting positively or negatively, depending on children's evaluation of the endorser" (p. 215). For example, R.P. Ross and colleagues (1984) found in addition to finding that live footage led to distorted perceptions among boys aged from 8 to 14 about a toy race car, that endorsement within a commercial by a famous race driver increased preference for the toy; that commercials with celebrities were better liked, led to higher product ratings, and the celebrities were perceived as more competent; and that these effects were principally attributable to teenagers.

Kunkel (1988b) provides evidence both in behalf of the effectiveness of endorsements and the policy against host-selling in which a character on a program vends a product. He found, among about 160 children aged from four to five or seven to eight, that commercials within episodes of the "Flintstones" and "Smurfs" featuring characters from each program were more effective among the older children in creating favorability and intent to ask a parent to purchase the advertised cereal, while at both ages such commercials were less frequently recognized as such than when they appeared embedded in a different program. Hoy, Young, and Mowen (1986) in contrast did not find any greater difficulty of recognition among about 80 children from three to seven in age when a host-selling commercial was embedded in its program, but they did find lowered recognition when the commercial followed the program and lesser recognition of selling intent—which in general was very low because of the ages of the children—for host-selling than nonhost commercials.

The evidence in behalf of the influence of endorsements, even when only implied, essentially documents the persuasive effectiveness of program-length commercials. In effect, it is testimony to the fundamental technique. Their characters self-endorse by implicitly bestowing, by their presence, approval upon each other and the devices they employ. This identifies these vehicles as commercials, if not by label, at least certainly in function.

We concur with Adler and colleagues that the evidence demonstrates that both explicit and implicit endorsements affect product evaluations by young viewers. We are less in accord with their conclusion that there is no evidence of effects on self-esteem.

The three major means by which commercials might adversely affect self-esteem are by portraying achievements, whether social, physical, or mental of which the young viewer is incapable; by portraying others in some way, socially, physically, or materially as better off than the young viewer; or, by portraying persons like the young viewer in roles socially inferior to those of other young persons. It is true that in the review by Rossiter (1980a) only one experiment is discussed that bears directly on the first, but we think that Atkin (1975a) at least shows the potential for such outcomes. He showed one group of children a commercial in which a child builds an immense and complex, intricate tower with building blocks, and showed another group a commercial in which the tower is modest. Those in the first condition displayed somewhat more anger and frustration when subsequently playing with the blocks. In regard to the second, we think there is sufficient research to suggest that portrayals in commercials of those who are somehow superior to the viewer can lower self-esteem at least among teenagers [we refer to the contrast effect discussed in connection with sex roles (Chapter IV)] and arguably then among all children old enough to understand their relative deprivation. In regard to the third, the data on gender-based responses to portrayals makes a *prima facie* case for such effects. Portrayals of the genders in nontraditional roles can increase the acceptability of such activities among both sexes (Chapter IV), portrayals of females in traditional and nontraditional roles can shift the thought and behavior of females toward accordance with the portrayals (Chapter IV), the linking in a portrayal of an activity with a gender decreases the likelihood that those of the opposite gender and increases the likelihood that those of the same gender will engage in it (Chapter I), and there is a tendency for more attention to be given to portrayals of the same sex (Chapter I). A decade ago, Welch, Huston-Stein, Wright, and Plehal (1979) found that gender portrayals in commercials were highly traditional, and while they have become somewhat less so since, they remain on the whole traditional (Bretl & Cantor, 1988). The implication is that they encourage acceptance of a role of lower status. In sum, portrayals in each of the three categories that would lower self-esteem are common in television commercials.

When commercials portray achievements at which the viewer is competent as valued, persons like the viewer as better off, or roles engaged in by the viewer as superior, the obverse occurs. Self-esteem is enhanced. However, given the present makeup of commercials, such effects would be far more common for males than for females.

A special case arises when advertising aimed at adults may influence young viewers. A portrayal of a child using a microwave in a commercial to demonstrate ease of operation would be an example. Imitation by a child could be hazardous, and such outcomes are what the various broadcast codes have tried to avoid by stipulating what kinds of appeals are acceptable and not acceptable. Two product categories advertised on television—drugs and alcohol—have been the focus of both considerable controversy and empirical inquiry in regard to: (a) legal and illegal drug use, and (b) alcohol consumption and abuse.

Contrary to some popular misgivings and a petition by 14 state attorneys general to the FCC to ban all drug advertising between 6 AM and 9 PM (Bellotti, 1975), teenage drug abuse does not seem to be encouraged by exposure to commercials for proprietary over-the-counter drugs. The argument was that such commercials portray drugs as a handy means of relief; thus, they promote illicit as well as licit drug use. Milavsky, Pekowsky, and Stipp (1975–76), however, did not find among 300 males aged 13–15 years, from whom data was obtained six times over a $3\frac{1}{2}$ year period, any association between cumulative exposure to drug commercials and illicit drug use, or between such exposure and an attitude favorable to taking drugs, although such an attitude was positively associated with use of both licit and illicit drugs. On the other hand, they did find that cumulative exposure was positively if modestly associated with use of proprietary drugs. This pattern is in accord with the interviews with almost 700 third-, fifth-, and seventh-grade boys and girls by Robertson, Rossiter, and Gleason (1979), with questionnaires from an almost equal number in the same grades obtained by Rossiter and Robertson (1980), and the questionnaires from about 260 boys and girls obtained by Atkin (1978b). As described in the review by Robertson (1980a):

1. Young persons' "beliefs, attitudes, and requests for medicines" are positively but modestly associated with exposure to television commercials for proprietary drugs.
2. Parental control over drugs results in no noteworthy association between exposure to drug commercials and drug use, except in the seventh grade when young persons are making their own decisions about proprietary medicines, when it becomes positive.
3. Young persons highly anxious about illness are a "vulnerable subgroup." They are more favorably inclined toward proprietary drugs, they are exposed to more commercials in their behalf, and there is a

decidedly positive association between such exposure and the holding of favorable beliefs about these drugs. Nevertheless, the correlation between exposure and use, although positive, was small.

4. Various differences in other subgroups (those younger, from households of lower socioeconomic status, and those more often ill) in favorability, exposure, use or their interrelationships, provide no evidence that exposure has any effects.

5. Parents do not typically discuss drugs and illness with their offspring very often, but such mediation is associated with more favorable beliefs and attitudes on the part of young persons toward drugs, suggesting that it occurs mostly as a means of getting children to take medicines.

Both Milavsky, Pekowsky, and Stipp (1975) and Robertson, Rossiter, and Gleason (1979) measured exposure by meticulously counting the frequency of drug commercials in programs reported as viewed, so their measures provide an accurate index of relative exposure. Thus, both give credible evidence in behalf of the view that proprietary drug advertising, although not aimed at young viewers, has some influence on them. However, the influence is confined to favorability toward, and at older ages use of, proprietary drugs. This is in agreement with the more recent finding of Thornton and Voight (1984) that, in a sample of 3500 between the ages of 11 and 17, amount of viewing was unassociated with illegal drug use.

We concur with Adler and colleagues that the available data are inconsistent with the facilitation of illegal drug use by exposure to commercials for proprietary over-the-counter drugs. The very modest positive effect in behalf of over-the-counter drugs hardly gives cause for alarm. Over-the-counter remedies are available by that means precisely because the risk they impose is so low, and even if many are less effective than the advertising and labeling in their behalf assert or imply, we would not wish to impugn the psychological effectiveness of a placebo.

Unfortunately for analytic tranquillity, these conclusions cannot simply be applied to alcohol consumption and abuse, because the two product categories vary in important ways. Unlike proprietary drugs, alcohol in our society has a symbolic role in the transition from child to young adult, with access a privilege of the latter; it is physiologically and psychologically rewarding to a degree unmatched by the most efficacious of over-the-counter remedies; it figures importantly in conflicts with parents; it has social functions in interacting with peers of both the same and opposite sexes; and it is frequently consumed by characters on television daytime and prime-time drama, with one expert (Greenberg, 1980) estimating that "conservatively, a youngster, too young to drink, will be exposed to 10 drinking acts on television during a day's viewing . . . this can be projected to more than 3,000 a year" (p. 145). Drugs and liquor also differ in the societal classification of their hard varietals. Hard drugs are illegal; hard liquor is not. Thus, the triangulation between product, society, and individual requires independent treatment.

The television advertising certainly differs from that for over-the-counter drugs in thematic emphasis. Drug ads emphasize chemical efficacy. Alcohol ads emphasize social interaction, having a good time, and partying. There is also a noteworthy dichotomy in what is advertised and what is shown in television programming. Only lighter alcoholic beverages are advertised on television: beer, ale, wines, and wine coolers. Anything, including hard liquor, may be consumed by the characters in programming. Finally, the advertisements typically do not show people drinking, only beverages of the advertised brand being served. This dichotomy and final nicety are self-imposed restraints to preclude public complaint or federal intervention.

Comprehensive and very recent reviews are provided by Atkin (1988a, 1988b). The evidence he presents, along with additional data, suggests:

1. While commercials for alcoholic beverages obviously never portray teenagers or children, they often employ famous athletes, and endorsements, implied or direct, have proven very effective with young viewers. Alcohol consumption in programming could prime the young viewer (that is, make drinking more salient and desirable) because most of it is done by high-status males who are favorably portrayed (Breed & DeFoe, 1981). Kotch, Coulter, and Lipsitz (1986) found, among about 40 aged 10–12 years, that boys who saw a montage of drinking scenes from a commercial program assigned somewhat more importance to the good than the bad effects of alcohol. Among those aged 8–10 years who saw a segment of "M.A.S.H." with three scenes with martinis, Rychtarik and colleagues (1983) found that more subsequently chose whiskey instead of water as appropriate to serve adults than those who saw the same sequence without the martini scenes or no "M.A.S.H." segment. Both the commercial and programming stimuli presumably would have a greater likelihood of affecting males because of the predominance of male models.

2. In two experiments described by Atkin (Kohn & Smart, 1984, 1987), there was some evidence of an effect of commercials on con-

sumption. In one, college-age males saw varying quantities of beer advertisements embedded in a video of a soccer match, in a comfortable group setting in a lounge; exposure to the commercials was associated with ordering beers sooner, but not with overall consumption. In another, college-age females similarly saw varying quantities of wine commercials in a similarly lengthy television program in the same setting, and exposure to the commercials was associated with somewhat greater consumption of wine. In another (Sobell *et al.*, 1986), the investigators conclude that neither exposure to commercials nor alcohol consumption in a program increased subsequent beer drinking during a supposed taste test, but we think Atkin is correct in dismissing these null findings on various methodological and conceptual grounds, with two particularly grievous missteps made in the sensitizing of the subject to alcohol use by administering a breatholator test before exposure and conducting the experiment at the Addiction Research Foundation laboratories.

3. A number of surveys record positive associations between exposure to television or other alcohol advertising and alcohol consumption. For example, Tucker (1985) found, among about 400 high school males, that heavy viewers consumed significantly more alcohol than light viewers, consumption was linearly associated with viewing, and the imposition of statistical controls for demographic variables led to a strengthened association between viewing and consumption. Atkin describes several major undertakings. Strickland (1983) found a very small positive association ($r = +.12$) between exposure to television alcohol commercials and consumption when controlling for demographics and total television viewing among about 775 teenagers in the seventh, ninth, and eleventh grades. The association was much stronger with having friends who were heavy drinkers and among those who identified with those portrayed in commercials or viewed commercials to learn about new products and modes of behavior. Atkin, Hocking, and Block (1984) found, among 665 young persons aged 12–17 years, that exposure to print and television alcohol advertising was associated positively if modestly with consumption of beer but not wine, even after a myriad of variables were controlled including, in addition to demographics, church attendance, social influences (such as parent and peer drinking), and exposure to other media (such as PSAs about alcohol or drinking in television entertainment). Those high in exposure were more likely to have tried advertised brands. Atkin, Neuendorf, and McDermott (1983) pooled the data for the younger persons from Atkin, Hocking, and Block (1984) with data from about the same number of young adults to examine abuse. They found a very

small positive association between total media advertising exposure and excessive drinking, when controlling for other variables, and a similar small positive association between such exposure and drinking while driving or otherwise in an automobile. Strickland (1983) reported a small, direct positive association between exposure to television alcohol advertising and only one (belligerence) of five misuse measures (such as drinking alone or rapidly), with any other contributions only possible indirectly through the small positive association with overall consumption, which in turn was associated positively to a modest degree with the abuse measures.

4. A post-Atkin analysis (Chirco, 1990) of data from about 2000 teenagers collected by the federally financed Monitoring the Future study found heavy drinking associated with having friends who drink and whose attitudes are favorable toward drinking, and with opportunities to drink. No association was found with television exposure, except possibly among a subset of young females who consumed excessive quantities of wine. The pattern for marijuana use was similar. This departs from what one would expect if commercials played a role in alcohol consumption, because the one is an advertised substance, and the other is not. Because it is a secondary analysis of data obtained for other purposes, the measures are not as elaborate or pointed as those employed by Strickland and by Atkin and colleagues, but the data are alone in representing a national sample.

The case for some influence of television on alcohol consumption is weaker, in our view, than that for drug commercials on over-the-counter drug use, but it is stronger than that for the influence of those latter commercials on illegal drug use. At first, this appears somewhat surprising, given the many factors (physiological, psychological, and social) not present for proprietary drugs, and present to a much reduced degree for illegal drugs, that would favor experimenting with or consuming alcohol.

The experimental literature is too sparse to be of much help, although there is a hint that for those with more established consumption patterns (males, in this instance), commercials may reduce inhibitions over deciding to drink, while among those with less established patterns (females), they may increase consumption somewhat. The one major test of overall television exposure with a national sample found no influence. We agree with Atkin that, on the whole, there is some evidence of a contribution by advertising. However, we conclude that the particular role of television, commercials or programming, appears to be minor, if present at all. If television does have any influence, it is, as Atkin argues, at the period when young persons decide whether or not to begin drinking, between the ages of 10 and 14. The many physiological and social factors that enhance the likelihood of alcohol use probably, in effect, delimit the role of the media and television in particular, for as we have seen, they have the greatest likelihood of influence when other factors are absent.

The products advertised on children's programming have displayed considerable stability over the decades, although there have been some noteworthy changes (Barcus, 1977, 1980; Condry, 1989; Condry *et al.*, 1988; Meringoff & Lesser, 1980; Rossiter, 1980b). Food has been predominant on the three major networks, with sugared cereals followed by candy and gum as most recurrent, except during the pre-Christmas weeks, when toy advertising becomes particularly frequent. Fast-food chains, despite the apparent ubiquity of certain logos, have always been a modest presence, about one-fifth of all food commercials at best. On independent stations, toys early were predominant. By the end of the 1980s, toy advertising had become more frequent outside the Christmas weeks on the networks, and there had been a large increase in the number of independent stations—about 150% over the past three decades (Comstock, 1989). The result is that as the 1990s begin, there are many more commercials directed at children than in past decades; toys have become increasingly prominent; food products, and particularly sugared cereals, candy, and gum, remain important; and fast foods, while maintaining their share of network food advertising, have become much diminished in overall presence.

Adler and colleagues, probably because of the substantial amount of empirical evidence presented in the review by Meringoff (1980b), reach a firm conclusion:

> Empirical evidence attests to the general effectiveness of food advertising to children. Children have been found to learn the information provided in food commercials, believe the product claims made about advertised foods, draw inferences about product benefits, and influence the purchase of the foods advertised to them. In the short-term, exposure to specific food commercials has produced significant increases in children's expressed preferences for the products promoted. (p. 217)

For example, Goldberg, Gorn, and Gibson (1978) manipulated the exposure of 80 first-grade children to commercials for sugared foods or PSAs for highly nutritional snacks, with both embedded in a television program. Those who saw the commercials chose more sugared foods; those who saw the PSAs chose more nutritional snacks (Table 5.3).

Table 5.3

Television Experience and Food Preferences and Requests

Mean number of sugared food choices following television exposure[a]

	Commercial	PSA	None
	12.58	8.70	10.20

Purchase influence attempts, commercial reinforcement, overall television reinforcement, and hours of television watched at home[b]

Purchase influence attempts	Television reinforcement (r_3)		Hours of television watched (r_3)	
	Commercial reinforcement ratio	Overall television reinforcement	Commercial	Noncommercial
Total	.52	.64	.31	−.06
Per minute in store	.53	.33	.35	−.09

Commercial exposure and ice cream flavor recognition and preference[c]

Condition	Correct flavor (percentage)	Brand preference (mean score)
One commercial	62	3.01
Three repetitions	70	
Five repetitions	47	
Three different commercials	85	4.05
Five different commercials	72	3.71

[a] From Goldberg, M.E., Gorn, G.J., & Gibson, W. (1978). TV messages for snacks and breakfast foods: Do they influence children's preferences? *Journal of Consumer Research, 5,* 73–81.

[b] Note: r_3 of ±.26 is significant at the .05 level of confidence (one-tail test); r_3 of ±.36 is significant at the .01 level of confidence (one-tail test).

From Galst, J.P., & White, M.A. (1976). The unhealthy persuader: The reinforcing value of television and children's purchase influence attempts at the supermarket. *Child Development, 47,* 1089–1096.

[c] Adapted from Gorn, G.J., & Goldberg, M.E. (1980). Children's responses to repetitive television commercials. *Journal of Consumer Research, 6*(4), 421–424.

Galst and White (1976) observed about 40 three- to five-year-old children and their mothers in the supermarket and found prior amount of television viewing positively associated with number of requests; the kinds of products requested were those more often advertised on children's programming. Goldberg and Gorn (1978) found that exposure of eight- to ten-year-old boys to a commercial for an unfamiliar brand of ice cream led to learning of the flavors offered and a preference for this brand, with the preference increasing with exposure to three different commercials instead of a single commercial in its behalf.

In a convincing demonstration, Gorn and Goldberg (1982) found, among 288 children aged from five to eight years, who saw for 14 days Saturday morning programs with fruit and fruit juice commercials, candy and Kool-Aid commercials, pronutritional PSAs, or no commercials, that the commercials made a decided difference in their choice of snacks immediately after viewing. Those who saw orange juice commercials chose that juice far more often than did those who saw Kool-Aid commercials, and the candy commercials resulted in more candy than fruit being chosen. This experiment is particularly credible because of the natural circumstances of viewing regular programming in groups, the free choice of snacks, and the fact that the groups did not differ in a postexperimental measurement of what they said they thought the experimenters wanted them to do; that is, there was no sign of so-called demand or experimenter effects.

Bolton (1983) provides evidence on long-term effects. Among about 260 children between the ages of 2 and 11, she found only small effects attributable to exposure to television food advertising compared to other factors, such as parents, but such exposure did increase, to a small degree, snacking and caloric intake, and overall slightly decreased quality of nutrition.

Nutritional behavior, however, cannot be said to be easily influenced by video presentations when the sought-for behavior is counter to what young viewers think is tasty. P. Zuckerman, Ziegler, and Stevenson (1978) found, among 110 second-, third-, and fourth-grade children, that attention to cereal commercials declines after the beginning, that a second commercial in a pair gets less attention than the first, and that before the age of nine, a single exposure is insufficient for many to recognize having seen the commercial. P.E. Peterson, Jeffrey, Bridgwater, and Dawson (1984) examined recall, information, preference, and behavioral choice by about 100 nursery school children after exposure daily for ten class days to a 20-minute video promoting consumption of nutritional foods, both by program content and PSAs, and found only recall and information affected, by implication challenging the effectiveness of brief disclaimers of commercials seen no more than once a day recommending product use as "part of a balanced breakfast." Galst (1980) found, among three to six year olds, that pronutritional commercials did not affect food choices unless followed by supportive recommendations by a live adult, while invariably the majority of choices were of low-nutritional sugared snacks. Stoneman and Brody

(1983b) found, among 90 pre-school, kindergarten, and second grade children, that exposure to cereal commercials increased recognition and interest in cereal products generally, so that television persuades children in behalf of whole classes of manufactured foods; they also found, as would be expected, that visual and audiovisual commercials were more effective than auditory only and that recognition increased with age. Faber, Meyer, and Miller (1984) found, among about 165 children ranging in age from 3 to 14, that exposure to a verbal health warning following a cereal or candy commercial led to considerable immediate recall even among the portion of the sample classified as younger, and a mild fear appeal was especially effective in this regard. Stoneman and Brody (1981a) found among 120 children in the fourth grade that preferences for a salty snack could be increased by a commercial in its behalf, and then further increased or decreased depending on whether a live peer pointed to a slide screen illustration of the snack or a nonsalty food item. On the whole, these findings lead to little optimism over altering the generic choices of children by television-based interventions, for pronutritional messages always will be overwhelmed in number by commercials for sugared and salted foods that children find highly pleasurable.

Amount of television viewing by young persons has been recorded as positively associated with obesity (Dietz, 1990) and negatively associated with measures of physical, psychological and social well-being (Tucker, 1986, 1987). We would not burden these specific correlations with even suggesting that television viewing causes lower levels of well-being, but we do find a suggestion that those who watch a great amount of television, and presumably greater quantities of commercials, may be at greater risk in regard to nutrition and health than those who typically view less. We find ourselves quite convinced by the evidence that television commercials play a role in the brand-based food choices of young persons, and that among younger children, premium offers may play a larger role than product attributes, including those that are health-related. Most of the foods advertised are certainly not ideal in their sugar and other contents, although they can hardly be faulted as a minor, enjoyable component of a regimen. However, young persons are not generally on a regimen; they eat, and commercials not only do not promote restraint in consumption, but also the emphasis on the role of advertised cereals as part of a balanced breakfast is at best unobtrusive and restrained. We see a cost measured by a lessening of the well-being of young persons, children and teenagers, by such advertising.

In regard to amount and frequency of exposure, we reach essentially the same conclusions as do Adler and colleagues on the basis of the review by Rossiter (1980b):

1. Repeated exposure by young viewers to the same commercial on Saturday mornings is remarkably modest, with about twice in one day the maximum likely to occur, and this not often.
2. Young viewers do not become more persuasible by television commercials as a function of their increasing cumulative exposure with age.
3. After one or very few viewings, repeated exposure to the same or different commercials for a product does not enhance product attractiveness; at best, repetition reintroduces or maintains salience of attitudes developed at the time of initial exposure(s).
4. As young persons grow older, they become increasingly critical of and negative toward commercials. Distrust begins to be expressed by the second grade, and becomes widespread by the sixth grade, with second graders primarily citing the unreality of something protrayed, such as a stomach with a window, while those in the sixth grade and beyond focused on persuasive intent; this is evidence that, even by the age when a majority of children can define a commercial, persuasion does not figure prominently in their thinking about commercials. However, there is no evidence that this results in any noteworthy decline in purchase requests or in the interest of young viewers in purchasing advertised products.

However, these qualifications appear to be suspended for a product class when it is extraordinarily salient, advertising is concentrated, and there is a decision date after which the commercials become comparatively irrelevant. That is, when circumstances create a "big build-up" for consumption. We reach this conclusion on the basis of Rossiter and Robertson's (1974) examination of the toy and game preferences of about 290 first-, third-, and fifth-grade children during the pre-Christmas advertising season. In early November, they found that children with superior affective and cognitive defenses against advertising selected fewer advertised toys, but by mid-December, defenses ceased to predict choice; among those with initially strong defenses, the choosing of advertised toys and games had increased. These findings could occur only if repetition of commercials for specific products under these particular circumstances made the commercials more effective.

Sanft (1985) found, among five and six year olds, that knowledgeability about advertising was associated with superior recall of product information in cereal commercials they were shown, suggesting that knowledgeability is not necessarily an effective defense. She found no immediate effects on preferences, but arguably the foundation for a later influence on consumer decision making had been laid. Brucks, Armstrong, and Goldberg (1988) found, among 102 children in the fourth grade, that counterarguing was enhanced by showing them two films accompanied by a discussion about how advertising works, but only markedly so when the salience of advertising was increased by a prior test about advertising. Even then the counterarguing was confined to the advertisement and did not include the product. They also conclude that direct questions about advertising act as cues that prime the verbalization of counterarguments, which implies that the frequent finding that skepticism and mistrust of advertising increases with age has scant relevance to the way it functions. Moschis and colleagues (Moschis 1987; Moschis & Moore, 1979, 1981; Moschis, Moore, & Stanley, 1984) found among teenagers that greater television exposure appeared to increase brand loyalty, and especially for products particularly pertinent to teenagers, although much of the possible range of brand loyalties, such as for food products, had been established earlier. We concur with their quoting of Rossiter (1979):

> Children's increasingly negative attitudes toward TV advertising do not mean much . . . (T)hey merely acquire an adult-like attitude against TV advertising as a social institution; an attitude that bears little relationship to advertising's actual effects. (p. 232)

3. Area #3

The frequency of children's purchase requests can be only crudely estimated, because the data reviewed by Robertson (1980b) consist of gross figures, and no better data have become available in intervening years. Thus, Atkin (1975c) found that among about 440 children ranging in age from preschool to fifth grade and identified as light viewers "a lot" was chosen to describe the frequency of their requests by 16% for toys and 24% for cereals, while 64 and 50% chose "sometimes" over "never" for a total of between 75 and 80% at least occasionally making requests. Among about 300 identified as heavy viewers, "a lot" was chosen by 40% for both toys and cereals; these data gain credence from their correspondence with the reports of about 300 of the children's mothers. Isler, Popper, and Ward (1987) found from diaries completed over four weeks by about 260 mothers of children between the ages of 3 and 11 that about one-sixth of all purchase requests were attributed to television advertising. Totality of requests decreased by age, with the average for those 3–4 about 25, those 5–7 about 13, and those 9–11 about 10; attribution of the request to television similarly declined, with figures of about 26, 18, and 9%. Caron and Ward (1975) found, among about 85 third- and fifth-grade children and their mothers, that television was the source of the children's Christmas gift requests about one-fourth of the time, with the figure about the same for friends. Rossiter and Robertson (1974) found television the most frequent source among their several hundred first through fifth graders. Data such as these lead to no better conclusion than that young persons typically ask with some regularity for products advertised to them on television.

The data of Isler and colleagues suggest that source of request varies by product. Television was said to be responsible for almost one-half of toy requests and almost one-third of cereal and other food requests. In contrast, for clothing the 39% for siblings and friends and the 26 for "saw in store" dwarfed the 7% for television; for candy and snack foods, saw in the store was preeminent (41 and 24% respectively, compared to 12 and 8 for television); and for sporting goods, siblings and friends were preeminent (41 versus 9 for television). This is a plausible pattern, for it represents the frequency of product appearances on television and the likelihood of exposure by other means.

The evidence on parental yielding is similarly imprecise (Table 5.4). If

Table 5.4
Purchase Requests by Children and Parental Yielding

Study	Product type	Percentage yielding
Ward & Wackman (1972)	Cereals	87
	Snack foods	63
	Games and toys	54
	Candy	42
	Toothpaste	39
	Shampoo	16
	Pet food	7
Atkin (1975b)	Cereal	62
Wells & LoScuito (1966)	Cereal	69
	Candy	57
Galst & White (1976)	Overall	45
Caron & Ward (1975)	Toys	31
Robertson & Rossiter (1977)	Christmas gift	43

Adapted from Adler, R.P., Lesser, G.S., Meringoff, L.K., Robertson, T.S., Rossiter, J.R., & Ward, S. (1980). *The effects of television advertising on children: Review and recommendations.* Lexington, MA: Lexington Books.

mothers are asked how often they yield, we have only a crude parental estimate of the outcome of an interaction that may range in frequency for a particular family from hardly ever to several times daily (Ward & Wackman, 1972). If we choose to observe parents and children in the supermarket or elsewhere, we have only a sampling of time and space that surely underestimates the number of requests and possibly the frequency of yielding (Atkin, 1975b; Galst & White, 1976; Wells & LoSciuto, 1966). Even if the metric were accurate, yielding would be an imperfect measure of the influence of children on consumption, because it excludes the first and fourth of the child consumer typology proposed two-and-a-half decades ago by Wells (1965):

1. By making direct, personal purchases using money given them by parents or somehow earned;
2. By directly requesting at home that a product be purchased;
3. By directly requesting in the store that a product be purchased; and
4. By "passive dictation," that is, by having communicated preferences to parents, the child has established a purchase agenda to which parents conform without further requests from the child.

Still, the varied data presented in the review by Robertson (1980b) are highly consistent. Yielding to cereal requests is most frequent, and a conservative estimate would place the proportion at about half the time or more (Fig. 5.1; Table 5.4). There is less yielding to requests for candy. In fact, yielding seems to be a function of category of product, with food items followed by games and sundries and items that children consume ranking above those consumed by others; thus, one survey (Ward & Wackman, 1972) found that 87% of mothers said they yielded to cereal requests, while only 7% said they yielded to requests for pet food. Although they found somewhat higher rates of yielding, with about two-thirds of the children's requests being acted on favorably, the more recent data of Isler and colleagues are essentially confirmatory; they also found somewhat more resistance when a television commercial was cited as the source than when a child simply asked for a product, and that frequency of requests declined with age—undoubtedly because as children grow older they begin to consume on their own except for food staples and household snacks.

The degree of conflict and disappointment that occurs when requests are denied also is difficult to gauge precisely, but the evidence is clear enough that it occurs more than rarely and probably somewhat more than warrants the term occasionally. Shiekh and Molesti (1977) and Goldberg and Gorn (1978) make a *prima facie* case for a fair amount of conflict. The former presented 72 boys and 72 girls in the first, third,

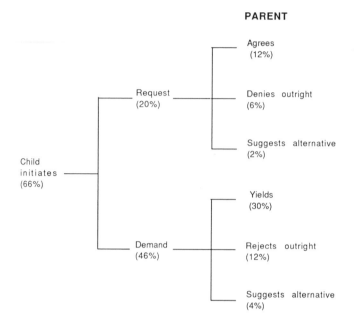

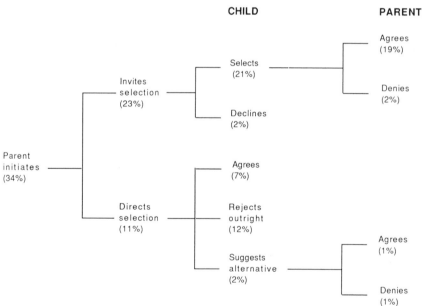

Fig. 5.1 Supermarket breakfast cereal interactions. Adapted from Atkin, C.K. (1978). Observations of parent–child interaction in supermarket decisionmaking. *Journal of Marketing, 42,* 41–45.

and fifth grades with a story about a child who watched a television program, saw a toy commercial, and asked that the toy be purchased. They asked the children what the child would do if the parents refused. About a third said the child would feel bad, about a fourth said the child would accept the decision, about a fourth said the child would become aggressive, and about one out of six said the child would persist. The latter manipulated exposure to a toy commercial among about 160 four and five year olds. Those who saw the commercial were more likely to believe that a child for whom the toy was not purchased by the father would not want to play with the father and would be unhappy. Two studies by Atkin (1975b, 1975c) provide some figures. In one, one-fifth of a sample of children said they became angry "a lot" when a toy request was denied, and one-sixth said they argued "a lot" in the same circumstance. The comparable figures for "sometimes" were two-fifths and one-third, which sum to half or more becoming angry or arguing over toy denials. Similar but slightly lower figures were recorded for cereal requests. In the other, observations of parents and children in supermarkets led to about two-thirds of denials recorded as evoking anger from the child and one half as inducing disappointment. Isler and colleagues (1987), relying on diary data from mothers, offer lower but not minute figures—a refusal was said to be met by disappointment about one-fourth of the time, by brief arguing in an additional one-sixth, and by extensive arguing in about one out of 20 instances. Stoneman and Brody (1981b) found, among 36 mothers and their preschool children, that exposure to television commercials embedded in a program before going shopping increased overall purchase requests and purchase requests for food products by the children. The mothers apparently took some offense at the obvious nature of the source of requests, for in this circumstance more often said no, replaced or had the child replace the item on the shelf, or offered alternatives. Wiman (1983) found among somewhat more than 200 mothers and their elementary school age children that discussions about television advertising were positively associated with requests by the children to purchase items, and that such requests increased as the attitudes of parents and children toward advertising diverged, hinting that such discussion is often a response to a child's high receptivity to advertising. Robertson, Ward, Gatignon, and Klees (1989) found, in a crosscultural comparison of 84 U.S., 118 Japanese, and 65 English families, that children's level of purchase requests and conflict with parents were greatest in the United States, were positively associated, and that requests were positively associated with amount of viewing. The major factor constraining anger, disappointment, or conflict is that many (and in the case of cereals, probably most) requests are met.

The quantitative data make it clear that families differ considerably in the communication that occurs in regard to consumption. Requests, the response to requests, and the degree of yielding all vary. Reid (1979) closely observed nine families that varied in the degree that parents instructed or coached children about consumer behavior. He concluded that the rules that parents have for behavior while viewing importantly affect children's responses to television advertising. For example, in some families interrupting viewing with a product request or the mimicking of a commercial is permitted; in others, it is not. The more immediate responses are permitted, the more likely there will be some longer term influence because recall will be enhanced. He argues that children's responses to commercials represent a transaction involving television, parents, and others in the viewing situation. We concur that the norms established by parents in regard to commercials figure importantly in any influence they have on a child, but we insist that the fundamental substance of any such transaction are the persuasive messages reaching children by the mass medium of television.

Consumer socialization has been defined by Ward (1980) as "the continuous, ongoing process by which children learn skills, knowledge, and attitudes relevant to their present and future behavior as consumers" (p. 185). Two types of models have emerged: (a) stage theories, which emphasize the increasing competencies in cognitive processing that occur with age, and (b) structural or outcome analyses, which emphasize the effects and role that advertising plays in the lives of children and teenagers.

The first ascribes the outcomes of exposure to advertising to developmental level, variously construed as cognitive ability (Piaget & Inhelder, 1967; Piaget, 1969), memory and retrieval skills (John & Whitney, 1986; Roedder, 1981), or recursive thinking about social interaction (Paget et al., 1984). Of these, the most widely applied in regard to advertising has been the first, of which transitions from preoperational (2–7 years) to concrete operational (7–11 years) to formal operational (11–15 years) are the major steps. Roughly, they carry the young person from (a) beginning to use language and mental imagery symbolically through (b) focusing on concrete attributes of objects and relations to (c) thinking abstractly and applying theories, values, and ideas to the present physical circumstances. These constructions have been extremely helpful in understanding how responses to advertising may change with age, and they have raised research questions of importance: the role in outcomes not only of age but also of mode of measurement, prior training, cues, and level of information. These latter four appear to interact to alter what can be concluded about children under the age of eight. For example, nonverbal or more probing verbal measurement lowers the age at which commercials become identifiable; training can increase comprehension; cues elicit prior training or skills, and their application often is dependent upon them; and superior information may improve the processing of a commercial, but cues may be necessary for its retrieval.

We prefer the second because it (a) places advertising at the forefront, (b) is not tied to any specific stage theory with concrete age ceilings or thresholds about what might be expected, and (c) explicitly introduces issues that have implications for policy. Adler and colleagues (1980, pp. 220–221) present a model from which we have gratefully and shamelessly borrowed, yet we have so rearranged it, relabeled its parts, and otherwise turned it to our own purposes that we doubt if more than passing acknowledgment would be welcome (Table 5.5).

One major departure is our rejection of the dichotomy between the *intended* and *unintended* effects of advertising, with the former including desire for, trial purchase, and continuing consumption of a product, and the latter encompassing the full range of alleged controversial outcomes, ranging from ignorance of persuasive intent to responses that are injurious to health. Although we can understand why such a pristine vocabulary might find ready use in the context in which they were working, we find it unctuous to imply that one motive of advertisers is to cast the product in a light more favorable than its competitors solely on its merits, thereby not taking advantage of any confusion, gullibility, or favorable impressions that may have been created, whatever their source. We certainly concur that no advertiser would wish to harm children; we are skeptical that certain outcomes classified by them as "unintended" are not an inevitable occurrence when advertising is directed at children. Thus, we prefer the distinction between *Primary Intended Effects, Secondary Effects—Desirable,* and *Secondary Effects—Undesirable,* which substitutes our judgment for the implied pure motives of advertisers.

We also reject what we take as the subtle implication that consumer socialization is confined to positive, edifying experiences. We are reminded of the short story by the late William Saroyan (1937), "The Sunday Zeppelin." Two boys send $1 to a Chicago firm for a flying machine pictured in the back pages of a periodical. The illustration shows two children aloft. As they wait for delivery, they increasingly speculate on where they will go, what people will think, and whether (and how many) freight cars will be necessary to bring it to them. When a brown envelope with a slight bulge arrives in the mail with the firm's return address, they realize the truth. "Those sons of bitches in Chi-

Table 5.5
Elements of Consumer Socialization

Stimulus properties

Amount and placement of advertising
Program–commercial separation practice
Nature of products advertised to children
Commercials not directed at children (drugs, etc.)
Content and techniques of commercials
   Format and audiovisual techniques (animation, music, pacing, special effects, etc.)
   Characters and spokespersons
   Product claims, disclosures, and disclaimers
   Premium offers

Mediating variables

Children's characteristics
   (age, cognitive development, sex, socioeconomic status, intelligence, etc.)
Child's viewing patterns—volume of exposure to advertising
Parent–child interactions
   (parental control of viewing, coviewing, control of consumption)
Other sources of consumer information
   (for example, peers, schools, stores, other TV content, other media)

Possible outcomes

Primary intended effects
   Attention to and recall of product brands and attributes
   Desire for advertised products
   Trial and repeat purchases of products or purchase requests to parents
Secondary effects—desirable
   Confusion between program and commercial materials; failure to understand selling
     intent of commercials
   Failure to comprehend product attributes or disclaimers (complexity of assembly or
     operation, role of a food product in a balanced diet, etc.)
   Incorrect (exaggerated) assessment of product performance or of satisfaction
     provided by product
Secondary effects—undesirable
   Encouragement of unsafe behavior through imitation
   Encouragement of inappropriate standard for consumer choices (sweetness or "fun"
     rather than nutritional value; premiums rather than product attributes, etc.)
   Promotion of parent–child communication and/or conflict
   Learning about workings of marketplace and advertising (for example, comparing
     advertising claims with actual product)
   Encouragement or reinforcement of unhealthy or hazardous behavior (for instance,
     poor nutritional habits, drug abuse)
   Encouragement or reinforcement of social values (for example, sex role or other
     stereotyping, distrust or cynicism toward society, unselfishness)
   Development of consumer skills

From Adler, R.P., Lesser, G.S., Meringoff, L.K., Robertson, T.S., Rossiter, J.R., & Ward, S. (1980). *The effects of television advertising on children: Review and recommendations.* Lexington, MA: Lexington Books.

cago!" says one. Ironically, the periodical was a Sunday school magazine.

Other studies that have become available since the work of Adler and colleagues (1980) reinforce earlier impressions or expand slightly the range of topics covered. With one exception, nothing has taken place that would lead us to different conclusions or emphases. Guidicatti and Stening (1980) report that, among 165 Australian children aged 6 to 8 and 9 to 12 years, not only age, and thus cognitive ability, but also socioeconomic class was positively associated with comprehending what commercials are and distinguishing them from programs. Rossano and Butter (1987) found that the beliefs of children between 8 and 11 years about proprietary medicines were essentially unaffected by exposure to actual commercials for specific drugs. T.P. Meyer and Hexamer (1981) asked about 200 Mexican–American teenagers why they disbelieved commercials and which products were truthfully advertised. For the former, more females named product experience; for the latter, more females and more of those older named products. Because the sample is within the same cognitive stage, the authors infer that differences in consumer experience affect the evaluation of advertising. Gorn and Florsheim (1985) found, among 70 nine- to ten-year-old girls, that exposure to a commercial for a product they expected to use in the future, lipstick, led to enhanced favorability toward the brand and product category; thus, adult commercials apparently can influence children, and exposure to them may affect choices later in life. Moschis and Moore (1982) obtained data from 230 young persons in the sixth through the twelfth grade on their television viewing and outlook as consumers at two points in time 14 months apart. They conclude that:

> (I)ncreasing advertising exposure seems to *decrease* the person's likelihood of performing socially desirable consumer behaviors, but only among those adolescents who are not likely to perform those activities in the first place. It does not seem to contribute to the development of materialistic values and traditional sex-role perceptions among those who have *not yet* developed such predispositions. (p. 285)

They base this conclusion on a cluster of associations: (a) among those low at the time of initial measurement in rational consumer decision making (such as comparing prices and product attributes), exposure to commercials was inversely associated with such behavior later, while (b) among those low in materialism (pursuit of "possessions and money for personal happiness") and sex-role stereotyping there was no comparable positive association with such views later.

Belk, Mayer, and Driscoll (1984) found among almost 400 fourth and sixth graders that stereotyping of the owners of youth-oriented products (such as Calvin Klein jeans) was greater among those older, females, and those from households higher in socioeconomic status; that the age, sex, and social class differences were increased when these variables were positively associated with product ownership; and that those likely to own a product ascribed more favorable attributes to others said to own that product. Soldow (1983) compared about 325 kindergarten and first graders with third graders in their ability to recognize later a product advertised in print, radio, or television. He predicted that those classified by individual test as having attained Piaget's concrete operational stage (the great majority of those older and a minority of those younger) would do better, which proved to be the case, and that those still in the preoperational stage would perform less well with radio, because it requires a transfer across modalities rather than merely recognizing an object previously displayed, which did not prove to be the case. These varied findings simply remind us of the importance of socioeconomic status and prior experience; the scant likelihood of influencing generic beliefs about products of low pertinence by brief television appeals; the pertinence of future expectations for present-day responses; the possibility that deleterious effects may occur among a subgroup, when not observable for the population as a whole; the tendency for young persons to use products as symbolic currency, with their own choices guiding favorability about others; and that cognitive stages do not always predict responses to the media.

The exception is M.L. Geis (1982), who analyzes the language of television advertising in regard to the outcomes that would be anticipated among children below the age of eight, given their cognitive and linguistic capabilities. Although arguments over whether verbal measures underestimate the ability of children to recognize television commercials have been frequent (Macklin, 1983), the linguistic practices of commercials directed at children previously received little attention. Geis reaches five conclusions:

1. The language of television advertising directed at children is often ungrammatical, uses difficult-to-understand terms and phrases, is condensed, elliptical, and requires reformulation to be understood. Given the constraints placed on decoding by a real-time medium such as television, these factors mean that many children cannot help but be deceived.

2. The language of disclaimers typically is unnatural and beyond a child's repertoire, such as (p. 170):
- *Partial assembly required,*
- *Artificially flavored,*
- *At participating stores;*

sometimes hides the critical phrase within a seemingly positive statement (p. 169):
- *Two 9-volt batteries not included provide the power;*

and sometimes converts a qualification into an advantage (p. 175):
- *You put it together.*

3. Commercials for fruit-flavored foods frequently use "language that entails or implies that these products contain fruit whether or not they actually do and whether or not the product is naturally or artificially flavored" (p. 244):
- *There's more orange. More lemon. More cherry. More lime.* (p. 202)
- *Cheer up, my porcupine pal, a fruitful [sic] breakfast we'll share right now.* (p. 196)

4. The qualification that advertised products should be part of a nutritionally balanced breakfast is often made in a way that usurps options so that the product is the only choice (p. 221):
- *(   ), a good part of any good breakfast.*
- *(   ) is part of a complete breakfast.*
- *Enjoy a complete breakfast with (   ).*

5. The argument that children are more limited linguistically than cognitively in understanding commercials is (a) invalid because abstract concepts cannot be understood without the use of language, and (b) if children are linguistically handicapped, then the use of language in advertising directed at them is hard to justify; thus, the arguments of the representatives of the advertising and television businesses and their supporters that children are linguistically limited, in effect, becomes a criticism of advertising as it currently is practiced.

D. POLICY OPTIONS

We begin with the implications of the evidence for self-regulation. We then turn to regulatory alternatives.

1. Self-Regulatory Codes

When Adler and colleagues (1980) were conducting their review, there were in place two business-wide codes, that of the NAB for broadcasters and that of the NAD for advertisers, as well as codes at each of the three networks. Two major subsequent changes have reduced the role of self-regulation (Comstock, 1989).

The first and most prominent has been the abandonment in the mid-1970s by the NAB of a business-wide code for television. In effect, the courts and the U.S. Department of Justice have held such joint agreements to be collusive and in violation of the antitrust statutes.

The second was the diminution in the late 1980s by each of the three networks of the broadcast standards departments, which reviewed commercials for their adherence to codes (Rotfeld, Abernethy, & Parsons, 1990). The marked reduction in the number of those engaged in enforcing network codes has meant the transfer of most responsibility from the networks to the advertisers.

Adler and colleagues gave considerable attention to whether the two codes were in accord with the empirical findings. This is a fruitless endeavor—logically, because there have never been clear goals by which to evaluate the codes (the evidence tells us about what advertising does, not what a specific stipulation achieves), and historically, because they have become less important.

2. Regulatory Alternatives

Extra-self-regulatory options are of far more interest because they go beyond the assumptions of self-regulation that directing television advertising at children is inherently legitimate, that undesirable outcomes can be avoided by prohibitions acceptable to advertisers and broadcasters, and that any harmful effects when such codes are adhered to are the responsibility of parents. Several were reviewed by the FTC in connection with the hearings in the late 1970s in Washington and San Francisco on the possibility of new federal action (Federal Trade Commission, 1978a, 1978b, 1978c). They included (in increasing severity):

1. Elimination of advertising for specific classes of product that are designed to appeal to children:
2. Limitations more stringent than industry codes on number and frequency of advertisements directed at children;
3. Elimination of advertising whose "dominant appeal" was to children below a specific age;
4. Elimination of advertising for products appealing primarily to or purchased primarily for children below a specific age; and
5. A ban effective only when children below some specified age constituted more than X percent of the audience and adults constituted less than Y percent.

The first is the least severe because it would foreclose only the advertising of one or more categories of product and thus probably not at all affect the revenues derived from children's programming. An example with scant if any effect on profits was the banning of commercials for children's vitamins. The second would reduce the totality of advertising directed at children without at all affecting the products advertised; revenues might be somewhat adversely affected, but the greater scarcity of television time to be sold would almost certainly lead to higher prices per time unit and thus lessen any such effect. The final three each attempt to identify large blocks of unacceptable advertising. The third invokes the techniques employed; presumably, two commercials for the same product could differ in acceptability depending on the degree they are judged to appeal to children. The fourth employs the product; regardless of technique, commercials for products of interest to children would be banned. The fifth rests on audience composition, with the threshold for barring commercials determined by the proportions of children and adults, which would exempt programs with substantial adult audiences regardless of viewing by children; a simpler formulation would simply use the proportion below a given age.

Among the specific remedies considered were

- A ban on all advertising of heavily sugared foods when the audience is made up primarily of children under age 12, on the grounds that consumption of such foods can contribute disproportionately to dental cavities, obesity, and otherwise place at risk the health and well-being of a child.
- A ban on all advertising directed at children below age eight, on the grounds that their lack of full understanding of the intent, nature, and purpose of advertising makes it unfair and deceptive.

The FTC took no action (Federal Trade Commission, 1981). On the one hand, it concluded that the evidence constituted a *prima facie* case that television advertising directed at children involved some risks, represented a social ill, and was a legitimate cause for concern. On the other, it concluded that there were no practical, effective remedies that could be imposed by FTC rule-making. As the final staff report (1981) said:

> The record developed during the rulemaking proceeding adequately supports the following conclusions regarding child-oriented television advertising and young children six years and under: (1) they place indiscriminate trust in televised advertising

messages; (2) they do not understand the persuasive bias in television advertising; and (3) the techniques, focus and themes used in child-oriented television advertising enhance the appeal of the advertising message and the advertised product. Consequently, young children do not possess the cognitive ability to evaluate adequately child-oriented television advertising. Despite the fact that these conclusions can be drawn from the evidence, the record establishes that the only effective remedy would be a ban on all advertisements oriented toward young children, and such a ban, as a practical matter, cannot be implemented (p. 2).

The practical barriers were fourfold. First, there was the difficulty of specifying the audience at risk: the ages, numbers, or proportions that would qualify. Second, there was the awkwardness of designating a class of products for action when the problem lay not with product attributes but with manner or quantity of use. Third, broadcasters might reshape their schedules to avoid qualifying for any stipulations. Fourth, if they did so, audience composition probably would change. Thus, neither content-based nor audience-based rules were judged feasible.

The FCC gave no indication that it would ameliorate the last two by mandating programming for children on Saturday mornings. In effect, it formally endorsed a "no mandate" position later when, after hearings on a possible rule-making requiring broadcasters to present weekday programming of cultural and educational value for children, it declined to take any action. As a result, restraints on television advertising directed at young persons have come to rest solely with the advertising and television businesses.

Whether or not a code is violated in a specific instance, of course, is often a subjective judgment. M.L. Geis (1982) concludes:

> The disregard of the NAB and ABC, NBC, and CBS television networks for the language of advertising broadcast to young children is rather puzzling, for some of the claims that pass their scrutiny are transparently false. It is difficult to escape the conclusion that responsible elements of these organizations simply don't care what advertisers say to children. If this is correct then I suspect that this is because the adults who monitor television advertisements for compliance with governmental and industry guidelines and rules are no more competent to cope with the fact that television advertising occurs in real time and use both the visual and auditory communications channels than are television viewers. (p. 244)

It is self-evident from the behavior so harshly described that most in the advertising and television businesses, and certainly those at the time responsible for the enforcement of codes, would have disagreed.

There is a wide range of views as to the degree of restraint required. Culley, Lazer, and Atkin (1976) queried three small groups of advertising executives, members of ACT, and government officials, and a larger sample of consumers about the effects of advertising on children and the means and mode of its regulation (Table 5.6). ACT members and the

Table 5.6
Beliefs about Television Advertising and Children[a]

Subject–attitude	ACT (n = 51)	Consumer (n = 455)	Government (n = 21)	Advertising (n = 71)
A. Effects on children				
Advertising helps develop a child's ability to make good consumer decisions	2	27	23	65
Commercials often persuade children to want things they do not really need	100	95	95	66
Television commercials lead to an increase in parent–child conflict	93	67	64	7
Television commercials often arouse anxieties and feelings of insecurity in children	75	51	41	3
B. Level of regulation				
Television advertising to children should be more regulated than it already is	100	77	91	23
Children's television advertising requires special regulation because of the nature of the viewing audience	98	89	86	61
Advertising on children's television programs should be banned completely	89	32	36	3
C. Mode of Regulation				
Commercials to children should be regulated by advertisers themselves	14	54	23	63
Commercials to children should be regulated by the government	70	30	50	11
It is up to the parents to regulate children's television viewing behavior	81	93	67	97

[a] Percentage agreement.
From Culley, J.D., Lazer, W., & Atkin, C.K. (1976). The experts look at children's television. *Journal of Broadcasting, 20*(1), 3–21.

advertising executives were at the extremes. The consumers and government officials were in between, with the latter somewhat more in favor of regulation and regulation by government, and the former assigning more responsibility to children and parents.

The historical record makes it evident that as long as the principle and fact of directing advertising at children are not threatened, those in the television and advertising businesses are willing to change their practices as long as they can do so without seriously affecting revenues adversely. The option chosen, then, has been a progressively enervated self-regulation. As a result, controversies about children and television advertising are likely to continue, because the circumstances that gave rise to them largely remain in place.

3. Marketplace Factors

In fact, the changes in the television marketplace described by Kunkel (1988b) make it likely that quarrels will escalate. Central to what has taken place are the increasing frequency of programs whose characters, the devices they use, and themes become the basis for products, or what have come to be called program-length commercials (and in some quarters but not here, PLCs). Kunkel defines this hybrid:

> The distinction between traditional program-related product licensing and the new trend known as program-length commercials rests, on the surface, on the question of which comes first: the program or the product. Traditionally, a program concept is conceived and evaluated solely on its merit for providing entertaining content that will attract large viewing audiences. If the program enjoys success, then its creator might subsequently consider engaging in licensing agreements with manufacturers of toys or other ancillary products. . . .
>
> In contrast, children's program-length commercials fit one of two molds: they "bring to life" on the television screen a line of toy characters already available, or they become part of a coordinated effort in which the program and its related products are introduced into the marketplace simultaneously. In either case, the program is *originally conceived* as a vehicle to provide product exposure to the child audience, in the hopes of stimulating product sales that in turn may help to sustain program popularity. (pp. 90–91)

As Englehardt (1987) describes them, they typically have three components. The first is the continuing introduction of elements (characters, devices, settings) that can be readily translated into products. The second is coordinated elements (teams and appendages), so that products have appeal not only singly but also in sets and combinations. The third is the display of such elements in combination so the program promotes the whole package.

Such programming can be lucrative. For example, it is estimated that in the mid-1980s a prototype of the genre, "He-Man and the Masters of the Universe," had more than $1 billion in annual licensed product sales. As Kunkel tells the tale, ABC withdrew the first of the genre, the animated "Hot Wheels" series based on the Mattel toy line, after the FCC in 1969 in a preliminary opinion said:

> There can be no doubt that in this program Mattel receives commercial promotion for its products beyond the time logged for commercial advertising. Nor is there any doubt that the program was developed with this promotional value . . . in mind.
> We find this pattern disturbing; more disturbing than the question of whether the commercial time logged is adequate. For this pattern subordinates programming in the interest of the public to programming in the interest of its saleability. (As quoted by Kunkel, 1988b, pp. 94–95)

Subsequently in 1974, the FCC issued a policy statement on children's television that, in regard to advertising, barred program-length commercials and called for audiovisual devices to help children identify commercials and a reduction in the amount of time devoted to advertising. What gave these admonitions force was the threat of explicit regulatory action such as inclusion of such criteria in license renewal; this has been called regulation "by raised eyebrow." Ten years later in 1984 the FCC, as part of its deregulatory policy, ceased to consider a station's commercial policies in license renewal and dropped the requirement that time devoted to commercials be logged. This made possible the reemergence of the program-length commercial.

Such commercialization of children's television has become increasingly conspicuous. It is part of a broader trend in broadcasting, with increases in number of messages (Condry et al., 1988) and nonprogram content (E.E. Cohen, 1988) on Saturday mornings, and increases in amount of time devoted to advertising throughout the schedule ("Television networks fatten. . . ," June 18, 1990). Program-length commercials were at first avoided by the three major networks, presumably because they feared public criticism, but by the late 1980s they had begun to appear on their schedules. They had been earlier and eagerly adopted by independent stations, which had grown enormously in importance and total audience shares, as their numbers increased dramatically between the 1970s and the end of the 1980s (Comstock, 1989). They provided fresh programming competitive with the networks in production values, or audiovisual quality, and they supplied it at reduced cost because of the subsidization of production by the company whose products would be promoted.

Subsidization has become increasingly important with the development of bartering, in which part of the fee paid by the station to the production company or distributor is paid in commercial time, which the latter uses or sells. In the case of "He-Man and the Masters of the Universe," all of the bartered time went to Mattel which, because the rules against host-selling prohibited advertising the program's characters, used it to promote its numerous other toys. Kunkel (1988b) reports that by the mid-1980s, over half of 19 newly syndicated children's programs were program-length commercials financed through barter, and that nine could be viewed in 80% or more of U.S. households (Table 5.7).

These trends toward commercialization are potentially enhanced by the proliferation of channel specialization made possible by cable. The

Table 5.7
Most Widely Distributed Syndicated Program-Length Commercials (1985–1986)

	Number of markets	Percentage of U.S. homes	Barter terms (ratio of station : producer commercial minutes)
G.I. Joe	110	87	4 : 2
GoBots	106	80	4 : 2
He-Man & the Masters of the Universe	111	81	5 : 1[a]
Jayce & the Wheeled Warriors	87	80	4 : 2
M.A.S.K.	80	80	5 : 1[a]
Robotech	93	82	4 : 2[b]
She-Ra	120	84	4 : 2
Thundercats	110	85	3 : 5 : 2.5[c]
Transformers	139	91	5 : 1[a]
Voltron	75	76	5 : 1[a]

[a] Plus cash.
[b] Cash terms available.
[c] 4 : 2 in fourth quarter.
From Kunkel, D. (1988). From a raised eyebrow to a turned back: The FCC and children's product-related programming. *Journal of Communication*, 38(4), 90–108.

road followed by the independents arguably will be followed by the cable channels presenting entertainment attractive to children, and for the same reasons. They too will find it profitable not only to direct advertising at children, but also to disseminate programming that itself promotes products. A number of writers (L. Brown, 1977; E.L. Palmer, 1988; Turow, 1981) in addition to Kunkel (1988b) have observed a secular pattern in network programming for children that, in our view, applies also to independent broadcasters and probably will apply to cable:

1. Initially, programming for children is employed to promote family use of the channel, with the result that it is comparatively plentiful.

2. Once channel use has stabilized, such promotion ceases to pay off, and the amount of such programming declines.

3. In order to maximize revenues, the programming available becomes increasingly commercialized.

VI BEHAVIOR

The most persistent and controversial of all questions regarding television and young viewers has concerned aggressive, antisocial, or delinquent behavior, and their link, if any, with violent television entertainment. Numerous college-level texts conclude that television violence facilitates aggressive behavior:

- In introductory psychology (Atkinson, Atkinson, Smith, & Hilgard, 1987; Darley, Glucksberg, Kamin, & Kinchla, 1981; Kagan & Havemann, 1980; McConnell, 1980; Mischel & Mischel, 1980; Smith, Sarason, & Sarason, 1982);
- In social psychology (Aronson, 1988; Jones, Hendrick, & Epstein, 1979; Myers, 1983; Oskamp, 1984; Penrod, 1983; Perlman & Cozby, 1983); and
- In developmental psychology (Elkind & Weiner, 1978; Evans & McCandless, 1978; Hetherington & Parke, 1979; Kopp & Krakow, 1982; R.M. Liebert & Wicks-Nelson, 1979

Nevertheless, more than a decade after the Surgeon General's advisory committee (1972) reached such a conclusion, a review appeared in the *Psychological Bulletin* (Freedman, 1984) that sought to correct these varied authors.

Our analysis is in accord with history by focusing on the behavioral effects of television (and by necessity, film) violence, with three important qualifications:

1. We organize the evidence around the behavior of teenagers and young adults. Among young viewers, they are the most likely to com-

mit seriously harmful antisocial or criminal acts, and much of the interest in and controversy over the evidence has centered on the contribution of violent portrayals to such behavior. The accumulation of evidence now makes it feasible to address this question.

2. We emphasize the role of assumptions, concepts, and theory in interpreting the evidence. We do so because they are as important as the empirical findings themselves in reaching conclusions. It is only by examining the framework on which interpretation rests that a judgment can be reached about its validity.

3. We develop a theory of effects that, because of the consistencies within and between the evidence on different types of outcomes, applies robustly to a wide range of behavior. In so doing, we endorse the maxim of Kurt Lewin (Marrow, 1969): "There is nothing so practical as a good theory."

A. THREE ISSUES

Three major scientific issues must be confronted in evaluating the empirical evidence. They are:

1. The implications for the behavior of young adults of the many experiments documenting unambiguously that within such a setting, exposure of subjects of nursery school age to violent television or film portrayals increases behavior categorized by the experimenters as aggressive or antisocial.

2. The external validity, or implications for everyday life, of the many experiments documenting unambiguously that within such a setting, exposure of subjects of college age to violent television or film portrayals increases behavior categorized by the experimenters as aggressive or antisocial.

3. The size of effect, if any; that is, the degree to which levels or frequencies of behavior categorized as antisocial or aggressive are altered by exposure to media violence.

In each instance, a fundamental factor is the character of the behavior under scrutiny: criminal, seriously harmful, disruptive, or acknowledged to be antisocial and aggressive, but of lesser significance.

The first two experiments demonstrating that exposure to violent portrayals can increase aggressiveness were published in 1963 in the *Journal of Abnormal and Social Psychology* (Bandura, Ross, & Ross, 1963a; Berkowitz & Rawlings, 1963). Since then, an enormous and varied literature has developed. It gives little comfort to those who assert that the findings are evenly divided, that ecologically or methodologically inferior studies are responsible for any association between exposure and behavior, or that there are not circumstances in which portrayals influence behavior. Nevertheless, different issues arise and differing qualifications and emphases are required, depending on the seriousness of the aggressive or antisocial behavior and the age of the population in question.

B. YOUNG CHILDREN

In one pioneer 1963 experiment, Bandura, Ross, and Ross (1963a) observed the behavior of nursery school children in a playroom with a Bobo doll and other toys, after they had seen either (a) no behavior involving a Bobo doll, or the Bobo doll attacked verbally and physically by (b) a live model in ordinary attire, (c) the same model in a film sequence, or (d) a female in a film sequence attired in a cat costume such as might appear in children's entertainment. To heighten the likelihood of aggressive behavior, they were first mildly frustrated by being taken away from a room full of attractive toys. Children in all three treatment groups (b, c, and d) displayed more aggressive behavior than those in the control condition. Nonimitative as well as imitative aggressive behavior was affected, although the effect was most prominent for imitative acts. The children exposed to the Cat Lady exhibited decidedly less aggression than those seeing the live model, but definitely more than those in the control condition.

In their next experiment, Bandura, Ross, and Ross (1963b) manipulated the exposure of children of nursery school age to film sequences involving young adults identified as Rocky and Johnny. In one version, Rocky successfully takes Johnny's toys away and is rewarded. In the other, Johnny successfully defends himself against Rocky, and Rocky, in effect, is punished. The first increased imitation of Rocky's play with the toys, and led to derogatory comments about Johnny as well as criticism of Rocky.

In the first experiment, behavior is a function of observation; in the second, of perceived efficacy. They are typical of the several dozen subsequent experiments, by Bandura and others, testing propositions derived from social learning theory, in regard to the influence of violent television and film portrayals on the aggressiveness of young children. This formulation holds that observation of the behavior of others will enhance or introduce the capability to act in a like manner, and will affect the appropriateness and efficacy attributed to a particular way of behaving.

These experiments have a strong claim to external validity for the behavior of young children. They approximate childhood experience—adults in charge, mild frustration involving toys, a little television, and an opportunity to act aggressively with little or no likelihood of punishment. Subjects at this age do not understand the concept of experimentation and thus could not practice guile or otherwise role play. Play is the context of most childhood aggressiveness (and much of that on the part of older persons as well).

External validity for those of about the same age also is enhanced by three other sources:

1. Experiments that introduce more naturalistic or ecologically valid elements but continue to produce positive results. Steuer, Applefield, and Smith (1971) and Josephson (1987) provide perhaps the most dramatic examples of this genre. In the former, a small group of children who viewed during nursery school recesses violent entertainment programs produced for such children became more aggressive in everyday playground interaction than a small group comparable in pretreatment playground aggressiveness who viewed nonviolent programs (Fig. 6.1).

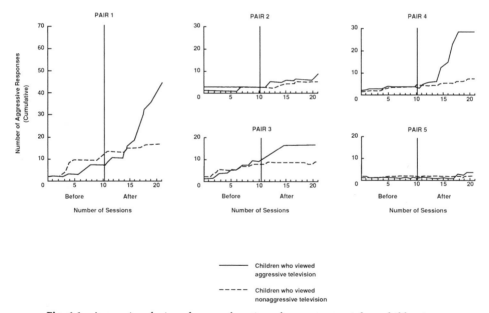

Fig. 6.1 Aggression during play as a function of exposure to violent children's programs. From Steuer, F.B., Applefield, J.M., & Smith, R. (1971). Televised aggression and interpersonal aggression of preschool children. *Journal of Experimental Child Psychology, 11,* 442–447.

In the latter, several hundred boys in grades two and three either watched a violent or nonviolent television program in groups of six; those who watched the violent program who typically were higher in aggressiveness subsequently displayed greater aggression while playing floor hockey, and the effect was heightened by exposure in conjunction with playing to a cue from the program. Analogously, children in circumstances so violent that one would expect the effects of the media to be overshadowed apparently remain subject to the influence of television. Both Day and Ghandour (1984) and McHan (1985) found that Arab boys between the ages of five and eight in Beirut, Lebanon, became more aggressive after seeing televised portrayals in experiments similar to those conducted by Bandura and colleagues although their real-life circumstances included street fighting, bombings of beach crowds, sporadic explosions, and the threat of invasion.

2. The three-community British Columbia experiment by T.M. Williams (1986) and colleagues in which the playground aggressiveness of children increased between the first and fourth grades in the community where television was introduced, but not in the two communities where television was already present (Fig. 6.2).

3. A series of studies by the Singers and their colleagues (D.G. Singer & J.L. Singer, 1980; J.L. Singer & D.G. Singer, 1980b, 1981, 1987; J.L. Singer et al., 1984; J.L. Singer et al., 1988; Desmond et al., 1985) in which the everyday aggression of young children—for the most part, of preschool age—was positively associated with the everyday viewing of violent television entertainment, with no evidence from the many variables measured that this association was attributable to something other than the influence of television on behavior.

These three sets of data have as a common strength the viewing of violent programs in an ordinary way, coupled with the measurement of aggressive behavior within a paradigm that either encourages causal inference (Steuer et al., 1971; T.M. Williams, 1986), or would permit the falsification of such a hypothesized relationship were another measured variable responsible (D.G. Singer & J.L. Singer, 1980; J.L. Singer & D.G. Singer, 1980b, 1981, 1987; J.L. Singer et al., 1984; Desmond et al., 1985). This use of data obtained by different means to assess the external validity of the findings of experiments in laboratory settings presages the model that will be applied to experiments using teenagers and young adults as subjects.

The issue of the external validity of experiments whose subjects were young children reminds us of an axiom: When real life approximates the circumstances of an experiment (however rarely), the challenge of

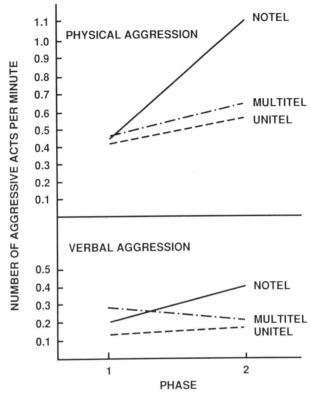

Fig. 6.2 Introduction of television and playground aggression. From Williams, T.M. (Ed.). (1986). *The impact of television. A natural experiment in three communities.* New York: Academic Press.

external validity is vanquished. We believe it applies to the viewing of much violent entertainment by young children.

C. TEENAGERS AND YOUNG ADULTS

In the other 1963 experiment by Berkowitz and Rawlings (1963), college-age subjects saw the prize fight sequence from the film *Champion*, in which Kirk Douglas is brutally beaten. Before viewing, subjects were given justification for hostility toward the experimental assistant by his insulting remarks while they took a bogus I.Q. test. The crucial comparison was between those who had been led to believe the portrayed beating was justified and those who had been led to believe it was unjustified. Subjects were thus alike in provocation, vicarious experience of violence, and opportunity to express hostility. A catharsis formulation (Feshbach, 1961) would predict no difference in expressed hostility, since both groups experienced the same vicarious violence. Berkowitz and Rawlings, however, predicted greater expressed hostility in the justified violence condition, on the grounds it would lower inhibitions over retributive aggression. The results, with ratings of the competency of the experimental assistant as a measure of hostility, supported them, and inhibition instead of catharsis became the accepted explanation when media portrayals appeared to reduce aggressive or antisocial behavior.

In subsequent experiments, Berkowitz and Geen (1966, 1967) manipulated the degree to which the experimental assistant was linked to the film by identifying him as either Bob or Kirk (the actor in the film). Anger was encouraged by the assistant's giving the subjects the maximal number of possible electric shocks as feedback in solving a problem. Aggression was measured by the number of electric shocks delivered to the assistant by the subject when roles were reversed. Aggression was greater among those subjects for whom the assistant was so linked.

Berkowitz and Alioto (1973) and Geen and Stonner (1972) in later experiments employing the same paradigm manipulated the motives ascribed to those engaged in the portrayed behavior. In two instances, boxers were described as engaged either in a professional encounter or in a grudge match in which their goal was injury; in another, football teams were so distinguished. Subjects told that the behavior was motivated by an intent to injure engaged in higher levels of aggressiveness.

These findings exemplify the dimensions of normativeness and pertinence. Normativeness of aggressive and hostile behavior is strongly implied when portrayed events are described as merited retribution or the motive attributed to participants is injury to one another. Pertinence represents the degree to which a portrayal is linked by a viewer to real life, in this instance achieved by the commonality of cues in the portrayal and real life: the name of the target.

Susceptibility, of course, was heightened by the induced anger as it was by the toy deprivation in the Cat Lady experiment. That there sometimes may be subtle links between the factors involved is apparent from Geen and Stonner's (1972) finding that the relationship between vengeful motive and greater aggressiveness occurred only among angered subjects; among nonangered subjects, the "professional" condition evoked greater aggression. Anger apparently was necessary for the normativeness imputed to vengeful violence by the portrayal to have an influence; in the absence of anger, such behavior might have been dismissed as irrelevant. Thus, pertinence would appear to have a pervasive role in linking these concepts.

The role of excitation transfer or arousal is demonstrated in an experiment by Zillmann (1971). Using the same paradigm employed by Berkowitz and colleagues (provocation followed by the manipulation), college students were shown either a violent sequence, an erotic sequence, or a bland sequence with neither element; electric shock delivery was greatest in the erotic condition, followed by the violent condition. Later, Zillmann, Johnson, and Hanrahan (1973) demonstrated that subsequent aggressiveness was greater when a violent sequence was unresolved than when it was resolved by a happy ending. In these instances, behavioral effects are attributable to the excitation induced and not subsequently alleviated by the portrayals.

These experiments are typical of the several dozen testing varied propositions derived from the disinhibition and cue (of which the "Kirk" manipulation is an example) and the arousal formulations regarding the influence of violent television and film portrayals on teenagers and young adults. The former holds that portrayals may alter the restraint imposed on an internal state, such as anger or the impulse to behave in a particular way, or the response elicited by an external stimulus, while the latter holds that stimulating portrayals may lead to excitation transfer, in which whatever behavior is engaged in subsequently is heightened in intensity. Each predicts distinct outcomes not explainable by the other, as does social learning. That is, neither justified nor unjustified aggression has a superior claim to excitation, and excitation hardly explains imitation. Thus, the formulations are complementary.

Effects on teenagers and young adults occur repeatedly in the laboratory setting. Since numerous and a decisive majority of experiments (Andison, 1977; Comstock *et al.*, 1978) demonstrate that a variety of types of violent portrayals increase aggressive or antisocial behavior, the inhibitory capability of media violence is far from invariably or arguably even very regularly exercised.

The challenges to external validity are serious, however. The experimental setting for teenagers and young adults departs from the everyday in the perceptions of the subjects, in the brevity of the television exposure, in the absence of the possibility of retaliation for aggression, in the exclusion of competing and countervailing communications, and in the criterion of immediacy as the measure of effects. Experiments are especially sensitive to detecting effects and may register outcomes that would not occur in everyday life; thus, there is some risk of a false impression of frequency, degree, seriousness, or even occurrence of an effect. The seemingly most plausible solution to the problem of external validity is the field experiment. Field experiments contrive to produce in naturalistic surroundings the factors on which causal inference in experimentation depend. These factors are comparability among groups and the manipulation of experience; if groups are comparable, subsequent differences between them can be attributed to differences in the experience imposed by the experimenter.

Unfortunately, comparability and the manipulation of experience are not easily achieved outside the laboratory. Random assignment is often impossible; experience may be difficult to control or manipulate. The consequence is that the price of increased naturalism often is decreased confidence in causal inference.

The several field experiments involving teenagers or young adults (Feshbach & Singer, 1971; Leyens & Camino, 1974; Leyens, Camino, Parke, & Berkowitz, 1975; Loye, Gorney, & Steele, 1977; Milgram & Shotland, 1973; Wells, 1973) are mixed in outcome, and the ambiguities courted by the method do not encourage attempting to discriminate between the more and less convincing. We agree with Cook, Kendzierski, and Thomas (1983) that as a body of evidence, they are uninterpretable.

Such a view is supported by the finding of Hearold (1986) in her meta-analysis that the average effect size for field experiments is virtually null (+.007, which can be interpreted as the proportion of the standard deviation by which treatment and control conditions differ) in contrast with the comparatively substantial (and for meta-analysis respectable) figures (of slightly greater than +.300) registered for laboratory-type experiments and surveys. These data make if clear that it is an analytic error to combine the results of field experiments with those of surveys—in effect, to subjectively average them—as measures of real-world outcomes as occasionally has been done (Freedman, 1984), because the first are open to methodological challenges to which the latter are not subject.

The remaining recourse is to seek evidence that reflects everyday events from a source other than field experiments. Such evidence is available from a series of surveys that began to influence conclusions about the effects of television and film violence when the first of the genre were published as part of the research sponsored by the Surgeon General's 1972 inquiry (Chaffee, 1972; Comstock, 1983b, 1986; Comstock et al., 1978). They divide into seven groups:

1. The large Maryland and national samples in the Surgeon General's inquiry (McIntyre & Teevan, 1972; Robinson & Bachman, 1972), with the former made up of 2270 males and females from 13 high schools,

and the latter, a probability sample of 1559 19-year-old males drawn from 87 high schools scattered across the country;

2. The Wisconsin sample of 600 high school boys and girls in the Surgeon General's inquiry (McLeod *et al.*, 1972a, 1972b), whose data parallel a portion of that for the Maryland survey to make up a joint Wisconsin–Maryland sample;

3. A series of studies by Eron, Lefkowitz, and colleagues in which data were obtained from the same samples at times as distant from one another as a decade (Lefkowitz, Eron, Walder, & Huesmann, 1972), as well as over briefer spans (Huesmann, Lagerspetz, & Eron, 1984), with the former involving several hundred upstate New York boys and girls who were teenagers at the time of second measurement;

4. A survey of 3500 males and females in the third through the twelfth grade in a large southern metropolitan area (Thornton & Voight, 1984) and a survey of about 750 young persons ranging in age from early preadolescence (about 11) to early adulthood (early twenties) in New York (McCarthy, Langner, Gersten, Eisenberg, & Orzeck, 1975).

5. A survey of 1500 London male teenagers (Belson, 1978);

6. A panel survey spanning $3\frac{1}{2}$ years in the lives of more than 2,000 boys and girls and several hundred male teenagers (Milavsky, Kessler, Stipp, & Rubens, 1982a, 1982b); and

7. A set of panel surveys conducted in roughly parallel fashion spanning three years in the lives of samples of boys and girls in six different countries: Australia, Finland, Israel, the Netherlands, Poland, and the United States (Huesmann *et al.*, 1984; Huesmann & Eron, 1986; Wiegman, Kuttschreuter, & Baarda, 1986).

There are numerous differences in procedures and findings among these seven bodies of evidence, but a discernible, consistent, and interpretable pattern emerges. These very differences make their commonalities convincing, and each set adds progressively to the evidence.

The Maryland (McIntyre & Teevan, 1972) and national (Robinson & Bachman, 1972) samples measured violence exposure by the degree of violence among four named favorites, with the programs scored by a panel of viewers. The former found both serious delinquency and less serious misbehavior positively associated with the violence-viewing scores for both boys and girls, when socioeconomic status and alienation were taken into account. The latter found interpersonal aggression among those earlier recorded as high in that respect, and serious delinquency (property damage and hurtful aggression) positively associated with violence-viewing scores.

The Wisconsin sample (McLeod *et al.*, 1972a, 1972b) documented a modest positive association (the typical $r = .30$) between viewing violent television programs and behaving aggressively. The exposure measure weighted self-reported frequency of viewing programs by a program violence score provided by a viewer panel. The aggression measure encompassed such interpersonal incursions as fighting, hitting, and name-calling, and was obtained by self-report and by the ratings of classmates. The data permitted the test of several hypotheses about the likelihood that television contributed causally:

1. The association represents the preference of aggressive youths for violent entertainment;
2. The association represents the influence of age, intelligence, race, school achievement, sex, and socioeconomic status, variables that might be responsible for higher degrees of both violence exposure and aggression; and
3. The association represents the influence of earlier viewing.

The first could be addressed by the Maryland measure of favorite programs. If the behavior correlated equally or better with a declared preference for violent programs, Hypothesis 1 would gain support. In fact, the opposite occurred, with behavior much more strongly correlated with exposure than with preference.

The second represents a further range of possible artifacts. For example, youths doing poorly in school might well be more aggressive because of that failure, and also might watch more television, and thereby view a greater amount of violence. In fact, no variable encompassed in Hypothesis 2 fully explained the association.

The third examines the plausibility of a developmental or cumulative sequence. In these data, the association with aggression was about as strong for earlier as for current exposure. This implies that the relationship in fact is stronger with earlier viewing because of the lower reliability likely for the measurement of past viewing. Hypothesis 3 thus received some support.

The national, Wisconsin, and Maryland samples are typical in several ways. They overall report positive associations, these associations withstand tests for artifactuality, and the data are suggestive of a developmental or cumulative sequence. However, each of the sets of data makes a contribution to the pattern.

Eron, Lefkowitz, and colleagues concluded from their ten-year panel data that earlier exposure of boys to television violence caused increased later teenage aggressive and antisocial behavior, as measured by the ratings of peers. We reject their interpretation because of the decline in the credibility placed in cross-lagged correlation (Cook & Campbell,

1979; Rogosa, 1980), and questions over suitability of the data for that model (Chaffee, 1972; Comstock, 1978). Nevertheless, these data significantly increase the credence that can be extended to the proposition that exposure to television violence increases such behavior in real life. They do so by adding to the positive correlations of the cross-sectional surveys, a positive correlation across a decade. This is not only larger than the early synchronous correlation within this sample, but one not reduced to null by eliminating the influence of aggression at the time of initial measurement (the third grade) and thereby the influence on the over-time relationship of any factors affecting aggressiveness at that time.

These circumstances are consistent with some causal contribution by television to the increase in the behavior in question at a later date. The type of aggression measured was essentially the same as in the Wisconsin and Maryland samples, and while not criminal, borders on the seriously harmful and certainly qualifies as antisocial within teenage society. The result held only for males; the outcome would be more compelling had it occurred for both males and females. It is still impressive, given the weak measure of violence exposure (mothers' reports of three favorite programs), and if a weaker relationship among females is assumed, that weakness of measurement may explain why a parallel outcome was not found for them.

Thornton and Voight (1984) drew a probability sample of 3500 males and females. Their measure of antisocial behavior was a 27-item delinquency scale and of television behavior the degree of violence among four favorite programs and the amount of television viewed. Despite this comparatively imprecise measure of violence exposure, they recorded statistically significant modest associations between the preference measure and delinquency. The associations were somewhat stronger for the most serious forms of antisocial behavior, such as criminal damage to property and hurtful aggression. The overall pattern is consistent with a causal interpretation, although neither they nor we venture to take such a step. This pattern includes a negative association for amount of weekday viewing, which clearly places the onus on type of content viewed; no association for drug- or alcohol-related delinquency, which rules out an artifact for delinquency *per se;* and the associations remained significant and positive when a variety of variables were taken into account, including in addition to demographics various "social control" variables, such as attachment to school and parents, involvement in activities, and belief in the legal system, all of which were strongly and negatively associated with delinquency.

McCarthy and colleagues (1975) obtained data from the mothers of a probability sample of 732 males and females between the ages of 11 and 23 living in Manhattan between Houston and 125th Street. This was a followup subsample of more than 1000 young persons from ages 6 to 18 on whom data had been obtained from these mothers five years earlier. The television exposure measure was the degree of violence in the four programs reported as favorites at the time of the second measurement. Behavioral indices were contructed from the mothers' reports for fighting, delinquency, mental health and alertness, and desirable experiences. The latter two were inversely associated with the measure for television violence exposure. Fighting and delinquency were positively associated. Delinquency encompasses getting in trouble with the police and engaging in rash acts.

The Belson (1978) survey is the most substantial to date on the topic of television violence and aggressive and antisocial behavior. The sample of 1565 London males between the ages of 12 and 17 is large, and its representativeness is exemplary, since probability methods were used. This stands in contrast to the surveys discussed so far which, while employing methods to preclude bias, could not be said to employ samples representative of any particular larger population. Exposure and behavior were measured by clinical interview. Judges were employed not only to score programs for violence, but also to score hypothetical acts for seriousness. The scales include behavior that is unambiguously criminal and seriously harmful, such as attempted rape, attacking someone with a tire iron, and falsely reporting bomb plantings to the police.

Belson concluded that

> The evidence gathered through this investigation is very strongly supportive of the hypothesis that high exposure to television violence increases the degree to which boys engage in serious violence. Thus for serious violence by boys: (i) heavier viewers of television violence commit a great deal more serious violence than do lighter viewers of television violence who have been closely equated to the heavier viewers in terms of a wide array of empirically derived matching variables; (ii) the reverse form of this hypothesis is *not* supported by the evidence. (p. 15)

It is not necessary to place such an inferential burden on these data to assign them importance. The validity of such a causal inference depends on overcoming the fundamental limitations of (a) measures obtained essentially within the same time span, for which time order cannot be unambiguously established, and (b) the possibility of an alternative explanation for the observed concordance. The data pose fewer ambiguities for interpretation when they are assessed in terms of association (in contrast to causation) and the degree to which the pattern of associations is consistent with, as contrasted with indicative of, a causal role for exposure to violent television programs. From this perspective, the major findings are:

1. Male teenagers who had viewed a substantially greater quantity of violent television programs than males otherwise like them in measured characteristics and attributes committed a markedly greater number of seriously harmful antisocial and criminal acts. As with the Maryland and Wisconsin data (McLeod *et al.*, 1972a, 1972b), there was little to suggest that this association could be attributed to the seeking out of more violent entertainment as a consequence of such behavior (Table 6.1).

2. Each of two less serious categories of aggressive and antisocial behavior also were positively associated with greater exposure to television violence (Table 6.1), as were two specific forms of antisocial and aggressive behavior, (a) aggressiveness in sports and play and (b) swearing and the use of bad language. More serious behavior was associated with exposure to violence in comic books and theater films, and less serious behavior with exposure to violence in newspapers, comic books, and theater films. The reverse hypothesis, that the expo-

Table 6.1
Seriousness of Antisocial Behavior and Exposure to Violent Television Entertainment

Level of behavior	Number of acts by mean score		Percentage difference [(heavy–light/light]
	Heavy viewers	Light viewers	
Original analysis			
Most serious acts only	7.48	5.02	49.0
All excluding most trivial	114.10	100.85	13.1
All including most trivial	294.10	265.03	11.0
Adjusted by seriousness			
Most serious	7.48	5.02	49.0
Moderately serious	106.62	95.83	11.2
[All − (Most serious + most trivial)]			
Least serious	180.00	164.18	9.6
[All − (Most serious + moderately serious)]			

Adapted from Belson, W.A. (1978). *Television violence and the adolescent boy*. Westmead, England: Saxon House, Teakfield Limited.

sure is the consequence of the behavior, could not be dismissed with as much confidence as in the first instance, but neither could it be said to explain these associations.

3. Associations for behavioral and cognitive variables were not symmetrical, as no notable associations were recorded between exposure to television violence and attitudes favoring or accepting of violence, such as preoccupation with such behavior, expressed willingness to engage in such behavior, belief that such behavior is a way to solve problems, or perceiving such behavior as human nature.

The Belson data parallel those for the earlier surveys. What they add is the positive association not readily explainable except by the influence of television between exposure and seriously harmful and criminal behavior.

The survey by Milavsky *et al.* (1982a, 1982b) spans 3½ years in the lives of about 2400 boys and girls in the second through sixth grades and about 800 male teenagers in Fort Worth and Minneapolis. Measures of aggressive and antisocial behavior and television exposure were obtained six times from the elementary school sample and five times from the teenage sample. Exposure was measured as in the Maryland and Wisconsin surveys. In the elementary school sample, aggression was measured by peer ratings as by Eron, Lefkowitz, and colleagues, and in the teenage sample, by responses to a questionnaire about four types of misbehavior: "personal," "property," "teacher," and "delinquency," with the first paralleling the elementary school measure.

Respondents entered and left the sample depending on whether they were available on the day of data collection, with graduation the major cause of attrition, and respondents in some waves were added. Over time, the number from whom data were collected at two times decreases markedly as the span of time lengthens; for example, among elementary school males with 3 months between measurements, $n = 497$; 9 months, 356; 2 years, 211; 3 years, 112.

The consequence is a body of data resembling in some respects the Wisconsin and Maryland surveys of McLeod and associates (exposure measures, peer reports, interpersonal aggression), the survey by Lefkowitz and colleagues (measurement of the same sample over a span of time, peer reports), and the Belson survey (measurement of antisocial behavior serious enough to qualify as criminal or delinquency). The major findings:

1. For both elementary school boys and girls and for the teenage males, there were, within each wave of measurement, small positive

correlations that achieved statistical significance between exposure to television violence and interpersonal aggression.

2. When the over-time associations were examined, positive associations remained more frequent, but to a more marked degree, among the elementary school boys and the teenage males. Among the elementary school boys, the associations were uniformly positive and noticeably larger in size for the 5 of the 15 wave pairings that represent the longest spans of time between measurement (two years or more). Several of the correlations for the lengthier spans are larger in magnitude than those that achieved significance when the spans were shorter and the numbers of respondents, much larger (Table 6.2).

3. When the over-time associations in the elementary school sample of boys were examined among 95 subgroups formed on the basis of 43 social and personal attributes, a majority were positive, and 9% achieved statistical significance ($p < .05$); similar results occurred for the girls.

4. The model employed for the over-time analyses eliminates the influence of all other variables, and thus encourages causal attribution when correlations between earlier viewing and later behavior are positive. However, this is a very conservative model (Cook et al., 1983), because among those variables is any contribution by still earlier viewing. When the investigators impose criteria for the number of significant positive correlations that would lead them to such an inference (a step they argue is necessary because of the large number of coefficients calculated, which increases the likelihood that one or more would achieve significance as the result of sampling variability, and by the lack of independence between many of the wave pairs, which could result in anomalies making multiple appearances—although they are silent on the possibility that a fluke could work equally well against meeting such criteria), they regularly find the outcome at the border of their criteria.

Milavsky and colleagues (1982a, 1982b) interpret these data as inconsistent with the view that exposure to violent television programming increases the likelihood of subsequent greater aggressive or antisocial behavior. They argue that (a) the synchronous correlations, although all positive and significant, are not relevant to causal inference because time order cannot be established; (b) the over-time analyses fail in the number of positive correlations meeting conventional levels of statistical significance; and (c) significance in all cases is vulnerable to the introduction of socioeconomic status as a control variable.

Table 6.2
Exposure to Television Violence and Aggression over $3\frac{1}{2}$ Years[a]

Wave pair	Duration	Earlier aggression coefficients[b]		Earlier TV violence exposure coefficients		n
		b	beta	b	beta	
Elementary school boys						
III–IV	3 months	.921*	.857	.167*	.063	497
II–III	4 months	.852*	.844	.091	.038	413
I–II	5 months	.713*	.686	−.070	−.026	364
II–IV	7 months	.844*	.771	.244*	.094	409
I–III	9 months	.710*	.671	−.016	−.006	356
I–IV	1 year	.699*	.632	.065	.023	349
IV–V	1 year	.723*	.734	−.070	−.026	301
V–VI	1 year	.688*	.723	.154	.058	188
III–V	1 year, 3 months	.727*	.734	.016	.007	291
II–V	1 year, 7 months	.737*	.665	.038	.016	240
I–IV	2 years	.685*	.594	.176	.067	211
IV–VI	2 years	.673*	.708	.125	.049	161
III–VI	2 years, 3 months	.620*	.642	.281**	.121	147
II–VI	2 years, 7 months	.765*	.677	.152	.065	121
I–VI	3 years	.644*	.543	.306	.113	112
Elementary school girls						
III–IV	3 months	.891*	.784	.138*	.081	491
II–III	4 months	.754*	.762	.082	.060	426
I–II	5 months	.616*	.676	−.062	−.037	391
II–IV	7 months	.766*	.662	.168*	.105	408
I–III	9 months	.555*	.634	−.008	−.005	384
I–IV	1 year	.612*	.636	.036	.020	369
IV–V	1 year	.504*	.501	.120	.062	296
V–VI	1 year	.499*	.585	.153	.101	153
III–V	1 year, 3 months	.694*	.614	−.043	−.028	292
II–V	1 year, 7 months	.672*	.602	.005	.004	245
I–V	2 years	.437*	.484	.103	.062	236
IV–VI	2 years	.573*	.679	−.017	−.011	134
III–VI	2 years, 3 months	.659*	.616	.135	.094	133
II–VI	2 years, 7 months	.622*	.606	.215*	.157	123
I–VI	3 years	.541*	.596	−.049	−.029	113

[a] Basic model regression coefficients for over-time associations between earlier exposure to violent television programs and aggression—without controls for intervening TV variables.

[b] "b" refers to *metric* partial regression coefficients; "beta" refers to *standardized* partial regression coefficients.

* Coefficients approach or exceed twice their standard errors.

** Coefficient = 1.94 its standard error.

From Milavsky, J.R., Kessler, R., Stipp, H.H., & Rubens, W.S. (1982b). *Television and aggression: A panel study.* New York: Academic Press.

Critics (Comstock, 1986; Cook *et al.*, 1983; Huesmann, 1984; D.A. Kenny, 1984; McGuire, 1986; Turner, Hess, & Peterson-Lewis, 1986) have reached quite different conclusions. They fault Milavsky and colleagues for:

1. Using the school as the basis for ascribing socioeconomic status for a portion of the sample, thereby not in fact effectively controlling for it as a factor in individual television viewing and behavior.

2. Adopting an asymmetrical and insensitive set of criteria that favors the null hypothesis, by neglecting borderline cases.

3. Ignoring the fact that it is the diminishment in number of cases and not the size of the coefficients that leads to nonsignificance for most of those representing longer time spans, when the obtained coefficients are the best estimates available of what they would be, were there no attrition.

4. Dismissing the frequency of significant positive correlations within subgroups when the number is about twice what would be expected by chance, and the number of cases within these cells is so small that significance is hard to achieve.

5. Employing a model for over-time data analysis that masks any influence on current aggression of prior influence of television violence on prior aggression.

6. Failing to take into account the possibility that data quality or validity across all waves is not equal, so that some wave pairings provide more meaningful outcomes than others.

When Cook and colleagues (1983) arrayed the data by the time span between waves and averaged the coefficients for each wave, there were two important outcomes (Fig. 6.3). First, the increasing degree of association with lengthening of span observed for the five lengthiest spans among the elementary school boys appears to hold generally, and for both boys and girls, except for spans of middling length, which represent an anomaly. Second, the likelihood that the trend is an artifact of socioeconomic status, with males of lower socioeconomic status registering by that fact higher on viewing and aggressiveness, is eliminated by the outcome for middle class girls (about 70% of the entire female sample) which displays the same pattern as that for the males.

When they isolated what they judged to be the data of highest quality for the teenage male sample, they found (a) for personal aggression, nonnegative coefficients that increase with the span of time between waves; (b) for teacher aggression, nonnegative coefficients unrelated in size to the time spanned; (c) for property aggression, inconsistent results; and (d) for delinquency aggression, nonnegative coefficients that

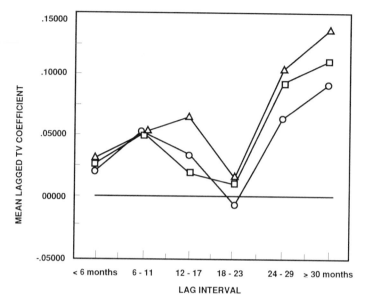

Fig. 6.3   Span between waves and over-time coefficients. Boys = square; girls = circle; middle-class girls = triangle. From Cook, T.D., Kendzierski, D.A., & Thomas, S.V. (1983). The implicit assumptions of television research: An analysis of the 1982 NIMH report on *Television and Behavior. Public Opinion Quarterly, 47*(2), 161–201.

increase with the span of time between waves. Thus, in two of four instances, an adjudication of the data produces results consistent with the pattern for the elementary school sample, and the two include the personal aggression that parallels the elementary school measure. Turner, Hesse, and Peterson-Lewis (1986) argue that young viewers attracted to violent series at the beginning of a television season may be affected by what they see as the season progresses. They thus propose that the correct comparisons are between the measures of exposure in the fall and later behavior within the same season, thus treating the season as an experimental manipulation. When they so confine the analysis, they conclude that the data of Milavsky and colleagues support the hypothesis that television violence increases aggressiveness, although this outcome appears to be largely attributable to a single age cohort (Kang, 1990).

In our view, the data of Milavsky and colleagues confirm earlier findings in regard to positive associations, positive associations over time, and positive associations with serious forms of antisocial behavior. We base this conclusion on the overall pattern in which positive associations are in the majority, increase in frequency with time span, and are not clearly absent for serious behavior. Because of the analytic model employed, the over-time associations in fact encourage causally attributing subsequent aggression to earlier violence viewing.

On the whole, these data are consistent with and add to the support given by the data from other surveys for the proposition that greater exposure to violent television entertainment heightens subsequent aggressive and antisocial behavior. They also give some (although very modest) support to the major findings of the Belson (1978) and Thornton and Voight (1984) surveys, that the association in question extends to seriously harmful and criminal behavior.

The six-country data, although not without ambiguities and conflicts (including some of the latter among the investigators over interpretation), on the whole parallel those for the similar, earlier United States surveys by Eron, Lefkowitz, and colleagues. Although some group and cultural distinctions appear, the major finding is that the positive association between some measures of involvement with violent entertainment and aggressive behavior travels well.

In sum, the surveys document:

1. Small positive synchronous correlations between both interpersonal aggression and delinquency and a weak and ambiguous measure of exposure (number of violent programs among stated favorites);

2. Modest positive synchronous correlations with a valid measure of exposure (frequency of viewing weighted by program violence) for interpersonal aggression;

3. Modest over-time correlations involving the same valid exposure measure and interpersonal aggression;

4. Repeated instances in which such exposure and behavioral associations synchronously and over time have been found;

5. No persistent or compelling demonstration that these associations are wholly explained by a set of variables that does not include a causal contribution by television exposure;

6. Interpersonal aggression as the type of behavior most convincingly associated with exposure, as it has been measured repeatedly and correlations have regularly ranged from small to modestly positive, both synchronously and over time; and

7. In the six instances in which measured behavior clearly exceeded the threshold of seriously harmful behavior, (a) a marked positive correlation between exposure to violent television programs and seriously harmful and criminal behavior (Belson, 1978), (b) modest positive correlations between a declared preference for violent programs and seri-

ous delinquency including property damage and hurtful aggression (McCarthy *et al.*, 1975; McIntyre & Teevan, 1972; Robinson & Bachman, 1972; Thornton & Voight, 1984), and (c) some evidence of a positive correlation between actual violence viewing and such behavior's increasing over time. (Cook *et al.*, 1983).

Survey data have important properties for causal inference. As in the present instance, they can establish whether an association implied by experimentation occurs in everday life, and they can heighten or diminish the likelihood of causation by examining alternative explanations and the consistency of the data with a causal explanation. These survey data, therefore, extend substantial external validity to the relationships documented in the experiments with teenagers and young adults as their subjects.

D. INTERPRETING THE EXPERIMENTS

The experiments in which the subjects were very young children have implications for the behavior of teenagers and young adults in two respects. First, they identify circumstances among young children on which the influence of exposure to violent television and film portrayals on aggressive and antisocial behavior are contingent, and thereby factors involved in any early developmental contribution by television. Second, by investigating what are for the most part basic, largely age-indifferent means by which human behavior is shaped, these experiments also identify those circumstances for teenagers and young adults.

The experiments in which the subjects were of college age also have two implications for the behavior of teenagers and young adults. First, their survival of the challenge to external validity offered by the surveys bestows some credence as reflecting real-life causation. Second, as with the experiments with younger subjects, they also identify factors that play a role in effects.

Taken together, the two bodies of experiments lead to a catalog of such contingencies. They include:

1. Reward or lack of punishment for the portrayed perpetrator of violence (Bandura, 1965; Bandura *et al.*, 1963b; Rosekrans & Hartup, 1967);

2. Portrayal of the violence as justified (Berkowitz & Rawlings, 1963; T.P. Meyer, 1973);

3. Cues in the portrayal of violence that resemble those likely to be encountered in real life, such as a victim in the portrayal with the same

name or characteristics as someone toward whom the viewer holds animosity (Berkowitz & Geen, 1966, 1967; Donnerstein & Berkowitz, 1981; Geen & Berkowitz, 1967) or exposure in real life to a cue from a previously seen violent portrayal (Josephson, 1987);

4. Portrayal of the perpetrator of violence as similar to the viewer (Rosekrans, 1967; Lieberman Research, 1975);

5. Involvement with the portrayed aggressor, such as imagining themselves in his or her place (Turner & Berkowitz, 1972);

6. Depiction of behavior ambiguous as to intent as motivated by the desire to inflict harm or injury (Berkowitz & Alioto, 1973; Geen & Stonner, 1972);

7. Violence portrayed so that its consequences do not stir distaste or arouse inhibitions over such behavior, such as violence without pain, suffering, or prolonged hurt on the part of the victim, sorrow among friends and lovers, or remorse by the perpetrator (Berkowitz & Rawlings, 1963);

8. Violence that is depicted realistically or in a lifelike manner rather than as fantasy or made up or violence portrayed as representing real events rather than events concocted for a fictional film (Atkin, 1983; Bandura *et al.*, 1963a; Feshbach, 1972; Geen & Rakosky, 1973; Hapkiewicz & Stone, 1974);

9. Portrayed violence that is not the subject of critical or disparaging commentary (Lefcourt, Barnes, Parke, & Schwartz, 1966);

10. Portrayals of violence whose commission particularly pleases the viewer (Ekman *et al.*, 1972; Slife & Rychiak, 1982);

11. Portrayals in which the violence is not interrupted by violence in a light or humorous vein (Lieberman Research, 1975);

12. Portrayed abuse that includes physical violence and aggression instead of or in addition to verbal abuse (Lieberman Research, 1975);

13. Portrayals, violent or otherwise, that leave the viewer in a state of unresolved excitement (Zillmann, 1971; Zillmann *et al.*, 1973);

14. Viewers who are in a state of anger or provocation before seeing a violent portrayal (Berkowitz & Geen, 1966; Caprara *et al.*, 1987; Donnerstein & Berkowitz, 1981; Geen, 1968; Thomas, 1982); and

15. Viewers who are in a state of frustration after viewing a violent portrayal, whether from an extraneous source or as a consequence of viewing the portrayal (Geen, 1968; Geen & Berkowitz, 1967; Worchel, Hardy, & Hurley, 1976).

We argue that these contingencies represent four dimensions: (a) *efficacy* (reward or lack of punishment); (b) *normativeness* (justified, consequenceless, intentionally hurtful, physical violence); (c) *perti-*

nence (commonality of cues, similarity to the viewer, absence of humorous violence); and (d) *susceptibility* (pleasure, anger, frustration, absence of criticism). Whatever heightens these four conditions (the first three of which are dependent on perceptions of, but governed to a large degree by media content, and the fourth of which is the internal state of the viewer) within a portrayal or in real life in regard to a way of behaving, increases the likelihood that this experience will contribute to behaving in such a way in the future.

The experimental examinations of aggression of males of college age against females (Donnerstein & Barrett, 1978; Donnerstein & Berkowitz, 1981; Donnerstein & Hallam, 1978; Donnerstein *et al.*, 1987) in connection with violent erotica essentially exemplify the application of these general principles. Circumstances that enhance the likelihood of such aggression include (a) the portrayal of physical aggression against a female by a male engaged in sexual conquest, (b) the portrayal of forcible rape in which the victim suffers when the real-life target has previously angered the subject, and (c) the portrayal of forcible rape that the victim eventually enjoys, whether or not the subject has previously been angered. Although some admixture is likely, these primarily represent, respectively, the manipulation of normativeness, pertinence, and efficacy.

The wide applicability of the experimental findings has been questioned because of the frequent presence of prior provocation or frustration. The argument is that such a state approaches a necessary condition and that, as a result, effects would be rare. Quite apart from the fact that the provocations and frustrations in the experiments are the peccadilloes encountered daily—rudeness and minor deprivation—Hearold's meta-analysis (1986) documents that effects occur in the absence of frustration or provocation, although they are typically greater when such a state is present, and at their maximum when it is present only for those in the treatment condition. Thus, the effects recorded in the experiments are not an artifact of frustration or provocation, but are attributable to differences in the television and film stimuli experienced by the subjects.

Variation by gender was prominent in the early experiments by Bandura and colleagues (Bandura *et al.*, 1963a, 1963b; Bandura, 1973), with girls invariably displaying less aggressive behavior. The meta-analysis of Hearold (1986) finds that the effect size associated with exposure to antisocial portrayals in fact is about the same for very young boys and girls. At this age, the data come entirely from experiments. At later ages, when the data come from surveys as well as experiments, the sexes diverge, with the effect size for males beyond elementary school increasing with age over that recorded for very young boys, and the effect size for females declining with age over that for very young girls. This pattern presumably reflects the progressive adoption of sex-appropriate norms and the greater frequency of violent male models in the media.

Although the surveys record somewhat stronger patterns of association (both synchronously and over time) between exposure to violent television programs and aggressive or antisocial behavior for males than for females, this is not universally so, and the patterns for the females on the whole resemble those for the males. Thus, the divergence in effect size implies a more limited, but not null, association of exposure and behavior for females.

The experimental findings, in fact, lead precisely to such an expectation. They record that gender of model and viewer interact (Bandura, 1965, 1973; Bandura *et al.*, 1963a, 1963b; Berkowitz & Rawlings, 1963). Among boys, males are more effective than females as models; among girls, males and females are about equally effective, with the pairing least likely to alter behavior the female model and the male subject. Apparently, status, which would favor the male, and appropriateness of behavior, which in the case of aggression would also favor the male, take precedence over the experimentally demonstrated influence of similarity between model and viewer. The expectation, then, would be that females would be less frequently or less strongly influenced than males by violent television and film entertainment because of the preponderance of males among aggressive models. Nevertheless, these male models would not be without their influence on females. The influence of violent entertainment on females would increase with two important social changes: the increasing number of aggressive female models in entertainment, and the increasing degree to which behavior once considered the province of males is perceived as unisexual.

The operation of the four basic dimensions would depend on the particular presentation(s) in question, as well as on the individual viewer and the social circumstances of viewing. Violent cartoons clearly have been implicated in the aggression of young children. Cautionary parental comments about such portrayals, which might have a mitigating effect, are few, because parental mediation is at its minimum when parents and children are viewing such programs. Certainly, superior comprehension of the adverse consequences of aggressive and antisocial behavior would be an inhibiting factor, and thus age might be supposed to mitigate effects. Both the secondary analysis by Kang (1990) of the data on elementary school males of Milavsky and colleagues, and the effect sizes recorded for the same age range for males and females in the meta-analysis by Hearold, are supportive of such an interpretation, but the increase with increasing age in effect size among teenage males in the meta-analysis suggests that other factors may overwhelm or render irrelevant any such cognitive influence. Certainly, much in popular entertainment runs counter to the theme of adverse consequences, such as the glorification of behavior that is antisocial or easily, if emulated, could become such: the complex heist, daring crime, team violence, ruthlessness, and retribution. The demonstrated influence of justified aggression (Berkowitz & Rawlings, 1963; Hearold, 1986) certainly provides no comfort over the frequent television and film dramas with retributive and vigilante themes. The same must be said of those with themes involving the harassment and victimization of women, given the role of cues (Berkowitz & Geen, 1966, 1967; Geen & Berkowitz, 1967); and particularly when, as is so often the case, there is an erotic undertone to the pursuit, given the demonstrated facilitation of aggression against women by portrayals in which males abuse females in a sexual context (Donnerstein, 1980; Donnerstein & Barrett, 1978; Donnerstein & Berkowitz, 1981; Donnerstein & Hallam, 1978; Donnerstein & Malamuth, 1984; Malamuth, Feshbach, & Jaffee, 1977).

There is also the familiar ascendancy of immediate over delayed consequences in their influence on behavior. Whatever the eventual outcome, television and film dramas supply numerous instances in which aggressive and antisocial behavior is rewarding in the short term, both with the characters portrayed and with the viewer highly gratified. Viewers can easily disassemble the plot or the theme, recasting certain elements so that when punishment is eventual, the behavior for which it is imposed is made independent; after all, the mistake, the miscue, the accident, or the flaw that brought ruin was not inevitable.

Finally, it should be remembered that the experiments, regardless of the age of the subjects, investigate the circumstances on which effects are contingent, even if those effects are rare. By sensitively examining factors difficult to disentangle in the everyday flow of experience, and by doing so in a way that permits causal inference, they provide an incipient empirical psychology of response to the mass media in regard to aggressive and antisocial behavior. This psychology would still be pertinent to effects involving seriously harmful and criminal behavior, even if they occurred so rarely as to make no noteworthy difference in any recorded national crime statistic.

E. SIZE OF EFFECT

Both the 10-year (Lefkowitz et al., 1972) and the 3½ year (Milavsky et al., 1982a, 1982b) panel surveys encourage a developmental interpretation by the strength of their associations over long periods of time. We specify "early and then continuing high exposure" because in the data of Milavsky and colleagues (1982b) for both the elementary school males and females there are (a) consistently significant positive cross-sectional or synchronous correlations, (b) the correlations are decidedly larger for the longest time spans, and (c) those longer span correlations are on the average larger when prior exposure to television violence is not controlled for (Table 6.1 and 6.2, pp. 126–127; Tables 8.14 and 8.15, pp. 239–240). A developmental interpretation is further encouraged by the data of Huesmann, Eron, Lefkowitz, & Walder (1984), which add one more decade, and those of Huesmann, Eron, Dubow, & Seebaur (summarized in Eron and Huesmann, 1987), which add two decades to the 10-year panel study (Lefkowitz *et al.*, 1972). There were two major findings among males, who are of primary interest because it was only among the male sample that the earlier positive significant correlations over time were recorded: (a) the early exposure to television violence had a consistently positive association with aggressive behavior 20 years and 30 years as well as 10 years later, and (b) aggression at the end of the initial decade was positively associated with aggression 10 and 20 years later. These associations survived the control of initial aggressiveness, socioeconomic status, and intelligence. Among the components of greater aggressiveness among these men as adults was harsher punitiveness toward their children. The aggressiveness of the children and their preference for violent entertainment, in turn, were positively correlated. The implication is that early media experiences may have a significant role in establishing stable modes of behavior that affect subsequent childrearing. Eron and Huesmann (1987) argue that:

> It is not claimed that the specific programs these adults watched when they were 8 years old still had a direct effect on their behavior. However, the continued viewing of these programs probably contributed to the development of certain attitudes and norms of behavior and taught these youngsters ways of solving interpersonal problems which remained with them over the years. Observation of aggressive sequences on the television screen provided scripts which then were continually rehearsed and easily elicited when the subjects found themselves in situations bearing some resemblance to the ones observed on the screen. (p. 196)

The data of Milavsky and colleagues (1982a, 1982b) suggest that any such developmental contribution occurs primarily before the teenage years, because the increases in size of coefficient over the $3\frac{1}{2}$ years of their study was greater for the elementary school than for the teenage male sample.

The question of whether a portion (and if so how great) of the positive association between the viewing of violent entertainment and aggressive and antisocial behavior is attributable to young persons higher in such behavior seeking out that type of diversion remains open. Chaffee's 1972 analysis of the set of surveys conducted in conjunction with the Surgeon General's inquiry indicated that any contribution was null or minor, with the most likely explanation a contribution by viewing to behavior. Belson (1978) repeatedly examined the issue and concluded that there was one instance, for the most serious of antisocial acts, in which the plausibility of a behavior-to-viewing explanation was nil, no instance for which the opposite could be said, and none for which such an explanation could be said to be better than an equal or somewhat inferior rival. Milavsky and colleagues (1982a, 1982b) did not examine the issue, but a secondary analysis of their data (Kang, 1990) finds greater support for viewing than behavior as the causal factor, and while in some waves of their panel, aggression predicts viewing, in no wave does each predict the other, which is the criterion for unambiguous reciprocity (Granger, 1969). In contrast, Huesmann (1982) and Huesmann and Eron (1986) conclude that more recent data suggest some reciprocity. Atkin, Greenberg, Korzenny, and McDermott (1979) found, among about 225 fourth, sixth, and eighth graders over a one-year period, that earlier aggressive inclinations, measured by the combined replies of mothers and their children about what the young person would do in hypothetical situations, predicted increased later consumption of violent programming. In sum, some of the association may be attributable to the influence of behavior on viewing, but it is unlikely that any such influence is as large as that of viewing on behavior, and unlikely that such influence entirely explains the association.

There is also the question of whether those who are more aggressive are more affected by television violence. Bryant (1989), elaborating on Bryant, Comisky, and Zillmann (1981), presents evidence that males who are more aggressive derive greater pleasure from portrayals of sports violence while those who are less aggressive are essentially indifferent to the degree of violence in televised sports, and that such aggressive viewers derive particular pleasure from the violence and injury rendered a target whom (or in the case of a team, which) they dislike. The Surgeon General's Scientific Advisory Committee on Television and Social Behavior (1972) concluded that young persons who were more aggressive were more likely to increase their aggressive behavior as a consequence of exposure to violent television portrayals, but this conclusion was primarily based on the circuitous and possibly irrelevant evidence that the correlations between present-day aggres-

sion and prior aggressiveness were markedly greater than those between everyday exposure to violent programming and contemporary
aggression, a common finding in the survey literature (Milavsky *et al.*,
1982). Paik (1991) in a meta-analysis of 1087 instances in which the
association between exposure to violent television and aggressive behavior was examined found the average effect sizes greater among those
scoring higher on some measure of aggressive predisposition.

Nevertheless, there is a plausible rationale for skepticism over such
an interaction. Those who are more aggressive obviously have the skills
to so act and clearly are less inhibited over so behaving. One might
expect that for precisely these reasons media influence would be less
frequent or strong; these individuals do not need the lessons of the
media in regard to efficacy, normativeness, or pertinence or specific
aggressive acts and their levels of aggression are probably already as
high as prudence over self-preservation would permit. Such reasoning
leads to the hypothesis that those low in behaving aggressively would
be most affected because of the greater opportunity for a larger degree of
influence on an individual.

In fact, the evidence supports the view that both those higher and
lower in initial aggressiveness may be influenced depending on the
circumstances. Josephson (1987) found in a naturalistic experiment in
which about 400 second- and third-grade boys played floor hockey after
viewing either a violent or nonviolent television sequence that only
among those groups with boys high in initial aggression did those
seeing the violent portrayal behave more aggressively. Celozzi, Kazelskis, and Gutsch (1981) found, among about 80 high school seniors,
that those scoring higher in trait aggression increased more than those
scoring low in their scores on a measure of hostility after seeing a
10-minute sequence from a violent hockey game. On the other hand,
the outcomes of the many experiments, in which the subjects on the
whole represent ordinary levels of everyday aggressiveness, and the
persistence in the surveys of positive correlations after levels of initial
aggressiveness are partialled out (that is, controlled for) make it clear
that a predisposition toward or a greater level of initial aggressiveness is
not a necessary condition for media effects.

We would argue that whether or not those more aggressive are more
affected depends upon how efficacy, normativeness, pertinence, and
susceptibility interact in the specific situation. Individuals who are
more aggressive probably more readily respond to aggressive stimuli
with thoughts supportive of such behavior; thus, Josephson found that
a cue from the violent television portrayal reproduced in real life
heightened aggression among the more aggressive groups beyond the

effect achieved by the television portrayal alone. On the other hand, these dimensions might often be more resistant to any influence because of their already high levels among the more aggressive. Still, the portrayal of successful violence administered to a hateful and morally justified recipient of punishment will almost certainly have more influence on the already aggressive when such a party turns out to be available as a target in real life because of the stronger associations with aggressive thought and behavior that such a cue will evoke and the superior repertoire of aggressive acts that the viewer will possess. We conclude that those more aggressive are particularly likely to be affected when there are a conjunction of factors that override the boundary imposed by the already high level of aggressive behavior, while otherwise we would expect effects to be more likely among those initially less aggressive. In our view, the process by and not the degree to which the trait of aggressiveness is prominent in an individual's television experience is determinative of the medium's influence on such behavior. For example, Rowe and Herstand (1986) found, among about 125 pairs of siblings of high school age, that aggressiveness was uncorrelated with amount of viewing crime and action–adventure programs (the signs were positive but the coefficients did not achieve statistical significance) while there was a positive association with a scale measuring degree of involvement with such programming and the belief that television viewing is a means of learning about the world and a negative association with the belief that aggression would have negative consequences for oneself, and these findings occurred for both males and females. To us, these (roughly) reflect normativeness and pertinence and (clearly) efficacy.

If one accepts (a) the applicability of the experiments with young children to their contemporary behavior, (b) the confirmation of the external validity of the experiments with young adults by the pattern of outcomes from surveys, (c) the joint contribution of the two bodies of experiments to a catalog of contingent conditions, and (d) the plausibility of a developmental pattern, the remaining question concerns effect size. How big is the contribution of television to the aggressive and antisocial behavior of teenagers and young adults?

The most unusual instance in which an estimate of size of effect is offered is the archival examination by Hennigan and colleagues of shifts in crime statistics associated with the introduction of television in the United States in the late 1940s and early 1950s (Hennigan *et al.*, 1982). These investigators took advantage of the immense natural experiment, produced by the FCC's freeze on television station licensing in the late 1940s, to conduct an interrupted time-series analysis with switching replications, in which the roles of the treatment and control sites reverse over time (Cook & Campbell, 1979). This is the same design employed to assess the effects of the introduction of television on library circulation (Chapter II).

Hennigan and colleagues (1982) encompassed data from two distinct pools, cities and states. Statistics for reported crimes of four types were examined: (a) crimes involving violence; (b) larceny theft; (c) auto theft; and (d) burglary. Larceny theft is defined as:

> The unlawful taking, carrying, leading, or riding away of property from the possession or constructive possession of another. Thefts of bicycles, automobile accessories, shoplifting, pocket-picking, or any stealing of property or article which is not taken by force and violence or by fraud. Excluded embezzlement, "con" games, forgery, worthless checks, etc. (p. 465)

Burglary is distinguished from larceny by breaking and entering.

The results are striking (Table 6.3; Fig. 6.4). No significant shifts were found for violent crimes or burglary. Two significant positive shifts were found for auto thefts, both for the sites acquiring television before the licensing freeze. For larceny theft, all four shifts are significant and positive. The data for the prefreeze cities, the prefreeze states, the postfreeze cities, and the postfreeze states display the identical pattern.

The authors conclude that the multiple replications demand the inference that the introduction of television increased larceny thefts, and for the lack of the same, they refrain from an inference about auto thefts. These data are pertinent to the present inquiry because of the substantial portion of such offenses committed by youths and young adults, particularly males, and they document an increase in crime associated with the introduction of television.

When the investigators estimate the size of the effects on larceny theft, they range from 5.5 to 18%, with an average of 12.7%. A conservative (if arbitrary) approach would be to accept the smallest estimate as the lower limit, and take the average of the remaining three as the upper limit, leading to a range of 5.5 to 15.1%, with a midpoint of 10.3%.

By the very nature of the design, nothing is revealed about process. Process is the province of research different in kind—experiments that permit examination of the effects of manipulations, or survey data in which associations between pertinent variables can be examined. One prominent candidate is relative deprivation induced either by the emphases of television programming and advertising on material well-being or by the availability without universal affordability of the most

Table 6.3
Changes in Crime Rates and Introduction of Television

Type of crime and sample	Significance[a]	Estimated percentage increase
Violent crime		
Prefreeze cities	0	
Postfreeze cities	0	
Prefreeze states	0	
Postfreeze states	0	
Larceny theft		
Prefreeze cities	+ +	13.3
Postfreeze cities	+ +	5.5
Prefreeze states	+ +	14.1
Postfreeze states	+ +	18.0
Auto theft		
Prefreeze cities	+	
Postfreeze cities	0	
Prefreeze states	+ +	
Postfreeze states	0	
Burglary		
Prefreeze cities	0	
Postfreeze cities	0	
Prefreeze states	0	
Postfreeze states	0	

[a] 0 = null, $+ < .05$, $++ < .01$.

From Hennigan, K.M., Heath, L., Wharton, J.D., Del Rosario, M.L., Cook, T.D., & Calder, B.J. (1982). Impact of the introduction of television on crime in the United States: Empirical findings and theoretical implications. *Journal of Personality and Social Psychology, 42*(3), 461–477.

rapidly adopted major home appliance of all time, the television set. The authors favor this interpretation, on the grounds that television portrayed many murders and much violence, but there was no increase in violent crime. Others are social learning and disinhibition, with the actual behavior at a level where the likelihood of apprehension and the severity of punishment would be minimal. We conclude that both general explanations are equally plausible and that, in fact, they are inseparable, because the translation of dissatisfaction into behavior might well rest on social learning and disinhibition; in this view, relative deprivation heightens suceptibility, while the other two give it direction. More importantly, the present analysis leads us to conclude that the effect, however explained, is probably a recurring one. We favor

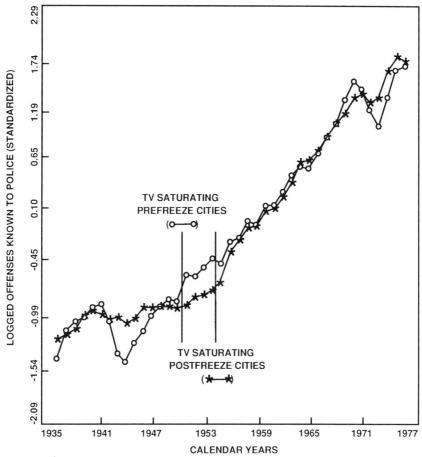

Fig. 6.4   Larceny theft rates 1936–1976 and introduction of television: City data. From Hennigan, K.M., Heath, L., Wharton, J.D., Del Rosario, M.L., Cook, T.D., & Calder, B.J. (1982). Impact of the introduction of television on crime in the United States: Empirical findings and theoretical implications. *Journal of Personality and Social Psychology, 42*(3), 461–477.

the latter over a one-time historical shift attributable to the enormous increase in pertinent stimuli because of the many ever-present factors on which effects are contingent, and the variations in exposure that lead to sizable quantitative differences among individuals.

This is not the sole instance outside of the survey evidence in which a positive association between portrayals and behavior in everyday life has been reported. It is of particular interest because of the large populations involved, the strength of the design with multiple replications, and the clarity of outcome. Others include the matching of about 50 prison inmates with noninmates on age, race, and teenage neighborhood by Heath, Kruttschnitt, and Ward (1986), and a body of time-series analyses in which public statistics are examined in conjunction with media portrayals (Bollen & Phillips, 1982; Gould & Shaffer, 1986; Phillips, 1986; Phillips & Carstensen, 1986; Phillips & Hensley, 1984). In the former, the viewing of violent television programs when younger was positively associated with the commission in later years of violent crime among those who, in their earlier years, had been abused by their parents. These data support a developmental sequence, but add the possibility that for any influence on later seriously harmful antisocial behavior, the earlier viewing must be accompanied by physical and psychological environmental stress. In the latter, it has been reported that teenage suicides have risen after suicides have received attention in television news and fiction; suicides overall have risen after coverage of prominent suicides; and the homicide rate has risen among males of the same race as the losing fighter after the televising of championship boxing matches. The most dramatic example is the cross-cultural analysis by Centerwall (1989), in which the introduction of television just about everywhere is said to have been followed by a substantial and sustained increase in homicides. J.N. Baron and Reiss (1985) offer a comprehensive methodological critique of such aggregate analyses that covers problematical aspects of the role of concepts, theory, and statistical techniques, while Kessler, Downey, Milavsky, and Stipp (1988) offer analyses using some of the same data sources that partially conflict with some of these findings and would not lead to the same conclusions about media influence. We do not draw on any of these sources in reaching our conclusions, because they are logically unnecessary to our paradigm, and thus need not attempt to resolve these issues.

We respect the aggregate analysis of Messner (1986) in which he consistently found negative associations between the estimated amount of exposure to violent programs within 281 Standard Metropolitan Statistical Areas (SMSAs) and rates of four types of crime, homicide, rape, robbery, and aggravated assault for the rigorous logic and thoroughness of the analysis. However, while we agree that one should be conservative in extrapolating from experiments reflecting effects on interpersonal aggression and surveys documenting associations with interpersonal aggression to seriously harmful, criminal behavior, we believe the evidence as a whole justifies the expectation that violent television entertainment does contribute to some small degree to such behavior. We do not think television exposure in general or to violence in particular varies enough for the amount of variation in the independent variable to be a valid measure of greater or lesser exposure, and we doubt whether analysis of cross-sectional or synchronous exposure and behavior at the SMSA level tells us much except that fewer crimes occur in areas where television viewing is somewhat greater than average and more occur where it is lower than average. Curious, because there are correlates with individual amount of viewing that in the aggregate are correlates of crime rates (in particular being black or a member of a household of lower socioeconomic status), but not particularly revealing about the influence of violent television entertainment; our explanation, *post hoc,* is that the correlates of Nielsen estimates of viewing within SMSAs are inversely associated with crime.

In this context, we would not take the very high, positive correlations between the estimates of the viewing of violent programs and television viewing in general as validating the estimate of violence viewing as Messner does because the association between the two is at best moderate (Chaffee, 1972) except in cases where the viewing measure represents an oversampling of violent programs (for example, Milavsky, Kessler, Stipp, & Rubens, 1982a, 1982b); rather, we would take it as supporting the interpretation that what at best is measured is overall television viewing and not meaningful differences in exposure to violence. We do accept two of his explanations as independently valid. As he points out young persons are likely to be socialized to act criminally by association with peers who behave in such a way, and such persons are more likely to be spending their time on the streets or in other locales where crime is possible than viewing television, essentially an at home activity. He also argues in our view correctly that greater than average amounts of television viewing may suppress the convergence in time and space of offenders, plausible victims, and the absence of guardians that makes crime possible. This leads us to expect that if exposure to television violence has any influence on seriously harmful, criminal acts one means is through the rare imitating of a portrayal particularly compelling to the individual and another is through the greater exposure to violent television entertainment of a small number of persons already within the category of regular offenders or delinquents, as was the case in the Belson (1978) survey.

When 22 separate estimates of effect size were collated from the various surveys (Comstock, 1986; Table 6.4), they did not diverge dramatically from this range, although they are on the whole somewhat smaller. When the measure is variance explained, the range is between 4 and 10%; other modes of estimation produce similar results. The

Table 6.4

Selected Estimates of Size and Association between Exposure to Violent Programs and Aggressive and Antisocial Behavior

Source	Behavior measure	Association	Time span	Other variables controlled	Sample
Wisconsin & Maryland surveys (McLeod, Atkin, & Chaffee, 1972a, 1972b)	Self-reported interpersonal aggression	$r = .30$**	Synchronous	None	68 seventh- and 83 tenth-grade males and females ($N = 151$); Wisconsin sample
	Self-reported interpersonal aggression	$r = .32$**	Synchronous	None	248 seventh- and 243 tenth-grade males and females ($N = 473$); Maryland sample
	Self-reported interpersonal aggression	$r = .24$**[a]	Synchronous	Total television viewing time	68 seventh- and 83 tenth-grade males and females ($N = 151$); Wisconsin sample
	Self-reported interpersonal aggression	$r = .28$**[a]	Synchronous	Total television viewing time	248 seventh- and 243 tenth-grade males and females ($N = 473$); Maryland sample
10-year survey (Lefkowitz, Eron, Walder, & Huesmann, 1977)	Peer-rated interpersonal aggression	$r = .21$**	Synchronous	None	184 males, modal age = 9

Peer-rated interpersonal aggression	$r = .31^{***}$	10 years	None	184 males, modal age = 19
Peer-rated interpersonal aggression	$r = .25^{**}$	10 years	Peer-rated interpersonal aggression at initial wave of measurement 10 years earlier	184 males, modal age = 19
London survey (Belson, 1978) Seriously harmful antisocial and criminal behavior	49%, or an average of 1.42, more acts by treatment than control population during preceding 6 months*	Synchronous	All major correlates with aggressive and antisocial behavior	1565 males, ages 12–17
All aggressive and antisocial behavior measured, except the most trivial	13%, or an average of 13.25 more, acts by treatment than control population during preceding 6 months*	Synchronous	All major correlates with aggressive and antisocial behavior	1565 males, ages 12–17
All aggressive and antisocial behavior measured, including the most trivial	11%, or an average of 29.07, more acts by treatment than control population during preceding 6 months*	Synchronous	All major correlates with aggressive and antisocial behavior	1565 males, ages 12–17

269

Table 6.4
(*Continued*)

Source	Behavior measure	Association	Time span	Other variables controlled	Sample
Three-year multiwave survey (Milavsky, Kessler, Stipp, & Rubens, 1982)	Peer-rated interpersonal aggression	Unweighted average for six individual waves of measurement, $r = .173^{*b}$	Synchronous	None	533, 428, 510, 546, 406, and 236 elementary school males and females per wave, in order of date of measurement[c]
	Peer-rated interpersonal aggression	Unweighted average for five wave pairs with longest time spans, $b = .208^d$ $B = .083^e$	2–3 years	Aggression at time of pair's initial wave	211, 161, 147 121, and 112 elementary school males per wave pair, in order of increasing span of time between waves
	Peer-rated interpersonal aggression	Unweighted average for five wave pairs with longest time time spans, $b = .077, B = .055$	2—3 years	Aggression at time of pair's initial wave	236, 134, 133, 123, and 113 elementary school females per wave pair, in order of increasing span of time between waves

Measure	Statistic	Time span	Controls	Sample
Self-reported interpersonal aggression	Average of five individual waves, $r = .13^{*f}$	Synchronous	None	389, 561, 561, 672, and 636 teenage males per wave in order of date of measurement
Self-reported interpersonal aggression	$b = .016^*$ $B = .094$	19 months; longest span of survey	All prior measures of aggression; all prior television measures; association between the television measure and aggression measure in the preceding wave	285 teenage males
Self-reported teacher aggression	$b = .009$ $B = .051$	Average for waves of 5, 7, and 9 months[g]		272 teenage males
Seriously harmful and criminal behavior	P = probability of committing such an act for percentile standing in prior television exposure *Percentile* P 5th .212* 10th .229* 50th .304* 90th .436* 95th .508*	25 months	Prior seriously harmful and criminal behavior	172 teenage males

(continued)

Table 6.4
(*Continued*)

Source	Behavior measure	Association	Time span	Other variables controlled	Sample
Interrupted time series with switching replications (Hennigan, Heath, Wharton, Del Rosario, Cook, & Calder, 1982)	Larceny thefts reported to police	5.5–12.7%[b]	Shifts associated with introduction of television	Time-specific social and historical events; crime trends	Prefreeze and postfreeze cities; prefreeze and postfreeze states
Meta-analysis (Hearold, 1986)	Antisocial behavior as measured by investigators	.30 effect size[i]	Varied		528 comparisons from all genres of method
	Antisocial behavior as measured by investigators	.20 effect size	Varied		159 comparisons, studies rated highest in quality of methodology

| Antisocial behavior as measured by investigators | .34 effect size | Mostly immediate | 290 comparisons from all laboratory experiments |
| Antisocial behavior as measured by investigators | .32 effect size | Mostly synchronous | 165 comparisons from all surveys |

[a] Partial correlations.

[b] Corrected for unreliability of measurement; $p < .05$ for all six waves.

[c] Valid data only; children reporting viewing an unusually large number of nonexistent television programs excluded.

[d] b refers to metric partial correlations.

[e] B (beta) refers to standardized partial regression coefficients.

[f] $p < .05$ for four of the five waves.

[g] Coefficients for longest time spans are reported for interpersonal aggression and seriously harmful and criminal behavior, because the coefficients increased with time span; average is reported for teacher aggression because the pattern was positive, but no increase over time occured.

[h] Minimum estimate plus average of three higher estimates.

[i] Effect size = average difference in scores between treatment and control populations expressed as a proportion of the standard deviation for the control population.

* $p < .05$.

** $p < .01$

*** $p < .001$

From Comstock, G. (1986). Television and film violence. In S.J. Apter & A. Goldstein (Eds.), *Youth violence: Programs and prospects* (pp. 178–218). Elmsford, NY: Pergamon.

explanation of variance for girls is less consistent than for boys, and on the whole, the explained variance is somewhat smaller.

The size of the association over the span of the 10-year panel survey by Eron, Lefkowitz, and colleagues (1972) does not encourage discarding the 4 to 10% range for smaller figures. It implies, in fact, that in the multiwave 3½-year panel survey of Milavsky and colleagues (1982a, 1982b), the association for personal aggression for the teenage males would have been greater had a longer time been involved. It thus hints that the associations for the more serious types of misbehavior might similarly increase.

The London teenage data (Belson, 1978) do not suggest that the association of exposure to violent television programs with the most serious aggressive and antisocial behavior is insignificant or in any meaningful way less substantial in social importance than that for the two lesser levels of such behavior. In these data, the association with exposure to violent programs is proportionately much greater for the most serious than for less serious behavior (49% more acts, versus 11.2% and 9.6%, in descending order of seriousness of behavior; Table 6.1). The high-television-violence group exceeds the matched low-exposure group in acts committed over the previous 6 months by an average of 2.46 for the most serious behavior; the figures for less serious behavior, in descending order, are 10.79 and 15.82. The discrepancy between proportions and frequencies is attributable to the fortunate fact that the most serious aggressive and antisocial behavior is not common among young males. Thus, a small increase in frequency produced a very large percentage increase, while with less serious forms of deviance, large frequency increases registered as modest proportions.

The least serious behavior is typified by "I wrote in big letters on the side of a building." At the next highest level, the least serious included "I hit a boy with bare fists in a fight." At the highest level, the least serious are (in ascending order) "I twisted a boy's arm until he yelled with pain," "I broke into a house and smashed everything I could find," and "I threw the cat into the fire."

The two less serious categories are hardly benign in their implications for others. Nevertheless, the association between the latter category and exposure is the most impressive because of its degree, the destructiveness of the behavior, and confidence with which television can be said to have some causal influence. It is this third element that precludes interpreting the data as documenting a weaker influence of viewing on more serious than on less serious behavior.

The various estimates lead us to conclude that the amount of aggressive and antisocial behavior involved is small, but enough to qualify for social significance, if even the lower limit of the probable range is taken as the best estimate. The measures of interpersonal aggression qualify as representing behavior unpleasant, unwelcome, and disruptive for others. Measures more definitively above the threshold of seriously harmful and criminal behavior do not display a pattern markedly or consistently different from those for interpersonal aggression.

It is tempting to attribute less explained variance to television for more serious than for less serious behavior. However, neither the data of Thornton and Voight (1984), Milavsky and colleagues (1982a, 1982b) nor those of Belson (1978), which are the three instances that permit comparisons, encourage such an interpretation. The former found slightly stronger relationships with more serious forms of delinquency, even when other variables were controlled. Within the teenage sample of Milavsky and colleagues, the size of the association for personal aggression is greater, but not markedly so, than for the more serious teacher and delinquency measures. Belson, of course, found the largest proportional and inferentially most convincing difference for the most serious offenses.

There are two reasons to suspect that the measures of association underestimate the actual degree of relationship. One is technical; the other, social; both are statistical. Unreliability of measurement means that any estimate of association will be less than the true figure, and measures of exposure and behavior have a degree of unreliability. Television is near-ubiquitous, so those "low" in exposure have had a substantial degree; associations will be depressed when the range of scores on a variable are truncated. Thus, the central tendency implied for the effect of exposure to violent television programs on aggressive and antisocial behavior is positive, probably modest or small, not exclusive of seriously harmful and criminal behavior, certainly inclusive of behavior unwelcome by others, socially significant, and possibly greater in magnitude than the figures obtained.

F. OTHER TYPES OF BEHAVIOR

The principles developed in regard to aggressive and antisocial behavior apply to other types of behavior. Such effects have consistently been found experimentally, and the factors on which they are contingent essentially are identical (Comstock et al., 1978; Rushton, 1979, 1980, 1982). These principles have application to socialization generally (Bandura, 1986); that is, they can be extended beyond television and film to other media and other sources of information. They also apply to certain instances of psychotherapy (Bandura & Menlove, 1968; G.T.

Wilson & O'Leary, 1980); for example, desensitization by visual media can be used to reduce phobias, and exposure to portrayals can be employed in the rehearsing of responses inhibitory or counter to antisocial behavior (such as the unwelcome public display of genitals). They represent the foundations of the health-belief model (Becker, 1974; Becker & Maiman, 1975), which has been the basis of numerous programs employing the media along with other interventions to change the health-related practices of persons of all ages and in a variety of settings, including several government-sponsored multimillion dollar campaigns in which the mass media have had a central role (Comstock, 1983a; Farquhar et al., 1977; Flora, Maccoby, & Farquhar, 1989; N. Maccoby & Solomon, 1981).

More directly pertinent, there have been a number of laboratory-type experiments that examine the effects of television portrayals that cannot be said to contain violent, aggressive, or antisocial content. Many would assign them the label *prosocial.* Examples include altruism; acceptance of others; behavior in accord with safety or health; book buying; cooperation; environmental protection; obeying of norms and rules; respecting the law; social interaction; and the like.

We can present the evidence succinctly because of the meta-analysis of Hearold (1986), which aggregated the data on both prosocial and antisocial portrayals. We first examine the contents of portrayals (Table 6.5) and then the average size of effect recorded (Table 6.6).

The range of portrayals investigated has been quite wide, and the results have been analogous for the two categories. Exposure to violent and antisocial portrayals is associated with higher levels of such behavior and lower levels of constructive, positive, or altruistic behavior; exposure to portrayals of constructive, positive, or altruistic behavior is associated with lower levels of aggressive and antisocial behavior and higher levels of such prosocial behavior. These results, although reduced in magnitude, hold up when the studies are scored for quality and for ecological validity (i.e., the presence of elements corresponding to ordinary television exposure); that is, the pattern remains the same when the analysis is confined to the studies highest in quality and ecological validity. This refutes the claim that reported behavioral outcomes have been an artifact of poor quality or low ecological validity.

Comstock and Paik (1990) updated the meta-analysis to the present for violent portrayals and aggressive behavior and, because of developments in the technique, introduced tests of statistical significance and, because of more recent data, criminal and seriously harmful behavior as an outcome. Almost half of the total outcomes were post-Hearold. The

Table 6.5
Principal Anti- and Prosocial Stimuli Employed in Television
Effects Research

Antisocial behavior	Number	Percentage
Mixture	132	19.4
Detective–crime	129	19.0
Demonstrated behavior	119	17.5
Drama	110	16.2
Cartoon	51	7.5
News	34	5.0
Western	31	4.6
Consumerism	26	3.8
Cartoons and comedy	10	1.5
Mixed movies	10	1.5
"Sanford and Son" and "All in the Family"	8	1.2
Other	19	2.8
Total	679	100

Prosocial behavior	Number	Percentage
Demonstrated behavior	48	25.3
"Mister Rogers' Neighborhood"	42	22.1
Drama	31	16.3
Public service ads and programs	21	11.0
Mixture	13	6.8
"Lassie"	6	3.2
"Big Blue Marble"	6	3.2
Comedy	4	2.6
"Patrik and Putrik"	4	2.1
Other	14	7.4
Total	190	100

Adapted from Hearold, S. (1986). A synthesis of 1043 effects of television on social behavior. In G. Comstock (Ed.), *Public communication and behavior* (Vol. 1, pp. 65–133). New York: Academic Press.

earlier results were confirmed with decidedly positive associations between exposure and the behavior in question for both experiments, mostly of the laboratory type, and for correlational studies, which were mostly surveys. Statistical significance was verified, and at high levels. In addition, positive and statistically significant associations were found for exposure to violent portrayals and criminal and seriously harmful acts.

The symmetry in the Hearold data is confined to directionality. The effect size for exposure to prosocial portrayals and like behavior is

Table 6.6
Meta-Analysis Outcomes by Treatment and Study Characteristics

Exposure to anti- and prosocial stimuli and associated anti- and prosocial behavior

Treatment type	Average effect size[a]	SD	SE$_M$	Number of effects
Antisocial treatments				
Demonstrated behavior	.69	.77	.10	62
News	.67	.92	.20	21
Commercials	.46	.84	.17	25
Cartoons	.41	.66	.13	27
Mixed movies	.40	.28	.11	6
Westerns	.35	.39	.09	19
Sports	.27	.60	.30	4
Mixture of cartoons and comedy	.26	.60	.27	5
Crime–detective	.25	.81	.11	57
"All in the Family" and "Sanford and Son"	.25	.19	.07	7
Drama	.16	.76	.09	77
Mixed	.14	.35	.03	104
Prosocial treatments				
Demonstrated behavior	1.02	1.04	.33	10
Simulated programs (usually drama)	.79	.95	.26	13
Public service ads	.79	.64	.15	19
TV programs	.59	.98	.14	49
"Lassie" (animal)	1.16	.82	.33	6
"Mister Rogers' Neighborhood"	.68	1.21	.25	23
"Sesame Street" and "Electric Company"	.58	.37	.19	4
"Big Blue Marble"	.57	.45	.18	6
Comedy	.54	.39	.28	2
Mixed programs	.18	.37	.15	6
"Patrik and Putrik"	− .73	1.06	.75	2

Ecological validity, study quality, and meta-analytic effect sizes

	Average effect size			
	Ecological validity		Study quality	
Comparison	All	Highest external validity	All	Highest quality
Antisocial behavior				
Antisocial versus other	0.45	0.23	0.30	0.20
Prosocial versus other	0.41	−0.17	−0.20	−0.41
Prosocial behavior				
Antisocial versus other	0.28	0.08	−0.01	−0.27
Prosocial versus other	1.25	0.36	0.63	0.62

[a] The reported effect sizes are for the treatment comparisons antisocial versus other and prosocial versus other.
Adapted from Hearold, S. (1986). A synthesis of 1043 effects of television on social behavior. In G. Comstock (Ed.), *Public communication and behavior* (Vol. 1, pp. 65–133). New York: Academic Press.

double that for antisocial portrayals and like behavior. There proportionately were more young children in the prosocial studies, but we do not think that is primarily responsible, because age does not seem to make a major difference in experimental response to portrayals. We also doubt whether prosocial portrayals enjoy an inherent advantage, because such behavior, while socially approved by adults, is not clearly normative for young children, and compared with antisocial portrayals, might not be so attention-getting and might require more generalizing from what was portrayed. We point to two other factors. First, "behavior demonstrations," defined as portrayals designed to influence, have the largest effect sizes for both types of behavior (Table 6.6) but are far more frequent in occurrence among the prosocial studies (Table 6.5) with, unlike the case for antisocial portrayals, even some ordinary programs such as "Mister Rogers' Neighborhood" in fact qualifying. Second, there is the greater frequency with which the portrayed behavior and the outcome measure were identical. This would enhance the likelihood of effects with very young children by overcoming their lesser ability to generalize from one example of prosocial behavior to another (Hearold, 1986) and by ensuring an opportunity to behave in accord with what had been viewed (Comstock *et al.*, 1978). Thus, we attribute the advantage of prosocial portrayals to (a) the much greater proportion of demonstrated behavior among the portrayals, and (b) an interaction between age and the identicality of the independent and dependent variables. It is not the type of behavior that makes the difference, but the mode of portrayal and, at least with very young children, mode of measurement.

We conclude then that on balance, despite the evidence of Hearold (1986), antisocial and aggressive have the advantage over prosocial portrayals and especially so for younger children and those with less skill at cognitive processing. This is because prosocial portrayals may require more demanding generalization to the new circumstances—the translation of an act of generosity to one expressing empathy or help—and for most young people such behavior does not bestow the intrinsic reward of acting out impulses or giving way to the temptation to violate a taboo. Probably fundamental to the differences between the two domains is that antisocial and aggressive behavior consistently and from very early in life are labeled as undesirable while positive reinforcement of prosocial acts is less consistent, leading to greater generalization or increased likelihood that an act different from what was portrayed but falling in the same category of behavior will be performed. Probably similarly fundamental is that while behavior in both domains can be complex, indirect, and nonphysical, antisocial and aggressive acts are more often simple, physical, and direct both in their portrayal and in their everyday performance, and this would apply especially to the television watched by and the behavior engaged in by children and especially young children.

The symmetry implies that two social costs result from violent children's programming and violent entertainment viewed by young persons. One is higher levels of antisocial behavior. The other is lower levels of beneficial, constructive, and desirable behavior. The emphasis on antisocial portrayals in children's programming (Greenberg, 1980) means that aggressive behavior is not inhibited when it might be, and that it is unnecessarily explicitly encouraged. We concur, then, with Hyman's (1973) argument that television may facilitate socially constructive responses. He singled out pity and concern for human suffering, which he argued could be enhanced by the calamities so persistently portrayed in news and drama, but the same argument could be applied to such frequently portrayed behavior as bravery, readiness to intervene in an emergency, loyalty to others, persistence, and pursuit of justice. He insightfully argued what experimental research has since confirmed—that violent drama may instead contribute to antisocial behavior by ignoring the consequences of such behavior. The problem, then, with popular entertainment that is violent is that often the positive elements are encapsulated in a formula in which antisocial influences predominate. For example, Potter and Ware (1987) found during prime time that antisocial acts were prevalent not only on the part of both heroes and villains, but also among secondary characters, and these generally were rewarded, justified, and voluntarily adopted as normative means to achieve goals, rather than imposed by circumstances. Liss and colleagues (Liss & Reinhardt, 1980; Liss, Reinhardt, & Fredriksen, 1983) found that in children's cartoons not only did morally positive superheroes commit much violence, but also that among young children, the mixture of violence with prosocial exhortations and acts led to less comprehension of the prosocial message, lessened prosocial, and increased aggressive behavior compared with prosocial portrayals without the violent element.

G. IMPLICATIONS

Several assumptions have guided this analysis:

1. Research evidence is dynamic and not static as a literature grows; credibility and validity initially increase sharply as mutually supportive findings and confirmations of theory-based hypotheses multiply.

2. Laboratory-based experimentation has implications for real-world

occurrences when their manipulations successfully simulate factors conceptually important in those occurrences (Brewer, 1985).

3. Distinctive genres of method—such as laboratory experiments, field experiments, surveys, and time series—must be assessed separately because of their unique attributes, and only synthesized subsequently.

4. Occasional departures from a pattern of findings do not constitute inconsistencies among results.

5. An occasional conflict between findings does not render a body of evidence or even those findings themselves uninterpretable.

6. Research concerned with possible social harms must be sensitive to detecting such outcomes; that is, the legitimate concern for Type II error (accepting a hypothesis when it is false) must be modulated in such cases by a particular sensitivity to Type I error (rejecting a hypothesis when it is true).

These assumptions on the whole depart from those underlying the contrary review by Freedman (1984), and this explains his somewhat different conclusions (for other comments, see Freidrich-Cofer and Huston, 1986, and Freedman, 1986). He confines the role of laboratory-based experiments to demonstrating the possibility of real-world effects, and ignores the implications of their overall congruence, contribution to theory, consistency with survey results, and examination of factors with real-life implications (1 and 2). He arraigns field experiments, surveys, and time series as if each were comparable independent tests of a real-world relationship that can be subjectively averaged; the meta-analysis of Hearold documents a genre-based difference between field experiments and surveys that logically precludes such treatment (3). He makes much of departures from the majority of, and of conflicts among, the findings without searching for a plausible, empirically based resolution (4 and 5), and exemplifies an anxiety over Type II error (6) by his mystifying conclusion that, "First, there is a consistent, small positive correlation between viewing television violence and aggressiveness; second, there is little convincing evidence that in natural settings viewing television violence causes people to be more aggressive" (p. 227), without specifying the criterion by which the first, based on evidence from natural settings, translates into the second.

More recently, social learning has been elaborated as social-cognitive theory (Bandura, 1986), and disinhibition and cue as cognitive neoassociation (Berkowitz, 1984, 1990). The former emphasizes the role of cognitive elements, and particularly beliefs and perceptions, while the latter focuses on the semantic linking together of such elements by labels and codes autonomically applied by the individual. Both encompass the articulatable and conscious, as well as less readily verbalizable components of thought, but the emphasis is greater on the first in social cognitive and on the second in neoassociation theory. In both, external and internal cues are central. The revisions encompass lengthier and more varied sequences of behavior than the single acts, which to some, the original theories might have seemed to be addressed, and in effect postulate that the earlier formulations sum to scenarios and sets of expectations based on direct and vicarious experience, reflecting our first three dimensions—efficacy, normativeness, and pertinence.

The view that one way in which television affects behavior is through internalized, learned, if variable behavioral sequences (variable because they would be dependent on subsequent cues and the probabilistic vagaries of semantic linkages) followed when circumstances present cues, leading to the retrieval of initiating acts and associated thoughts, receives overlooked support from the Belson data. Exposure to violent programs was not correlated with beliefs favorable to violence, with high regard for its use, or with callousness. Such exposure was also unassociated with being irritating, annoying, or argumentative, and with committing violence in the company of other boys. These findings suggest that consciously articulatable beliefs, hostile personality traits, or some form of contagion are not means by which television influences behavior. Instead, television's influence in this sample apparently lay in scripts sporadically retrieved in response to environmental cues.

The experiment of Thomas (1982), in which college-age subjects became more aggressive after seeing a 15-minute highly violent condensation of a "Mannix" episode, but had a lowered pulse rate while aggressing, certainly makes a case for processes that can operate in the absence of physiological arousal. Arousal is a facilitative but not a necessary factor. Social cognitive and neoassociation theory essentially lead to the same predictions. The former more clearly applies when behavior is essentially imitated or articulatable beliefs and perceptions play a role, and the latter, when behavior diverges markedly from what has been portrayed or less articulatable elements come into play, but we can neither find nor invent an outcome that one but not the other could be said to explain. For example, without a citation, it would be impossible to identify from which of the two formulations the following contingencies derive:

> The ideas the observers have at the time they were exposed to the communication, their interpretations as to whether the witnessed actions are appropriate, profitable, or morally justified, the

nature of the available targets, and whether the depicted incident is real or fictional. (Berkowitz, 1984, p. 410)

This does not mean that one or the other is not the better or more parsimonious explanation for one or another set of circumstances, or that the varying interplay of affective and cognitive factors within each does not merit further investigation. For example, Josephson (1987) found neo-association the best explanation for the enhancement of aggression among more aggressive boys by the real-life presentation of a cue from a just-viewed violent portrayal. Reeves, Lang, Thorson, and Rothschild (1989) found the processing of television scenes asymmetrical, with violent scenes likely to arouse negative affect processed by the nonverbal right, and humorous scenes, by the verbal left hemisphere. The implication is that at least *some* violent portrayals (those that trigger primarily negative emotions) may be processed initially outside the verbal realm, with the result that behavior may be primed (Berkowitz, 1986) with little or no intervention by articulatable beliefs. Less emotion-arousing positive behavior would be processed within a more verbal framework, and effects would be more within the viewer's direct control. These findings would favor neoassociation over social cognitive theory in explaining effects of some types of portrayed violence. However, the authors argue convincingly that such asymmetry may disappear when violence invites approach by inspiring anger. Neither formulation requires that a portrayal be perceived as antisocial or aggressive to facilitate such behavior. Quite the opposite. The less social stigma attached to the portrayed behavior, the more likely it is to be taken as a guide; thus, the dimension of normativeness clearly posits that not attaching a label with negative valence to behavior enhances the likelihood that it will be engaged in. Neither also requires much in the way of cognitive skills; the fact that imitation occurs as early as 14 months (Meltzoff, 1988) and the subjects in most of the experiments testing social learning theory were five to six year olds unambiguously testifies to this for one of them. In fact, both would predict that the greater the cognitive skills and the more active and analytic, or beta wave left brain the processing, the less likely an effect because of the greater likelihood the fictionalized character of the portrayal, the realization that those portrayed may not really resemble oneself, possible adverse consequences, social taboos, and alternatives will be given some weight. Primitive levels of processing are not only sufficient but a circumstance that makes effects more likely. Our view is that future research will clarify their preeminent territoriality while depriving neither of a domain.

We advocate, then, a three-factor explanation of the influence of television and film violence on antisocial and aggressive behavior:

1. *Nonredundancy.* When violent portrayals are nonredundant with real-life experience or what is experienced through the media, they may influence behavior. In effect, they provide new information. When such effects occur, one would expect the portrayal to have been particularly compelling to the viewer. This implies that highly promoted, emotional, dramatic narratives are particularly likely to have such effects, because they would have the advantages of high attention, arousal, and involvement.

2. *Social cognition.* By presenting repetitive, inevitably somewhat redundant portrayals of aggression, retributive justice, and violence, such portrayals contribute to the development of expectations and perceptions. These expectations and perceptions will guide behavior when an event, person, activity, or other cue makes them pertinent. Television helps formulate scripts and scenarios; these are the maps that provide the crude and uneven paths for behavior.

3. *Developmental.* Violent portrayals not only encourage concurrent increases in such behavior among children, but they also may contribute to the acquisition of fairly stable enduring traits. We agree with Eron and Huesmann (1987) that the role of television in establishing traits occurs primarily before adolescence. The contribution of television to traits apparently begins remarkably early, because Meltzoff (1988) found that children as young as 14 and 24 months would imitate what they saw on a television screen, and that they could do so even after a 24-hour delay.

These factors emphasize both the unusual and compelling and the banal and continuing aspects of television as they are experienced while growing up. They lead us to believe there are synchronous contributions at all ages, and over-time contributions in the establishing of traits. Taken together, the three theories—social cognitive, cognitive neoassociation, and excitation transfer—hold that television may heighten or lower the likelihood of behavior varying widely in type or character, depending on what television portrays and the circumstances in which the viewer finds himself or herself (Berkowitz, 1986; Geen & Thomas, 1986; Huesmann, 1986; Malamuth & Briere, 1986; Rule & Ferguson, 1986).

These principles of the psychology of media effects on behavior apply to news and sports as well as to entertainment programming. What differs among the genres, as well as within them, are the placements that a portrayal would achieve on our major dimensions. For example, news may affect perceived efficacy by whether a particular act is said to have succeeded or failed; pertinence inherently is high because events are real, but would be sharply diminished by events distant geographically, politically, or socially; and the emphases on conflict, disaster, and disruption may enhance the degree to which normativeness is ascribed to them. News accounts occasionally are emotionally arousing, and this heightened excitation may not be diminished until some time after the end of the report. Analogous comments can be made about sports, except that such programming typically would place higher in regard to arousal. No one would dispute their many differences, but the three genres also have much in common. Much of news (Levy, 1978), as well as sports, is received by the audience as entertainment. Both news and sports are designed to entertain (Comstock, 1989; Robinson & Levy, 1986). Visual depictions, an important contributor to media effects, are present in all three. Thus, we would err to think that, because news is presumably information and sports are events, they cannot affect behavior in a manner comparable to that of entertainment.

Thus, the implications of the evidence on television and behavior fall into three broad categories:

1. prescriptions for the analyses of large, varied, and complex bodies of data where there is some element of public risk;

2. substantive conclusions about the effects of television and film violence; and

3. theories and concepts that explain and predict the influence of television and other media on a wide range of behavior.

KNOWLEDGE, FOR WHAT?

The questioning of the usefulness of the social and behavioral sciences, the attempt to apply them to important real-life issues, and the urging that such application be given high priority have enjoyed a long—and, we suspect, cyclical—history. We have chosen a title used 50 years ago by Robert S. Lynd (1939), the sociologist who was coauthor with his wife of *Middletown* (1929) and *Middletown in Transition* (1937), for his plea that more be made of what was known and could be discovered, to emphasize that our concluding concern is with what we should make of the evidence.

The empirical investigation of the relationships between children, teenagers, and television over the past two decades (a period that encompasses the federal inquiry into television violence by the Surgeon General's Scientific Advisory Committee on Television and Social Behavior (1972)) when added to the findings previously recorded, has created a sizable and varied body of evidence, enlarged importantly on issues previously investigated, and introduced data on new topics. This represents scientific progress of a substantial order. But what meaning should we assign to this progress?

A. EXPERT OPINION

One way of creating knowledge is to survey experts. The results may be construed in at least two ways. They may be taken as valid advice or as the documentation of informed conventional wisdom. The evidence then can serve as a test of the veracity of such wisdom.

Two such surveys on the effects of television on young persons are available. Murray (1983) queried 109 persons who had published articles or reports on television and young viewers about a single issue, television violence and aggressive behavior. Bybee, Robinson, and Turow (1982a) asked 784 college-level teachers and scholars (drawn from the membership lists of the Association for Education in Journalism and Mass Communication and the Speech Communication Association, two of the major professional organizations to which communications professors belong) to rank television for its influence on 18 possible outcomes.

In the first instance, Murray asked his sample by mail whether they agreed or disagreed, and if so whether they did so strongly or moderately, with a statement in the 1982 report prepared by a select committee under the auspices of the National Institute of Mental Health, *Television and Behavior: Ten Years of Scientific Progress and Implications for the Eighties* (Pearl, Bouthilet, & Lazar, 1982a, 1982b):

> The consensus among most of the research community is that violence on television does lead to aggressive behavior by children and teenagers who watch the programs. This conclusion is based on laboratory experiments and on field studies. Not all children become aggressive, of course, but the correlations between violence and aggression are positive. In magnitude, television violence is as strongly correlated with aggressive behavior as any other behavioral variable that has been measured. The research question has moved from asking whether or not there is an effect to seeking explanations for the effect. (Pearl *et al.*, 1982a, p. 6)

Sixty-eight responded. More than 80% strongly or moderately agreed. This means that at least half of the total sample agreed, for it is obviously an excessively conservative assumption to calculate all those not replying as disagreeing.

In the second instance, Bybee, Robinson, and Turow asked their sample, also by mail, whether they judged television to have been *the* cause, an important cause, somewhat of a cause, not a cause, or did not know, in regard to 18 outcomes. Four hundred eighty-six responded. The most agreed-upon outcome was an increase in world knowledge. More than nine out of ten thought that television had had such an effect (Table 7.1). Next was an increase in buying behavior, with more than eight out of ten agreeing that television had had such an effect. About eight out of ten agreed that effects of television included decreased physical activity, increased reinforcement of social values, and decreased reading. About three-fourths thought that television had increased the desire for immediate gratification. Others in the top ten,

Table 7.1
Experts Rank the Effects of Television on Children

Effect	Television's contribution[a] (percentage saying)				Total citing television as a cause
	Don't know	No relationship	Somewhat important or important cause	The cause	
Increased world knowledge	6.0	2.7	82.3	9.1	91.4
Increased buying behavior	9.7	6.2	76.8	7.4	84.2
Decreased physical activity	8.2	11.9	73.9	6.0	79.9
Increased social value reinforcement	11.2	8.8	76.8	2.7	79.5
Decreased reading	6.8	13.8	69.3	10.1	79.4
Increased desire for immediate gratification	11.7	12.8	67.7	7.8	75.5
Increased curiosity	12.6	17.7	67.3	2.5	69.8
Increased aggressive behavior	10.5	23.9	65.0	.8	65.8
Increased ethnic stereotyping	12.1	22.2	61.9	3.7	65.6
Increased verbal ability	10.9	23.7	62.7	2.7	65.4
Decreased attention span	21.6	20.0	51.2	7.2	58.4
Increased interest in sex	11.5	30.0	56.5	1.9	58.4
Decreased creativity	13.8	28.0	51.9	6.4	58.3
Increased distorted political perceptions	16.5	25.5	54.5	3.5	58.0
Increased prosocial behavior	19.1	28.8	51.4	.6	52.0
Increased alienation	22.6	30.2	45.7	1.4	47.1
Increased sex stereotyping	7.6	11.1	44.0	1.2	45.2
Decreased social values	17.1	40.7	40.5	1.6	42.1

[a] N = 486 college-level communications teachers and scholars.

From Bybee, C., Robinson, D., & Turow, J. (1982). *Mass media scholars' perceptions of television's effects on children*. Unpublished paper presented to the annual convention of the American Association for Public Opinion Research, Hunt Valley, MD.

with each cited by more than six out of ten: increased curiosity, increased aggressive behavior, increased ethnic stereotyping, and increased verbal ability. Almost six out of ten held television responsible for a decreased attention span, an increased interest in sex, decreased creativity, and an increase in "distorted" political perceptions. About half thought that television had increased prosocial behavior, while about the same number thought it had increased alienation. More than four out of ten thought that television had increased sex stereotyping and had had a negative effect on social values.

Thus, four out of ten or more were willing to ascribe at least some or greater causal influence to television for each of these outcomes. If the list had been somewhat different, the scores for the less-subscribed-to outcomes, whatever they might have been, probably would have been about the same, for evidently substantial numbers of the ostensibly well informed believe television has had wide-ranging effects.

As any reasonable person would expect, extremely large majorities ascribing influence (about 90% or more) thought that other factors also were involved. Only seven outcomes had a noteworthy proportion (5% or more) citing television as *the* cause: decreased reading (10.1%), increased world knowledge (9.1%), increased desire for immediate gratification (7.8%), increased buying behavior (7.4%), decreased attention span (7.2%), decreased creativity (6.4%), and decreased physical activity (6.0%). Given the options, these proportions are striking. Two, because they are not in the top ten overall, reflect unusually strong opinions among a few: decreased attention span and decreased creativity. On the whole, then, television was seen as part of and a contributor to social change in a direction also furthered by other factors.

Interpretation is occasionally ambiguous. It is difficult to say what the respondents had in mind in regard to "social values" or "political perceptions," and "reading" could refer to the ability, the behavior, or both. However, for the most part what they were being queried about is clear enough, and even in ambiguous cases, it is clear that many think, because of television, something in some way is not what it once was or could be.

Most of the effects are agreed upon by a majority. Those adverse include several intrinsic to scholastic achievement: reading, immediate gratification, attention span, and creativity. Positive effects include the increase in world knowledge, which as a phenomenon is subscribed to almost universally and in which television almost universally is said to have played a part, curiosity, and verbal ability. These experts essentially think television has harmed achievement in school while bringing other benefits.

The evidence variously supports, qualifies, calls into question, and has little to say about the veracity of the experts. The negative correlations between television viewing and scholastic achievement in mathematics, reading, and writing (Chapter III) certainly are consistent with the view that television has reduced reading ability and interfered with achievement by suppressing attention span and creativity and encouraging immediate gratification. Some and conceivably most or all of these relationships are certainly explained by the greater attention of less able or less disciplined pupils to television, leaving any causal contribution probably modest at most. However, we think the evidence on the whole suggests a small negative effect on achievement. If impulsivity is taken as a crude proxy for attention span, then there is some evidence that television viewing increases the former and thus, by implication, decreases the latter. There is little evidence that television has adversely affected creativity.

If the topics covered in regard to "knowledge, beliefs, and perceptions" (Chapter IV) are defined as "world knowledge," then the opinion of the experts has some claim to validity. All three have been recorded as associated in various ways with television viewing, and in some instances, causal contributions by television have been documented or at least arguably are the most plausible interpretation. The findings sum to a case for television as an important contributor to what children know, believe, and perceive.

Particularly impressive is the evidence in behalf of the effectiveness of counterstereotypical, nonconventional portrayals in changing the thinking of young persons about the acceptability of social roles, and of favorable portrayals in changing their thinking about those different in ethnicity. However, the evidence also supports the view that television contributes to what young persons think by its repetition of characters by type as well as by persona, similarity of themes across and within programs, and its overall conventionality. Nevertheless, when these findings are placed in the context of the evidence that involvement in television viewing is typically low, and active cognitive processing of what is viewed is not often pronounced, the conclusion is difficult to escape that much that would seem to be disseminated by the medium is not absorbed by its young audience.

Schramm, Lyle, and Parker (1961), in evaluating the effects of the introduction of television in the United States on young viewers, concluded that they were more knowledgeable and better informed than in decades past, but were skeptical that television independently made much of a contribution. Their specific findings were that most of the increased vocabulary and factual knowledge associated with television availability represented people and things prominent in its programming. The two-thirds who agreed that television increases vocabulary probably are right, but much or all of the contribution consists of the language of the medium. This interpretation is supported by the finding of the Canadian three-community experiment (T.M. Williams, 1986) that scores on standardized vocabulary tests were not increased by the introduction of television.

The definition given world knowledge, and the age and mental ability of the young persons referred to, become critical in evaluating the opinion of the experts. If by world knowledge we mean the kind taught by the schools, then a greater amount of television viewing typically does not contribute much, if anything. If we mean incidental knowledge reflecting the content of television entertainment, advertising, sports and news, then certainly exposure has some influence. If we mean the inculcation of knowledge, beliefs, and perceptions in harmony with what is portrayed with some consistency on television, then there is arguably some modest influence.

Young children high in mental ability consume large amounts of television because it is one of the means by which they satisfy their curiosity. Television gives direction to curiosity; it may arouse interest in various topics by what it portrays; it is highly doubtful that it increases curiosity as a trait. These children turn increasingly to print as they get older because television comparatively becomes increasingly less satisfying. Those of lower mental ability remain comparatively high in consumption of television, but we would not expect any effects beyond some threshold of exposure, because of the redundancy among what is viewed. For those at all ages and levels of ability, when programming is not redundant with itself or other sources, the likelihood of some influence is enhanced.

Television has certainly increased the exposure of children to news, and while children aged 2 to 11 typically are not news followers, the proportion in the average audience (their ratings) is actually a full two-thirds that for adults aged from 18 to 49 (Comstock *et al.*, 1978), so world knowledge in the sense of current events (even allowing for a largely passive and indifferent young audience) undoubtedly has been increased. This applies, to a somewhat lesser extent, to teenagers, because many at that age turn to print media so that television has a reduced role as a sole source.

The experts can make a strong case in regard to buying behavior. Analogous to the role of television in bringing the news to children, television arguably has greatly increased the amount of advertising reaching children, although, as that Saroyan short story reminds us (Chapter V), advertising directed at children was far from unknown long before children had access to television. Television brings an enormous number of commercials to children annually, with the ratio about nine to one in favor of products marketed to general audiences. Saturday morning and other programming aimed at young viewers present their audiences with a very large number of products for which young viewers will be the user and final consumer, if not always the purchaser. The appeal of the medium to young viewers, the sizable portion of time devoted to commercials, and the development of Saturday morning at the three major networks and elsewhere as an island for children's programming have combined to increase greatly the attention that young viewers give to products. The evidence (Chapter V) says that commercials aimed at young viewers are effective in creating desires for products.

However, television is only part of a larger set of changes since World War II that have increased the role of consumption in the lives of young persons. These factors include increases, despite recessions and stock crashes, in affluence and general prosperity that have made it possible for young persons to participate more directly and fully in the allocation of family resources; the growth of the suburbs, which favored the proliferation of shopping malls where parents could shop conveniently with children and which older children and teenagers could frequent by themselves; the emergence of the supermarket, whose parking lots, wide aisles, shopping carts, and brand-name shelf displays combined to make children companions and participants in food and houseware shopping; and the continuing elaboration of a child and particularly teenage culture based on products, brand names, advertising, music, and entertainment that made of them an important market.

Certainly the evidence on behavior, both aggressive and prosocial, supports the majority view that television has increased both. There are good reasons to agree with the experts that aggression has been more affected than has prosocial behavior. Such portrayals are more frequent, and especially on the Saturday morning programming aimed at young viewers (Greenberg, 1980); such behavior as portrayed is generally physical or verbal. The opportunity and range of possibilities for emulation are abundant, while prosocial responses do not generalize readily from one type to another, and emulation depends more on the match between portrayal and subsequent opportunity (Hearold, 1986).

As for ethnic and sex-role stereotyping, the evidence is mixed. Blacks and other minorities, as has been the case for Caucasians, in television portrayals are typically middle or upper-middle class (Comstock *et al.*, 1978); this inversion of the actual social pyramid, a feature of television from its early days (Head, 1954), is false to reality but cannot be said to further any generally held stereotype about minorities. Sex-role stereotypes present a somewhat different picture. While the same distortion of the social hierarchy occurs, men outnumber women in major roles, women take orders from but seldom give them to men (although they may give them to other women), and conventional roles of housewife and object of sexual attraction predominate (Cassata & Skill, 1983;

Comstock *et al.*, 1978; Greenberg, 1980). We find it difficult not to believe that this emphasis on conventional roles does not reinforce them, especially when the evidence is so strong in behalf of the effectiveness of counterstereotypical portrayals where the possibility of detecting an exposure-related shift is so much greater. Thus, we think the experts are wrong about ethnic stereotyping, probably right about sex-role stereotyping, and certainly wrong to give more emphasis to the former than the latter.

If alienation is taken as meaning the sort of pessimism that has been found to be positively associated with greater exposure to television, and particularly to television programming that emphasizes the threatening elements of life (Chapter IV), then the half of the experts who believe television has increased such an outlook are probably right. In our view, the rationale for such a conclusion is that it is difficult to imagine pretelevision alternatives that would have exposed young viewers to so much bad news (and not only in the news) in such a graphic, attention-getting way.

Our opinion is that television has not reduced the physical activity of young viewers. We acknowledge that amount of television viewing is negatively correlated (Chapter V) with general well-being, physical, mental, and social, and positively correlated with body weight (which at some threshold translates into obesity). We also recall the findings that television displaces sedentary but not nonsedentary activities (Chapter III), that it does not seriously depress engaging in most activities except reading (Chapter II), and that attending events outside the home may be somewhat reduced, but any such effect is circumscribed by the high importance some of these activities have for young persons and particularly teenagers (Chapter II). This amounts to a *prima facie* case for television viewing as what people do who do not have anything else they prefer doing, and viewing thus as a correlate and not a contributor. Thus, we disagree with four out of five of the experts.

We find no evidence that bears in any informative way on increased reinforcement of social values, increased interest in sex, increased distortions of political perceptions, and decreased social values. In the case of the first, third, and fourth, we are not sure what anyone might have had in mind. The ambiguity of the first was empirically documented when the investigators subjected their data to a factor analysis (Bybee, Robinson, & Turow, 1982b), because this item split between the two main dimensions, anti- and prosocial, which conformed to our subjective description. The first and the fourth could be taken as opinions in conflict, although we can see how one could be construed as referring to the strengthening of predominant values, and the other, as a lowering in the quality of such values. An increased interest in sex among young persons is in our view an extremely heavy historical burden to place on any mass medium, and among technological innovations, we would nominate the Ford Model-T instead. The response in regard to political perceptions puzzles us. Although correlations between television exposure and political perceptions among adults have been reported (Gerbner, Gross, Morgan, & Signorielli, 1982, 1984), we cannot believe that this sample has a view of the medium overall as so politicized or politically relevant, and if an increase in exposure to what is labeled news is responsible, there is not only a paradox but an indictment of television as a news medium. These responses say no more than that the effects attributed to television by some are wide-ranging.

Much of the data pertaining to the outcomes about which the experts expressed their opinions are ahistorical. They do not reflect circumstances before and after the widespread adoption of television, but circumstances within the television era. The use of such data to infer historical changes attributable to television depends on the alternative activity that would have been engaged in had television (unthinkably) not become part of our lives. Nevertheless, our judgment on the basis of the evidence is that the experts, while correct some of the time, overrate the breadth of the influence of television. Thus, the evidence, while informative on many questions, is more convincing in regard to contemporary effects (the type of question addressed to his sample by Murray) than about television's role in secular change (the types of questions addressed to their sample by Bybee, Robinson, and Turow).

B. CHILDREN'S PROGRAMMING

We began with Turow's (1981) excellent account of scheduled children's series on the three major networks between the introduction of the medium in the late 1940s and the end of the 1970s. It ignores little, because network audience shares were between 80 and 90% or better, cable initially was nil, and only about 20% of households were subscribers by the end of the period. Because there is now much other than network television, we collected our own data for 1989–1990 (Misiolek, 1990) replicating Turow and adding specials, local programming, independent stations, cable including pay channels, and public television. In addition, we have drawn on recent analyses of what cable disseminates (Siemicki, Atkin, Greenberg, & Baldwin, 1986) and what is available in a well-served community (Wartella *et al.*, 1990).

Children's programming is defined as that intended for a young audience. This excludes the general audience programming that annually accounts for about half of the ten programs most popular with children. Principal trends of interest include amount available, diversity, and quality.

Our conclusions are that:

1. There has been a decline over the past decade in series programming for children at the three major networks. The decline is particularly sharp when we examine unduplicated hours of weekend programming. Those in the television business may protest that unduplicated hours give a falsely miserly impression. Our reply, other than pointing to its use in the CBS-sponsored national surveys (Bower, 1973, 1985) to depict the choices available to viewers, is that it is the proper measure when programs within a genre are much alike and differences with other genres are great.

2. There also has been a decline over the four decades in the diversity of such network programming, by which we mean subject matter and modes of presentation (action–adventure versus other; live versus animated; animal versus human, etc.). Action–adventure and animation, with the former somewhat modulated by a shift from superheroes toward animals in the late 1980s, and the latter marginally diminished by one of the periodic renaissances of live action, have been predominant. Historically, live action increases or declines as a function of cost. Animation invariably has remained preeminent because of technological advances that maintain its competitiveness, such as partial animation with its sharply reduced frames per sequence, and its more certain record in attracting young viewers.

3. Quality is more subjective, unless production cost per hour adjusted for inflation were used—absurd, in our opinion. The declines in quantity and diversity, and especially the latter, imply a decline in quality, in the absence of programs with some claim to unusual features. We find little that would qualify for the latter, and certainly none that could be said to be particularly educational or socially or psychologically beneficial. Kunkel (1988b) and Turow (1980) argue that meaningful innovations largely have been in response to the threat of regulatory action. For example, Turow observes that such nonfiction programs as "Discovery," "One, Two, Three—Go!," "Exploring," and "Reading Room" in the early 1960s were a response to the pressures created by then FCC Commissioner Newton Minow, still famous for his "vast wasteland" characterization of the medium, and Senator Thomas Dodd, chairman of the subcommittee on juvenile delinquency that held protracted hearings on television violence. There have been no comparable initiatives in recent years, and thus there has been a retreat from such programming.

4. There has been an enormous increase in the amount of programming available (Table 7.2). This has come about through the growth of cable, with its basic and pay options, and the large increase during the

1980s in independent stations with most of the new ones in large markets. This development has several characteristics:

a. The superheroes once preeminent on network programming have been recycled to the independents, and one of the principal roles of cable is to make several independents available to subscribers.

b. Educational and instructional programming is almost wholly confined to public television.

c. Program-length commercials have become a notable presence among what has been available.

The amount available to those with access to cable in a well-served market is impressive. The situation becomes far less so when unduplicated hours, diversity, and quality are taken into account. We concur with Wartella and colleagues (1990) that there is almost no diversity among broadcast sources, except for the educational programming provided by public television, and that cable makes some additions, but not substantially so, until premium channels are added; on the basis of our own observation, we do not think even The Disney Channel adds much in the way of variety and diversity. The contribution of cable in regard to independent channels is limited to areas otherwise without such service, because they are essentially redundant to one another. Independents themselves do not provide much if anything beyond reruns and other content redundant to the networks. The basic cable channels aimed at young viewers or families provide a great deal of general audience programming popular with young viewers, such as western and situation comedy reruns, but little in the way of children's programming. The arguable exception is The Discovery Channel, which provides informational programming for general audiences, some (and sometimes quite a bit) of which would be of interest to children and teenagers. We find the situation disappointing.

As Turow recounts, the critics of the 1970s faulted commercial children's programming for the small quantity of nonfiction; the absence of educational content; the emphases on action–adventure, animation, and fantasy; and the preponderance of superheroes. Television as a business and a medium has changed, but there have been no changes in children's programming that would render these criticisms invalid. The ascendancy of the program-length commercial merely gives added currency to his ironic title of a decade ago: *Entertainment, Education, and the Hard Sell.*

C. POLICY RECOMMENDATIONS

We reject the argument sometimes offered by those in the television and advertising businesses—that of a marketplace, technological solu-

Table 7.2

Percentage Children's Programming by Genre on Broadcast and Cable Television in One Market*

Genre	Weekdays				Weekends			
	Commercial broadcast	Public broadcast	Basic cable	Pay cable	Commercial broadcast	Public broadcast	Basic cable	Pay cable
Animated–toy-related	63.7	0	12.7	0	27.2	0	4.1	0
Animated–non-toy related	36.3	0	37.6	0	57.5	0	52.1	49.7
Live-action comedy–drama	0	0	12.3	12.7	3.0	44.4	15.0	19.5
Quiz–game	0	0	3.3	0	0	0	1.3	0
Variety–concert–circus	0	30.0	28.5	40.8	12.1	11.1	20.5	15.1
Exercise	0	0	0.2	10.0	0	0	0	11.6
Instructional–educational	0	70.0	5.0	10.0	0	44.4	4.1	3.9
Other	0	0	0	0	0	0	2.7	0
Total hours of programs	27.5	25.0	148.75	49.66	16.5	4.5	36.5	17.0

* Champaign-Urbana, Illinois, November 1–7, 1987.

Adapted from Wartella, E., Heintz, K.E., Aidman, A.J., & Mazzarella, S.R. (1990). Television and beyond: Children's video media in one community. *Communication Research, 17*(1), 45–64.

tion. The proliferation of sources allegedly will provide diversity and quality as well as quantity. Ducey (1988) is fairly representative:

> The video marketplace in children's television is prolific and dynamic. The viewing environment is such that the great preponderance of children have a large number of broadcast, cable and home video viewing options. Some of these options are advertiser-supported, some are subscriber-supported. The typical child (and his or her parent) has a virtual wealth of video options from which to make viewing choices.
>
> The children's video marketplace consists of three major parts, the broadcast, cable and home video segments. Each of these segments interacts and affects the other, both in terms of programming and economically. These segments are substitutable and thus competitive. From a public policy perspective, this is a fundamental observation. In order to preserve this competitiveness among the three major segments of the children's video marketplace, policymakers should bear in mind that these segments do not operate in isolation. (p. 20)

What is described here is true enough for many children (Table 7.3) but not true for a substantial proportion. Noncable households, which account for about 40%, are dependent on broadcast sources unless they own a VCR. VCR households, more than 60% of the total, are limited in access to programming for children by software costs. Independent stations, basic cable, and Fox on the whole add quantity, but not variety or better quality, to what is available from the three major networks. There is a thriving marketplace, but not much in meaningful differences in subject matter, treatment, or quality among which young viewers can choose. Only the costly addition of premium cable truly expands choice, which confines this benefit to slightly more than half of households and other than Disney to movies most of which were made for the adolescent or adult markets.

This view is consistent with the statistical portrait drawn by Huston and colleagues (1990) representing three years of viewing by several hundred young children who were aged three to five and five to seven when data collection began. The Disney Channel increased viewing of nonanimated entertainment. Cable increased the viewing of children's programming, and of general audience comedies. With the increased competition from acceptable entertainment, cable actually decreased slightly the viewing of children's educational programming. Additional public television channels made available by cable did not increase diversity of such programming, because the programs on the different channels were the same.

Table 7.3
Channel Access and Use

	Prime-time audience shares (percentage)				1991 (est.)[a]
	1983	1985	1987		
Networks	80	77	72	21 ABC 23 CBS 27 NBC	68
Independents and PBS	17	20	23	18 Independent 5 PBS	25
Basic cable	4	6	8		9
Pay cable	6	6	5		6

	Number of channels available (percentage of U.S. households)			
Number of channels available	1964	1972	1985	1991 (est.)
1–4	41	17	3	1
5–10	51	52	22	18
11–29	8	31	31	57
30 or more	—	—	19	24

	U.S. TV households (percentage)	
	1987	1991 (est.)
TV only	28	18
TV + VCR	23	27
TV + basic cable	12	7
TV + VCR + basic cable	10	19
TV + basic cable + pay cable	9	6
TV + VCR + basic cable + pay cable	18	23

	Overall audience shares (percentage)		
Program source	1983	1987	1991 (est.)
Network affiliates	70	62	59
Independent stations	19	19	20
Basic cable	7	14	15
Pay cable	5	6	7
Public television	3	4	4

[a] 1991 estimates are based on calculations by the principal author.
Adapted from Lichty, L.W. (1989). Television in America: Success story. In P.S. Cook, D. Gomery, & L.W. Lichty (Eds.), *American media: The Wilson Quarterly reader* (pp. 159–176). Washington, DC: The Wilson Center Press; and Carey, J. (1989). Public broadcasting and federal policy. In P.R. Newberg (Ed.), *New directions in telecommunications policy. Vol. 1: Regulatory policy: Telephony and mass media* (pp. 192–221). Durham, NC: Duke University Press.

It must be recognized that access to superior programming for young viewers is a function of socioeconomic status. This is because the technologies on which it depends have (sometimes substantial) costs. Inequality between strata will persist even as overall access increases, and those most disadvantaged will be those as a class most reliant on television for entertainment and information.

Schramm, Lyle, and Parker (1963) concluded their *Television in the Lives of Our Children* with a series of questions to broadcasters, parents, schools, the federal government, and researchers as to whether they were doing all they could to make television a better experience for young viewers. They counseled, on grounds of political philosophy, against regulatory reforms unless "the media and the public cannot solve the problems" (p. 186). Because media no longer appear to be frail entities in need of protection from big government, children's programming in the past three decades has not changed for the better, and the evidence that television plays an important role in their lives has accumulated, we focus on what the federal government might do.

We have had the benefit of eight recent policy-oriented analyses in regard to young viewers: the articles in the *American Psychologist* by Huston, Watkins, and Kunkel (1989), in the *Federal Communications Law Journal* by Aufderheide (1989), in the *Journal of Public Policy and Marketing* by G.M. Armstrong and Brucks (1988), in *The Journal of Broadcasting & Electronic Media* by Kunkel and Watkins (1987), the chapter by Kunkel in *Television and the American Family* (Bryant, 1990), and *Television and America's Children* (1988) by the Palmer who helped develop "Sesame Street," *Children in the Cradle of Television* (1987) by the Palmer who is a professor of psychology at Davidson College, and *The Psychology of Television* by Condry (1989). We have benefited and borrowed; however, the blame for what we say is ours.

1. Program Content

The adverse effects of some types of program content on young viewers has been a debated policy issue almost since the introduction of the medium. The first Congressional hearing on television content occurred in 1952, and the topic was the portrayal of sex and violence and the influence on young viewers. Concern over violence escalated in the late 1950s when television began to shift toward violent serials as a staple of evening programming (Comstock, 1983b).

The National Commission on the Causes and Prevention of Violence in 1969 included, among its many conclusions about the factors responsible for violent urban racial conflict, the judgment, based on reviews of the available research, that television violence contributed to aggressive and antisocial behavior. The Surgeon General's Scientific Advisory Committee on Television and Social Behavior in 1972 concluded, based largely on new research conducted in its behalf, that the aggressive and antisocial behavior of at least some young viewers was increased by television violence. Subsequent research has reinforced these conclusions.

One response was the 1976 "family viewing" policy. It took the form of an industry-wide code subscribed to by the three major networks, the NAB, and almost all stations, that required that the two hours before 9 PM be suitable for viewing by all family members. It came about through the ex-officio persuasive efforts of the then-FCC chairman, Richard Wiley. Ironically, by the time the courts and the Justice Department were through, the entire NAB code had been judged as a variant of collusion under the antitrust statutes.

We are in favor of the Congressional initiative ("Violence bill debated . . . ," February 5, 1990) to exempt broadcasters from antitrust legislation for the purpose of cooperating on standards for violence and other content arguably problematic in regard to young viewers. We are not dissuaded by the evidence (Cramer & Mechem, 1982) that the NAB code made little difference in the amount of violence in children's cartoons, because we are not recommending reestablishing an old document but developing a new set of shared standards for the full spectrum of the broadcast day. The evidence makes it clear that there is reason to be concerned, not merely about the quantity of violence, but about the way in which it is depicted. Portrayals of violence likely to encourage antisocial behavior can be constrained only through sensitive interaction with those who market and produce programming. The same applies to other questionable content; there are no simple rules. For example, in their review of the code employed by the Motion Picture Association of America, Wilson, Linz, and Randall (1990) identify four different categories of content with empirically documented possible adverse consequences for young viewers, "horror," "violence," "sex," and "sex and violence," and for each three different age brackets (3–7, 8–12, and 13–17) with different implications for concerns and remedies. This is a task feasible only for their principal clients, the three major networks. It has not been performed recently, as in decades past, because the networks in effect have dismantled their broadcast standards departments (Comstock, 1989), while making a show of good intentions. The congressional initiative is a signal that this responsibility cannot be passed so readily by those who disseminate to those who make television.

This courts a partial, irregular, and imperfect solution. It is 15 years too late, for with each passing year the hegemony of broadcasting and the three major networks as sources of programming has become lessened. However, when we examine how television works, and what cable television disseminates, we do not find this a persuasive criticism. What the major networks disseminate as original programming often will be recycled again and again as reruns through syndication. This programming then becomes a major portion of what cable brings into the home. The current electronic marketplace thus argues for rather than against such a step.

We do not argue in behalf of a replication of the family viewing policy. The formulation is unworkable and in the end would increase rather than decrease both the quantity and severity of violent television entertainment.

The later hours by implication become "adult viewing." The almost certain result would be an increased emphasis on violence and sexual provocativeness after the stipulated boundary. Such content has a useful role in attracting viewers, and we would expect the medium to act rationally by taking advantage of a new opportunity. Such an expectation is in accord with the original family viewing experience, when the level of violence was measurably greater after than before 9 PM.

At the minimum, the later hours would become an attractive nuisance for young viewers, either through direct exposure or by recording for later playback. The effects probably would be more far-reaching. The new late programming eventually would become available for broadcast at all parts of the day by independents, and by affiliates when not accepting a network feed. These signals, in turn, constitute a significant portion of what is disseminated by cable.

The outcome, then, would be a newly created factory for the manufacture of television entertainment more violent and sexually provocative than hitherto available, while the three major networks and presumably many other broadcasters maintained more stringent standards for the early evening. Instead, we think the statutory exemption should bring the networks, including the novice Fox, together with the NAB, which represents the industry as a whole, to establish general standards and criteria for identifying the unacceptable throughout the schedule, with typical audience composition a factor, but not one that leads to a demarcation between one and another type of programming or part of the day.

Competition among the media, however, ensures that violence (as well as other questionable content) in television, as well as in film drama, in the future will not be lower overall in quantity than today, and for the same reason may become more graphic and ferocious. Remedy, if arguably to some degree the responsibility of the media, thereby necessarily also falls to the home, the school, and the community.

Huesmann, Eron, Klein, Brice, and Fischer (1983) have demonstrated that a calculated, forceful, and quite explicit indoctrination program on the character and possible effects of television violence can reduce aggressive effects among first and third-grade children. The indoctrination emphasized the lack of reality of television violence, the undesirability of imitating it, and involved the children in such self-persuasion and role-playing as writing brief essays on these themes. McLeod and colleagues (1972a, 1972b) found that the correlations between exposure to television violence and aggressiveness were markedly lower when parents were perceived as disapproving of such behavior for resolving conflicts. There are three implications:

1. The apparent effect of exposure to television violence on aggressive and antisocial behavior is somewhat amenable to intervention and remedy.
2. Effective interventions may focus either on (a) increasing the undesirability of the behavior or (b) increasing skepticism and knowledge about the medium.
3. The key to effective intervention lies in raising or lowering the likelihood that a young viewer will attribute efficacy, normativeness, or pertinence to the portrayed behavior, and altering the degree to which he or she is rendered more or less susceptible by a particular experience.

There have been numerous demonstrations of success in increasing the sophistication and knowledge of young persons about the way television operates as a medium, the factors that govern content, and the techniques employed in production, by specialized educational interventions (J. Anderson, 1980; L. Baron, 1985; Dorr et al., 1980; Rapaczynski, Singer, & Singer, 1982; D.G. Singer, Zuckerman, & Singer, 1980b). Abelman and Courtright (1983), after observing that most of the interventions had centered on countering adverse effects, devised an instructional sequence (for which they documented some success) to make young viewers more sensitive to and cognizant of the many examples of constructive, positive behavior that are portrayed on television. There is, however, little evidence that this increased understanding of television modulates any influence on cognitions or behavior. Dorr, Graves, and Phelps (1980), for example, reported that such special instruction increased comprehension of the medium among young children between kindergarten and second grade in age, but there was no evidence of any effects on beliefs that television might influence. Huesmann and colleagues (1983) in our view are the exception, precisely because they focused narrowly on a particular outcome in a way that would affect the psychological process by which the effect in question comes about. As Eron (1986) warns,

> Aggression is a problem-solving behavior learned early in life, usually learned well and therefore quite resistant to change. (p. 155)

Interventions face a difficult challenge; aggression is likely in Eron's terminology to be "intractable," and television-facilitated aggression especially so because the source, violence in television and film entertainment, is itself so intractable. Thus, we would not emphasize so much instruction *about* television as manipulation by whatever means of the factors on which effects are contingent, which, for behavior, are perceived efficacy, pertinence, normativeness, and susceptibility.

2. Commercial Programming

We posit three criteria for commercial children's programming:

- *quantity and scheduling* sufficient to ensure wide availability on weekends and weekday afternoons;
- *content, themes, and formats* varied enough so as not to be largely redundant; and
- *specific attributes* that educate, instruct, or provide some psychological or social benefit beyond entertainment.

The ideal "children's hour" could serve all of these purposes. Our expectation is that they would be served variously by programs scattered about the schedule. The criteria call for weekday scheduling in the late afternoons or early evenings, and weekend scheduling on Sunday mornings and afternoons and Saturday afternoons, in addition to the present concentration on Saturday mornings. Many of these offerings presumably would be regular series. Our criteria call for a large change, for as Kunkel and Watkins (1987) reported in the late 1980s, there was not at that time a single regularly scheduled weekday children's series on any of the three major networks. They imply a substantial proportion of nonfiction, and of fiction that is realistic and live, rather than animated. Within programming that is unambiguously fantasy, they imply forms other than animation, such as puppetry and live drama. They do not imply an end to entertainment.

The most plausible option is statutory action by the Congress, because of the lack of prior effective action in this area by the FCC (Kunkel, 1990), but certainly an independent brave step by this agency would suffice. Legislation requiring that broadcasters serve the needs of children was vetoed by President Reagan at the end of his final term on First Amendment grounds, although it was modest enough in its requirements that it had the approval of the NAB (motivated no doubt by the desire to preempt a sterner measure). We think the disposition of such measures should be left to the courts when and if a challenge is offered.

There are two mutually exclusive avenues. The first would require, as did the vetoed legislation, that broadcasters serve the needs of children without specifying when or how this might be accomplished. The implication is that a broadcaster could comply with general audience programming that is popular among young viewers. The second would specify when and what type of programming would suffice. The broadcaster thereby could be restrained from relying entirely either on general audience programming or children's entertainment.

Enforcement would fall to the FCC. One purpose of the legislation would be to stir the agency from the indifference, inconsistency, and (although the former have been so pronounced that there has been only modest opportunity for) retreat in this area. The question then becomes the framework for evaluating performance.

Again, there are two mutually exclusive options. The first would employ the television market. The second, the individual licensee at renewal (which occurs every five years). We reject the first as unworkable. The market permits ready tabulation of program availability, but otherwise eludes practical action. When an adopted standard was not met, who would be asked to alter their behavior? How could an accord be reached voluntarily on joint action without violating the federal antitrust statutes? Individual review is the sole means of effective enforcement. Each broadcaster should be expected to make some contribution. Overall marketplace availability now takes on an important role. We would expect that what would be considered satisfactory performance during a given part of the day would vary by what is available from other sources at the same time. Such a focus provides what the market does not—the ability to assign responsibility and to specify what would constitute conformity.

These are critical elements for the success of a regulatory venture. Turow (1980) documents that the 1974 policy statement by the FCC calling for more nonfiction programs for children—"educational and informational programming" encompassing "history, science, literature, the environment, drama, music, fine arts, human relations, other cultures and languages, and basic skills such as reading and mathematics which are crucial to a child's development" (FCC, November 6, 1974 as quoted in Turow, 1980, p. 437)—failed to increase such programming. He suggests, and we agree, that a major reason was the reliance on self-regulatory response without concrete guidelines or evaluative record-keeping.

Historically, there is no reason to think that inadequate performance at the time of initial review by the FCC would result in more than a warning, and every reason to think that broadcasters will attempt to err on the side of compliance. The raised eyebrow works when accompanied by some muscle.

3. Advertising

No one can shield children or teenagers from advertising. Children and teenagers annually are exposed to many thousands of commercials directed at them. Some are persuaded to want the products, to ask parents to buy them, and to give them preference over alternatives for the allocation of attention, money, and time. Those for adult products may arouse favorable expectations about future use. Parents yield some of the time, but not invariably. Whether the desires contributed to by television advertising lead to the consumption of types of products parents would prefer to ignore, but purchase in the interest of domestic tranquility, has not been addressed; yielding within a product category essentially is trivial except to the advertiser and the young person. Surely some young viewers are hurt if not harmed by their exclusion from what they know at least some others are enjoying; such effects are inevitable. All one can ask is that television advertising not be deceptive or exploitative, or in some way place children and teenagers at risk.

If we apply to children the standards applied to adults in regard to print advertising, those under the age of eight are deceived because they cannot comprehend the persuasive and selling intent, for it is to ensure such comprehension that print advertisements ambiguous in format are clearly so labeled. We agree with the FTC that it is not feasible to ban all advertising from children's programming, and thus there is no way to exclude very young viewers from exposure to commercials for some products they might wish to consume.

We turn to presumptive relief. We suggest that federal guidelines require one hour on Saturday mornings of commercial-free programming with special cultural or educational merit, and that advertisements directed at younger children not be allowed at any time. Predominant age of consumers and ages of those portrayed would guide the latter, and because premium offers play an inordinate role among younger children, they would receive particular scrutiny. The FCC has acknowledged the legitimacy of distinctions within the young audience based on age by promulgating different rules for those 16 and those 12 and under ("FCC endorses . . . ," April 15, 1991), and the same kind of discrimination can be employed within the 12-and-under category. We also argue that:

1. The ban on host selling (a principal character or personality in a program advocates purchase of or endorses a product) within children's

programming should be either abandoned or extended from the program and adjacent minutes (those not separated by another program) to all time periods; there is no evidence that points to any noteworthy diminution in the effectiveness or deceptiveness attributable to such commercials as a consequence of placement, and thus no justification for such a distinction.

2. Separators ostensibly designed to help young viewers distinguish between programs and commercials should be discarded until demonstrated as effective for their intended purpose; otherwise, they may serve as ambiguous sequences that confuse rather than clarify the distinction.

3. Programs derived from and inextricably linked to a plan for the joint marketing of toys and other program-linked paraphernalia are deceptive to younger children if not all young persons in regard to intent, are inconsistent with the rationales for no-host selling and for separators, violate thereby the separation of program content from advertising, and thus even by some criteria endorsed by the FCC are exploitative of the young audience. Such program-length commercials were once barred by the FCC (Chapter V); the question is whether the agency can do so again. The recent FCC "ban" (Andrews, 1991) is meaningless because it defines "program-length commercials" as programs that *also* carry paid-for advertisements for the featured products. This in effect is no more than a restatement of the prohibition against host selling and presumably for this reason, as well perhaps as the fear of arousing public displeasure and regulatory ire, advertisers and broadcasters largely avoid such a combination. The FCC has acknowledged that the regulation of commercial television in this respect poses no threat to the sale of toys and educational items associated with such public television offerings as "Sesame Street" ("FCC endorses . . . ," April 15, 1991). Nevertheless, the FCC's reversal of its opposition of more than a decade-and-a-half ago has led to so many prominent specimens that formulating a restrictive rule at this time could be awkward—although a ban on commercials for program-linked products at any time would be simple, enforceable, and discouraging to the development of program-length commercials. Otherwise, the FCC may have to admit that the artful language and careful draftsmanship once so surely within its grip to preclude the vending of products to young persons under the guise of entertainment has fallen from its grasp.

4. Stringent guidelines and review should be required for commercials directed at children because the language of television advertising has a high likelihood of being ambiguous, deceptive, and hard to interpret for young viewers.

5. The criterion for degree of commercialization should include not only product commercials but promotions for other programs, since

these are commercials in behalf of the broadcaster; the two account for about 80% of nonprogram material (Condry & Scheibe, 1989), which places the average of 13 minutes per hour of such content recently recorded by the NAB (E.E. Cohen, 1988) well in excess (about 12%) of the 9.5 minutes stipulated by the now-abandoned NAB code as the limit on product commercials during children's weekend programming.

6. The minutes-per-hour criterion should be uniform, with weekday and weekend programming required to meet the same standards; if the rationale for prescription is serving the child audience, logic requires no less.

The promoting of heavily sugared foods and other products, questionable to some on nutritional grounds, can be ameliorated only through reductions in the proportion of time devoted to advertising, more stringent standards of language and presentation, the elimination of advertising from some quantity of programming, and the promotion by PSAs and other means of nutritional practices. They are not analogous to cigarettes in being harmful *per se*; only abuse makes them so.

The evidence does not lead to other prohibitions on quantity or repetition. Young viewers do not often see the same commercial repeatedly within a day, and generally repetitive exposure does not enhance persuasion, but merely reinstates the degree of favorability or unfavorability achieved with one or two viewings. This heightening of salience is what advertisers are paying for, and where advertising is legitimate, is simply the way it functions.

The enforcement of federal guidelines would fall to the FCC and FTC; however, we think self-regulation could serve in many areas. The appropriate entity, although we apologize for perhaps multiplying its burdens, would be the Children's Advertising Review Unit which functions within the National Advertising Division of the National Council of Better Business Bureaus, Inc. It was established by the advertising business in 1974 to monitor self-regulatory programs with respect to children and has since adjudicated complaints on a case-by-case basis. Its guidelines, first issued in 1975 (although preceded by an earlier version by the Association of National Advertisers in 1972), are now in their third edition (Children's Advertising Review Unit, 1983) and in our view are quite strict—sufficiently so that we suspect many would spot what they think are violations on any given Saturday morning. For example, commercials encouraging children to call "900" numbers for an entertaining message implicitly violate the common code provision that advertising aimed at children should not exhort them to ask parents for products, because the child in effect can make the purchase without resort to the parent; the principle of not intervening directly in the relationship between parents and children is violated. We think a more vigorous stance on its part, combined with more frequent and aggressive challenges, should be given a trial.

Our arguments in behalf of greater federal as well as self-regulatory strictness in regard to overall content, children's programming, and advertising directed at children on proprietary channels are in accord with those of Aufderheide (1989). She argues that increased regulation (such as ceilings on minutes of nonprogram content on children's programming and linking license renewal to meeting criteria for serving children) would only restate values inherent in such activity in the past, and would not constitute any new intrusion in the First Amendment rights of broadcasters. As she points out, these values have not been diminished by new technology, even if it has made enforcement more problematic. Our arguments in two respects also are in accord with the recent 24-hour ban on indecency by the FCC, which essentially implements legislation passed by Congress in 1988 ("FCC votes . . . ," July 16, 1990, pp. 30–31)—the renewed acknowledgment that children may merit special consideration, and the recognition that segmenting the broadcast day, as was the case with family viewing, may be unrealistic. The step itself is cosmetic in regard to television. Even if it survives the inevitable challenges on First Amendment grounds, which is doubtful, such a narrow prohibition will be of little use when the practice against which it is directed is engaged in by few if any television broadcasters. It may have some restraining effect on radio talk show content and vocabulary and rock-and-roll lyrics, which have been the subject of some controversy. It does not address the fundamental conformity of broadcast performance to the "public interest, convenience, and necessity" as stipulated by the Federal Communications Act of 1934.

4. Public Television

In his analysis (1988), the Palmer who was a "Sesame Street" pioneer argues that public television has failed to serve children well because of limited resources, uncertain and inconsistent financing, and competition for the few dollars available. When he compares expenditures on public television systems in the United States, Great Britain, and Japan, he finds those of the United States to be startlingly less. When he examines the sources for public television programming, it becomes apparent that the most reasonable solution would be increased federal support (Table 7.4).

We agree that such programming should change with the changing interests and needs of children as they grow older (in contrast to commercial programs, which are designed to attract as large an audience and thus as wide a range of ages as possible) and with his proposal that

Table 7.4
Augmenting Children's Programming by Federal Support

Support for public television in three countries			
	United States (PTV)	Britain (BBC)	Japan (NHK)
Population[*]	239	56	120
Public broadcasting revenues[*]	$1096	$904	$1420
Per capita support	$4.58	$16.14	$11.83

[*] Funding shown in U.S. dollars; all figures in millions, for 1985.

Age group	Initial yearly costs for proposed national children's TV schedule[a,b]				
	Scheduled hours each year	New hours each year	Cost per new hour[c] (thousands)	Yearly total (millions)	Annual cost per child
2–5	260	60	$200	$12.0	$0.86
6–9	260	65	$375	$24.4	$1.74
10–13	260	65	$400	$26.0	$1.86
Total	780	190		$62.4	$1.49 (ave.)

[a] The calculations are based on 14 million children per four-year age group, for a total of 42 million, as a convenient approximation.

[b] A factor of 50% has been added to production, to cover the activities of series development, curriculum planning, preproduction research and child testing, pilot production and review, and audience building.

Current expenditure and needed federal funding[a]		
Funder categories	Dollar amount (millions)	Program hours (approximate)
Nongovernment contributors		
Children's Television Workshop	$ 7.299	
Business and industry	$ 0.350	
Foundations	$ 0.020	
PTV (Stations Program Cooperative)	$ 5.739	
PTV (CPB Program Fund)	$ 6.470	
Other	$ 4.433[b]	
Total nongovernment contribution	$24.3	75
Current annual government contribution	4.4	13
Additional new funding needed (to be contributed mostly by government)	33.7	102
Total annual funding and hours required	62.4	190

[a] All figures are for the 1984–1985 broadcast year, and reflect uncommitted amounts which may fluctuate from year to year.

[b] This figure includes $4.276 million in funding support from "WonderWorks" coproducers and $157 thousand from Bank Street College for "The Voyage of the Mimi."

Adapted from Palmer, E.L. (1988). *Television and America's children: A crisis of neglect.* New York: Oxford University Press.

for planning purposes the child audience be segmented into three age groups: 2–5, 6–9, and 10–13. He sets the goal for each group at one hour of programming per weekday, which sums to 260 hours per year per group, and suggests that each year one-fourth of this sum be newly produced. The first four years would be spent building the inventory, and thereafter the one-fourth deemed less appealing, effective, popular, or topical would be replaced. The minimum new fund required sums to about $64 million (Table 7.4). It is estimated that such a bold program would cost an estimated $1.50 to $1.75 per American child per year.

We think this is sensible and modest. The focus on weekdays is correct, because that has been a continually sparse time segment in the schedules of the networks and other disseminators for children's programming, despite occasional laudatory network specials. The 25% annual rate of new production is excellent, because we would expect this to exceed the amount of programming meriting discard, and thus there would be a growing inventory that could serve weekend mornings and afternoons, additional weekday hours, and dissemination systems other than public television.

The measured advanced by Senator Daniel Inouye of Hawaii and passed into law by Congress late in 1990 went considerably beyond the legislation vetoed near the end of his presidency by Reagan. It requires the FCC to consider at license renewal the service rendered the "educational and informational needs" of young persons 16 and under, and while we think it could have been more specific in regard to how this would be achieved and the criteria for compliance, it is a long-needed, positive step. Obviously, it falls far short of our proposals in placing a ceiling on commercials of 10.5 minutes per hour weekends and 12 minutes weekdays, and establishing an endowment of $2 million the first year and $4 million the second year for children's educational and informational programming in a two-year trial. Nevertheless, it is a bold maneuver that may prove quite astute on the part of Senator Inouye, who originally proposed a $10 million endowment for the first year, because it is a step toward establishing a precedent for direct statutory action by the Congress in this area.

Teenagers, after the first two or three years, are essentially adults in media-related behavior, and no special policies are necessary, with one arguable exception. There are topics related to psychological and social development that are unlikely to be adequately if at all treated by commercial entertainment. Federal and foundation support for such programming is justified because it serves the goals of education outside what can be done in the classroom. Examples of this type of programming for younger persons include "Sesame Street," "3–2–1 Contact," "Vista Alegre," and "Freestyle," the 13-episode series discussed earlier (Chapter IV) as having had some success in reducing sex-role stereotypes among 9–12 year olds. The current "DeGrassi Junior High" is a teenage example. Such programming in effect is part of special education, a legitimate government and public responsibility. We concur, then, with the Inouye legislation that the obligation of all parties is now toward children and teenagers.

5. *Parents*

We reject the contention by some in the television and advertising businesses that the responsibility for how young viewers respond to television rests entirely with parents. It is an unreasonable task when a majority of households have more than one television set; there is a substantial proportion of single-parent households, and many of these single parents are employed; in many two parent households, both parents are employed. Parents can only work with what they are provided with by television. Nevertheless, we do believe that parents should (a) set some guidelines for when, how much, and what is viewed, and especially so for younger children; (b) encourage the viewing of superior fiction and nonfiction, however they define them; and, (c) make their views known about programs viewed, the behavior portrayed, and the values implied.

Parents can make a difference. The centrality extended to television by parents is a major factor in determining how much will be viewed. The use of television when alternative activities are not more desirable, interesting, or important means that when parents succeed in shifting viewing to better quality programming, the amount of lesser quality consumed is reduced absolutely, and when they succeed in encouraging other activities, the total amount consumed is reduced. If there are effects on scholastic achievement, they are a function of how much and what is viewed, and these are amenable to parental influence. When parents express their opinions and judgments, these will take precedence over what television presents in affecting thought or behavior. Television is not a dictator of but a servant to the milieu established within the home.

Of all the technological developments of recent years, the VCR offers the greatest likelihood of making the television experience of children and teenagers more varied and, for better or ill, more motivated and more cognitively and emotionally involving. However, we think the medium, commercial and public, should be asked to serve better the interests of young viewers. Everyone has set forth goals, such as ending the commercial exploitation of children; some have advanced means for selective ends; we have tried to offer, in addition, concrete suggestions that cover the full range of issues and adhere closely to the evidence. We have chosen to letter distinctly rather than scrawl imposingly.

■ REFERENCES

Abelman, R. (1985). Styles of parental disciplinary practices as a mediator of children's learning from prosocial television portrayals. *Child Study Journal, 17*, 46–57.

Abelman, R. (1987). Child giftedness and its role in the parental mediation of television viewing. *Roeper Review, 9*(4), 217–220, 246.

Abelman, R. (1989). From here to eternity: Children's acquisition of understanding of projective size. *Human Communication Research, 15*(3), 463–481.

Abelman, R. (1990). Determinants of parental mediation of children's television viewing. In J. Bryant (Ed.), *Television and the American family* (pp. 311–326). Hillsdale, NJ: Erlbaum.

Abelman, R., & Courtright, J. (1983). Television literacy: Amplifying the cognitive level effects of television's prosocial fare through curriculum intervention. *Journal of Research and Development in Education, 17*(1), 46–57.

Abelman, R., & Pettey, G.R. (1989). Child attributes as determinants of parental television-viewing mediation: The role of child giftedness. *Journal of Family Issues, 10*(2), 251–266.

Abelson, R.P. (1976). Script processing in attitude formation and decision making. In J. Carroll & J. Payne (Eds.), *Cognition and social behavior.* Hillsdale, NJ: Erlbaum.

Abelson, R.P. (1981). Psychological status of the script. *American Psychologist, 36*, 715–729.

Acker, S.R. (1983). Viewers' perceptions of velocity and distance in televised events. *Human Communication Research, 9*, 335–348.

Acker, S.R., & Tiemens, R.K. (1981). Children's perceptions of changes in size of televised images. *Human Communication Research, 7*, 340–346.

Adler, R.P., Lesser, G.S., Meringoff, L.K., Robertson, T.S., Rossiter, J.R., & Ward, S. (1980). *The effects of television advertising on children: Review and recommendations.* Lexington, MA: Lexington Books.

Adoni, H., Cohen, A.A., & Mane, S. (1984). Social reality and television news: Perceptual dimensions of social conflict in selected life areas. *Journal of Broadcasting, 28*(1), 33–49.

Alexander, A. (1985). Adolescents' soap opera viewing and relational perceptions. *Journal of Broadcasting & Electronic Media, 29*(3), 295–308.

Alexander, A., Ryan, M., & Munoz, P. (1984). Creating a learning context: Investigations on the interactions of siblings during television viewing. *Critical Studies in Mass Communication, 1*, 345–364.

Alexander, A., Wartella, E., & Brown, D. (1981). Estimates of children's television viewing by mother and child. *Journalism Quarterly, 25*(3), 243–252.

313

Allen, C. (1965). Photographing the audience. *Journal of Advertising Research, 5,* 2–8.

Allen, R.C. (1985). *Speaking of soap operas.* Chapel Hill: University of North Carolina Press.

Alper, W.S., & Leidy, T.R. (1970). The impact of information transmission through television. *Public Opinion Quarterly, 33*(2), 556–562.

Alvarez, M.M., Huston, A.C., Wright, J.C., & Kerkman, D.D. (1988). Gender differences in visual attention to television form and content. *Journal of Applied Developmental Psychology, 9,* 459–475.

Alwitt, L.F., Anderson, D.R., Lorch, E.P., & Levin, S.R. (1980). Preschool children's visual attention to attributes of television. *Human Communication Research, 7*(1), 52–67.

Anderson, B., Mead, N., & Sullivan, S. (1986). *Television: What do National Assessment results tell us?* Princeton, NJ: Educational Testing Service.

Anderson, C., & McGuire, T. (1978). The effect of TV viewing on the educational performance of thirteen elementary school children. *The Alberta Journal of Educational Research, 24,* 156–163.

Anderson, C.C. (1982). Some correlates of TV viewing. *The Alberta Journal of Educational Research, 28,* 58–68.

Anderson, D.R., Choi, H.P., & Lorch, E.P. (1987). Attentional inertia reduces distractability during young children's TV viewing. *Child Development, 58,* 798–806.

Anderson, D.R., & Collins, P.A. (1988). *The impact on children's education: Television's influence on cognitive development.* Washington, DC: U.S. Department of Education.

Anderson, D.R., Field, D.E., Collins, P.A., Lorch, E.P., & Nathan, J.G. (1985). Estimates of young children's time with television: A methodological comparison of parent reports with time-lapse video home observation. *Child Development, 56*(5), 1345–1357.

Anderson, D.R., Levin, S., & Lorch, E. (1977). The effects of TV program pacing on the behavior of preschool children. *AV Communication Review, 25,* 159–166.

Anderson, D.R., & Lorch, E.P. (1983). Looking at television: Action or reaction. In J. Bryant & D.R. Anderson (Eds.), *Children's understanding of television: Research on attention and comprehension* (pp. 1–34). New York: Academic Press.

Anderson, D.R., Lorch, E.P., Field, D.E., Collins, P.A., & Nathan, J.G. (1986). Television viewing at home: Age trends in visual attention and time with TV. *Child Development, 57,* 1024–1033.

Anderson, D.R., Lorch, E.P., Field, D.E., & Sanders, J. (1981). Television viewing at home: Age trends in visual attention and time with TV. *Child Development, 57,* 1024–1033.

Anderson, D.R., Lorch, E.P., Smith, R., Bradford, R., & Levin, S.R. (1981). Effects of peer presence on preschool children's television-viewing behavior. *Developmental Psychology, 17*(4), 446–453.

Anderson, J. (1980). The theoretical lineage of critical viewing curricula. *Journal of Communication, 30*(3), 64–70.

Anderson, W.H., Jr., & Williams, B.M. (1983). TV and the Black child: What Black children say about the shows they watch. *The Journal of Black Psychology, 9,* 27–42.

Andison, F.S. (1977). TV violence and viewer aggression: A cumulation of study results. *Public Opinion Quarterly, 41,* 314–331.

Andrews, E.L. (1991). F.C.C. limits ads on TV shows aimed at children. *The New York Times,* D6, April 10.

Argenta, D.M., Stoneman, Z., & Brody, G.H. (1986). The effects of three different television programs on young children's peer interactions and toy play. *Journal of Applied Developmental Psychology, 7,* 355–371.

Armstrong, G.B., & Greenberg, B.S. (1990). Background television as an inhibitor of cognitive processing. *Human Communication Research, 16*(3), 355–386.

Armstrong, G.M., & Brucks, M. (1988). Dealing with children's advertising: Public policy issues and alternatives. *Journal of Public Policy & Marketing, 7,* 98–113.

Aronfreed, J. (1976). Moral development from the standpoint of a general psychological theory. In T. Lickona (Ed.), *Moral development and behavior theory, research and social issues.* New York: Holt, Rinehart & Winston.

Aronson, E. (1988). *The social animal* (5th ed.). San Francisco: Freeman.

Atkin, C. (1975a). *Effects of television advertising on children—First year experimental evidence.* Report #1. East Lansing, MI: Department of Communication, Michigan State University.

Atkin, C. (1975b). *Effects of television advertising on children—Parent-child communication in supermarket breakfast selection.* Report #7. East Lansing, MI: Department of Communication, Michigan State University.

Atkin, C. (1975c). *Effects of television advertising on children—Survey of children's and mothers' responses to television commercials.* Report #8. East Lansing, MI: Department of Communication, Michigan State University.

Atkin, C. K. (1977). Effects of campaign advertising and newscasts on children. *Journalism Quarterly 54*(3), 503–508.

Atkin, C.K. (1978a). Observations of parent–child interaction in supermarket decisionmaking. *Journal of Marketing, 42,* 41–45.

Atkin, C.K. (1978b). Effects of proprietary drug advertising on youth. *Journal of Communication, 28,* 71–79.

Atkin, C.K. (1983). Effects of realistic TV violence vs. fictional violence on aggression. *Journalism Quarterly, 60,* 615–621.

Atkin, C.K. (1988a). *A critical review of media effects on alcohol consumption patterns.* A report to the Alcoholic Beverage Medical Research Foundation, Baltimore, MD. East Lansing, MI: Department of Communication, Michigan State University.

Atkin, C.K. (1988b). Mass communication effects on drinking and driving. In *Surgeon General's Workshop on Drunk Driving* (pp. 15–34). Washington, DC: U.S. Department of Health and Human Services.

Atkin, C.K., & Block, M. (1983). Effectiveness of celebrity endorsers. *Journal of Advertising Research, 23,* 57–61.

Atkin, C.K. & Gantz, W. (1978). Television news and political socialization. *Public Opinion Quarterly, 42,* 183–198.

Atkin, C.K., Greenberg, B.S., Korzenny, F., & McDermott, S. (1979). Selective exposure to televised violence. *Journal of Broadcasting, 23*(1), 5–13.

Atkin, C.K., Greenberg, B.S., & McDermott, S. (1983). Television and race role socialization. *Journalism Quarterly, 60,* 407–414.

Atkin, C.K., Hocking, J., & Block, M. (1984). Teenage drinking: Does advertising make a difference? *Journal of Communication, 34*(2), 157–167.

Atkin, C.K., Murray, J.P., & Nayman, O.R. (1971). *Television and social behavior: An annotated bibliography of research focusing on television's impact on children.* Washington, DC: Government Printing Office.

Atkin, C.K., Neuendorf, K., & McDermott, S. (1983). The role of alcohol advertising in excessive and hazardous drinking. *Journal of Drug Education, 13,* 313–325.

Atkin, D., Heeter, C., & Baldwin, T. (1989). How presence of cable affects parental mediation of television viewing. *Journalism Quarterly, 66*(3), 557–578.

Atkinson, R.L., Atkinson, R.C., Smith, E.E., & Hilgard, E.R (1987). *Introduction to psychology* (9th ed.). New York: Harcourt Brace Jovanovich.

Atwood, R., Allen, R., Bardgett, R., Proudlove, S., & Rich, R. (1982). Children's realities in television viewing: Exploring situational information seeking. In M. Burgoon (Ed.), *Communication Yearbook 6* (pp. 605–625). Newbury Park, CA: Sage.

Aufderheide, P. (1989). Reregulating children's television. *Federal Communications Law Journal, 42*(1), 87–106.

Austin, E.W., Roberts, D.F., & Nass, C.I. (1990). Influences of family communication on children's television-interpretation processes. *Communication Research, 17*(1), 545–564.

Babrow, A.S. (1989). An expectancy-value analysis of the student soap opera audience. *Communication Research, 16*(2), 155–178.

Babrow, A.S., O'Keefe, B.J., Swanson, D.L., Meyers, R.A., & Murphy, M.A. (1988). Person perception and children's impressions of television and real peers. *Communication Research, 15*(6), 680–698.

Baggaley, J.P. (1985). Design of a TV character with visual appeal for preschool children. *Journal of Educational Television, 11*(1), 41–48.

Ball, S., & Bogatz, G.A. (1970). *The first year of "Sesame Street": An evaluation.* Princeton, NJ: Educational Testing Service.

Ball, S., & Bogatz, G.A. (1975). Some thoughts on this secondary evaluation. In T.D. Cook, H. Appleton, R.F. Conner, A. Shaffer, G. Tamkin, & S.J. Weber, *"Sesame Street" revisited* (pp. 387–403). New York: Russell Sage Foundation.

Ballard-Campbell, M. (1983). *Children's understanding of television advertising: Behavioral assessment of three developmental skills.* Unpublished doctoral dissertation, University of California, Los Angeles.

Ball-Rokeach, S.J., Rokeach, M., & Grube, J.W. (1984). *The great American values test.* New York: The Free Press.

Bandura, A. (1965). Influence of model's reinforcement contingencies on the acquisition of imitative responses. *Journal of Personality and Social Psychology, 1,* 589–595.

Bandura, A. (1973). *Aggression: A social learning analysis.* Englewood Cliffs, NJ: Prentice-Hall.

Bandura, A. (1978). Social learning theory of aggression. *Journal of Communication, 28*(3), 12–29.

Bandura, A. (1986). *Social foundations of thought and action: A social cognitive theory.* Englewood Cliffs, NJ: Prenctice-Hall.

Bandura, A., & Menlove, F. (1968). Factors determining vicarious extinction of avoidance behavior through symbolic modeling. *Journal of Personality and Social Psychology, 8*(2), 99–108.

Bandura, A., Ross, D., & Ross, S.A. (1961). Transmission of aggression through imitation of aggressive models. *Journal of Abnormal and Social Psychology, 63,* 3–11.

Bandura, A., Ross, D., & Ross, S.A. (1963a). Imitation of film-mediated aggressive models. *Journal of Abnormal and Social Psychology, 66*(1), 3–11.

Bandura, A., Ross, D., & Ross, S.A. (1963b). Vicarious reinforcement and imitative learning. *Journal of Abnormal and Social Psychology, 67*(6), 601–607.

Bantz, C.R. (1982). Exploring uses and gratifications: A comparison of reported uses of television and reported uses of favorite program type. *Communication Research, 9*(2), 352–379.

Barcus, F.E. (1977). *Children's television: An analysis of programming and advertising.* New York: Praeger.

Barcus, F.E. (1980). The nature of television advertising to children. In E. Palmer & A.

Dorr (Eds.), *Children and the faces of television: Teaching, violence, selling* (pp. 273–286). New York: Academic Press.

Baron, J.N., & Reiss, P.C. (1985). Same time, next year: Aggregate analyses of the mass media and violent behavior. *American Sociological Review, 50,* 347–363.

Baron, L. (1985). Social class determinants of children's television understanding and use. *International Review of Applied Psychology, 34,* 443–453.

Baron, L.J. (1985). Television literacy curriculum in action: A long-term study. *Journal of Educational Television, 11*(1), 49–55.

Barrow, L.C., & Westley, B.H. (1959, Winter). Comparative teaching effectiveness of radio and television. *AV Communication Review,* entire.

Barwise, T.P. (1986). Repeat-viewing of prime-time TV series. *Journal of Advertising Research, 26,* 9–14.

Barwise, T.P., & Ehrenberg, A.S.C. (1988). *Television and its audience.* Newbury Park, CA: Sage.

Barwise, T.P., Ehrenberg, A.S.C., & Goodhardt, G.J. (1982). Glued to the box?: Patterns of TV–repeat viewing. *Journal of Communication, 32*(4), 22–29.

Beagles-Roos, J., & Gat, I. (1983). Specific impact of radio and television on children's story comprehension. *Journal of Educational Psychology, 75,* 128–135.

Bechtel, R.P., Achelpohl, C., & Akers, R. (1972). Correlates between observed behavior and questionnaire responses on television viewing. In E.A. Rubinstein, G.A. Comstock, & J.P. Murray (Eds.), *Television and social behavior: Vol. 4. Television in day-to-day life: Patterns of use* (pp. 274–344). Washington, DC: Government Printing Office.

Becker, M.H. (Guest Ed.). (1974). The health belief model and personal health behavior. *Health Education Monographs, 2*(4).

Becker, M.H., & Maiman, L.A. (1975). Sociobehavioral determinants of compliance with health and medical care recommendations. *Medical Care, 13,* 10–24.

Beentjes, J.W.M., & Van der Voort, T.J.A. (1988). Television's impact on children's reading skills: A review of research. *Reading Research Quarterly, 23*(4), 389–413.

Belk, R., Mayer, R., & Driscoll, A. (1984). Children's recognition of consumption symbolism in children's products. *Journal of Consumer Research, 10,* 386–397.

Bellotti, F.X. (1975, July). Petition before the F.C.C. of the Attorneys General of Massachusetts, Alaska, Colorado, Delaware, Hawaii, Illinois, Maryland, Nebraska, New Hampshire, North Carolina, Maine, Pennsylvania, Rhode Island, and Wyoming to promulgate a rule restricting the advertising of over-the-counter drugs. Washington, D.C.: US House of Representatives.

Belson, W.A. (1959). Effects of television on the interests and initiative of adult viewers in Greater London. *British Journal of Psychology, 50,* 145–158.

Belson, W.A. (1978). *Television violence and the adolescent boy.* Westmead, England: Saxon House, Teakfield Limited.

Berkowitz, L. (1962). *Aggression: A social psychological analysis.* New York: McGraw-Hill.

Berkowitz, L. (1964). The effects of observing violence. *Scientific American, 21*(2), 35–41.

Berkowitz, L. (1973). Words and symbols as stimuli to aggressive responses. In J.F. Knutson (Ed.), *Control of aggression: Implications from basic research.* Chicago: Aldine-Atherton.

Berkowitz, L. (1984). Some effects of thoughts on anti- and prosocial influences of media events: A cognitive-neoassociation analysis. *Psychological Bulletin, 95*(3), 410–427.

Berkowitz, L. (1986). Situational influences on reactions to observed violence. *Journal of Social Issues, 42*(3), 93–106.

Berkowitz, L. (1990). On the formation and regulation of anger and aggression: A cognitive-neoassociationistic analysis. *American Psychologist, 45*(4), 494–503.

Berkowitz, L., & Alioto, J.T. (1973). The meaning of an observed event as a determinant of aggressive consequences. *Journal of Personality and Social Psychology, 28,* 206–217.

Berkowitz, L., & Geen, R.G. (1966). Film violence and the cue properties of available targets. *Journal of Personality and Social Psychology, 3,* 525–530.

Berkowitz, L., & Geen, R.G. (1967). Stimulus qualities of the target of aggression: A further study. *Journal of Personality and Social Psychology, 5,* 364–368.

Berkowitz, L., & Rawlings, E. (1963). Effects of film violence on inhibitions against subsequent aggression. *Journal of Abnormal and Social Psychology, 66,* 405–412.

Berkowitz, L., & Rogers, K.H. (1986). A priming effect analysis of media influences. In J. Bryant & D. Zillmann (Eds.), *Perspectives on media effects* (pp. 57–81). Hillsdale, NJ: Erlbaum.

Berman, D.R., & Stookey, J.A. (1980). Adolescents, television, and support for government. *Public Opinion Quarterly, 66,* 330–340.

Beuf, A. (1974). Doctor, lawyer, household drudge. *Journal of Communication, 24,* 142–145.

Beville, H.M., Jr. (1988). *Audience ratings: Radio, television, cable* (rev. ed.). Hillsdale, NJ: Erlbaum.

Birnbaum, D.W., & Croll, W.L. (1984). The etiology of children's stereotypes about sex differences in emotionality. *Sex Roles, 10*(9/10), 677–690.

Blatt, J., Spencer, L., & Ward, S. (1972). A cognitive developmental study of children's reactions to television advertising. In E.A. Rubinstein, G.A. Comstock, & J.P. Murray (Eds.), *Television and social behavior: Vol. 4. Television in day-to-day life: Patterns of use* (pp. 452–467). Washington, DC: U.S. Government Printing Office.

Blosser, B.J., & Roberts, D.F. (1985). Age differences in children's perceptions of message intent: Responses to TV news, commercials, educational spots, and public service announcements. *Communication Research, 12*(4), 455–484.

Bogart, L. (1972a). Negro and white media exposure: New evidence. *Journalism Quarterly, 49,* 15–21.

Bogart, L. (1972b). *The age of television* (3rd ed.). New York: Frederick Ungar.

Bogatz, G.A., & Ball, S. (1971). *The second year of "Sesame Street": A continuing evaluation* (Vols. 1 & 2). Princeton, NJ: Educational Testing Service.

Bollen, K.A., & Phillips, D.P. (1982). Imitative suicides: A national study of the effects of television news stories. *American Sociological Review, 47,* 802–809.

Bolton, R.N. (1983). Modeling the impact of TV food advertising on children's diets. *Current Issues and Research in Advertising, 6*(1), 173–199.

Bower, R.T. (1973). *Television and the public.* New York: Holt, Rinehart & Winston.

Bower, R.T. (1985). *The changing television audience in America.* New York: Columbia University Press.

Boyanowsky, E.O., Newston, D., & Walster, E., (1974). Film preferences following a murder. *Communication Research, 1,* 32–43.

Breed, W., & DeFoe, J.R. (1981). The portrayal of the drinking process on prime-time television. *Journal of Communication, 31*(1), 58–67.

Bretl, D.J., & Cantor, J. (1988). The portrayal of men and women in U.S. television commercials: A recent content analysis and trends over 15 years. *Sex Roles, 18*(9/10), 595–609.

Brewer, M.B. (1985, August). *Experimental research and social psychology: Must it be rigor less relevance?* Presidential Address delivered at the Annual Meeting of the American Psychological Association, Los Angeles.

Brody, G.H., Stoneman, Z., & Sanders, A. (1980). Effects of television viewing on family interactions: An observational study. *Family Relations, 29*, 216–220.

Bronfenbrenner, U. (1970). *Two worlds of childhood: U.S. and U.S.S.R.* New York: Russell Sage Foundation.

Brown, D., & Bryant, J. (1990). Effects of television on family values and selected attitudes and behaviors. In J. Bryant (Ed.), *Television and the American family* (pp. 253–274). Hillsdale, NJ: Erlbaum.

Brown, J.D., Childers, K.W., Bauman, K.E., & Koch, G.G. (1990). The influence of new media and family structure on young adolescents' television and radio use. *Communication Research, 17*(1), 65–82.

Brown, J.R., Cramond, J.K., & Wilde, R.J. (1974). Displacement effects of television and the child's functional orientation to media. In J.G. Blumler & E. Katz (Eds.), *The uses of mass communications: Current perspectives on gratifications research.* Newbury Park, CA: Sage.

Brown, L. (1971). *Television: The business behind the box.* New York: Harcourt Brace Jovanovich.

Brown, L. (1977). *The New York Times encyclopedia of television.* New York: Times Books.

Brown, M.H., Skeen, P., & Osborn, D.K. (1979). Young children's perception of the reality of television. *Contemporary Education, 50*(3), 129–133.

Brucks, M., Armstrong, G.M., & Goldberg, M.E. (1988). Children's use of cognitive defenses against television advertising: A cognitive response approach. *Journal of Consumer Research, 14*, 471–482.

Bryant, J. (1989). Viewers' enjoyment of televised sports violence. In L.A. Wenner (Ed.), *Media, sports, & society* (pp. 270–289). Newbury Park, CA: Sage.

Bryant, J. (Ed.) (1990). *Television and the American family.* Hillsdale, NJ: Erlbaum.

Bryant, J., & Anderson, D.R. (Eds.) (1983). *Understanding TV: Research in children's attention and comprehension.* New York: Academic Press.

Bryant, J., Carveth, R.A., & Brown, D. (1981). Television viewing and anxiety: An experimental examination. *Journal of Communication, 31*(1), 106–119.

Bryant, J., Comisky, P., & Zillmann, D. (1981). The appeal of rough-and-tumble play in televised professional football. *Communication Quarterly, 29*, 256–262.

Bryant, J., & Zillmann, D. (1984). Using television to alleviate boredom and stress: Selective exposure as a function of induced excitational states. *Journal of Broadcasting, 28*(1), 1–20.

Bryant, J., Zillmann, D., & Brown, D. (1983). Entertainment features in children's educational television: Effects on attention and information acquisition. In J. Bryant & D.R. Anderson (Eds.), *Children's understanding of television: Research on attention and comprehension* (pp. 221–240). New York: Academic Press.

Buerkel-Rothfuss, N.L., Greenberg, B.S., Atkin, C.K., & Neuendorf, K. (1982). Learning about the family from television. *Journal of Communication, 12*(3), 191–201.

Burton, S., Calonico, J., & McSeveney, D. (1979). Growing up with television: Effects of preschool television watching on first-grade children. *Journal of Communication, 30*, 164–170.

Butter, E. J., Popovich, P.M., Stackhouse, R.H., & Garner, R. K. (1981). Discrimination of television programs and commercials by preschool children. *Journal of Advertising Research, 21*(2), 53–56.

Bybee, C., Robinson, D., & Turow, J. (1982a). *Mass media scholars' perceptions of television's effects on children.* Unpublished paper presented at the Annual Convention of the American Association for Public Opinion Research, Hunt Valley, MD.

Bybee, C., Robinson, D., & Turow, J. (1982b). Determinants of parental guidance of children's television viewing for a special subgroup: Mass media scholars. *Journal of Broadcasting, 26,* 697–710.

Cairns, E., Hunter, D., & Herring, L. (1980). Young children's awareness of violence in Northern Ireland: The influence of Northern Irish television in Scotland and Northern Ireland. *British Journal of Social and Clinical Psychology, 19,* 3–6.

California Assessment Program. (1980). *Student achievement in California schools. 1979–1980 annual report: Television and student achievement.* Sacramento: California State Department of Education.

California Assessment Program. (1982). *Survey of sixth grade school achievement and television viewing habits.* Sacramento: California State Department of Education.

California Assessment Program. (1988). *Annual report, 1985–1986.* Sacramento: California State Department of Education.

Calvert, S.L. (1988). Television production feature effects on children's comprehension of time. *Journal of Applied Developmental Psychology, 9,* 263–273.

Calvert, S.L., & Gersh, T.L. (1987). The selective use of sound effects and visual inserts for children's television story comprehension. *Journal of Applied Developmental Psychology, 8,* 363–375.

Calvert, S.L., Huston, A.C., & Wright, J.C. (1987). Effects of television preplay formats on children's attention and story comprehension. *Journal of Applied Developmental Psychology, 8,* 329–342.

Calvert, S.L., & Scott, M.C. (1989). Sound effects for children's temporal integration of fast-paced television content. *Journal of Broadcasting & Electronic Media, 33*(3), 233–246.

Campbell, T.A., Wright, J.C., & Huston, A.C. (1987). Form cues and content difficulty as determinants of children's cognitive processing of televised educational messages. *Journal of Experimental Child Psychology, 43,* 311–327.

Cantor, J., & Hoffner, C. (1990). Children's fear reactions to a televised film as a function of perceived immediacy of depicted threat. *Journal of Broadcasting & Electronic Media, 34*(4), 421–442.

Cantor, J., & Reilly, S. (1982). Adolescents' fright reactions to television and films. *Journal of Communication, 32*(1), 87–99.

Cantor, J., & Wilson, B.J. (1984). Modifying fear responses to mass media in preschool and elementary school children. *Journal of Broadcasting, 28,* 431–443.

Cantor, J., Wilson, B.J., & Hoffner, C. (1986). Emotional responses to a televised nuclear holocaust film. *Communication Research, 13*(2), 257–277.

Caplow, T., Bahr, H.M., Chadwick, B.A., Hill, R., & Williamson, M.H. (1982). *Middletown families.* Minneapolis: University of Minnesota Press.

Caprara, G.V., D'Imperio, G., Gentilomo, A., Mammucari, A., Renzi, P., & Travaglia, G. (1987). The intrusive commercial: Influence of aggressive TV commercials on aggression. *European Journal of Social Psychology, 17,* 23–31.

Carey, J. (1989). Public broadcasting and federal policy. In P.R. Newberg (Ed.), *New directions in telecommunications policy. Vol. 1: Regulatory policy: Telephony and mass media* (pp. 192–221). Durham, NC: Duke University Press.

Carlson, J.M. (1983). Crime show viewing by preadults. The impact on attitudes and civil liberties. *Communication Research, 10*(4), 529–552.

Caron, A., & Ward, S. (1975, August). Gift decisions by kids and parents. *Journal of Advertising Research, 15,* 12–50.

Carveth, R., & Alexander, A. (1985). Soap opera viewing motivations and the cultivation process. *Journal of Broadcasting & Electronic Media, 29*(3), 259–273.

Cash, T.F., Cash, D.M., & Butters, J.W. (1983). "Mirror, mirror, on the wall . . . ?": Contrast effects and self-evaluations of physical attractiveness. *Journal of Experimental Research in Personality, 6,* 76–83.

Cassata, M., & Skill, T. (1983). *Life on daytime television: Tuning-in American serial drama.* Norwood, NJ: Ablex.

Celozzi, M.J., II, Kazelskis, R., & Gutsch, K.U. (1981). The relationship between viewing televised violence in ice hockey and subsequent levels of personal aggression. *Journal of Sport Behavior, 4*(4), 157–162.

Centerwall, B.S. (1989). Exposure to television as a cause of violence. In G. Comstock (Ed.), *Public communication and behavior* (Vol. 2, pp. 1–58). New York: Academic Press.

Chaffee, S.H. (1972). Television and adolescent aggressiveness (overview). In G.A. Comstock & E.A. Rubinstein (Eds.), *Television and social behavior: Vol. 3. Television and adolescent aggressiveness* (pp. 1–34). Washington, DC: U.S. Government Printing Office.

Chaffee, S.H., Jackson-Beeck, M., Durall, J., & Wilson, D. (1977). Mass communication in political socialization. In S.A. Renshon (Ed.), *Handbook of political socialization: Theory and research* (pp. 223–258). New York: The Free Press.

Chaffee, S.H., & McLeod, J.M. (1972). Adolescent television use in the family context. In G.A. Comstock & E.A. Rubinstein (Eds.), *Television and social behavior: Vol. 3. Television and adolescent aggressiveness* (pp. 149–172). Washington, DC: U.S. Government Printing Office.

Chaffee, S.H., McLeod, J.M., & Atkin, C.K. (1971). Parental influences on adolescent media use. *American Behavioral Scientist, 14,* 323–340.

Chaffee, S.H., McLeod, J.M., & Wackman, D.B. (1973). Family communication patterns and adolescent political participation. In J. Dennis (Ed.), *Socialization to politics: A reader.* New York: Wiley.

Chaffee, S.H., & Miyo, Y. (1983). Selective exposure and the reinforcement hypothesis: An intergenerational panel study of the 1980 campaign. *Communication Research, 10,* 3–36.

Chaffee, S.H., Ward, S., & Tipton, L.P. (1970). Mass communication and political socialization. *Journalism Quarterly, 47,* 647–659, 666.

Chall, J.S. (1983). *Stages of reading development.* New York: McGraw-Hill.

Chaney, D.C. (1970). Involvement, realism, and the perception of aggression in television programmes. *Human Relations, 23,* 373–381.

Char, C.A., & Meringoff, L. (1981). *The role of story illustrations: Children's story comprehension in three different media.* Harvard Project Zero, Technical Report No. 22. Cambridge, MA: Harvard University.

Charters, W.W. (1933). *Motion pictures and youth: A summary.* New York: Macmillan.

Children's Advertising Review Unit. (1983). *Self-regulatory guidelines for children's advertising* (3rd ed.). New York: National Advertising Division, Council of Better Business Bureaus, Inc.

Children's television: Saturday morning live. (1988, Oct. 17). *Broadcasting,* pp. 53–54.

Children's Television Workshop. (1989). *"Sesame Street" research bibliography.* New York: CTW.

Chirco, A.P. (1990). *An examination of stepwise regression models of adolescent alcohol and marijuana use with special attention to the television exposure–teen drinking issue.* Unpublished doctoral dissertation, Syracuse University, Syracuse, NY.

Christenson, P.G. (1982). Children's perceptions of TV commercials and products: The effects of PSAs. *Communication Research, 9*(4), 491–524.

Christenson, P.G. (1985). Children and commercials: The relationship between general trust and specific influence. *Communication Research Reports, 2*(1), 41–45.

Christenson, P.G., & Roberts, D.F. (1990). *Popular music in early adolescence.* Washington, DC: Carnegie Council on Adolescent Development.

Cline, V.B., Croft, R.G., & Courrier, S. (1973). Desensitization of children to television violence. *Journal of Personality and Social Psychology, 27,* 360–365.

Cobb, C.J. (1986). Patterns of newspaper readership among teenagers. *Communication Research, 13*(2), 299–326.

Cobb, N.J., Stevens-Long, J., & Goldstein, S. (1982). The influence of televised models on toy preference in children. *Sex Roles, 8*(10), 1075–1080.

Coffin, T.E. (1955). Television's impact on society. *American Psychologist, 10,* 630–641.

Cohen, A.A., Adoni, H., & Drori, G. (1983). Adolescents' perceptions of social conflicts in television news and social reality. *Human Communication Research, 10*(2), 772–780.

Cohen, A.A., & Cohen, S. (1989). Big eyes but clumsy fingers: Knowing about and using technological features of home VCRs. In M. Levy (Ed.), *The VCR age* (pp. 135–147). Newbury Park, CA: Sage.

Cohen, A.A., Harrison, R.P., & Wigand, R.T. (1974, August). *Affect and learning in TV news viewing by children.* (Final report to the National Institute of Mental Health, MH 24496-01). East Lansing, MI: Department of Communication, Michigan State University.

Cohen, A.A., Levy, M.R., & Golden, K. (1988). Children's uses and gratifications of home VCRs: Evolution or revolution. *Communication Research, 15*(6), 772–780.

Cohen, E.E. (1988, February). *Children's television commercialization survey.* Washington, DC: National Association of Broadcasters.

Cohen, J. (1977). *Statistical power analysis and behavioral science.* New York: Academic Press.

Cohen, M.E., Brown, J.D., & Clark, S. (1981). Canadian public television and preschool children: Predictors of viewers and nonviewers. *Communication Research, 8*(2), 205–231.

Collins, W.A. (1981). Recent advances in research on cognitive processing television viewing. *Journal of Broadcasting, 25*(4), 327–334.

Collins, W.A. (1983). Interpretation and inference in children's television viewing. In J. Bryant & D.R. Anderson (Eds.), *Children's understanding of television: Research on attention and comprehension* (pp. 125–150). New York: Academic Press.

Collins, W.A., Sobol, B.L., & Westby, S. (1981). Effects of adult commentary on children's comprehension and inferences about a televised aggressive portrayal. *Child Development, 52,* 158–163.

Collins, W.A., & Wellmann, H.M. (1982). Social scripts and developmental patterns in comprehension of televised narratives. *Communication Research, 9,* 380–398.

Collins, W.A., Wellman, H.M., Keniston, A.H., & Westby, S.D. (1978). Age-related aspects of comprehension and inference from a televised dramatic narrative. *Child Development, 49,* 389–399.

Columbia Broadcasting System. (1974). *A study of messages received by children who viewed an episode of "Fat Albert and the Cosby Kids."* New York: Columbia Broadcasting System, Office of Social Research.

Comstock, G. (1978). An overview: The state of the art of television research and the young adolescent. In M. Marmony (Ed.), *Televised role models and young adolescents: An ACT research workshop.* Newtonville, MA: Action for Children's Television.

Comstock, G. (1982a). Television and American social institutions. In D. Pearl, L. Bouthilet, & J. Lazar (Eds.), *Television and behavior: Ten years of scientific inquiry and implications for the eighties: Vol. 2. Technical reviews* (pp. 334–348). Washington, DC: U.S. Government Printing Office.

Comstock, G. (1982b). Violence in television content: An overview. In D. Pearl, L. Bouthilet, & J. Lazar (Eds.), *Television and behavior: Ten years of scientific inquiry and implications for the eighties: Vol. 2. Technical reviews* (pp. 108–125). Washington, DC: U.S. Government Printing Office.

Comstock, G. (1983a). The mass media and social change. In E. Seidman (Ed.), *Handbook of social intervention* (pp. 268–288). Newbury Park, CA: Sage.

Comstock, G. (1983b). Media influences on aggression. In A. Goldstein (Ed.), *Prevention and control of aggression* (pp. 241–272). Elsmford, NY: Pergamon.

Comstock, G. (1986). Television and film violence. In S.J. Apter & A. Goldstein (Eds.), *Youth violence: Programs and prospects* (pp. 178–218). Elmsford, NY: Pergamon.

Comstock, G. (1988). Today's audiences, tomorrow's media. In S. Oskamp (Ed.), *Applied social psychology annual: Vol. 8. Television as a social issue* (pp. 324–345). Newbury Park, CA: Sage.

Comstock, G. (1989). *The evolution of American television.* Newbury Park, CA: Sage.

Comstock, G., Chaffee, S., Katzman, N., McCombs, M., & Roberts, D. (1978). *Television and human behavior.* New York: Columbia University Press.

Comstock, G., & Cobbey, R. (1979). Television and the children of ethnic minorities. *Journal of Communication, 29*(1), 104–115.

Comstock, G., & Fisher, M.L. (1975). *Television and human behavior: A guide to the pertinent scientific literature.* Santa Monica, CA: The Rand Corporation.

Comstock, G., & Paik, H. (1990). *The effects of television violence on aggressive behavior: A meta-analysis.* A preliminary report to the National Research Council for the Panel on the Understanding and Control of Violent Behavior. Syracuse, NY: S.I. Newhouse School of Public Communications, Syracuse University.

Condry, J. (1989). *The psychology of television.* Hillsdale, NJ: Erlbaum.

Condry, J., Bence, P., & Scheibe, C. (1988). Nonprogram content of children's television. *Journal of Broadcasting, 32*(3), 255–270.

Conway, M., Stevens, J., & Smith, R. (1975). The relation between media use and children's civic awareness. *Journalism Quarterly, 52,* 531–538.

Cook, T.D., Appleton, H., Conner, R., Shaffer, A., Tamkin, G., & Weber, S.J. (1975). *"Sesame Street" revisited: A study in evaluation research.* New York: Russell Sage Foundation.

Cook, T.D., & Campbell, D.T. (1979). *Quasi-experimentation: Design and analysis issues for field settings.* Chicago: Houghton Mifflin.

Cook, T.D., & Curtin, T.R. (1986). An evaluation of the models used to evaluate television series. In G. Comstock (Ed.), *Public communication and behavior* (Vol. 1: pp. 1–64). New York: Academic Press.

Cook, T.D., Kendzierski, D.A., & Thomas, S.A. (1982). *Television research for science and policy: An alien perspective on the NIMH Report on Television and Behavior.* Unpublished manuscript prepared for the Committee on Research and Law Enforcement and the Administration of Justice of the National Research Council of the National Academy of Sciences, Northwestern University, Evanston, IL.

Cook, T.D., Kendzierski, D.A., & Thomas, S.A. (1983). The implicit assumptions of television research: An analysis of the1982 NIMH report on *Television and Behavior. Public Opinion Quarterly, 47*(2), 161–201.

Cooney, J.G. (1968, February 19). Television for preschool children: A proposal. New York: Children's Television Workshop.

Cooper, E., & Jahoda, M. (1947). The evasion of propaganda. *Journal of Psychology, 33,* 15–25.

Corder-Bolz, C.R. (1980). Mediation: The role of significant others. *Journal of Communication, 30*(3), 106–118.

Cordau, G.D., McGraw, K.O., & Drabman, R.S. (1979). Doctor or nurse: Children's perception of sex typed occupations. *Child Development, 50,* 590–593.

Courtright, J.A., & Baran, S.J. (1980). The acquisition of sexual information by young people. *Journalism Quarterly, 57,* 107–114.

Cramer, P., & Mechem, M.B. (1982). Violence in children's animated television. *Journal of Applied Developmental Psychology, 3,* 23–39.

Crouch, C. (1989). Television and primary school children in Northern Ireland 1: Television program preferences. *Journal of Educational Television, 15*(3), 163–170.

Culley, J.D., Lazer, W., & Atkin, C.K. (1976). The experts look at children's television. *Journal of Broadcasting, 20*(1), 3–21.

Cunningham & Walsh. (1958). *Videotown, 1948–1957.* New York: Author.

Danowski, J.A., & Ruchinskas, J.E. (1983). Period, cohort, and aging effects: A study of television exposure in presidential election campaigns, 1952–1980. *Communication Research, 10*(1), 77–96.

Darley, J.M., Glucksberg, S., Kamin, L.J., & Kinchla, R.A. (1981). *Psychology.* Englewood Cliffs, NJ: Prentice-Hall.

Dates, J. (1980). Race, racial attitudes, and adolescent perceptions of black television characters. *Journal of Broadcasting, 24*(4), 549–560.

Davidson, E.S., Yasuna, A., & Tower, A. (1979). The effects of television cartoons on sex-role stereotyping in young girls. *Child Development, 50,* 597–600.

Davis, D.K., & Abelman, R. (1983). Families and television: An application of frame analysis theory. *Journal of Family Issues, 4,* 385–404.

Day, R.C., & Ghandour, M. (1984). The effect of television-mediated aggression and real-life aggression on the behavior of Lebanese children. *Journal of Experimental Child Psychology, 38,* 7–18.

DeFleur, M.L., & DeFleur, L.B. (1967). The relative contribution of television as a learning source for children's occupational knowledge. *American Sociological Review, 32,* 777–789.

Dennis, J. (1986). Preadult learning of political independence. *Communication Research, 13*(3), 401–433.

Desmond, R.J., Hirsch, B., Singer, D., & Singer, J. (1987). Gender differences, mediation, and disciplinary styles in children's responses to television. *Sex Roles, 16*(7/8), 375–389.

Desmond, R.J., Singer, J.L., & Singer, D.G. (1990). Family mediation: Parental communication patterns and the influences of television on children. In J. Bryant (Ed.), *Television and the American family* (pp. 293–310). Hillsdale, NJ: Erlbaum.

Desmond, R.J., Singer, J.L., Singer, D.G., Calam, R., & Colimore, K. (1985). Family mediation patterns and television viewing: Young children's use and grasp of the medium. *Human Communication Research, 11*(4), 461–480.

Dietz, W.H. (1990). You are what you eat—what you eat is what you are. *Journal of Adolescent Health Care, 11*(1), 76–81.

DiLeo, J.C., Moely, B.E., & Sulzer, J.L. (1979). Frequency and modifiability of children's preferences for sex-typed toys, games, and occupations. *Child Study Journal, 9*(2), 141–159.

Dominick, J.R. (1974). Children's viewing of crime shows and attitudes on law enforcement. *Journalism Quarterly, 51*, 5–12.

Dominick, J.R., & Greenberg, B.S. (1970). Three seasons of blacks on television. *Journal of Advertising Research, 10*(2), 21–27.

Dominick, J.R., & Greenberg, B.S. (1972). Attitudes toward violence: The interaction of television, exposure, family attitudes, and social class. In G.A. Comstock & E.A. Rubinstein (Eds.), *Television and social behavior: Vol. 5. Television and adolescent aggressiveness.* Washington, DC: Government Printing Office.

Donnerstein, E. (1980). Pornography and violence against women: Experimental studies. In F. Wright, D. Bahn, & R.W. Reiber (Eds.), *Annals of the New York Academy of Sciences: Vol. 347. Forensic psychology and psychiatry* (pp. 277–288). New York: The New York Academy of Sciences.

Donnerstein, E. (1984). Pornography: Its effect on violence against women. In N. Malamuth & E. Donnerstein (Eds.), *Pornography and sexual aggression* (pp. 53–81). New York: Academic Press.

Donnerstein, E., & Barrett, G. (1978). The effects of erotic stimuli on male aggression against women. *Journal of Personality and Social Psychology, 36*, 180–188.

Donnerstein, E., & Berkowitz, L. (1981). Victim reactions in aggressive erotic films as a factor in violence against women. *Journal of Personality and Social Psychology, 41*, 710–724.

Donnerstein, E., Donnerstein, M., & Evans, R. (1975). Erotic stimuli and aggression: Facilitation or inhibition. *Journal of Personality and Social Psychology, 32*, 236–244.

Donnerstein, E., & Hallam, J. (1978). The facilitating effects of erotica on aggression against women. *Journal of Personality and Social Psychology, 36*(11), 1270–1277.

Donnerstein, E., Linz, D., & Penrod, S. (1987). *The question of pornography: Research findings and policy implications.* New York: The Free Press.

Donnerstein, E., & Malamuth, N. (Eds.). (1984). *Pornography and sexual aggression.* New York: Academic Press.

Donohue, T.R., Henke, L.L., & Donohue, W.A. (1980). Do kids know what TV commercials intend? *Journal of Advertising Research, 20*, 51–57.

Donohue, T.R., Henke, L.L., & Meyer, T.P. (1983). Learning about television commercials: The impact of instructional units on children's perceptions of motive and intent. *Journal of Broadcasting, 27*(3), 251–261.

Doob, A.N., & MacDonald, G.E. (1979). Television viewing and fear of victimization: Is the relationship causal? *Journal of Personality and Social Psychology, 37*, 170–179.

Dorr, A., Graves, S.B., & Phelps, E. (1980). Television literacy for young children. *Journal of Communication, 30*(3), 71–83.

Dorr, A., Kovaric, P., & Doubleday, C. (1989). Parent-child coviewing of television. *Journal of Broadcasting & Electronic Media, 33*(1), 35–51.

Dorr, A., & Kunkel, D. (1990). Children and the media environment: Change and constancy amid change. *Communication Research, 17*(1), 5–25.

Drabman, R.S., Robertson, S.J., Patterson, J.M., Jarvie, G.J., Hammer, D., & Cordua, G. (1981). Children's perceptions of media-portrayed sex roles. *Sex Roles, 12*, 379–389.

Drabman, R.S., & Thomas, M.H. (1974). Does media violence increase children's toleration of real-life aggression? *Developmental Psychology, 10*, 418–421.

Drew, D.G., & Reeves, B. (1980). Children and television news. *Journalism Quarterly, 57*, 45–54, 114.

Drew, D.G., & Reeves, B. (1984). Children's learning from a television newscast. *Journalism Quarterly, 61*, 83–88.

Ducey, R.V. (1988). *The children's video marketplace.* Washington, DC: National Association of Broadcasters.

Durkin, K. (1984). Children's accounts of sex-role stereotypes in television. *Communication Research, 11,* 341–362.

Eisenstock, B. (1984). Sex-role differences in children's identification with counter stereotypical televised portrayals. *Sex Roles, 10,* 417–430.

Ekblad, S. (1986). Social determinants of aggression in a sample of Chinese primary school children. *Acta Psychiatrica Scandinavica, 73,* 515–523.

Ekman, P., Liebert, R.M., Friesen, W.V., Harrison, R., Zlatchin, C., Malstrom, E.J., & Baron, R.A. (1972). Facial expressions of emotion while watching televised violence as predictors of subsequent aggression. In G.A. Comstock, E.A. Rubinstein, & J.P. Murray (Eds.), *Television and social behavior: Vol. 5. Television's effects: Further explorations* (pp. 22–58). Washington, DC: Government Printing Office.

Elkind, D., & Weiner, I.B. (1978). *Development of the child.* New York: Wiley.

Elliott, W.R., & Slater, D. (1980). Exposure, experience and perceived TV reality for adolescents. *Journalism Quarterly, 57,* 409–414, 431.

Englehardt, T. (1987). Children's television: The shortcake strategy. In T. Gitlin (Ed.), *Watching television* (pp. 68–110). New York: Pantheon Books.

Eron, L.D. (1986). Interventions to mitigate the psychological effects of media violence on aggressive behavior. *Journal of Social Issues, 42*(3), 155–169.

Eron, L.D., & Huesmann, L.R. (1987). Television as a source of maltreatment of children. *School Psychology Review, 16*(2), 195–202.

Eron, L.D., Huesmann, L.R., Brice, P., Fischer, P., & Mermelstein, R. (1983). Age trends in the development of aggression, sex typing, and related television habits. *Developmental Psychology, 19*(1), 71–77.

Evans, E.D., & McCandless, B.R. (1978). *Children and youth.* New York: Holt, Rinehart & Winston.

Evra, J.V. (1990). *Television and child development.* Hillsdale, NJ: Erlbaum.

Faber, R.J., Meyer, T.P., & Miller, M.M. (1984). The effectiveness of health disclosures within children's television commercials. *Journal of Communication, 28,* 463–476.

Faber, R.J., Perloff, R.M., & Hawkins, R.P. (1982). Antecedents of children's comprehension of television advertising. *Journal of Broadcasting, 26*(2), 575–584.

Farquhar, J.W., Maccoby, N., Wood, P.D., Alexander, J.K., Breitrose, H., Brown, B.W., Jr., Haskell, W.L., McAlister, A.L., Meyer, A.M., Nash, J.D., & Stern, M.P. (1977, 4 June). Community education for cardiovascular health. *Lancet, 1,* 1192–1195.

FCC endorses children's TV act. (1991). *Broadcasting, 120*(15), 90–92.

FCC votes 5–0 for indecency ban. (1990, July 16). *Broadcasting,* 30–31.

Federal Communications Commission. (1974, November 6). Children's television report and policy statement. *Federal Register, 39*(215), para. 22.

Federal Trade Commission. (1978a, April). Children's advertising: Proposed trade regulation rulemaking and public hearing. *Federal Register, 43*(82), 17967–17972.

Federal Trade Commission. (1978b). *Federal Trade Commission news summary, 3*(24).

Federal Trade Commission. (1978c, February). *Staff report on television advertising to children.* Washington, DC: Author.

Federal Trade Commission. (1981, March 31). *FTC final staff report and recommendation.* Washington, DC: Author.

Feilitzen, C., & Linne, O. (1975). Identifying with television characters. *Journal of Communication, 25*(4), 51–55.

Feshbach, S. (1961). The stimulating versus cathartic effects of a vicarious aggressive activity. *Journal of Abnormal and Social Psychology, 63,* 381–385.

Feshbach, S. (1972). Reality and fantasy in filmed violence. In J.P. Murray, E.A. Rubinstein, & G.A. Comstock (Eds.), *Television and social behavior: Vol. 2. Television and social learning* (pp. 318–345). Washington, DC: Government Printing Office.

Feshbach, S., & Singer, R.D. (1971). *Television and aggression: An experimental field study.* San Francisco: Jossey-Bass.

Fetler, M. (1984). Television viewing and school achievement. *Journal of Communication, 34,* 104–118.

Field, D. (1987). *Child and parent coviewing of television: Relationships to cognitive performance.* Unpublished doctoral dissertation, University of Massachusetts, Amherst.

Field, D., & Anderson, D. (1985). Instruction and modality effects on children's television attention and comprehension. *Journal of Educational Psychology, 77,* 91–100.

Flavell, J.H., Everett, B.A., Croft, K., & Flavell, E.R. (1981). Young children's knowledge about visual perception: Further evidence for the level 1–level 2 distinction. *Developmental Psychology, 17,* 99–103.

Flavell, J.H., Flavell, E.R., Green, F.L., & Korfmacher, J.E. (1990). Do young children think of television images as pictures or real objects? *Journal of Broadcasting & Electronic Media, 34*(4), 399–419.

Flerx, V.C., Fidler, D.S., & Rogers, R.W. (1976). Sex role stereotypes: Developmental aspects and early intervention. *Child Development, 47,* 998–1007.

Flora, J.A., Maccoby, N., & Farquhar, J.W. (1989). Communication campaigns to prevent cardiovascular disease: The Stanford community studies. In R.E. Rice & C.K. Atkin (Eds.), *Public communication campaigns* (2nd ed.). Newbury Park, CA: Sage.

Fosarelli, P. (1986). In my opinion . . . Advocacy for children's appropriate viewing of television: What can we do? *CHC, 15*(2), 79–80.

Frank, R.E., & Greenberg, M.G. (1980). *The public's use of television.* Newbury Park, CA: Sage.

Freedman, J.L. (1984). Effect of television violence on aggressiveness. *Psychological Bulletin, 96*(2), 227–246.

Freedman, J.L. (1986). Television violence and aggression: A rejoinder. *Psychological Bulletin, 100*(3), 372–378.

Freeman, H.E. (1975). Forward. In T.D. Cook, H. Appleton, R.F. Conner, A. Shaffer, G. Tamkin, & S.J. Weber, *"Sesame Street" revisited* (pp. ix–xv). New York: Russell Sage Foundation.

Freuh, T., & McGhee, P.E. (1975). Traditional sex role development and amount of time spent watching television. *Developmental Psychology, 11,* 109.

Friedlander, B.Z., Wetstone, J.S., & Scott, C.S. (1974). Suburban preschool children's comprehension of an age-appropriate informational television program. *Child Development, 45,* 561–565.

Friedrich, L., & Stein, A.H. (1973). Aggressive and prosocial television programs and the natural behavior of preschool children. *Monographs of the Society for Research in Child Development, 38*(4, Serial No. 151).

Friedrich-Cofer, L., & Huston, A.C. (1986). Television violence and aggression: The debate continues. *Psychological Bulletin, 100*(3), 364–371.

Gadberry, S. (1980). Effects of restricting first graders' TV viewing on leisure time use, I.Q., change, and cognitive style. *Journal of Applied Developmental Psychology, 1,* 161–176.

Gaddy, G.D. (1986). Television's impact on high school achievement. *Public Opinion Quarterly, 50,* 340–359.

Galst, J.P. (1980). Television food commercials and pronutritional public service announcements as determinants of young children's snack choices. *Child Development, 51,* 935–938.

Galst, J.P., & White, M.A. (1976). The unhealthy persuader: The reinforcing value of television and children's purchase influence attempts at the supermarket. *Child Development, 47,* 1089–1096.

Gantz, W., & Masland, J. (1986). Television as babysitter. *Journalism Quarterly, 63,* 530–536.

Geen, R.G. (1968). Effects of frustration, attack, and prior training in aggressiveness upon aggressive behavior. *Journal of Personality and Social Psychology, 9,* 316–321.

Geen, R.G., & Berkowitz, L. (1967). Some conditions facilitating the occurrence of aggression after the observation of violence. *Journal of Personality, 35,* 666–676.

Geen, R.G., & Rakosky, J. (1973). Interpretations of observed violence and their effects on GSR. *Journal of Experimental Research in Personality, 6,* 289–292.

Geen, R.G., & Stonner, D. (1972). Context effects in observed violence. *Journal of Personality and Social Psychology, 25,* 145–150.

Geen, R.G., & Thomas, S.L. (1986). The immediate effects of media violence on behavior. *Journal of Social Issues, 42*(3), 2–27.

Geis, F.L., Brown, V., Jennings, J., & Corrado-Taylor, D. (1984). Sex vs status in sex-associated stereotypes. *Sex Roles, 11*(9/10), 771–785.

Geis, F.L., Brown, V., Jennings (Walstedt), J., & Porter, N. (1984). TV commercials as achievement scripts for women. *Sex Roles, 10*(7/8), 513–525.

Geis, M.L. (1982). *The language of advertising.* New York: Academic Press.

Gentner, D. (1975). Evidence for the psychological reality of semantic components: The verbs of possession. In D. Norman & D. Rumelhart (Eds.), *Explorations in cognition* (pp. 211–246). San Francisco: W.H. Freeman.

Gerbner, G., & Gross, L. (1976). Living with television: The violence profile. *Journal of Communication, 26*(2), 172–199.

Gerbner, G., Gross, L., Eleey, M.F., Jackson-Beeck, M., Jeffries-Fox, S., & Signorielli, N. (1977). *Violence profile no. 8: Trends in network television drama and viewer conceptions of social reality, 1967–1976.* Philadelphia: The Annenberg School of Communications, University of Pennsylvania.

Gerbner, G., Gross, L., Jackson-Beeck, M., Jeffries-Fox, S., & Signorielli, N. (1978). Cultural indicators: Violence profile No. 9. *Journal of Communication, 28*(3), 176–207.

Gerbner, G., Gross, L., Morgan, M., & Signorielli, N. (1980). The "mainstreaming" of America: Violence profile no. 11. *Journal of Communication, 30*(3), 10–29.

Gerbner, G., Gross, L., Morgan, M., & Signorielli, N. (1981a). A curious journey into the scary world of Paul Hirsch. *Communication Research, 8,* 39–72.

Gerbner, G., Gross, L., Morgan, M., & Signorielli, N. (1981b). Final reply to Hirsch. *Communication Research, 8,* 259–280.

Gerbner, G., Gross, L., Morgan, M., & Signorielli, N. (1984). Political correlates of television viewing. *Public Opinion Quarterly, 48,* 283–300.

Gerbner, G., Gross, L., Morgan, M., Signorielli, N., & Jackson-Beeck, M. (1979). The demonstration of power: Violence profile no. 10. *Journal of Communication, 29*(3), 177–196.

Gerbner, G., Gross, L., Signorielli, N., & Morgan, M. (1986, September). *Television's mean world: Violence profile no. 14–15.* Unpublished manuscript, The Annenberg School of Communications, The University of Pennsylvania, Philadelphia.

Gerbner, G., Gross, L., Signorielli, N., Morgan, M., & Jackson-Beeck, M. (1979). The demonstration of power: Violence profile no. 10. *Journal of Communication, 29*(3), 177–196.

Gibbons, J., Anderson, D.R., Smith, R., Field, D.E., & Fischer, C. (1986). Young children's recall and reconstruction of audio and audiovisual narratives. *Child Development, 57*, 1014–1023.

Gilmore, M., Evans, K., & Schleuter, G. (1989, August). *The television marketing of sex, booze, and unsafe driving.* Unpublished paper presented at the American Psychological Association annual meeting, New Orleans.

Gitlin, T. (1983). *Inside primetime.* New York: Pantheon.

Glass, G.V. (1978). Integrating findings: The meta-analysis of research. *Review of Research in Education, 5*, 351–379.

Glass, G.V., McGaw, B., & Smith, M.L. (1981). *Meta-analysis in social research.* Newbury Park, CA: Sage.

Goldberg, M.E., & Gorn, G.J. (1978). Some unintended consequences of TV advertising to children. *Journal of Consumer Research, 5*, 22–29.

Goldberg, M.E., Gorn, G.J., & Gibson, W. (1978). TV messages for snacks and breakfast foods: Do they influence children's preferences? *Journal of Consumer Research, 5*, 73–81.

Gorn, G.J., & Florsheim, R. (1985). The effects of commercials for adult products on children. *Journal of Consumer Research, 11*, 962–967.

Gorn, G.J., & Goldberg, M.E. (1980). Children's responses to repetitive television commercials. *Journal of Consumer Research, 6*(4), 421–424.

Gorn, G.J., & Goldberg, M.E. (1982). Behavioral evidence of the effects of televised food messages on children. *Journal of Consumer Research, 9*, 200–205.

Gorn, G.J., Goldberg, M.E., & Kanungo, R.N. (1976). The role of educational television in changing intergroup attitudes of children. *Child Development, 47*, 277–280.

Gould, M.S., & Shaffer, D. (1986). The impact of suicide in television movies: Evidence of imitation. *The New England Journal of Medicine, 315*(11), 690–694.

Granger, C.W. (1969). Investigating causal relations by econometric models and cross-spectral methods. *Econometrica, 37*, 424–438.

Graves, S.B. (1975). *Racial diversity in children's television: Its impact on racial attitudes and stated program preferences.* Unpublished doctoral dissertation, Harvard University.

Graves, S.B. (1980). Psychological effects of black portrayals on television. In S.B. Withey & R.P. Abeles (Eds.), *Television and social behavior: Beyond violence and children* (pp. 259–289). Hillsdale, NJ: Erlbaum.

Greenberg, B.S. (1972). Children's reactions to TV blacks. *Journalism Quarterly, 47*, 277–280.

Greenberg, B.S. (1980). *Life on television.* Norwood, NJ: Ablex.

Greenberg, B.S., Abelman, R., & Cohen, A. (1990). Telling children not to watch television. In R.J. Kinkel (Ed.), *Television and violence: An overview* (pp. 2–22). Detroit: Mental Health Association of Michigan.

Greenberg, B.S., & Dervin, B. (1970). *Use of the mass media by the urban poor.* New York: Praeger.

Greenberg, B.S., & Dervin, B. (1973). Mass communication among the urban poor. In C.D. Mortensen & K.K. Sereno (Eds.), *Advances in communication research* (pp. 388–397). New York: Harper & Row.

Greenberg, B.S., & Gordon, T.F. (1972a). Social and racial differences in children's perceptions of television violence. In G.A. Comstock, E.A. Rubinstein, & J.P. Murray (Eds.),

Television and social behavior: Vol. 5. Television's effects: Further explorations (pp. 185–210). Washington, DC: Government Printing Office.

Greenberg, B.S., & Gordon, T.F. (1972b). Children's perceptions of television violence: A replication. In G.A. Comstock, E.A. Rubinstein, & J.P. Murray (Eds.), *Television and social behavior: Vol. 5. Television's effects: Further explorations* (pp. 211–230). Washington, DC: Government Printing Office.

Greenberg, B.S., & Heeter, C. (1987). VCRs and young people. *American Behavioral Scientist, 30*(5), 509–521.

Greenberg, B.S., & Lin, C. (1989). Adolescents and the VCR boom: Old, new, and non-users. In M.R. Levy (Ed.), *The VCR age* (pp. 73–91). Newbury Park, CA: Sage.

Greenberg, B.S., & Reeves, B. (1976). Children and the perceived reality of television. *Journal of Social Issues, 32*(4), 86–97.

Greenfield, P. (1984). *Mind and media: The effects of television, video games, and computers.* Cambridge, MA: Harvard University Press.

Greenfield, P., & Beagles-Roos, J. (1988). Television versus radio: The cognitive impact on different socio-economic and ethnic groups. *Journal of Communication, 38*(2), 71–92.

Greenfield, P., Bruzzone, L., Koyamatsu, Satuloff, W., Nixon, K., Brodie, M., & Kingsdale, D. (1987). What is rock music doing in the minds of our youth? A first experimental look at the effects of rock music lyrics and music videos. *Journal of Early Adolescence, 7*(3), 315–329.

Greenfield, P., Farrar, D., & Beagles-Roos, J. (1986). Is the medium the message?: An experimental comparison of the effects of radio and television on imagination. *Journal of Applied Developmental Psychology, 7,* 201–218.

Greer, D., Potts, R., Wright, J., & Huston, A.C. (1982). The effects of television commercial form and commercial placement on children's social behavior and attention. *Child Development, 53,* 611–619.

Guidicatti, V., & Stening, B.W. (1980). Socioeconomic background and children's cognitive abilities in relation to television advertisements. *The Journal of Psychology, 106,* 153–155.

Gunter, B. (1979). Recall of brief television news items. *Journal of Educational Television and Other Media, 5,* 57–61.

Gunter, B. (1980). Remembering television news: Effects of picture content. *Journal of General Psychology, 102,* 127–133.

Gunter, B. (1986). *Television and sex role stereotyping.* London: John Libbey.

Gunter, B. (1987a). *Poor reception: Misunderstanding and forgetting broadcast news.* Hillsdale, NJ: Erlbaum.

Gunter, B. (1987b). *Television and fear of crime.* London: John Libbey.

Haefner, M.J., & Wartella, E.A. (1987). Effects of sibling coviewing on children's interpretations of television programs. *Journal of Broadcasting & Electronic Media, 31*(2), 153–168.

Halpern, W. (1975). Turned-on toddlers. *Journal of Communication, 25*(4), 66–70.

Hapkiewicz, W.G., & Stone, R.D. (1974). The effect of realistic versus imaginary aggressive models on children's interpersonal play. *Child Study Journal, 4*(2), 47–58.

Harris, Louis and Associates, Inc. (1974). *A survey on aging: Experience of older Americans vs. public expectation of old age.* Conducted for the National Council on Aging. New York: Author.

Harrison, L., & Williams, T.M. (1986). Television and cognitive development. In T.M. Williams (Ed.), *The impact of television: A natural experiment in three communities* (pp. 87–142). New York: Academic Press.

Harvey, M.G., & Rothe, J.T. (1985–1986). Video cassette recorders: Their impact on viewers and advertisers. *Journal of Advertising Research, 25*(6), 19–27.

Hawkins, R.P., & Pingree, S. (1980). Some processes in the cultivation effect. *Communication Research, 7,* 193–226.

Hawkins, R.P., & Pingree, S. (1981). Uniform messages and habitual viewing: Unnecessary assumptions in social reality effects. *Human Communication Research, 7*(4), 291–301.

Hawkins, R.P., & Pingree, S. (1982). Television's influence on construction of reality. In D. Pearl, L. Bouthilet, & J. Lazar (Eds.), *Television and behavior: Ten years of scientific progress and implications for the eighties: Vol. 2. Technical reviews* (pp. 224–247). Washington, DC: Government Printing Office.

Hawkins, R.P., Pingree, S., & Adler, I. (1987). Searching for cognitive processes in the cultivation effect: Adult and adolescent samples in the United States and Australia. *Human Communication Research, 13*(4), 553–577.

Hayes, D.S., & Birnbaum, D.W. (1980). Preschoolers' retention of televised events: Is a picture worth a thousand words? *Developmental Psychology, 16,* 410–416.

Hayes, D.S., & Kelly, S.B. (1984). Young children's processing of television: Modality differences in the retention of temporal relations. *Journal of Experimental Child Psychology, 38,* 505–514.

Hayes, D.S., & Kelly, S.B. (1985). Sticking to syntax: The reflection of story grammar in children's and adults' recall of radio and television shows. *Merrill-Palmer Quarterly, 31*(4), 345–360.

Hayes, D.S., Kelly, S.B., & Mandel, M. (1986). Media differences in children's story synopses: Radio and television contrasted. *Journal of Educational Psychology, 78,* 341–347.

Head, S.W. (1954). Content analysis of television drama programs. *Quarterly of Film, Radio, and Television, 9,* 175–194.

Hearold, S. (1986). A synthesis of 1043 effects of television on social behavior. In G. Comstock (Ed.), *Public communication and behavior* (Vol. 1, pp. 65–133). New York: Academic Press.

Heath, L., Kruttschnitt, C., & Ward, D. (1986). Television and violent criminal behavior: Beyond the Bobo doll. *Violence and Victims, 1,* 177–190.

Heeter, C. (1985). Program selection with abundance of choice: A process model. *Human Communication Research, 12*(1), 126–152.

Henderson, R.W., & Rankin, R.J. (1986). Preschoolers' viewing of instructional television. *Journal of Educational Psychology, 78,* 44–51.

Henke, L.L. (1985). Perceptions and use of news media by college students. *Journal of Broadcasting & Electronic Media, 29*(4), 431–436.

Hennigan, K.M., Heath, L., Wharton, J.D., Del Rosario, M.L., Cook, T.D., & Calder, B.J. (1982). Impact of the introduction of television on crime in the United States: Empirical findings and theoretical implications. *Journal of Personality and Social Psychology, 42*(3), 461–477.

Hetherington, E.M., & Parke, R.D. (1979). *Child psychology: A contemporary viewpoint.* New York: McGraw-Hill.

Heyns, B. (1976). *Exposure and the effects of schooling.* Washington, DC: National Institute of Education.

Himmelweit, H.T., Oppenheim, A.N., & Vince, P. (1958). *Television and the child.* London: Oxford University Press.

Himmelweit, H.T., & Swift, B. (1976). Continuities and discontinuities in media usage and taste: A longitudinal study. *Journal of Social Issues, 32*(4), 133–156.

Hirsch, B.Z., & Kulberg, J.M. (1987). Television and temporal development. *Journal of Early Adolescence, 7*(3), 331–344.

Hirsch, P. (1980a). On Hughes' contribution: The limits of advocacy research. *Public Opinion Quarterly, 44*(3), 411–413.

Hirsch, P. (1980b). The "scary world" of the nonviewer and other anomalies: A reanalysis of Gerbner et al.'s findings of cultivation analysis. Part I. *Communication Research, 7*, 403–456.

Hirsch, P. (1981a). On not learning from one's own mistakes: A reanalysis of Gerbner et al.'s findings on cultivation analysis, part 2. *Communication Research, 8*, 3–37.

Hirsch, P. (1981b). Distinguishing good speculation from bad theory: A rejoinder to Gerbner et al. *Communication Research, 8*, 73–95.

Hoff-Ginsberg, E., & Shatz, M. (1982). Linguistic input and the child's acquisition of language. *Psychological Bulletin, 92*, 3–26.

Hoffner, C., & Cantor, J. (1985). Developmental differences in responses to a television character's appearance and behavior. *Developmental Psychology, 21*(6), 1065–1074.

Hoffner, C., & Cantor, J. (1990). Forewarning of a threat and prior knowledge of outcome: Effects on children's emotional responses to a film sequence. *Human Communication Research, 16*(3), 323–354.

Hoffner, C., Cantor, J., & Thorson, E. (1988). Children's understanding of a televised narrative: Developmental differences in processing video and audio content. *Communication Research, 15*(3), 227–245.

Hoffner, C., Cantor, J., & Thorson, E. (1989). Children's responses to conflicting auditory and visual features of a televised narrative. *Human Communication Research, 16*(2), 256–278.

Hofman, R.J., & Flook, M.A. (1980). An experimental investigation of the role of television in facilitating shape recognition. *The Journal of Genetic Psychology, 136*, 305–306.

Hollander, N. (1971). Adolescents and the war: The sources of socialization. *Journalism Quarterly, 58*, 472–479.

Hollenbeck, A., & Slaby, R. (1979). Infant visual and vocal responses to television. *Child Development, 50*, 41–45.

Hopkins, N.M., & Mullis, A.K. (1985). Family perceptions of television viewing habits. *Family Relations, 34*, 177–181.

Hornik, R. (1978). Television access and the slowing of cognitive growth. *American Educational Research Journal, 15*, 1–15.

Hornik, R. (1981). Out-of-school television and schooling: Hypotheses and methods. *Review of Educational Research, 51*(2), 193–214.

Horst, D.P., & Tallmadge, G.K. (1976). *A practical guide to measuring project impact on student achievement.* Washington, DC: U.S. Office of Education.

Hoy, M.G., Young, C.E., & Mowen, J.C. (1986). Animated host-selling advertisements: Their impact on young children's recognition, attitudes, and behavior. *Journal of Public Policy and Marketing, 5*, 171–184.

Huesmann, L.R. (1982). Television violence and aggressive behavior. In D. Pearl, L. Bouthilet, & J. Lazar (Eds.), *Television and behavior: Ten years of scientific inquiry and implications for the eighties: Vol. 2. Technical reviews* (pp. 126–137). Washington, DC: U.S. Government Printing Office.

Huesmann, L.R. (1984). Ally or enemy? A review of Milavsky et al. *Contemporary Psychology, 29*(4), 283–285.

Huesmann, L.R. (1986). Psychological processes promoting the relation between exposure to media violence and aggressive behavior by the viewer. *Journal of Social Issues, 42*(3), 125–139.

Huesmann, L.R., & Eron, L.D. (Eds.) (1986). *Television and the aggressive child: A cross-national comparison.* Hillsdale, NJ: Erlbaum.

Huesmann, L.R., Eron, L.D., Klein, R., Brice, P., & Fischer, P. (1983). Mitigating the imitation of aggressive behaviors by changing children's attitudes about media violence. *Journal of Personality and Social Psychology, 44*(5), 899–910.

Huesmann, L.R., Eron, L.D., Lefkowitz, M.M., & Walder, L.O. (1984). The stability of aggression over time and generations. *Developmental Psychology, 20*(6), 1120–1134.

Huesmann, L.R., Lagerspetz, K., & Eron, L.D. (1984). Intervening variables in the TV violence–aggression relation: Evidence from two countries. *Developmental Psychology, 20*(5), 746–775.

Hughes, M. (1980). The fruits of cultivation analysis: A reexamination of the effects of television watching on fear of victimization, alienation, and the approval of violence. *Public Opinion Quarterly, 44*(3), 287–302.

Hunter, J., Schmidt, F.L., & Jackson, G.B. (1982). *Meta-analysis: Cumulating research findings across studies.* Newbury Park, CA: Sage.

Hur, K.K. (1978). Impact of "Roots" on black and white teenagers. *Broadcasting, 22*(3), 289–298.

Hur, K. K., & Robinson, J.P. (1978). The social impact of "Roots." *Journalism Quarterly, 55,* 19–24, 83.

Husson, W., & Krull, R. (1983). Nonstationarity in children's attention to television. In R.N. Bostrom (Ed.), *Communication yearbook 7* (pp. 304–340). Newbury Park, CA: Sage.

Huston, A., Greer, D., Wright, J.C., Welch, R., & Ross, R. (1984). Children's comprehension of televised formal features with masculine and feminine connotations. *Developmental Psychology, 20,* 707–716.

Huston, A., Watkins, B.A., & Kunkel, D. (1989). Public policy and children's television. *American Psychologist, 44*(2), 424–433.

Huston, A., & Wright, J.C. (1989). The forms of television and the child viewer. In G. Comstock (Ed.), *Public communication and behavior* (Vol. 2, pp. 103–159). New York: Academic Press.

Huston, A.C., Wright, J.C., Rice, M.L., Kerkman, D., Seigle, J., & Bremer, M. (1983). *Family environment and television use by preschool children.* Paper presented at the biennial meeting of the Society for Research in Child Development, Detroit, MI.

Huston, A.C., Wright, J.C., Rice, M.L., Kerkman, D., & St. Peters, M. (1990). Development of television viewing patterns in early childhood: A longitudinal investigation. *Developmental Psychology, 26*(3), 409–420.

Huston-Stein, A., Fox, S., Greer, D., Watkins, B.A., & Whitaker, J. (1981). The effects of TV action and violence on children's social behavior. *The Journal of Genetic Psychology, 138,* 183–191.

Hyman, H. H. (1973). Mass communication and socialization. *Public Opinion Quarterly, 37,* 524–540.

Isler, L., Popper, E.T., & Ward, S. (1987). Children's purchase requests and parental responses: Results from a diary study. *Journal of Advertising Research, 27*(5), 28–39.

Jackson-Beeck, M. (1979). Interpersonal and mass communication in children's political socialization. *Journalism Quarterly, 56,* 48–53.

Jacoby, J., & Hoyer, W.D. (1982). Viewer miscomprehension of televised communication: Selected findings. *Journal of Marketing, 46,* 12–26.

James, N.C., & McCain, T.A. (1982). Television games preschool children play: Patterns, themes, and uses. *Journal of Broadcasting, 26*(4), 783–800.

Janis, I.L. (1980). The influence of television on personal decision-making. In S.B. Withey

& R.P. Abeles (Eds.), *Television and social behavior: Beyond violence and children* (pp. 161–189). Hillsdale, NJ: Erlbaum.

Jennings, M.K., & Niemi, R.G. (1968). The transmission of political values from parent to child. *American Political Science Review, 62,* 443–467.

John, D.R., & Whitney, J.C., Jr. (1986). The development of consumer knowledge in children: A cognitive structure approach. *Journal of Consumer Research, 12,* 406–417.

Johnson, N.R. (1973). Television and politicization: A test of competing models. *Journalism Quarterly, 50,* 447–455.

Johnston, J., & Ettema, J.S. (1982). *Positive images: Breaking stereotypes with children's television.* Newbury Park, CA: Sage.

Jones, R.A., Hendrick, C., & Epstein, Y.M. (1979). *Introduction to social psychology.* Sunderland, MA: Sinauer Associates.

Josephson, W.L. (1987). Television violence and children's aggression: Testing the priming, social script, and disinhibition predictions. *Journal of Personality and Social Psychology, 53*(5), 882–890.

Joy, J., Kimball, M., & Zabrack, M. (1977, June). *Television exposure and children's aggressive behaviour.* Paper presented at the meeting of the Canadian Psychological Association, Vancouver, B.C.

Kagan, J., & Havemann, E. (1980). *Psychology: An introduction.* New York: Harcourt Brace Jovanovich.

Kalisch, P.A., & Kalisch, B.J. (1984). Sex-role stereotyping of nurses and physicians on prime-time television: A dichotomy of occupational portrayals. *Sex Roles, 10*(7/8), 533–553.

Kang, N. (1990). *A critique and secondary analysis of the NBC study on television and aggression.* Unpublished doctoral dissertation, Syracuse University, Syracuse, NY.

Katzman, N. (1972). Television soap operas: What's been going on anyway? *Public Opinion Quarterly, 36,* 200–212.

Keith, T.Z., Reimers, T.M., Fehrmann, P.G., Pottebaum, S.M., & Aubey, L.W. (1986). Parental involvement, homework, and TV time: Direct and indirect effects on high school achievement. *Journal of Educational Psychology, 78*(5), 373–380.

Kenny, D.A. (1984). The NBC study and television violence: A review (with comment by Milavsky et al., and response by Kenny). *Journal of Communication, 34*(1), 176–188.

Kenny, J.F. (1985). *The family as a mediator of television use and the cultivation phenomenon among college students.* Unpublished doctoral dissertation, Syracuse University, Syracuse, NY.

Kenrick, D.T., & Gutierres, S.E. (1980). Contrast effects and judgments of physical attractiveness: When beauty becomes a social problem. *Journal of Personality and Social Psychology, 38,* 131–140.

Kenrick, D.T., Gutierres, S.E., & Goldberg, L. (1989). Influence of popular erotica on interpersonal attraction judgments: The uglier side of pretty pictures. *Journal of Personality and Social Psychology, 25*(2), 159–167.

Kessler, R.C., Downey, G., Milavsky, J.R., & Stipp, H. (1988). Clustering of teenage suicides after television news stories about suicides: A reconsideration. *American Journal of Psychiatry, 145*(11), 1379–1383.

Kessler, R.C., & Stipp, H. (1984). The impact of fictional television suicide stories on U.S. fatalities: A replication. *American Journal of Sociology, 90*(1), 151–164.

Kim, W.Y., Baran, S.J., & Massey, K. (1988). Impact of the VCR on control of television viewing. *Journal of Broadcasting & Electronic Media, 32,* 351–357.

Klopfenstein, B.C. (1989). The diffusion of the VCR in the United States. In M. Levy (Ed.), *The VCR age* (pp. 21–39). Newbury Park, CA: Sage.

Koblinsky, S.G., Cruse, D.F., & Sugaware, A.I. (1978). Sex role stereotypes and children's memory for story content. *Child Development, 49,* 452–458.

Kohn, P.M., & Smart, R.G. (1984). The impact of television advertising on alcohol consumption: An experiment. *Journal of Studies on Alcohol, 45,* 295–301.

Kohn, P.M., & Smart, R.G. (1987). Wine, women, suspiciousness, and advertising. *Journal of Studies on Alcohol, 48,* 161–166.

Kopp, C.B., & Krakow, J.B. (1982). *The child: Development in a social context.* Reading, MA: Addison-Wesley.

Kotch, J.B., Coulter, M., & Lipsitz, A. (1986). Does televised drinking influence children's attitudes toward alcohol? *Addictive Behaviors, 11,* 67–70.

Krafka, C.L. (1985). *Sexually explicit, sexually violent, and violent media: Effects of multiple naturalistic exposures and debriefing on female viewers.* Unpublished doctoral dissertation, University of Wisconsin, Madison.

Kraus, S. (1972). Modifying prejudice: Attitude change as a function of the race of the communicator. *Audiovisual Communication Review, 10*(1).

Krendl, K.A., & Watkins, B. (1983). Understanding television: An exploratory inquiry into the reconstruction of narrative content. *Educational Communication & Technology Journal, 31,* 201–212.

Krull, R. (1983). Children learning to watch television. In J. Bryant & D.R. Anderson (Eds.), *Children's understanding of television: Research on attention and comprehension* (pp. 103–123). New York: Academic Press.

Kubey, R.W. (1986). Television use in everyday life: Coping with unstructured time. *Journal of Communication, 36*(3), 108–123.

Kubey, R.W. (1990). Television and family harmony among children, adolescents, and adults: Results from the experience sampling method. In J. Bryant (Ed.), *Television and the American family* (pp. 73–88). Hillsdale, NJ: Erlbaum.

Kubey, R.W. (in press). Television and the quality of family life. *Communication Quarterly, 38*(3).

Kubey, R.W., & Czikszentmihalyi, M. (1990). *Television and the quality of life. How viewing shapes everyday experience.* Hillsdale, NJ: Erlbaum.

Kubey, R.W., & Larson, R. (1990). The use and experience of the new video media among children and young adolescents. *Communication Research, 17*(1), 107–130.

Kunkel, D. (1988a). Children and host-selling television commercials. *Communication Research, 15*(1), 71–92.

Kunkel, D. (1988b). From a raised eyebrow to a turned back: The FCC and children's product-related programming. *Journal of Communication, 38*(4), 90–108.

Kunkel, D. (1990). Child and family television regulatory policy. In J. Bryant (Ed.), *Television and the American family* (pp. 349–368). Hillsdale, NJ: Erlbaum.

Kunkel, D., & Watkins, B. (1987). Evolution of children's television regulatory policy. *Journal of Broadcasting & Electronic Media, 31*(4), 367–389.

Lambert, W.E., & Klineberg, O. (1967). *Children's views of foreign peoples: A cross-national study.* New York: Appleton-Century-Crofts.

Larsen, O., Gray, L.N., & Fortis, J.G. (1963). Goals and goal achievement in television content: Models for anomie? *Sociological Inquiry, 33,* 180–196.

Larson, R., & Kubey, R. (1983). Television and music: Contrasting media in adolescent life. *Youth and Society, 15,* 13–31.

Larson, R., Kubey, R., & Colletti, J. (1990). Changing channels: Early adolescent media choices and shifting investments in family and friends. *Journal of Early Adolescence, 18*(1), 583–599.

Lawrence, F.C., & Wozniak, P.H. (1989). Children's television viewing with family members. *Psychological Reports, 65,* 396–400.

Lefcourt, H.M., Barnes, K., Parke, R., & Schwartz, F. (1966). Anticipated social censure and aggression–conflict as mediators of response to aggression induction. *Journal of Social Psychology, 70,* 251–263.

Lefkowitz, M.M., Eron, L.D., Walder, L.O., & Huesmann, L.R. (1972). Television violence and child aggression: A followup study. In G.A. Comstock & E.A. Rubinstein (Eds.), *Television and social behavior: Vol. 3. Television and adolescent aggressiveness* (pp. 35–135). Washington, DC: Government Printing Office.

Lefkowitz, M.M., Eron, L.D., Walder, L.O., & Huesmann, L.R. (1977). *Growing up to be violent: A longitudinal study of the development of aggression.* Elmsford, NY: Pergamon.

Lemish, D., & Rice, M.L. (1986). Television as a talking picture book: A prop for language acquisition. *Journal of Child Language, 13,* 251–274.

Lesser, G.S. (1972). Learning, teaching, and television production for children: The experience from "Sesame Street." *Harvard Educational Review, 42,* 232–272.

Lesser, G.S. (1974). *Children and television: Lessons from "Sesame Street."* New York: Random House.

Levin, S.R., Petros, T.V., & Petrella, F.W. (1982). Preschoolers' awareness of television advertising. *Child Development, 53,* 933–937.

Levy, M.R. (1978). The audience experience with television news. *Journalism Monographs, 55.*

Leyens, J.P., & Camino, L. (1974). The effects of repeated exposure to film violence on aggressiveness and social structure. In J. DeWit & W.P. Hartup (Eds.), *Determinants and origins of aggressive behavior.* The Hague, Netherlands: Mouton.

Leyens, J.P., Camino, L., Parke, R.D., & Berkowitz, L. (1975). Effects of movie violence on aggression in a field setting as a function of group dominance and cohesion. *Journal of Personality and Social Psychology, 32*(2), 346–360.

Lichty, L.W. (1989). Television in America: Success story. In P.S. Cook, D. Gomery, & L.W. Lichty (Eds.), *American media* (pp. 159–176). Washington, D.C.: Wilson Center Press.

Lieberman Research. (1975). *Children's reactions to violent material on television* (Report to the American Broadcasting Company). New York: Author.

Liebert, D., Sprafkin, J., Liebert, R., & Rubinstein, E. (1977). Effects of television commercial disclaimers on the product expectations of children. *Journal of Communication, 27*(1), 118–124.

Liebert, R.M., & Wicks-Nelson, R. (1979). *Developmental psychology.* New York: McGraw-Hill.

Lin, C.A., & Atkin, D.J. (1989). Parental mediation and rulemaking for adolescent use of television and VCRs. *Journal of Broadcasting & Electronic Media, 33*(1), 53–67.

Lindlof, T.R., & Shatzer, M.J. (1990). VCR usage in the American family. In J. Bryant (Ed.), *Television and the American family* (pp. 89–109). Hillsdale, NJ: Erlbaum.

Lindlof, T.R., Shatzer, M.J., & Wilkinson, D. (1988). Accomodation of video and television in the American family. In J. Lull (Ed.), *World families watch television* (pp. 158–192). Newbury Park, CA: Sage.

Linz, D. (1985). *Sexual violence in the media: Effects on male viewers and implications for society.* Unpublished doctoral dissertation, University of Wisconsin, Madison.

Linz, D., Donnerstein, E., & Adams, S.M. (1989). Physiological desensitization and judgments about female victims of violence. *Human Communication Research, 15*(4), 509–522.

Linz, D., Donnerstein, E., & Penrod, S. (1984). The effects of multiple exposures to filmed violence against women. *Journal of Communication, 34*(3), 130–147.

Linz, D., Donnerstein, E., & Penrod, S. (1988). Effects of long-term exposure to violent and sexually degrading depictions of women. *Journal of Personality and Social Psychology*, *55*(5), 758–768.

Liss, M.B. (1981). Children's television selections: A study of indicators of same-race preferences. *Journal of Cross-Cultural Psychology*, *12*(1), 103–110.

Liss, M.B., & Reinhardt, L.C. (1980). Aggression on prosocial television programs. *Psychological Reports*, *46*, 1065–1066.

Liss, M.B., Reinhardt, L.C., & Fredriksen, S. (1983). TV heroes: The impact of rhetoric and deeds. *Journal of Applied Developmental Psychology*, *4*, 175–187.

List, J.A., Collins, W.A., & Westby, S.D. (1983). Comprehension inferences from traditional and nontraditional sex-role portrayals on television. *Child Development*, *54*, 1579–1587.

Loehlin, J.C., & Nichols, R.C. (1976). *Heredity, environment and personality.* Austin: University of Texas Press.

Long, B.H., & Henderson, E.H. (1973). Children's use of time: Some personal and social correlates. *Elementary School Journal*, *73*, 193–199.

Lorch, E.P., Anderson, D.R., & Levin, S.R. (1979). The relationship of visual attention to children's comprehension of television. *Child Development*, *50*, 722–727.

Lorch, E.P., Bellack, D.R., & Augsbach, L.H. (1987). Young children's memory for televised stories: Effects of importance. *Child Development*, *58*, 453–463.

LoSciuto, L.A. (1972). A national inventory of television viewing behavior. In E.A. Rubinstein, G.A. Comstock, & J.P. Murray (Eds.), *Television and social behavior: Vol. 4. Television in day-to-day life: Patterns of use* (pp. 33–86). Washington, DC: Government Printing Office.

Lovibond, S.H. (1967). The effect of media stressing crime and violence upon children's attitudes. *Social Problems*, *15*, 91–100.

Loye, D., Gorney, R., & Steele, G. (1977). Effects of television: An experimental field study. *Journal of Communication*, *27*(3), 206–216.

Lull, J. (1985). On the communicative properties of music. *Communication Research*, *12*, 363–372.

Lull, J. (1990). Families' social uses of television as extensions of the household. In J. Brant (Ed.), *Television and the American family* (pp. 59–72). Hillsdale, NJ: Erlbaum.

Lyle, J. (1975). *The people look at television 1974.* Washington, DC: The Corporation for Public Broadcasting.

Lyle, J., & Hoffman, H.R. (1972a). Children's use of television and other media. In E.A. Rubinstein, G.A. Comstock, & J.P. Murray (Eds.), *Television and social behavior: Vol. 4. Television in day-to-day life: Patterns of use* (pp. 129–256). Washington, DC: Government Printing Office.

Lyle, J., & Hoffman, H.R. (1972b). Explorations in patterns of television viewing by preschool-age children. In E.A. Rubinstein, G.A. Comstock, & J.P. Murray (Eds.), *Television and social behavior: Vol. 4. Television in day-to-day life: Patterns of use* (pp. 257–273). Washington, DC: Government Printing Office.

Lynd, R.S. (1939). *Knowledge for what?* Princeton, NJ: Princeton University press.

Lynd, R.S., & Lynd, H.M. (1929). *Middletown: A study in American culture.* New York: Harcourt and Brace.

Lynd, R.S., & Lynd, H.M. (1937). *Middletown in transition: A study in cultural conflicts.* New York: Harcourt and Brace.

Maccoby, E.E. (1954). Why do children watch television? *Public Opinion Quarterly*, *18*, 239–244.

Maccoby, E.E. (1964). Effects of the media. In M. Hoffman & L.W. Hoffman (Eds.), *Review of child development research* (Vol. 1, pp. 323–348). New York: Russell Sage Foundation.

Maccoby, E.E., & Wilson, W.C. (1957). Identification and observational learning from films. *Journal of Abnormal and Social Psychology, 55,* 76–87.

Maccoby, E.E., Wilson, W.C., & Burton, R.V. (1958). Differential movie-viewing behavior of male and female viewers. *Journal of Personality, 26,* 259–267.

Maccoby, N., & Solomon, D. (1981). Experiments in risk reduction through community health education. In M. Meyer (Ed.), *Health education by television and radio* (pp. 140–166). New York: K.G. Saur (Munich).

Macklin, M.C. (1983). Do children understand TV ads? *Journal of Advertising Research, 23*(Feb/March), 63–69.

Macklin, M.C. (1985). Do young children understand the selling intent of commercials? *The Journal of Consumer Affairs, 19*(2), 293–304.

Macklin, M.C. (1987). Preschoolers' understanding of the informational function of television advertising. *Journal of Consumer Research, 14,* 229–239.

Malamuth, N.M. (1984). Aggression against women: Cultural and individual causes. In N.M. Malamuth & E. Donnerstein (Eds.), *Pornography and sexual aggression* (pp. 19–52). New York: Academic Press.

Malamuth, N.M. (1989). Sexually violent media, thought patterns, and antisocial behavior. In G. Comstock (Ed.), *Public communication and behavior* (Vol. 2, pp. 159–204). New York: Academic Press.

Malamuth, N.M., & Billings, V. (1986). The functions and effects of pornography: Sexual communication versus the feminist models in light of research findings. In J. Bryant & D. Zillmann (Eds.), *Perspectives on media effects* (pp. 83–108). Hillsdale, NJ: Erlbaum.

Malamuth, N.M., & Briere, J. (1986). Sexual violence in the media: Indirect effects on aggression against women. *Journal of Social Issues, 42*(3), 75–92.

Malamuth, N.M., Feshbach, S., & Jaffe, T. (1977). Sexual arousal and aggression: Recent experiments and theoretical issues. *Journal of Social Issues, 33*(2), 110–133.

Mandler, J.M. (1983). Representation. In J.H. Flavell & E.M. Markman (Eds.), *Handbook of child psychology: Volume III. Cognitive development* (pp. 33–62). Hillsdale, NJ: Erlbaum.

Marrow, A.J. (1969). *The practical theorist: The life and work of Kurt Lewin* (Reprint, 1980). New York: Basic Books.

Mayes, S.L., & Valentine, K.B. (1979). Sex role stereotyping in Saturday morning cartoons. *Journal of Broadcasting, 23,* 41–50.

Mays, L., Henderson, E.H., Seidman, S.K., & Steiner, V.S. (1975). *An evaluation report on "Vegetable Soup": The effects of a multi-ethnic children's television series on intergroup attitudes of children.* Unpublished manuscript, New York State Department of Education.

McAllister-Johnson, P. (1977). *Interpersonal communication effects of viewing "Roots."* Unpublished doctoral dissertation, University of Wisconsin, Madison.

McArthur, L. Z., & Resko, B. G. (1975). The portrayal of men and women in American television commercials. *The Journal of Social Psychology, 97,* 209–220.

McCarthy, E.D., Langner, T.S., Gersten, J.C., Eisenberg, J.G., & Orzeck, L. (1975). Violence and behavioral disorders. *Journal of Communication, 25,* 71–85.

McConnell, J.V. (1980). *Understanding human behavior.* New York: Holt, Rinehart & Winston.

McDermott, S.T., & Greenberg, B.S. (1984). Black children's esteem: Parents, peers, and television. In R.N. Bostrom (Ed.), *Communication yearbook 8* (pp. 164–177). Newbury Park, CA: Sage.

McDonald, D.G. (1986). Generational aspects of television coviewing. *Journal of Broadcasting & Electronic Media, 30*(1), 75–85.

McGhee, P.E., & Freuh, T. (1980). Television viewing and the learning of sex-role stereotypes. *Sex Roles, 6,* 179–188.

McGuire, W.J. (1986). The myth of massive media impact: Savagings and salvagings. In G. Comstock (Ed.), *Public communication and behavior* (Vol. 1, pp. 173–257). New York: Academic Press.

McHan, E.J. (1985). Imitation of aggression by Lebanese children. *The Journal of Social Psychology, 125*(5), 613–617.

McIlwraith, R.D., & Josephson, W.L. (1985). Movies, books, music, and adult fantasy life. *Journal of Communication, 35*(2), 167–179.

McIlwraith, R.D., & Schallow, J. (1982–83). Television viewing and styles of children's fantasy. *Imagination, Cognition and Personality, 2*(4), 323–331.

McIlwraith, R.D., & Schallow, J. (1983). Adult fantasy life and patterns of media use. *Journal of Communication, 33*(1), 78–91.

McIntyre, J.J., & Teevan, J.J., Jr. (1972). Television violence and deviant behavior. In G.A. Comstock & E.A. Rubinstein (Eds.), *Television and social behavior: Vol. 3. Television and adolescent aggressiveness* (pp. 383–435). Washington, DC: Government Printing Office.

McLeod, J.M., Atkin, C.K., & Chaffee, S.H. (1972a). Adolescents, parents, and television use: Adolescent self-report measures from Maryland and Wisconsin samples. In G.A. Comstock & E.A. Rubinstein (Eds.), *Television and social behavior: Vol. 3. Television and adolescent aggressiveness* (pp. 173–238). Washington, DC: Government Printing Office.

McLeod, J.M., Atkin, C.K., & Chaffee, S.H. (1972b). Adolescents, parents, and television use: Self-report and other-report measures from the Wisconsin sample. In G.A. Comstock & E.A. Rubinstein (Eds.), *Television and social behavior: Vol. 3. Television and adolescent aggressiveness* (pp. 239–313). Washington, DC: Government Printing Office.

McLuhan, M. (1964). *Understanding media: The extensions of man.* New York: McGraw-Hill.

Meadowcroft, J.M. (1986). Family communication patterns and political development: The child's role. *Communication Research, 13*(4), 603–624.

Meadowcroft, J.M., & Reeves, B. (1989). Influence of story schema development on children's attention to television. *Communication Research, 16*(3), 352–374.

Medrich, E.A., Roizen, J., Rubin, V., & Buckley, S. (1982). *The serious business of growing up: A study of children's lives outside school.* Los Angeles: University of California Press.

Meltzoff, A.N. (1988). Imitation of televised models by infants. *Child Development, 59,* 1221–1229.

Meringoff, L. (1970). A story a story: The influence of the medium on children's comprehension of stories. *Journal of Educational Psychology, 72,* 240–244.

Meringoff, L.K. (1980a). The influence of the medium on children's story apprehension. *Journal of Educational Psychology, 72,* 240–249.

Meringoff, L.K. (1980b). The effects of children's television food advertising. In R.P. Adler, G.S. Lesser, L.K. Meringoff, T.S. Robertson, J.R. Rossiter, & S. Ward, *The effects of television advertising on children: Review and recommendations* (pp. 123–152). Lexington, MA: Lexington Books.

Meringoff, L.K., & Lesser, G.S. (1980). The influence of format and audiovisual techniques on children's perceptions of commercial messages. In R.P. Adler, G.S. Lesser, L.K. Meringoff, T.S. Robertson, J.R. Rossiter, & S. Ward, *The effects of television advertis-*

ing on children: Review and recommendations (pp. 43–60). Lexington, MA: Lexington Books.

Meringoff, L.K., Vibbert, M.M., Char, C.A., Ferme, D.E., Banker, G.S., & Gardner, H. (1983). How is children's learning from television distinctive? Exploiting the medium methodologically. In J. Bryant & D.R. Anderson (Eds.), *Children's understanding of television: Research on attention and comprehension* (pp. 151–179). New York: Academic Press.

Messaris, P. (1983). Family conversations about television. *Journal of Family Issues, 4,* 293–308.

Messaris, P., & Kerr, D. (1983). Mothers' comments about TV: Relation to family communication patterns. *Communication Research, 10,* 175–194.

Messaris, P., & Kerr, D. (1984). TV-related mother–child interaction and children's perceptions of TV characters. *Journalism Quarterly, 61,* 662–667.

Messaris, P., & Sarett, C. (1981). On the consequences of television-related parent–child interaction. *Human Communication Research, 7*(3), 226–244.

Messner, S.F. (1986). Television violence and violent crime: An aggregate analysis. *Social Problems, 33*(3), 218–235.

Meyer, B. (1980). The development of girls' sex-role attitudes. *Child Development, 51,* 508–415.

Meyer, T.P. (1973). Children's perceptions of favorite television characters as behavioral models. *Educational Broadcasting Review, 7*(1), 25–33.

Meyer, T.P., & Hexamer, A. (1981). Perceived truth and trust in television advertising among Mexican-American adolescents. *Journal of Broadcasting, 25*(2), 139–153.

Milavsky, J.R., Kessler, R., Stipp, H.H., & Rubens, W.S. (1982a). Television and aggression: Results of a panel study. In D. Pearl, L. Bouthilet, & J. Lazar (Eds.), *Television and social behavior: Ten years of scientific progress and implications for the eighties: Vol. 2. Technical reviews* (pp. 138–157). Washington, DC: Government Printing Office.

Milavsky, J.R., Kessler, R., Stipp, H.H., & Rubens, W.S. (1982b). *Television and aggression: A panel study.* New York: Academic Press.

Milavsky, J.R., Pekowsky, B., & Stipp, H. (1975–76). TV drug advertising and proprietary and illicit drug use among teenage boys. *Public Opinion Quarterly, 39,* 457–481.

Milgram, S., & Shotland, R.L. (1973). *Television and antisocial behavior: A field experiment.* New York: Academic Press.

Miller, M.M., & Reeves, B. (1976). Dramatic TV content and children's sex-role stereotypes. *Journal of Broadcasting, 20,* 35–50.

Mischel, W., & Mischel, H.N. (1980). *Essentials of psychology.* New York: Random House.

Misiolek, N.I. (1990). Memorandum to principal author on children's network television programming, 1989–1990. Syracuse, NY: SI Newhouse School, Syracuse University.

Morgan, M. (1980). Television viewing and reading: Does more equal better? *Journal of Communication, 30*(1), 159–165.

Morgan, M. (1982). Television and adolescents' sex-role stereotypes: A longitudinal study. *Journal of Personality and Social Psychology, 43*(5), 947–955.

Morgan, M. (1987). Television, sex role attitudes, and sex role behavior. *Journal of Early Adolescence, 7*(3), 269–282.

Morgan, M. (1988). Cultivation analysis. In E. Barnouw (Ed.), *International encyclopedia of communication* (Vol. 1, pp. 430–433). New York: Oxford University Press.

Morgan, M., Alexander, A., Shanahan, J., & Harris, C. (1990). Adolescents, VCRs, and the family environment. *Communication Research, 17*(1), 83–106.

Morgan, M., & Gross, L. (1980). Television viewing, IQ, and academic achievement. *Journal of Broadcasting, 24,* 117–133.

Morgan, M., & Gross, L. (1982). Television and educational achievement and aspiration. In D. Pearl, L. Bouthilet, & J. Lazar (Eds.), *Television and behavior: Ten years of scientific progress and implications for the eighties: Vol. 2. Technical reviews* (pp. 78–90). Washington, DC: Government Printing Office.

Morison, P., Kelly, H., & Gardner, H. (1981). Reasoning about the realities on television: A developmental study. *Journal of Broadcasting, 25*(3), 229–241.

Moschis, G.P. (1987). *Consumer socialization: A life-cycle perspective.* Lexington, MA: Lexington Books.

Moschis, G.P., & Moore, R.L. (1979). Decision making among the young: A socialization perspective. *Journal of Consumer Research, 6,* 101–112.

Moschis, G.P., & Moore, R.L. (1981). *A model of brand preference formation.* Unpublished manuscript, Georgia State University, Atlanta, GA.

Moschis, G.P., & Moore, R.L. (1982). A longitudinal study of television advertising effects. *Journal of Consumer Research, 9,* 279–286.

Moschis, G.P., Moore, R.L., & Stanley, T.J. (1984). An exploratory study of brand loyalty development. In T.C. Kinnear (Ed.), *Advances in consumer research. Proceedings of the annual conference of the Association for Consumer Research* (Vol. 11, pp. 412–417). Urbana, IL: Association for Consumer Research.

Mulac, A., Bradac, J.J., & Mann, S.K. (1985). Male/female language differences and attributional consequences in children's television. *Human Communication Research, 11*(4), 481–506.

Murray, J.P. (1980). *Television and youth: 25 years of research and controversy.* Boys Town, NB: Boys Town Center for the Study of Youth Development.

Murray, J.P. (1983). *Results of an informal poll of knowledgeable persons concerning the impact of TV violence.* Unpublished paper presented to the APA Monitor, American Psychological Association, Washington, DC.

Murray, J.P., & Kippax, S. (1977). Television diffusion and social behavior in three communities: A field experiment. *Australian Journal of Psychology, 29*(1), 31–43.

Murray, J.P., & Kippax, S. (1978). Children's social behavior in three towns with differing television experience. *Journal of Communication, 28*(4), 19–29.

Myers, D.G. (1983). *Social psychology.* New York: McGraw-Hill.

National Commission on the Causes and Prevention of Violence. (1969). *To establish justice, to ensure domestic tranquility.* Washington, DC: U.S. Government Printing Office.

Neuman, S.B. (1980). Listening behavior and television viewing. *Journal of Educational Research, 74,* 15–18.

Neuman, S.B. (1988). The displacement effect: Assessing the relation between television viewing and reading performance. *Reading Research Quarterly, 23*(4), 414–440.

Neuman, S.B., & Prowda, P. (1982). Television viewing and reading achievement. *Journal of Reading, 25,* 666–670.

Neuman, W.R. (1982). Television and American culture: The mass medium and the pluralistic audience. *Public Opinion Quarterly, 46*(4), 471–487.

Newcomb, A.F., & Collins, W.A. (1979). Children's comprehension of family role portrayals in televised dramas: Effects of socioeconomic status, ethnicity, and age. *Developmental Psychology, 15*(4), 417–423.

Newcomb, H. (1988). One night of prime time: An analysis of television's multiple voices. In J. Carey (Ed.), *Media, myths, and narratives: Television and the press.* Newbury Park, CA: Sage.

Nie, N.H., Verba, S., & Petrocik, J.R. (1976). *The changing American voter.* Cambridge, MA: Harvard University Press.

A.C. Nielsen and Company. (1986). *1986 Nielsen Report on television.* New York: Author.

A.C. Nielsen and Company. (1988). *1988 Nielsen Report on television.* Northbrook, IL: Author.

O'Keefe, G.J., & Reed-Nash, K. (1987). Crime news and real-world blues: The effects of the media on social reality. *Communication Research, 14*(2), 147–163.

Oskamp, S. (1984). *Applied social psychology.* Englewood Cliffs, NJ: Prentice-Hall.

Paget, K.F., Kritt, D., & Bergemann, L. (1984). Understanding strategic interactions in television commercials: A developmental study. *Journal of Applied Developmental Psychology, 5*, 145–161.

Paik, H. (1991). *The effects of television violence on aggressive behavior: A meta-analysis.* Unpublished doctoral dissertation, Syracuse University, Syracuse, NY.

Palmer, E.L. (1987). *Children in the cradle of television.* Lexington, MA: Lexington Books.

Palmer, E.L. (1988). *Television and America's children.* New York: Oxford University Press.

Palmer, E.L., & McDowell, C.N. (1979). The program/commercial separators in children's television programming. *Journal of Communication, 29*(3), 197–201.

Palmer, E.L., Hockett, A.B., & Dean, W.W. (1983). The television family and children's fright reactions. *Journal of Family Issues, 4*, 279–292.

Palmer, P. (1986). *The lively audience.* Boston: Allen and Unwin.

Parker, E.B. (1960). *The functions of television for children.* Unpublished doctoral dissertation, Stanford University, Palo Alto, CA.

Parker, E.B. (1963). The effects of television on library circulation. *Public Opinion Quarterly, 27*(4), 578–589.

Pearl, D., Bouthilet, L., & Lazar, J. (Eds.). (1982a). *Television and behavior: Ten years of scientific progress and implications for the eighties: Vol. 1. Summary report.* Washington, DC: Government Printing Office.

Pearl, D., Bouthilet, L., & Lazar, J. (Eds.) (1982b). *Television and behavior: Ten years of scientific progress and implications for the eighties: Vol. 2. Technical reviews.* Washington, DC: Government Printing Office.

Peirce, K. (1983). Relation between time spent viewing television and children's writing skills. *Journalism Quarterly, 60*, 445–448.

Penrod, S. (1983). *Social psychology.* Englewood Cliffs, NJ: Prentice-Hall.

Perlman, D., & Cozby, P.C. (1983). *Social psychology.* New York: Holt, Rinehart & Winston.

Perloff, R.M. (1977). Some antecedents of children's sex-role stereotypes. *Psychological Reports, 40*, 947–955.

Peterson, C.C., Peterson, J.L., & Carroll, J. (1987). Television viewing and imaginative problem solving during preadolescence. *The Journal of Genetic Psychology, 147*(1), 61–67.

Peterson, P.E., Jeffrey, B.J., Bridgwater, C.A., & Dawson, B. (1984). How pronutritional television programming affects children's dietary habits. *Developmental Psychology, 20*(1), 55–63.

Peterson, R.C., & Thurstone, L.L. (1933). *Motion pictures and the social attitudes of children.* New York: Macmillan.

Pezdek, K., & Hartman, E.F. (1983). Children's television viewing: Attention and comprehension of auditory versus visual information. *Child Development, 54*, 1015–1023.

Pezdek, K., Lehrer, A., & Simon, S. (1984). The relationship between reading and cognitive processing of television and radio. *Child Development, 55*, 2072–2082.

Pezdek, K., Simon, S., Stoeckert, J., & Kiley, J. (1985). *Individual differences in television comprehension.* Paper presented at the annual meeting of the Psychonomic Society, Boston.

Pezdek, K., & Stevens, E. (1984). Children's memory for auditory and visual information on television. *Developmental Psychology, 20*(2), 212–218.

Phair, A.J. (1976). Comparison of cognitive learning from a 16 mm motion picture, a 35 mm sound filmstrip, sound track only, and printed narration, using immediate and delayed retention scores in sixth grade social studies. *Dissertation Abstracts International, 36*(8-A), 4968.

Phillips, D.P. (1986). The found experiment: A new technique for assessing the impact of mass media violence on real-world aggressive behavior. In G. Comstock (Ed.), *Public communication and behavior* (Vol. 1, pp. 260–307). New York: Academic Press.

Phillips, D.P., & Carstensen, L.L. (1986). Clustering of teenage suicides after television news stories about suicide. *The New England Journal of Medicine, 315*(11), 685–689.

Phillips, D.P., & Hensley, J.E. (1984). When violence is rewarded or punished. *Journal of Communication, 34*(3), 101–116.

Piaget, J. (1969). *The mechanism of perception.* New York: Basic Books.

Piaget, J. (1971). The theory of stages in cognitive development. In D.R. Geen et al. (Eds.), *Measurement and Piaget* [Proceedings] (pp. 1–11). New York: McGraw-Hill.

Piaget, J., & Inhelder, B. (1956). *The child's conception of space.* London: Routledge and Kegan Paul. [Reissued by Norton, 1967]

Piaget, J., & Inhelder, B. (1969). *The psychology of the child.* New York: Basic Books.

Pillow, B.H., & Flavell, J.H. (1986). Young children's knowledge about visual perception: Projective size and shape. *Child Development, 57*, 125–135.

Pingree, S. (1978). The effects of nonsexist television commercials and perceptions of reality on children's attitudes about women. *Psychology of Women Quarterly, 2*, 262–277.

Pingree, S. (1986). Children's activity and television comprehensibility. *Communication Research, 13*(2), 239–256.

Pingree, S., with Hawkins, R.P., Rouner, D., Burns, J., Gikonyo, W., & Neuwirth, C. (1984). Another look at children's comprehension of television. *Communication Research, 11*(4), 477–496.

Pinon, M.F., Huston, A.C., & Wright, J.C. (1989). Family ecology and child characteristics that predict young children's educational television viewing. *Child Development, 60*(4), 846–856.

Plomin, R., Corley, R., DeFries, J.C., & Fulker, D.W. (1990). Individual differences in television viewing in early childhood: Nature as well as nurture. *Psychological Science, 6*(1), 371–377.

Plomin, R., & DeFries, J.C. (1985). *Origins of individual differences in infancy: The Colorado Adoption Project.* New York: Academic Press.

Poindexter, P.M., & Stroman, C.A. (1981). Blacks and television: A review of the research literature. *Journal of Broadcasting, 25*, 103–122.

Potter, W.J. (1987). Does television viewing hinder academic achievement among adolescents? *Human Communication Research, 14*(1), 27–46.

Potter, W.J., & Ware, W. (1987). An analysis of the contexts of antisocial acts on prime-time television. *Communication Research, 14*(6), 664–686.

Potts, R., Huston, A.C., & Wright, J.C. (1986). The effects of television form and violent content on boys' attention and social behavior. *Journal of Experimental Child Psychology, 41*, 1–17.

Quarforth, J.M. (1979). Children's understanding of the nature of TV characters. *Journal of Communication, 29*(3), 210–218.

Rapaczynski, W., Singer, D.G., & Singer, J.L. (1982). Teaching television: A curriculum for young children. *Journal of Communication, 32,* 46–55.

Rarick, D.L., Townsend, J.E., & Boyd, D.A. (1973). Adolescent perceptions of police: Actual and as depicted in TV drama. *Journalism Quarterly, 50,* 438–446.

Reep, D.C., & Dambrot, F.H. (1987). Television's professional women: Working with men in the 1980s. *Journalism Quarterly, 64*(2), 376–381.

Reeves, B., Lang, A., Thorson, E., & Rothschild, M. (1989). Emotional television scenes and hemispheric specialization. *Human Communication Research, 15*(4), 493–508.

Reid, L.N. (1979). Viewing rules as mediating factors of children's responses to commercials. *Journal of Broadcasting, 23*(1), 15–26.

Reid, L.N., & Frazer, C.F. (1980). Children's use of television commercials to initiate social interaction in family viewing situations. *Journal of Broadcasting, 24*(2), 149–158.

Reilly Group, Inc., The Gene. (1973). Assumption by the child of the role of consumer. *The Child, 1.*

Reitzes, K.A., & White, M.A. (1982). Children's expectations for television entertainment vs. television news events. *Journal of Applied Communication Research, 10,* 168–173.

Rice, M.L. (1983). The role of television in language acquisition. *Developmental Review, 3,* 211–224.

Rice, M.L. (1984). The words of children's television. *Journal of Broadcasting, 28,* 445–461.

Rice, M.L., Huston, A.C., Truglio, R., & Wright, J.C. (1990). Words from "Sesame Street": Learning vocabulary while viewing. *Developmental Psychology, 26*(3), 421–428.

Rice, M.L., Huston, A.C., & Wright, J.C. (1983). The forms of television: Effects on children's attention, comprehension, and social behavior. In E. Wartella, D.C. Whitney, & S. Windahl (Eds.), *Mass communication review yearbook* (Vol. 4, pp. 37–41). Newbury Park, CA: Sage.

Rice, M.L., Huston, A.C., & Wright, J.C. (1986). Replays as repetitions: Young children's interpretation of television forms. *Journal of Applied Developmental Psychology, 7,* 61–76.

Rice, M.L., & Woodsmall, L. (1988). Lessons from television: Children's word learning when viewing. *Child Development, 59*(2), 420–429.

Ridley-Johnson, R., Cooper, H., & Chance, J. (1983). The relation of children's television viewing to school achievement and I.Q. *Journal of Educational Research, 76,* 294–297.

Ritchie, D., Price, V., & Roberts D. (1987). Television, reading, and reading achievement: A reappraisal. *Communication Research, 14,* 292–315.

Roberts, C. (1981). Children's and parents' television viewing and perceptions of violence. *Journalism Quarterly, 58,* 556–581.

Roberts, D.F., & Bachen, C.M. (1981). Mass communication effects. *Annual Review of Psychology, 32,* 307–356.

Roberts, D.F., Bachen, C.M., Hornby, M.C., & Hernandez-Ramos, P. (1984). Reading and television: Predictors of reading achievement at different age levels. *Communication Research, 11*(1), 9–49.

Roberts, D.F., Hawkins, R.P., & Pingree, S. (1975). Do the mass media play a role in political socialization? *The Australian and New Zealand Journal of Sociology, 11,* 37–42.

Roberts, D.F., Herold, C., Hornby, M., King, S., Whiteley, S., & Silverman, L.T. (1974). Earth's a Big Blue Marble: A report of the impact of a children's television series on children's opinions. Unpublished manuscript. Palo Alto, CA: Institute for Communication Research, Stanford University.

Robertson, T.S. (1980a). The impact of proprietary medicine advertising on children. In R.P. Adler, G.S. Lesser, L.K. Meringoff, T.S. Robertson, J.R. Rossiter, & S. Ward, *The effects of television advertising on children: Review and recommendations* (pp. 111–122). Lexington, MA: Lexington Books.

Robertson, T.S. (1980b). Television advertising and parent–child relations. In R.P. Adler, G.S. Lesser, L.K. Meringoff, T.S. Robertson, J.R. Rossiter, & S. Ward. *The effects of television advertising on children.* (pp. 195–212). Lexington, MA: Lexington Books.

Robertson, T.S., & Rossiter, J.R. (1977). Children's responsiveness to commercials. *Journal of Communication, 27*(1), 101–106.

Robertson, T.S., Rossiter, J.R., & Gleason, T.C. (1979). *Televised medicine advertising and children.* New York: Praeger.

Robertson, T.S., Ward, S., Gatignon, H., & Kless, D.M. (1989). Advertising and children: A cross-cultural study. *Communication Research, 16*(4), 459–485.

Robinson, J.P. (1969). Television and leisure time: Yesterday, today, and (maybe) tomorrow. *Public Opinion Quarterly, 33,* 210–233.

Robinson, J.P. (1972a). Television's impact on everyday life: Some cross-national evidence. In E.A. Rubinstein, G.A. Comstock, & E.A. Rubinstein (Eds.), *Television and social behavior: Vol. 4. Television in day-to-day life: Patterns of use* (pp. 410–431). Washington, DC: Government Printing Office.

Robinson, J.P. (1972b). Toward defining the functions of television. In E.A. Rubinstein, G.A. Comstock, & J.P. Murray (Eds.), *Television and social behavior: Vol. 4. Television in day-to-day life: Patterns of use* (pp. 568–603). Washington, DC: Government Printing Office.

Robinson, J.P. (1977). *How Americans use time.* New York: Praeger.

Robinson, J.P. (1990). Television's effects on families' use of time. In J. Bryant (Ed.), *Television and the American family* (pp. 195–210). Hillsdale, NJ: Erlbaum.

Robinson, J.P., & Bachman, J.G. (1972). Television viewing habits and aggression. In G.A. Comstock & E.A. Rubinstein (Eds.), *Television and social behavior: Vol. 3. Television and adolescent aggressiveness* (pp. 372–382). Washington, DC: U.S. Government Printing Office.

Robinson, J.P., & Converse, P.E. (1972). The impact of televison on mass media usages: A cross-national comparison. In A. Szalai (Ed.), *The use of time: Daily activities of urban and suburban populations in twelve countries* (pp. 197–212). The Hague, The Netherlands: Mouton and Co.

Robinson, J.P., & Levy, M.R. (1986). *The main source: Learning from television news.* Newbury Park, CA: Sage.

Roe, K. (1983). *Mass media and adolescent schooling: Conflict or co-existence?* Stockholm, Sweden: Almqvist & Wiksell International.

Roedder, D.L. (1981). Age differences in children's responses to television advertising: An information-processing approach. *Journal of Consumer Research, 8,* 144–153.

Rogosa, D. (1980). A critique of cross-lagged correlation. *Psychological Bulletin, 88,* 145–158.

Rolandelli, D.R. (1989). Children and television: The visual superiority effect reconsidered. *Journal of Broadcasting & Electronic Media, 33*(1), 69–81.

Rosekrans, M.A. (1967). Imitation in children as a function of perceived similarities to a social model of vicarious reinforcement. *Journal of Personality and Social Psychology, 7,* 305–317.

Rosekrans, M.A., & Hartup, W.W. (1967). Imitative influences of consistent and inconsistent response consequences to a model on aggressive behavior in children. *Journal of Personality and Social Psychology, 7*, 429–434.

Rosengren, K.E., & Windahl, S. (1989). *Media matter: TV use in childhood and adolescence.* Norwood, NJ: Ablex.

Rosenthal, R. (1984). *Meta-analytic procedures for social research.* Newbury Park, CA: Sage.

Rosenwasser, S.M., Lingenfelter, M., & Harrington, A.F. (1989). Nontraditional gender role portrayals on television and children's gender role perceptions. *Journal of Applied Developmental Psychology, 10*, 97–105.

Ross, L., Anderson, D.R., & Wisocki, P.A. (1982). Television viewing and adult sex-role attitudes. *Sex Roles, 8*(6), 589–592.

Ross, R.P., Campbell, T., Wright, J.C., Huston, A.C., Rice, M.L., & Turk, P. (1984). When celebrities talk, children listen: An experimental analysis of children's responses to TV ads with celebrity endorsement. *Journal of Applied Developmental Psychology, 5*, 185–202.

Rossano, M.J., & Butter, E.J. (1987). Television advertising and childrens' attitudes toward proprietary medicine. *Psychology and Marketing, 4*(3), 213–224.

Rossiter, J.R. (1979). Does television advertising affect children? *Journal of Advertising Research, 19*, 43–49.

Rossiter, J.R. (1980a). Source effects and self-concept appeals in children's television advertising. In R.P. Adler, G.S. Lesser, L.K. Meringoff, T.S. Robertson, J.R. Rossiter, & S. Ward, *The effects of television advertising on children: Review and recommendations* (pp. 61–94). Lexington, MA: Lexington Books.

Rossiter, J.R. (1980b). The effects of volume and repetition of television commercials. In R.P. Adler, G.S. Lesser, L.K. Meringoff, T.S. Robertson, J.R. Rossiter, & S. Ward, *The effects of television advertising on children: Review and recommendations* (pp. 153–184). Lexington, MA: Lexington Books.

Rossiter, J.R., & Robertson, T.S. (1974). Children's TV commercials: Testing the defenses. *Journal of Communication, 24*(4), 137–144.

Rossiter, J.R., & Robertson, T.S. (1980). Children's dispositions toward proprietary drugs and the role of television drug advertising. *Public Opinion Quarterly, 44*(3), 316–329.

Rotfeld, H.J., Abernethy, A.M., & Parsons, P.R. (1990). Self-regulation and television advertising. *Journal of Advertising, 19*(4), 18–26.

Rothschild, M.I., Thorson, E., Reeves, B., Hirsch, J.E., & Goldstein, R. (1986). EEG activity and the processing of television commercials. *Communication Research, 13*(2), 182–220.

Rothschild, N., & Morgan, M. (1987). Cohesion and control: Adolescents' relationships with parents as mediators of television. *Journal of Early Adolescence, 7*(3), 299–314.

Rovet, J. (1983). The education of spatial transformations. In D.R. Olson & E. Bialystok (Eds.), *Spatial cognition: The structures and development of mental representations of spatial relations* (pp. 164–181). Hillsdale, NJ: Erlbaum.

Rowe, D.C., & Herstand, S.E. (1986). Familial influences on television viewing and aggression: A sibling study. *Aggressive Behavior, 12*, 111–120.

Rubin, A.M. (1976). Television in children's political socialization. *Journal of Broadcasting, 20*(1), 51–60.

Rubin, A.M. (1977). Television usage, attitudes and viewing behaviors of children and adolescents. *Journal of Broadcasting, 21*(3), 355–369.

Rubin, A.M. (1978). Children and adolescent television use and political socialization. *Journalism Quarterly, 55*, 125–129.

Rubin, A.M. (1979). Television use by children and adolescents. *Human Communication Research, 5*(2), 109–120.

Rubin, A.M. (1983). Television uses and gratifications: The interactions of viewing patterns and motivations. *Journal of Broadcasting, 27*(1), 37–51.

Rubin, A.M. (1984). Ritualized and instrumental television viewing. *Journal of Communication, 34,* 67–77.

Rubin, A.M. (1986). Age and family control influences on children's television viewing. *The Southern Speech Communication Journal, 52,* 35–51.

Rubin, R.S. (1972). *An exploratory investigation of children's responses to commercial content of television advertising in relation to their stages of cognitive development.* Unpublished doctoral dissertation, University of Massachusetts, Amherst.

Ruble, D.M., Balaban, T., & Cooper, J. (1981). Gender constancy and the effects of sex-typed televised toy commercials. *Child Development, 52*(2), 667–673.

Rule, B.G., & Ferguson, T.J. (1986). The effects of media violence on attitudes, emotions, and cognitions. *Journal of Social Issues, 42*(3), 29–50.

Runco, M., & Pezdek, K. (1984). The effect of television and radio on children's creativity. *Human Communication Research, 11,* 109–120.

Rushton, J.P. (1979). Effects of prosocial television and film material on behavior of viewers. In L. Berkowitz (Ed.), *Advances in experimental social psychology* (Vol. 12, pp. 321–351). New York: Academic Press.

Rushton, J.P. (1980). *Altruism, socialization, and society.* Englewood Cliffs, NJ: Prentice-Hall.

Rushton, J.P. (1982). Television and prosocial behavior. In D. Pearl, L. Bouthilet, & J. Lazar (Eds.), *Television and social behavior: Ten year of research and implications for the eighties: Vol. 2. Summary reports* (pp. 248–257). Washington, DC: U.S. Government Printing Office.

Ryan, J., Bales, K., & Hughes, M. (1988). Television and the cultivation of adolescent occupational expectations. *Free Inquiry in Creative Sociology, 16*(1), 103–108.

Rychtarik, R.G., Fairbank, J.A., Allen, C.M., Foy, D.W., & Drabman, R.S. (1983). Alcohol use in television programming: Effects on children's behavior. *Addictive Behavior, 8,* 19–22.

Sanft, H. (1985). The role of knowledge in the effects of television advertising on children. In R.J. Lutz (Ed.), *Advances in consumer research.* Proceedings of the Association for Consumer Research. (Vol. 13, pp. 147–152). Urbana, IL: Association for Consumer Research.

Salomon, G. (1974). Internalization of filmic schematic operations in interaction with learner's aptitudes. *Journal of Educational Psychology, 66*(4), 499–511.

Salomon, G. (1979). *Interaction of media, cognition and learning.* San Francisco: Jossey-Bass.

Salomon, G. (1981a). *Communication and education: Social and psychological interactions.* Newbury Park, CA: Sage.

Salomon, G. (1981b). Introducing AIME: The assessment of children's mental involvement with television. In H. Kelly & H. Gardner (Eds.), *New directions for child development: Viewing children through television* (no. 13) (pp. 89–102). San Francisco: Jossey-Bass.

Salomon, G. (1983a). Beyond the formats of television: The effects of student preconceptions on the experience of televiewing. In M. Meyer (Ed.), *Children and the formal features of television.* Munich: K.G. Saur.

Salomon, G. (1983b). Television watching and mental effort: A social psychological view. In J. Bryant & D.R. Anderson (Eds.), *Children's understanding of television:*

Research on attention and comprehension (pp. 181–198). New York: Academic Press.

Salomon, G. (1984). TV is "easy" and print is "tough": The role of perceptions and attributions in the processing of material. *Journal of Educational Psychology, 76,* 647–658.

Salomon, G., & Leigh, T. (1984). Predispositions about learning from print and television. *Journal of Communication, 34,* 119–135.

Sapolsky, B.S., & Zillmann, D. (1981). The effect of soft-core and hard-core erotica on provoked and unprovoked hostile behavior. *Journal of Sex Research, 17,* 319–343.

Saroyan, W. (1937). *Little children.* New York: Harcourt, Brace and Company.

Schallow, J.R., & McIlwraith, R.D. (1986–1987). Is television viewing really bad for your imagination?: Content and process of TV viewing and imaginal styles. *Imagination, Cognition and Personality, 6*(1), 25–42.

Schank, R.C., & Abelson, R.P. (1977). *Scripts, plans, goals, and understanding.* Hillsdale, NJ: Erlbaum.

Schramm, W., Lyle, J., & Parker, E.B. (1961). *Television in the lives of our children.* Stanford, CA: Stanford University Press.

Selnow, G.W. (1986). Solving problems on prime-time television. *Journal of Communication, 36*(2), 63–72.

Selnow, G., & Bettinghaus, E. (1982). Television exposure and language development. *Journal of Broadcasting, 26,* 469–479.

Sheikh, A.A., & Moleski, M.L. (1977). Conflict in the family over commercials. *Journal of Communication, 27*(1), 152–157.

Shimp, T., Dyer, R., & Divita, S. (1976). An experimental test of the harmful effects of premium-oriented commercials on children. *Journal of Consumer Research, 3,* 1–11.

Siegel, H. (1973). McLuhan, mass media, and education. *Journal of Experimental Education, 41,* 68–70.

Siemicki, M., Atkin, D., Greenberg, B., & Baldwin, T. (1986). Nationally distributed children's programs: What cable TV contributes. *Journalism Quarterly, 63,* 710–718.

Sigel, R. (1965). Television and the reactions of schoolchildren to the assassination. In B. Greenberg & E. Parker (Eds.), *The Kennedy assassination and the American public* (pp. 175–198). Stanford CA: Stanford University Press.

Signorielli, N. (1989). Television and conceptions about sex roles: Maintaining conventionality and the status quo. *Sex Roles, 21*(5/6), 341–360.

Silverman-Watkins, L.T., Levi, S.C., & Klein, M.A. (1986). Sex-stereotyping as a factor in children's comprehension of television news. *Journalism Quarterly, 64,* 3–11.

Sims, J.B. (1989). VCR viewing patterns: An electronic and passive investigation. *Journal of Advertising Research, 29*(2), 11–17.

Singer, D.G., & Singer, J.L. (1980a). Television viewing and aggressive behavior in preschool children: A field study. *Annals of the New York Academy of Sciences, 347,* 289–303.

Singer, D.G., Zuckerman, D.M., & Singer, J.L. (1980). Helping elementary school children learn about TV. *Journal of Communication, 30*(3), 84–93.

Singer, J.L., & Singer, D.G. (1976). Can TV stimulate imaginative play? *Journal of Communication, 26,* 74–80.

Singer, J.L., & Singer, D.G. (1980b). Television viewing, family type and aggressive behavior in preschool children. In M. Green (Ed.), *Violence and the family.* Boulder, CO: Westview Press.

Singer, J.L., & Singer, D.G. (1981). *Television, imagination, and aggression: A study of preschoolers.* Hillsdale, NJ: Erlbaum.

Singer, J.L., & Singer, D.G. (1983). Psychologists look at television: Cognitive, developmental, personality, and social policy implications. *American Psychologist, 38*, 826–834.

Singer, J.L., & Singer, D.G. (1985). Television-viewing and family communication style as predictors of children's emotional behavior. *Journal of Children in Contemporary Society, 17*(4), 75–91.

Singer, J.L., & Singer, D.G. (1986). Family experiences and television viewing as predictors of children's imagination, restlessness, and aggression. *Journal of Social Issues, 42*(3), 107–124.

Singer, J.L., & Singer, D.G. (1987). Some hazards of growing up in a television environment: Children's aggression and restlessness. In S. Oskamp (Ed.), *Television as a social issue. Applied psychology annual* (Vol. 8, pp. 172–188). Newbury Park, CA: Sage.

Singer, J.L., Singer, D.G., Desmond, R., Hirsch, B., & Nicol, A. (1988). Family mediation and children's cognition, aggression, and comprehension of television: A longitudinal study. *Journal of Applied Developmental Psychology, 9*, 329–347.

Singer, J.L., Singer, D.G., & Rapaczynski, W.S. (1984). Family patterns and television viewing as predictors of children's beliefs and aggression. *Journal of Communication, 34*(2), 73–89.

Slaby, R.G., & Frey, K.S. (1975). Development of gender constancy and selective attention to same-sex models. *Child Development, 46*, 849–856.

Slater, D., & Elliott, W.R. (1982). Television's influence on social reality. *Quarterly Journal of Speech, 68*, 69–79.

Slater, D., & Thompson, T.L. (1984). Attitudes of parents concerning televised warning statements. *Journalism Quarterly, 61*(4), 853–859.

Slife, B.D., & Rychiak, J.F. (1982). Role of affective assessment in modeling behavior. *Journal of Personality and Social Psychology, 43*, 861–868.

Smith, R.E., Sarason, E.G., & Sarason, B.R. (1982). *Psychology: The frontiers of behavior.* New York: Harper & Row.

Smythe, D.W. (1954). Reality as presented by television. *Public Opinion Quarterly, 18*, 143–156.

Snow, R.P. (1974). How children interpret TV violence in play context. *Journalism Quarterly, 51*, 13–21.

Sobell, L.C., Sobell, M.B., Riley, D.M., Klajner, F., Leo, G.I., Pavan, D.C., & Cancilla, A. (1986). Effect of television programming and advertising on alcohol consumption in normal drinkers. *Journal of Studies on Alcohol, 47*, 333–340.

Soldow, G.F. (1983). The processing of information in the young consumer: The impact of cognitive developmental stage on television, radio and print advertising. *Journal of Advertising, 12*(3), 4–12.

Sparks, G.G. (1986). Developmental differences in children's reports of fear induced by the mass media. *Child Study Journal, 16*(1), 55–66.

Sparks, G.G., & Cantor, J. (1986). Developmental differences in fright responses to a television program depicting a character transformation. *Journal of Broadcasting & Electronic Media, 30*(3), 309–323.

Sprafkin, J., & Gadow, K.D. (1986). Television viewing habits of emotionally disturbed, learning disabled, and mentally retarded children. *Journal of Applied Developmental Psychology, 7*, 45–59.

Sprafkin, J., Gadow, K.D., & Grayson, P. (1984). Television and the emotionally disturbed, learning disabled, and mentally retarded child: A review. In K.D. Gadow (Ed.), *Advances in learning and behavioral disabilities* (Vol. 3, pp. 151–213). Greenwich, CT: JAI Press.

Sprafkin, J.N., & Liebert, R.M. (1978). Sex-typing and children's preferences. In G. Tuchman, A.K. Daniels, & J. Benet (Eds.), *Hearth and home: Images of women in the mass media* (pp. 288–339). New York: Oxford University Press.

Stein, A.H., & Friedrich, L.K. (1972). Television content and young children's behavior. In J.P. Murray, E.A. Rubinstein, & G.A. Comstock (Eds.), *Television and social behavior: Vol. 2. Television and social learning* (pp. 202–317). Washington, DC: U.S. Government Printing Office.

Steinberg, C. (1980). *TV facts.* New York: Facts on File.

Steiner, G.A. (1963). *The people look at television.* New York: Knopf.

Stern, B.L., & Harmon, R.R. (1984). The incidence and characteristics of disclaimers in children's television advertising. *Journal of Advertising, 13*(2), 12–16.

Steuer, F.B., Applefield, J.M., & Smith, R. (1971). Televised aggression and interpersonal aggression of preschool children. *Journal of Experimental Child Psychology, 11,* 442–447.

Stipp, H.H. (1975). *Validity in social research: Measuring children's television exposure.* Unpublished doctoral dissertation, Columbia University.

Stoneman, Z., & Brody, G.H. (1981a). Peers as mediators of television food advertisements aimed at children. *Developmental Psychology, 17*(6), 853–858.

Stoneman, Z., & Brody, G.H. (1981b). The indirect impact of child-oriented advertisements on mother–child interactions. *Journal of Applied Developmental Psychology, 2,* 369–376.

Stoneman, Z., & Brody, G.H. (1983a). Family interactions during three programs: Contextualist observations. *Journal of Family Issues, 4*(2), 349–365.

Stoneman, Z., & Brody, G.H. (1983b). Immediate and long-term recognition and generalization of advertised products as a function of age and presentation mode. *Developmental Psychology, 19*(1), 56–61.

Strickland, D.E. (1983). Advertising exposure, alcohol consumption and misuse of alcohol. In M. Grant, M. Plant, & A. Williams (Eds.), *Economics and alcohol: Consumption and controls* (pp. 201–222). New York: Gardner Press.

Stroman, C.A. (1986). Television viewing and self-concept among black children. *Journal of Broadcasting & Electronic Media, 30,* 87–93.

Stutts, M.A., & Hunnicutt, G.G. (1987). Can young children understand disclaimers in television commercials? *Journal of Advertising, 16*(1), 41–46.

Stutts, M.A., Vance, D., & Hudleson, S. (1981). Program–commercial separators in children's television: Do they help a child tell the difference between *Bugs Bunny* and the *Quik Rabbit. Journal of Advertising, 10,* 16–25, 48.

Surgeon General's Scientific Advisory Committee on Television and Social Behavior. (1972). *Television and growing up: The impact of televised violence.* Report to the Surgeon General, United States Public Health Service. Washington, DC: Government Printing Office.

Surlin, S.H. (1974). Bigotry on the air and in life: The Archie Bunker case. *Public Opinion Quarterly, 212,* 34–41.

Surlin, S.H. (1978). "Roots" research: A summary of findings. *Journal of Broadcasting, 22,* 309–320.

Surlin, S.H., & Dominick, J.R. (1970). Television's function as a "third parent" for black and white teen-agers. *Journal of Broadcasting, 15,* 55–64.

Swerdlow, J. (1981). What is television doing to real people? *Today's Education, 70,* 50–57.

Szalai, A. (Ed.). (1972). *The use of time: Daily activities or urban and suburban populations in twelve countries.* The Hague, The Netherlands: Mouton and Co.

Tallmadge, G.K. (1976). *Joint dissemination review panel, ideabook*. Washington, DC: National Institute of Education.

Tamborini, R., & Zillmann, D. (1985). Effects of questions, personalized communication style, and pauses for reflection in children's educational programs. *Journal of Educational Research, 79*(1), 19–26.

Tamborini, R., Zillmann, D., & Bryant, J. (1984). Fear and victimization: Exposure to television and perceptions of crime and fear. In R. Bostrom (Ed.), *Communication yearbook 8* (pp. 492–513). New Brunswick, NJ: ICA-Transaction Press.

Tan, A.S. (1979). TV beauty ads and role expectations of adolescent female viewers. *Journalism Quarterly, 56*, 283–288.

Tan, A.S., Raudy, J., Huff, C., & Miles, J. (1980). Children's reactions to male and female newscasters: Effectiveness and believability. *The Quarterly Journal of Speech, 66*, 201–205.

Tangney, J.P. (1988). Aspects of the family and children's television viewing content preferences. *Child Development, 59*, 1070–1079.

Tangney, J.P., & Feshbach, S. (1988). Children's television-viewing frequency: Individual differences and demographic correlates. *Personality and Social Psychology Bulletin, 14*(1), 145–158.

Tannenbaum, P.H., & Zillmann, D. (1975). Emotional arousal in the facilitation of aggression through communication. In L. Berkowitz (Ed.), *Advances in experimental social psychology* (Vol. 8, pp. 149–192). New York: Academic Press.

Television Information Office. (1987). *America's watching*. New York: Author.

Television networks fatten commercial calf. (1990, June 18). *Broadcasting*, pp. 21–22.

Thomas, M.H. (1982). Physiological arousal, exposure to a relatively lengthy aggressive film, and aggressive behavior. *Journal of Research in Personality, 16*, 72–81.

Thomas, M.H., Horton, R.W., Lippencott, E.C., & Drabman, R.S. (1977). Desensitization to portrayals of real-life aggression as a function of exposure to television violence. *Journal of Personality and Social Psychology, 35*, 450–458.

Thornton, W., & Voight, L. (1984). Television and delinquency. *Youth and Society, 15*(4), 445–468.

Thorson, E., Reeves, B., & Schleuder, J. (1985). Message complexity and attention to television. *Communication Research, 12*, 427–454.

Times Mirror Center for the People and the Press. (1990). *The age of indifference: A study of young Americans and how they view the news*. Washington, DC: The Times Mirror Center for the People and the Press.

Timmer, S.G., Eccles, J., & O'Brien, K. (1985). How children use time. In F.T. Juster & F.P. Stafford (Eds.), *Time, goods, and well-being* (pp. 353–382). Ann Arbor: Institute for Social Research, University of Michigan.

Tolley, H., Jr. (1973). *Children and war: Political socialization to international conflict*. New York: Teachers College Press, Columbia University.

Tower, R., Singer, D., Singer, J., & Biggs, A. (1979). Differential effects of television programming on preschoolers' cognition, imagination and social play. *American Journal of Orthopsychiatry, 49*, 265–281.

Tucker, L.A. (1985). Television's role regarding alcohol use among teenagers. *Adolescence, 20*(79), 593–598.

Tucker, L.A. (1986). The relationship of television viewing to physical fitness and obesity. *Adolescence, 21*(84), 797–806.

Tucker, L.A. (1987). Television, teenagers, and health. *Journal of Youth and Adolescence, 16*(5), 415–425.

Turner, C.W., & Berkowitz, L. (1972). Identification with film aggressor (covert role taking) and reactions to film violence. *Journal of Personality and Social Psychology,* *21,* 256–264.

Turner, C.W., Hesse, B.W., & Peterson-Lewis, S. (1986). Naturalistic studies of the long-term effects of television violence. *Journal of Social Issues, 42*(3), 51–73.

Turow, J. (1980). Non-fiction on commercial children's television: Trends and policy implications. *Journal of Broadcasting, 24*(4), 437–448.

Turow, J. (1981). *Entertainment, education, and the hard sell: Three decades of network children's television.* New York: Praeger.

Tyler, T.R. (1978). *Drawing inferences from experiences: The effect of crime victimization experiences upon crime-related attitudes and behaviors.* Unpublished doctoral dissertation, University of California, Los Angeles.

Tyler, T.R. (1980). The impact of directly and indirectly experienced events: The origin of crime-related judgments and behaviors. *Journal of Personality and Social Psychology, 39,* 13–28.

Tyler, T.R. (1984). Assessing the risk of crime victimization: The integration of personal victimization experience and socially-transmitted information. *Journal of Social Issues, 40,* 27–38.

Tyler, T.R., & Cook, F.L. (1984). The mass media and judgments of risk: Distinguishing impact on personal and societal level judgments. *Journal of Personality and Social Psychology, 47*(4), 693–708.

U.S. Commission on Civil Rights. (1977). *Window dressing on the set: Women and minorities in television.* Washington, DC: U.S. Government Printing Office.

U.S. Commission on Civil Rights. (1979). *Window dressing on the set: An update.* Washington, DC: U.S. Government Printing Office.

Vidmar, N., & Rokeach, M. (1974). Archie Bunker's bigotry: A study in selective perception and exposure. *Journal of Communication, 24*(1), 36–47.

Vig, S.R. (1980). The role of visual elements in the learning of television news by adolescents. *Dissertation Abstracts International, 40*(5-B), 1957–1958.

Violence bill debated in Washington, (1990, February 5). *Broadcasting,* 77–78.

Waite, C.H. (1976). The effects of pictorial, audio, and print television news messages on undergraduate students as measured by output, recall, error, and equivocation. *Dissertation Abstracts International, 36*(8-A), 4833.

Wakshlag, J.J., Bart, L., Dudley, J., Groth, G., McCutcheon, J., & Rolla, C. (1983). Viewer apprehension about victimization and crime drama programs. *Communication Research, 10*(2), 195–217.

Wakshlag, J.J., Vial, V., & Tamborini, R. (1983). Selecting crime drama and apprehension about crime. *Human Communication Research, 10*(2), 227–242.

Walberg, H.J., & Tsai, S. (1984–1985). Correlates of reading achievement and attitude: A national assessment study. *Journal of Educational Research, 78*(3), 159–167.

Ward, S. (1980). The effects of television advertising on consumer socialization. In R.P. Adler, G.S. Lesser, L.K. Meringoff, T.S. Robertson, J.R. Rossiter, & S. Ward, *The effects of television advertising on children: Review and recommendations* (pp. 185–194). Lexington, MA: Lexington Books.

Ward, S., Reale, G., & Levinson, D. (1972). Children's perceptions, explanations, and judgments of television advertising: A further exploration. In E.A. Rubinstein, G. Comstock, & J.P. Murray (Eds.), *Television and social behavior: Vol. 4. Television in day-to-day life* (pp. 468–490). Washington, DC: U.S. Government Printing Office.

Ward, S., & Wackman, D.B. (1972). Children's purchase influence attempts and parental yielding. *Journal of Marketing Research, 9,* 316–319.

Ward, S., & Wackman, D.B. (1973). Children's information processing of television advertising. In P. Clarke (Ed.), *New models for mass communication research* (pp. 119–146). Newbury Park, CA: Sage.

Wartella, E., Heintz, K.E., Aidman, A.J., & Mazzarella, S.R. (1990). Television and beyond: Children's video media in one community. *Communication Research, 17*(1), 45–64.

Watkins, B. (1985). Television viewing as a dominant activity of childhood: A developmental theory of television effects. *Critical Studies in Mass Communication, 2*, 323–337.

Watkins, B. (1988). Children's representations of television and real-life stories. *Communication Research, 15*(2), 159–184.

Watkins, B., Calvert, S., Huston-Stein, A., & Wright, J.C. (1980). Children's recall of television material: Effects of representation mode and adult labeling. *Developmental Psychology, 16*(6), 672–674.

Weaver, J., & Wakshlag, J. (1986). Perceived vulnerability to crime, criminal victimization experience, and television viewing. *Journal of Broadcasting & Electronic Media, 30*(2), 141–158.

Webster, J.G. (1986). Audience behavior in the new media environment. *Journal of Communication, 36*(3), 77–93.

Webster, J.G., Pearson, J.C., & Webster, D.B. (1986). Children's television viewing as affected by contextual variables in the home. *Communication Research Reports, 3*, 1–8.

Webster, J.G., & Wakshlag, J.J. (1983). A theory of television program choice. *Communication Research, 10*(4), 430–446.

Weigel, R.H., & Jessor, R. (1973). Television and adolescent conventionality: An explanatory study. *Public Opinion Quarterly, 37*(1), 76–90.

Welch, R.L., Huston-Stein, A., Wright, J.C., & Plehal, R. (1979). Subtle sex-role cues in children's commercials. *Journal of Communication, 29*(3), 202–209.

Wells, W.D. (1965). Communicating with children. *Journal of Advertising Research, 5*, 2–14.

Wells, W.D. (1973). *Television and aggression: Replication of an experimental field study.* Unpublished manuscript, Graduate School of Business, University of Chicago.

Wells, W.D., & LoScuito, L.A. (1966). Direct observation of purchasing behavior. *Journal of Marketing Research, 3*, 227–233.

Wiegman, O., Kuttschreuter, M., & Baarda, B. (1986). *Television viewing related to aggressive and prosocial behavior.* The Netherlands: Stitchting voor Orderzoek van het Onderwijs, Foundation for Educational Research in the Netherlands (SVO) & Department of Psychology, Technical University of Enshede (THT).

Wilkes, R.E., & Valencia, H. (1989). Hispanics and blacks in television commercials. *Journal of Advertising, 18*(1), 19–25.

Williams, F., LaRose, R., & Frost, F. (1981). *Children, television, and sex-role stereotyping.* New York: Praeger.

Williams, P.A., Haertel, E. H., Haertel, G.D., & Walberg, J. (1982). The impact of leisure-time television on school learning: A research synthesis. *American Educational Research Journal, 19*, 19–50.

Williams, T.M. (Ed.). (1986). *The impact of television: A natural experiment in three communities.* New York: Academic Press.

Wilson, B.J. (1987). Reducing children's emotional reactions to mass media through rehearsed explanation and exposure to a replica of a fear object. *Human Communication Research, 14*(1), 3–26.

Wilson, B.J. (1989a). Desensitizing children's emotional reactions to the mass media. *Communication Research, 16*(6), 723–745.

Wilson, B.J. (1989b). The effects of two control strategies on children's emotional reactions to a frightening movie scene. *Journal of Broadcasting & Electronic Media, 33*(4), 397–418.

Wilson, B.J., & Cantor, J. (1987). Reducing fear reactions to mass media: Effects of visual exposure and verbal explanation. In M. McLaughlin (Ed.), *Communication yearbook 10* (pp. 553–573). Newbury Park, CA: Sage.

Wilson, B.J., Linz, D., & Randall, B. (1990). Applying social science research to film ratings: A shift from offensiveness to harmful effects. *Journal of Broadcasting & Electronic Media, 34*(4), 443–468.

Wilson, G.T., & O'Leary, K.D. (1980). *Principles of behavior therapy.* Englewood Cliffs, NJ: Prentice-Hall.

Wiman, A.R. (1983). Parental influence and children's responses to television advertising. *Journal of Advertising, 12*(1), 12–18.

Windahl, S., Hojerback, I., & Hedinsson, E. (1986). Adolescents without television: A study in media deprivation. *Journal of Broadcasting & Electronic Media, 30,* 47–63.

Winn, M. (1977). *The plug-in drug.* New York: Viking Press.

Winston, B. (1986). *Misunderstanding media.* Cambridge, MA: Harvard University Press.

Wober, J.M. (1988). *The use and abuse of television: A social psychological analysis of the changing screen.* Hillsdale, NJ: Erlbaum.

Wober, J.M., & Gunter, B. (1988). *Television and social control.* New York: St. Martin's Press.

Wolf, M.A. (1987). How children negotiate television. In T.R. Lindlof (Ed.), *Natural audiences: Qualitative research of media uses and effects* (pp. 58–94). Norwood, NJ: Ablex.

Wolfe, K.M., & Fiske, M. (1954). Why they read comics. In W. Schramm (Ed.), *Process and effects of mass communication.* Urbana: University of Illinois Press.

Wolfenstein, M. (1965). Death of a parent and the death of a President: Children's reactions to two kinds of loss. In M. Wolfenstein & G. Kliman (Eds.), *Children and the death of a President: Multi-disciplinary studies* (pp. 70–90). New York: Doubleday.

Wolman, B.B. (1989). *Dictionary of behavioral science* (2nd ed.). New York: Academic Press.

Worchel, S., Hardy, T.W., & Hurley, R. (1976). The effects of commercial interruption of violent and nonviolent films on viewers' subsequent aggressiveness. *Journal of Experimental Psychology, 2,* 220–232.

Wright, J.C., & Huston, A.C. (1983). A matter of form: Potentials of television for young viewers. *Journal of Experimental Psychology, 2,* 220–232.

Wright, J.C., Kunkel, D., Pinon, M., & Huston, A.C. (1989). How children reacted to televised coverage of the space shuttle disaster. *Journal of Communication, 39*(2), 27–45.

Wright, J.C., Huston, A.C., Ross, R.P., Calvert, S.L., Rolandelli, D., Weeks, L.A., Raeissi, P., & Potts, R. (1984). Pace and continuity of television programs: Effects on children's attention and comprehension. *Developmental Psychology, 20,* 653–666.

Wroblewski, R., & Huston, A.C. (1987). Televised occupational stereotypes and their effects on early adolescents: Are they changing? *Journal of Early Adolescence, 7*(3), 283–297.

Zillmann, D. (1971). Excitation transfer in communication-mediated aggressive behavior. *Journal of Experimental Social Psychology, 7,* 419–434.

Zillmann, D. (1982). Television viewing and arousal. In D. Pearl, L. Bouthilet, & J. Lazar (Eds.), *Television and behavior: Ten years of scientific inquiry and implications for the eighties: Vol. 2. Technical reviews* (pp. 53–67). Washington, DC: U.S. Government Printing Office.

Zillmann, D. (1988). Mood management: Using entertainment to full advantage. In L. Donohew, H.E. Sypher, & E.T. Higgins (Eds.), *Communication, social cognition, and affect* (pp. 147–171). Hillsdale, NJ: Erlbaum.

Zillmann, D., & Bryant, J. (1982). Pornography, sexual callousness, and the trivialization of rape. *Journal of Communication, 32*(4), 10–21.

Zillmann, D., & Bryant, J. (1984). Effects of massive exposure to pornography. In N. Malamuth & E. Donnerstein (Eds.), *Pornography and sexual aggression* (pp. 115–138). New York: Academic Press.

Zillmann, D., & Bryant, J. (1986). *Pornography's impact on sexual satisfaction.* Unpublished manuscript, Indiana University, Bloomington.

Zillmann, D., & Sapolsky, B. (1977). What mediates the effect of mild erotica on annoyance and hostile behavior in males?. *Journal of Personality and Social Psychology, 35,* 587–596.

Zillmann, D., Bryant, J., Comisky, P.W., & Medoff, N.J. (1981). Excitation and hedonic valence in the effect of erotica on motivated intermale aggression. *European Journal of Social Psychology, 11,* 233–252.

Zillmann, D., Johnson, R.C., & Hanrahan, J. (1973). Pacifying effect of a happy ending of communications involving aggression. *Psychological Reports, 32,* 967–970.

Zoglin, R. (1990, June 4). The disappearing TV audience. *Time,* p. 80.

Zuckerman, D.M., Singer, D.G., & Singer, J.L. (1980a). Children's television viewing, racial and sex role attitudes. *Journal of Applied Psychology, 10,* 281–294.

Zuckerman, D.M., Singer, D.G., & Singer, J.L. (1980b). Television viewing, children's reading, and related classroom behavior. *Journal of Communication, 30*(1), 166–174.

Zuckerman, P., & Gianinno, L. (1981). Measuring children's responses to television advertising. In J. Esserman (Ed.), *Television advertising and children: Issues, research and findings* (pp. 83–93). New York: Child Research Service.

Zuckerman, P., Ziegler, M., & Stevenson, H.W. (1978). Children's viewing of television and recognition memory of commercials. *Child Development, 49,* 96–104.

AUTHOR INDEX

A

Abelman, R., 32, 50–51, 51, 87, 149, 186, 304, *313, 324, 329*
Abelson, R. P., 186, *313, 348*
Abernethy, A. M., 226, *346*
Achelpohl, C., 14, 19, 20, 21, 23, 26, 34, 51, *317*
Acker, S. R., 25, 29, *313*
Adams, S. M., 171, *336*
Adler, I., 182, *331*
Adler, R. P., 102, 194, 200, 202, 203, 216, 221, 222, 223, 225, *313*
Adoni, H., 145, *313,* 322
Aidman, A. J., 21, 52, 53–54, 196, 295, 296, 297, *353*
Akers, R., 14, 19, 20, 21, 23, 26, 34, 51, *317*
Alexander, A., 6, 51, 52, 53, 54, 65, 116, 162, 182, 184, *313, 320, 340*
Alexander, J. K., 276, *326*
Alioto, J. T., 240, 255, *318*
Allen, C., 14, 20, *314*
Allen, C. M., 207, *347*
Allen, R., 40, *316*
Allen, R. C., 159, *314*
Alper, W. S., 142, *314*
Alvarez, M. M., 24, *314*
Alwitt, L. F., 24, *314*
Anderson, B., 16, 71, 72, 90, 92, 143, *314*
Anderson, C., 109, *314*
Anderson, C. C., 63, *314*
Anderson, D., 126, *327*
Anderson, D. R., 20, 23, 24, 25, 26, 27, 34, 35–36, 37, 40, 66, 108, 117, 125, 127, 164, *314, 319, 329, 337, 346*

Anderson, J., 304, *314*
Anderson, W. H., 70, *314*
Andison, F. S., 241, *314*
Applefield, J. M., 237, *350*
Appleton, H., 33, 96, 98, 178, *323*
Argenta, D. M., 34, *314*
Armstrong, G. B., 126, 127, *315*
Armstrong, G. M., 215, 300, *315, 319*
Aronfreed, J., 149, *315*
Aronson, E., 234, *315*
Atkin, C., 201, 204, 215, 217, 219, *315*
Atkin, C. K., 10, 11, 44, 45, 143, 146, 150, 179, 205, 207, 208, 229, 243, 247, 255, 303, *315, 319, 321, 324, 339*
Atkin, D., 54, 295, *315, 348*
Atkin, D. J., 54, *336*
Atkinson, R. C., 234, *315*
Atkinson, R. L., 234, *315*
Atwood, R., 40, *316*
Aubey, L. W., 87, 90, 94, 122, 123, 125, 131, 138, *334*
Aufderheide, P., 300, 308, *316*
Augsbach, L. H., 27, *337*
Austin, E. W., 44, *316*

B

Baarda, B., 243, *353*
Babrow, A. S., 14, 140, *316*
Bachen, C. M., 122, 123, 125, 141, 150, *344*
Bachman, J. G., 242, 243, 254, *345*
Baggaley, J. P., 24, *316*
Bahr, H. M., 62, *320*
Balaban, T., 9, 159, *347*
Baldwin, T., 54, 295, *315, 348*

357

Campbell, T. A., 23, 28, *320*
Cancilla, A., 208, *349*
Cantor, J., 25, 37, 155, 156, 157, 176, 204, *318, 320, 332, 349, 354*
Caplow, T., 62, *320*
Caprara, G. V., 255, *320*
Carey, J., 64, 299, *320*
Carlson, J. M., 154, *320*
Caron, A., 216, *320*
Carroll, J., 116, *342*
Carstensen, L. L., 266, *343*
Carveth, R., 182, 184, *320*
Carveth, R. A., 184, 185, *319*
Cash, D. M., 171, *321*
Cash, T. F., 171, *321*
Cassata, M., 159, 163, 176, 293, *321*
Celozzi, M. J., 261, *321*
Centerwall, B. S., 266, *321*
Chadwick, B. A., 62, *320*
Chaffee, S., 1, 4, 11, 51, 66, 67, 70, 80, 99, 143, 146, 150, 275, 291, 292, 293, *323*
Chaffee, S. H., 10, 11, 143, 145, 146, 147, 150, 151, 242, 243, 245, 247, 267, 303, *321, 339*
Chall, J. S., 126, 127, *321*
Chance, J., 122, 123, 125, *344*
Chaney, D. C., 153, *321*
Char, C. A., 103, *340*
Charters, W. W., 177, *321*
Childers, K. W., 65, 74, *319*
Chirco, A. P., 209, *321*
Choi, H. P., 35–36, *314*
Christenson, P. G., 33, 53, 141, *322*
Clark, S., 70, *322*
Cline, V. B., 152, *322*
Cobb, C. J., 150, *322*
Cobb, N. J., 161, *322*
Cobbey, R., 10, 170, *323*
Coffin, T. E., 72, 79, *322*
Cohen, A., 51, *329*
Cohen, A. A., 54, 143, 145, *313, 322*
Cohen, E. E., 231, *322*
Cohen, J., 166, *322*
Cohen, M. E., 70, *322*
Cohen, S., 54, *322*
Colimore, K., 44, 70, 238, *324*
Collins, P. A., 20, 26, 51, 66, 87, 117, 125, 127, *314*
Collins, W. A., 23, 25, 26, 27, 28, 162, 186, *322, 341*

Columbia Broadcasting System, 141, 179, *322*
Comisky, P., 184, 185, *319*
Comisky, P. W., 173, *355*
Comstock, G., 1, 4, 10, 11, 14, 16, 22, 32, 33, 51, 57, 58, 61, 62, 63, 66, 67, 70, 80, 99, 143, 145, 146, 150, 151, 168, 170, 176, 181, 182, 210, 226, 232, 242–243, 245, 251, 267, 275, 276, 285, 291, 292, 293, 294, 301, 302, *322, 323, 340*
Condry, J., 67, 68, 157, 188, 210, 231, 300, *323*
Conner, R., 33, 96, 98, 178, *323*
Converse, P. E., 2, 62, 72, 74, *345*
Conway, M., 146, *323*
Cook, F. L., 184, *352*
Cook, T. D., 33, 76, 79, 80, 81, 95, 96, 98, 162, 178, 181, 224, 242, 249, 251, 254, 262, 263, 264, 265, *323, 331*
Cooney, J. G., 96, *324*
Cooper, E., 180, *324*
Cooper, H., 122, 123, 125, *344*
Cooper, J., 9, 159, *347*
Cordau, G., 160, 161, *325*
Cordau, G. D., 159, *324*
Corder-Bolz, C. R., 51, *324*
Corley, R., 37, *343*
Corrado-Taylor, D., 164, *328*
Coulter, M., 207, *335*
Courrier, S., 152, *322*
Courtright, J., 304, *313*
Courtright, J. A., 175, *324*
Cozby, P. C., 234, *342*
Cramer, P., 301, *324*
Cramond, J. K., 78, *319*
Croft, K., 32, *327*
Croft, R. G., 152, *322*
Croll, W. L., 159, *318*
Crouch, C., 10, *324*
Cruse, D. F., 9, *335*
Culley, J. D., 229, *324*
Cunningham, 72, 79, *324*
Curtin, T. R., 33, 95, 96, 162, *323*
Czikszentimihali, M., 20, 33, 45, *335*

D

Dambrot, F. H., 176, *344*
Danowski, J. A., 150, *324*
Darley, J. M., 234, *324*

■ SUBJECT INDEX

knowledge gained from, 139–152. **See also** Television news
media dependency and, 143
low level of involvement in, 16–18
as means of acknowledging commonalities, 33
mean world beliefs and, 182–184
mental ability and orientation toward, 104–108
mental effort invested in, 38–39
minutes spent, culture as factor in, 2t
miscomprehension as reflection of low level of involvement in, 17–18
monitoring as element of, 22–24
and nonviolent behavior, relationship between, 275–280
and obesity, relationship between, 213
occupational knowledge gained from, 140, 141t
and other activities, relationship between, 72–85
parental control of, policy recommendations on, 311–312
parental mediation as factor influencing children's, 45
parental mediation in, factors influencing, 50
passivity of, 36
perceptions of ethnicity from, 177–181. **See also** Ethnicity
perceptual dependence and, 35–36
perceptual responses affected by, 110–112
perseverance measurements after, 108–110
physical and mental responses to, 19–20
preferences, type of program and, 31t
principal factors affecting, 4
program alternatives as factor affecting, 4–5
program preferences and, 5–14. **See also** Program preferences
and reading achievement,
  environmental influences on, 129–134
  mechanism explaining negative relationship between, 125–138
  social influences on, 129–134

and reading for fun, relationship between, 83–85, 84t
reality perceptions affected by, 144–145
recall and comprehension in, mode of measurement as factor in determining, 40
repeat,
  by number of episodes, 15t
  weekday series and, 3t
  weekly series and, 4t
ritualistic, concept of, 41
and scholastic achievement. **See also** Scholastic achievement
summary of patterns correlating, 134–138
sexism scores and, 165t
and sex-role beliefs, summary on, 175–177
sex roles in, 158–177. **See also** Sex role(s)
social circumstances as factor in, 42–55
social cognition of, 181–187
social setting of, 43t
socioeconomic status as factor affecting, 71t
socio-orientation of children and, 149
spatial responses affected by, 113
as stable behavioral trait, 67–68
summary of mean world beliefs contributed by, 185–187
teenager mental ability and amount of, 105
temporal responses affected by, 113–114
time availability as factor in, 16–17
time of day as factor in degree of attention in, 39t
time use in, 1–3
traits affected by, 108–120
viewer behavior and, 14–22. **See also** Behavior, viewer
violence perceptions and, 152–158. **See also** Violence
vocabulary effects caused by, 101–103
weekday, 58–61
weekend, 58–61